STRANGERS IN A
STRANGE LAND

STRANGERS IN A
STRANGE LAND

Occidentalist Publics and Orientalist Geographies in
Nineteenth-Century Georgian Imaginaries

Paul MANNING

Boston 2012

Library of Congress Cataloging-in-Publication Data:
A catalog record for this title is available from the Library of Congress.

Copyright © 2012 Academic Studies Press
All rights reserved
ISBN 978-1-61811-831-8

Book design by Adell Medovoy
On the cover: Photo by Vasil Roinashvili (1879–1958). 1912.

Published by Academic Studies Press in 2012
28 Montfern Avenue
Brighton, MA 02135, USA

press@academicstudiespress.com
www.academicstudiespress.com

Figure 1: Photo by Vasil Roinashvili (1879–1958). 1912.

Georgian Dream Come True (1912). Mixed media, photography, and painting.
Self-portrait of photographer Vasil Roinashvili, represented lying in heaven while reading
a newspaper among the attributes of a Georgian supra, drinking horns, games and musical
instruments; in the background is a view of Mount Kazbek from the post station at Kazbek
(image courtesy of Giorgi Gersamia).

CONTENTS

List of Illustrations

Maps

ACKNOWLEDGMENTS

I would like to thank Ronald Suny for inspiring me to undertake this project and for encouraging me to complete it. Funds provided by the National Council for Eurasian and East European Research (NCEEER), under authority of a Title VIII grant from the U.S. Department of State, as well an NEH/ACTR fellowship, supported the work leading to this report in whole or in part. Neither NCEEER, the NEH or ACTR, nor the U.S. Government is responsible for the views expressed within this text. I also would to acknowledge the helpful advice and enthusiasm of the late Robert Huber, president of NCEEER, during the period of researching and writing this monograph.

This book took form over the period of more than a decade, and there are many people to thank. My research work in Georgia would not have been as productive as it was without the ongoing friendship, advice, and assistance of Paata Bukhrashvili and, in his name, his friends and family. I thank my research assistant, David Toklikishvili, for his uncanny abilities to do in a day what might have taken me weeks to do on my own. I thank Zaza Shatirishvili for his insightful comments helping me to frame this book, and I also thank him and his family and friendship "circle" not only for their hospitality, but also for helping me understand ethnographically what the term "intelligentsia" means in its best sense. I thank Tina Tseradze in particular for helping me do the crucial research that allowed me to complete this book.

Many of the chapters have benefited from the insightful comments of many people over a long time. In addition to those people mentioned above, I thank Kristof van Assche, Susan Gal, Victor Friedman, Erin Koch, Florian Muhlfried, Erin Pappas, Alejandro Paz, Stephanie Platz, Oliver Reisner, Hulya Sakarya, Michael Silverstein, Rupert Stasch, and Kevin Tuite, for listening, reading, and discussing parts of this book as a work in progress. I thank Hulya Sakarya for introducing me to the work of Roinashvili, in particular the image that graces the cover of this book. I thank Alaina Lemon for her general insights and particularly for encouraging me to not give up on this book. I thank Anne Meneley for her careful, critical, even caustic, comments on the work in progress and and for helping me "re-Orient" the framework and argument in a less Eurocentric direction. I thank Shunsuke Nozawa for inspiring me, in both his written work (2011, 2012) and in conversations, to rewrite this book to make "nobody" the hero of the story, as well as helping me understand the importance of nobodies and to see how many different ways there are of being nobody.

I give particular thanks to Bruce Grant, Michael Dylan Foster, Miyako Inoue, Stephen Jones, Brian Larkin, and especially Harsha Ram for encouragement and careful and insightful readings of the final draft. Lastly, I thank my editors, Sharona Vedol and Boris Wolfson, for their enthusiasm and advice, and the anonymous reviewer for their insightful comments.

Some of the material in Chapter 1 originally appeared in a different form in "Describing dialect and defining civilization in an early Georgian nationalist manifesto: Ilia Ch'avch'avadze's 'Letters of a Traveler'." *Russian Review* 63 (1) (2004), 26-47.

This book, which begins with travelers writing about the mountains of the Caucasus and ends with travelers who never go very far from home, is haunted by the absent presence of my late father, Harvey H. Manning, a wilderness writer and conservationist who first taught me how to appreciate the alpine sublime of the Cascades and whose travels over hill and dale, like those of Bavreli, never took him very far from home. I dedicate this book to him and the fellow travelers who shared the trails with him; my mother, Betty L. Manning; my sisters, Claudia, Penelope, and Rebecca; my nephew, Dylan; and one faithful hiking dog among many, Buffalo.

This book about nobodies is further dedicated to nobodies everywhere, and is inspired by those who act today in their non-name, in particular the Anonymous collectivity.

INTRODUCTION: EUROPE STARTED HERE

"Europe started here." The current slogan decorating the Web site of the Georgian Department of Tourism proposes a seemingly radical revisionist answer to the question that has haunted the Georgian intelligentsia since the nineteenth century: "Europe or Asia?" (Orjonikidze 1997).[1] While Georgians have long seen their modern predicament in terms of their ambiguous location within an Orientalist imaginative geography, few members of the intelligentsia have ever seriously proposed any answer to that question other than "Europe."

But this answer just raises further questions. In fact, the whole definition of that peculiar social formation, the intelligentsia (a collective noun in Russian, the singular form of which is *intelligent*, plural *intelligenty*), appears to be found in mediating the gap between "Europe" and "here," wherever "here" is. For each generation, the predicament is always a sense of nonidentity with Europe, which must be overcome, and overcoming this nonidentity is precisely what gives state or intelligentsia actors their mission. While the current tendency of Georgian state intellectuals of the Department of Tourism is to claim status as being *inventors* or *originators* of European civilization, in the nineteenth century, the more general consensus was that the civilizational narrative of Europe (the ideal "forms") would have to be imitated in the obdurate material of Georgia, and the intelligentsia public would be the Platonic demiurge (imitative craftsman rather than original creator) mediating between the ideal forms of Europe and the recalcitrant matter of Georgia and its people.[2] To do that, the intelligentsia not only aligned themselves with Europe (progress) and their people with Asia (stasis, obduracy); they recreated the opposition between enlightened society and the unenlightened people as an opposition between the (modern, European) public and the (traditional, Oriental) people.

Thus, the attempt by the Georgian intelligentsia to forge European-style publics in Georgia was at the same time a strong claim to European identity. It also produced an almost immediate crisis of self-definition, as European Georgia sent newspaper correspondents into newly reconquered Ottoman Georgia, only to discover that the people of these lands saw themselves, and increasingly were seen, as strangers to European Georgia. Georgian intelligentsia publics and the Georgian people became increasingly estranged in this encounter, and the community of "strangers" of European Georgian publics proved unable to convince the people of the "strange land" of Oriental Georgia of their belonging within a quasi-secular model of the Georgian nation. Georgian correspondents bore witness to the *muxajirat* (the Georgian/Russian spelling of *muhajirat*), hundreds of thousands of estranged Georgian Muslim "brothers" fleeing Russian-conquered territories to Ottoman lands. This crisis of nonrecognition between public and people, European and Oriental Georgia, figured in the *muxajirat*, produced both notions of Georgian public life and European identity that this book explores. It is the story of how Georgia became "modern" and "European" primarily by encountering its own "backward" and "Oriental" other.

This is a book about the attempt of the emergent Georgian intelligentsia to mediate two crucial binaries: state and people, and Europe and Asia. On the one hand, by constituting themselves as an intelligentsia, they sought to turn a received aristocratic notion of "society" based on embodied representative publicness into an explicitly European form of disembodied public sphere mediated by discourse alone. In doing so, the intelligentsia defined themselves as being in the service of "the people" as opposed to the "state." On the other hand, just as they defined themselves as a mediating group between the people and the state, they positioned themselves within an explicitly Orientalist and diffusionist model of civilizational progress in which there was a unitary civilization, located in Europe, which provided perfected models for progress elsewhere, and it was the historical mission of the intelligentsia to adapt those European models to the national "life" of the people. The Georgian intelligentsia then saw modern social imaginaries like "the public" as being part of a general set of European models for civilizational progress; newspapers like *Droeba* (1866–1885), like the intelligentsia writers and correspondents, were to mediate between European models and local conditions of "life."

By conflating modern social imaginaries (public, market, nation) with categories of imaginative geographies (European civilization), Georgian intelligentsia models anticipate similar conflations characteristic of popular and scientific literatures on Western modernity, usually following directly or indirectly from the European or Western material they are working from (Anderson 1991, Habermas 1991, Taylor 2002, Warner 2002). First of all, the Georgian intelligentsia shares with many contemporary theorists a sense that certain social forms (for example, modern social imaginaries) are European property by virtue of historical priority or productive elaboration (Asad 2003). Since European civilization is a narrative rather than a geographical category (Asad 2003, 166), there is always the question of historical priority, in which foundational categories of modernity turn out to be ancient European heirlooms. The claim of the Georgian Department of Tourism that "Europe started here" (and subsidiary claims illustrating specific institutions originated on Georgian soil) simply mimics a well-known European discourse in which concepts like "liberty" turn out to be European inventions which others would have to work hard to acquire (Van de Veer 2001, 158).

Second, European civilization as narrative is based on a Lockean model of appropriation via "productive elaboration" (Asad 2003, 167), so even if the raw materials are not original, the specific civilizational forms (social imaginaries like public, nation, market) worked out by European civilizational labor are products that belong to Europe (Asad 2003, 168) and then are "exported" or "pirated" elsewhere (e.g., Anderson 1991, 156–7), and sometimes the European brand is even counterfeited or "faked" in (Oriental) despotisms (Taylor 2002, 83). The point is that the "modular" products distinctive of European modernity (modern social imaginaries like nations, publics, markets, forms of subjectivity etc.) can be exported, imitated, or pirated. But like certain other products, they originated in the traditional *terroir* of Europe and bear a protected designation of origin.

The "civilization" of the nineteenth century was unitary, however. Many current theorists, like Charles Taylor, are willing to add the plural suffixes of pluralism to terms like "civilization" and "modernity" and then allow these discrete civilizations to enter into dialogue, thereby further reifying civilizational differences and avoiding questions of global narratives (see Van de Veer 2001, 160). But however much these are pluralized, the Lockean sense of property via productive elaboration remains intact; modernity may be multiple, but it is not multicentric. The European forms are purchased, pirated, borrowed, or creatively imitated, leading to a contemporary plurality of civilizations among which Europe is merely *primus inter pares*. "This means we finally get over seeing modernity as a single process of which Europe is the paradigm, and that we understand the European model as the first, certainly, as the object of some creative imitation, naturally, but as, at the end of the day, one model among many . . ." (Taylor 2002, 196). Not so much a social theory as a sophisticated rehearsal of a triumphalist European model of self-representation, I lay it out here because it explains both the contemporary Georgian assertion that "Europe started here" (claiming to be the very beginning of this narrative of productive elaboration) but also the explicitly diffusionist Georgian intelligentsia discourse by which they positioned themselves as mediators between European forms and Georgian realities. Both models assert a nonidentity between European civilization and Georgia in the present tense, but contemporary Georgians assert historical priority ("inventors" of Europe), while nineteenth-century Georgians sought to appropriate Europe via "imitation."

This diffusionist model is the enabling condition for civilizing projects, both imperial and intelligentsia civilizing missions, external and internal colonialisms. This is, in part, because while Europe is conceptualized as a narrative with certain distinctive products, for the most part, the Orient is not conceptualized as a civilization at all. To the extent that it is opposed to Europe as a civilization, it is as a quasi-civilization, a mere carrier civilization in opposition to the productive civilization of Europe (Asad 2003, 169). Europe, quite unlike all the other spatial categories of the Orientalist imaginative geography, is a narrative category of time, labor, and progress, while Asia belongs only to space and obduracy. As the Russian Romantic Marlinskii pithily summarizes this Orientalist commonplace (whose locus classicus is Hegel's *Philosophy of History*) in his novel of the Caucasus, *Ammalat Bek* (1843 [1831], chapter x), "Against Asia all attempts of improvement and civilization have broken like waves; it seems not to belong to time, but to place."

The models discussed so far, because they locate modern social imaginaries primarily as a development internal to a basically hermetically sealed European civilization, have a strong tendency to ignore global aspects of formation of that narrative in which metropole and colony, Europe and its others, both participate (if not the subsequent diffusion) (Van De Veer 2001, 160). Such accounts also ignore the way in which Europe's social and geographical others serve both as actual participants (Van de Veer 2001) and also as internalized imaginary others to create "symbolic fields of social alterity" (Coombe 1996, 212) against which social imaginaries define themselves. European civilization or modernity is defined by the drawing of borders: "These borders involve more than a confused geography. They reflect a history whose unconfused purpose is to separate Europe from alien times ('communism,' 'Islam') as well as alien places ('Islamdom,' 'Russia')" (Asad 2003, 171). While apologists for each sort of imaginary seek to define it by its internal progressive content or in terms of the historical unfolding of an internal logic or entelechy, it seems clear that, as Barth famously argued for ethnic groups (1969), all social imaginaries and "civilizations" are entities defined first and foremost at their boundaries: "Europe did not merely expand overseas; it made itself through that expansion" (Asad 2003, 172). Nowhere is this as clear as a would-be European country that is located at the absolute margins of Europe, like Georgia.

Both the narrative of the public and the narrative of European civilization have at their core a certain universalizing liberal narrative, one that gives Georgian intelligentsia of this period their historic mediating mission. Both the liberal narrative of the public and the liberal narrative of Europe have in common that their boundaries generate exclusions and then seek to overcome those exclusions (Asad 2003, 170). Civilizing narratives like colonialism and, of course, the parasitic Georgian intelligentsia discourse, are born in the gap between the haves and the have-nots of both narratives. This exclusion is temporary, but inclusion is endlessly deferred. The groups excluded from publics and public life in the imperial metropole (women, the working classes, the lower orders, children, etc.) are often, but not always, rhetorically placed in parallel with the exclusions generated by the colonial order. In a similar fashion, the self-definition of the Georgian intelligentsia as an enlightened public defined them both in service to, but in opposition to, the benighted "people" (first of rural west Georgia, then of Ottoman Georgia). But the fact that they represented an explicitly European civilizing mission to these people, the fact that some of these people were Ottoman, Muslims, Orientals, mapped this vertical division of social imaginary onto a horizontal opposition of imaginative geography. In the case at hand, the formation of modern print publics in Georgia occurs in tandem with a massive crisis of Georgian identity, as European Georgians (intelligentsia) encountered their Ottoman Georgian (people) and, in the shock of mutual nonrecognition, just as quickly parted ways.

This book deals with a crucial period in the development of Georgian print culture, the first continuously published Georgian newspaper, *Droeba* (1866–1885), focusing on the period leading up to the period of the Russian conquest of Ottoman Georgia and the aftermath of the conquest (1877–79). This period was decisive for the creation of an imagined community of self-described "intelligentsia" based on the circulation of the newspaper *Droeba*. It was also a period in which the imagined spatial horizons of Georgia expanded immensely with the addition of the "lost" territories of Ottoman Georgia after the Russian conquest and just as quickly contracted when correspondents from this newspaper discovered that there would be no happy story of instant mutual recognition and reunification between the sundered halves of the two Georgias, European and Asian. This case can show how print cultures are formed at their margins, as the discourse of seemingly infinite inclusiveness of Occidentalist social imaginaries encounters the discourse of unassimilable alterity of Orientalist imaginative geographies. Like the narrative of Europe, the narrative of publics was by definition unable to absorb the very alterity that it had created in order to define itself. Georgian print culture in this period provides an almost unique opportunity to see these two kinds of imaginings, the Occidentalist imagining of a public as a community of intimate strangers, the Orientalist imagining of strange lands, come to mutually construct one another at the moment of the birth of Georgian print culture. This was a moment when Georgians came to see themselves as an Occidentalist liberal public, a paradoxical community of like-minded strangers formed by being addressed by print discourse, and this public confronted the increasingly obdurate Orientalist strangeness of the land of Ottoman Georgia described by that print discourse.

Map 1: Regions of Georgia

Georgian print culture in the period of *Droeba* (1966–1885) confronted the same uneven geographic and social terrains that confronted Russian imperial administrators over the entire century from the moment of conquest in 1801.

First, geographically, Georgia is conventionally divided into a northern mountainous region of the main Caucasus range and a southern region that, while highly uneven topographically, is conventionally called "the plains." To the mountains belong regions like Svaneti, Racha, Xevi, Xevsureti, and Pshavi (see map 1), while the remaining regions are assigned to the "plains" (Charachidze 1968). The geographical opposition between "mountains" and "plains" subsumes a whole range of cultural differences, forms of imputed alterity, and attendant difficulties for Russian conquest and administration. The period under discussion here is one in which the "mountains" designated a zone of almost complete alterity to the plains. Aside from an early literary experiment by the writer Ilia Chavchavadze, it was not until the 1880s that Georgian novelists and ethnographers like Aleksandre Qazbegi, Vazha Pshavela, and Urbneli began to represent the lives of the mountaineers as being integral to Georgian identity. By 1892, as one commentator put it, Georgian mountain dwellers finally moved from being peripheral savages to becoming the highest representation of Georgian traditional culture, "our mountaineers" (Le Galcher Baron 1992).[3] While this book does not discuss this movement in any detail (but see Manning 2007), I argue that the preceding period of engagement and disappointment with the unassimilable alterity of Ottoman Georgia (1877–80) makes intelligible this abrupt change of interest from the Ottoman Southwest to the mountainous Northeast that characterized the 1880s.

The second relevant geographic and cultural division, and the one that is directly relevant to understanding the period in question, is the enduring political and cultural division between East Georgia (the primary city being Tbilisi or Tiflis) and West Georgia (the primary city being Kutaisi). In part, this division reflects a general cultural divide formed by centuries of Safavid Persian hegemony and conquest in the East and Ottoman dominance in the West (Suny 1988, chapter 3), but it was preserved and continued in Russian administrative divisions which divided Georgia into an eastern Tbilisi province and a Western Kutaisi province (Suny 1988, 62). The Russian conquest of Georgia recapitulated these divisions, beginning with Eastern Georgia in 1801, with portions of West Georgia (Mingrelia, Imereti) accepting Russian sovereignty in 1803–1804. Subsequently piecemeal conquests of West Georgia followed over a series of wars between the Russian and Ottoman empires. The period of the war of 1806–1812 brought the regions of Guria and Abkhazia into the Russian Empire. With the war of 1828–9, the rest of the regions of Mingrelia, Mesxeti, and Javaxeti (map 1), as well as the Armenian city of Erevan and with it Eastern Armenia, became permanent additions to the Russian Empire. With the war of 1877–1878, which happens in the middle of the period covered by this book, the historic regions of West Georgia that Georgians of the period called Ottoman Georgia—the regions of Ajaria (including the city of Batumi), Ardahan, and Kars—all became part of the Russian Empire.

The uneven and piecemeal nature of Russian conquest of Georgia produced a situation in which previous cultural divisions between East and West Georgia (Kutaisi province, also named Imereti after the central province) were preserved by Russian bureaucratic categories and ultimately came to inform Georgian print culture. The literary reconquest of Western Georgia in the pages of the newspaper *Droeba* essentially recapitulated the stages of the Russian conquest earlier in the century with articles of correspondence about Imereti (beginning in 1866),

Mingrelia (1867), Guria (1868), and Svaneti (1869), with nothing about Ottoman Georgia (Ajaria) until 1875.

Lastly, the newspaper *Droeba* represented and presupposed, by and large, the East Georgian viewpoints of the intelligentsia of Tbilisi or Tiflis, which was also the viceroy's capital for governing Caucasia. The opposition between rapidly urbanizing East Georgia and rural West Georgia then could also be stereotypically mapped onto the cultural geographic opposition between "the city" (Tbilisi/Tiflis) and the "country," and onto stereotypical associated images of persons: urban aristocrats or intelligentsia living in the primary city of the Caucasus, Tbilisi/Tiflis (the editors of *Droeba*), and the West Georgian peasants or Georgian mountain dwellers who are exemplars of Georgian rural backwardness. (I note here that the multilingual and multicultural terrain of the city of Tbilisi itself also represents an uneven cultural terrain in which Georgians were in a sense, visitors, but while I will tell fragments of this story, the story of the city would require a separate treatment.)[4]

Compared to the hegemonic East Georgians of the plains, the mountain dwellers and the inhabitants of West Georgia represented a form of unassimilated alterity: East Georgian plains-dwellers in a sense embodied the voice of the "writers" and "readers" of *Droeba*, and West Georgians and mountain-dwellers embodied the voice of those "written about." And if the region of West Georgia as a whole was coming to be represented as a hotbed of backwardness and superstition compared to the enlightened city-dwellers of Tbilisi, then the even more extreme alterity of recently conquered Ottoman Georgia would prove to be the limit of absolute unassimilable alterity. As I will show, it is as if the East Georgians, unable to incorporate the alterity of Ottoman Georgia into their sense of identity at the end of the 1870s, instead turned their attention to the mountains in the 1880s in compensation.

The period dealt with in this book (roughly the period of the publication of *Droeba*, the first continuously published Georgian newspaper, 1866–1885) is also a period of immense social reforms and upheavals. Most of the period of *Droeba* occurs during the reign of the reform-minded Alexander II (tsar from 1855 until assassinated in 1881), and these reforms provide both many of the enabling conditions and field of activity for a newly emergent group within Russian and Georgian society, the intelligentsia. This is a period in which a new generation of Russian and Georgian intelligentsia, the so-called men of the sixties, embraced new social and political ideologies of service to the people and associated themselves with aesthetic categories such as realism adequate to express their newfound critical and engaged role with respect to society (Paperno 1988, Frierson 1993). At the same time, they defined themselves in opposition to the political ideology of service to the state and aesthetic categories of Romanticism that were felt to characterize the "men of the forties," a generation in Georgia that was strongly associated with an upper nobility who had entered state service when their aristocratic rank was officially recognized (Suny 1988, chapter 4). Even as they did so, it remained that the Georgian intelligentsia emerged out of an urbanizing Georgian service aristocracy, and the sixties generation in Georgia remained much more solidly aristocratic in character than in Russia. But at the same time, reforms of the period which enabled the emergence of Georgian print culture also provided avenues for new additions to the intelligentsia from nonnoble backgrounds.

Official recognition of noble status (a lengthy process finally completed in 1859) and transformation into a largely urban service aristocracy was not the only historical change that changed the Georgian aristocracy's relationship to state and society (Suny 1988, chapter 4), equally important if not more so is the central reform of the period of the Great Reforms, the emancipation of the serfs, decreed for Russia in 1861. The emancipation in Georgia happened later than in Russia, decreed for Tbilisi/Tiflis province in 1864 and continued piecemeal into West Georgia over almost a decade (Suny 1988, chapter 5). In effect, the first decade of *Droeba* ("Times," beginning in 1866) is as much a chronicle of the "times" of the Emancipation (1864–1871) as it is an exploration of the alien "spaces" of West Georgia where the progress of emancipation continued very slowly through the period. The attempted cultural reconquest of Ottoman Georgia in the pages of *Droeba* at the end of the 1870s is simply a continuation of the mission of the cultural, geographic, and social conquest of West Georgia that defined *Droeba* from the very outset.

Starting from this period, this book centrally describes changes in the category "society" or "public" (*sazogadoeba*). The newspaper *Droeba* helped move this term from denoting the embodied, face-to-face "society" of the aristocracy displayed at court or at feasts, to the print-mediated "society" of strangers of the intelligentsia. The resulting form of public, when compared with Western publics, is familiar, yet strange, and thus produces questions for our general received literature on publics: however, rather than pluralistically posit a whole new (and potentially radically incommensurable) civilizational form, or an "alternate modernity," I prefer to see this uncanny doppelganger of Western modernity as being part of a single global process (especially since the Georgian intelligentsia saw it that way!) that produces strangely similar, yet different, siblings. The existence of state supervision in the form of censors constituting one of the audiences for this paper made the forms of address in this public multiple, addressed both to an intimate society of intelligentsia as well as the state censor. Unlike Western publics which can presuppose their own material infrastructure or channels of communication, the rather more picturesque technologies and infrastructures of the Russian Empire are always topical both for the self-definition of tsarist publics and as an exemplification of the predicament of the "people." Unlike paradigmatic Western publics, again, this public defines itself in terms of the people, but not as being identical with the people. In fact, this public continuously defines itself by either erasing or subsuming competing kinds of publics, in the case of "the people" by defining this public as being the primarily oral and illiterate quoted voice of the rural peasantry, subsumed in print under the quoting voice of the intelligentsia transcriber. Hence, genres emerge of intelligentsia dialogues with the rural people which continually deepen the inscription of otherness or alterity between the "public" and the "people" within Russian Georgia, and those genres in turn deepen the parallel opposition between Russian and Ottoman Georgia as the unbridgeable Orientalist opposition between Europe and Asia. Because of the uncanny familiarity crossed with strangeness of this form of public, the account seeks to determine how categories which often have the very same names ("people," "public") and often the same intentions in this context produces a result which is at first glance so familiar, but has consequences that are so strange. Here as elsewhere, Georgian reformers began with the explicit attempt to imitate and replicate, European categories of modernity, social imaginaries like "public." Their project foundered on their inability to reconcile this explicit Occidentalism with their own implicit Orientalism, concretely, in the obduracy of the lands and people of Ottoman Georgia to their project of reconciling the public and the people, European and Ottoman Georgia. The familiarity and strangeness of their categories result historically from this predicament. Analytically, the strangeness of these familiar categories allows us a unique perspective on the hidden presuppositions of theories of social imaginary and imaginative geography alike.

This book, then, attempts to critically engage the categories of by-now familiar models of (largely) Western publics (Anderson 1991, Habermas 1991, Taylor 2002, Warner 2002) from a defamiliarizing perspective provided by what we could call the "intelligentsia public" of Georgian print culture. (Lisa Wedeen (2008) also makes comparable critiques of this literature from the perspective of an equally peripheral public, but unfortunately arrived too late for me to incorporate comparisons into this book. See also Cody (2009, 2011a) for other defamiliarizing ethnographic and theoretical perspectives on the category of public that I have not been able to fully incorporate here, and Cody (2011b) for a survey of recent anthropological perspectives on the concept). The encounter between these familiar models and this unfamiliar case provides a critical perspective that both illuminates blind spots and presuppositions of the Western model (which was, of course, the model that the intelligentsia publics themselves sought to imitate and in terms of which they judged themselves and found themselves wanting) as well as sheds light on the commonalities and specificities of these peripheral publics. The book engages the presuppositions of these dominant Occidentalist models of publics by bringing them together with other literatures that are seldom explored in tandem, notably the literature on Orientalist imaginative geographies (for example, Asad 1973, 2003, Said 1978), in order to show how the categories of Western social imaginaries are always cultural models of the Occidental self which are defined implicitly against a recalcitrant residuum of Orientalist alterity. Obviously the Georgian intelligentsia, finding themselves on the ambiguous periphery of Europe and Asia, had to make explicit the Orientalist oppositions which Western publics left implicit, here, Georgian print culture is valuable in the way that thematizes and makes explicit the latent presuppositions of its Western print culture model.

Another important critical perspective is provided by a varied literature drawn from Science and Technology Studies (for example, Latour 1992, 2005, Law 1987, Laurier and Philo 2007, Bier 2008) , and in particular an influential group of recent studies that explore the perennially neglected category of "infrastructure" (Star 1999, Otter 2002, Robbins 2007, Larkin 2008, Elyachar 2010). Just as the addition of the literature on Orientalist constructions of alterity complicates and corrects the sometimes triumphalist rehearsal of Occidentalist liberal narratives found in the literature on publics, so the "flat ontology" and "principle of symmetry" in the technology studies literature produces a level playing field in which humans and nonhumans both figure symmetrically as actors. This move corrects the rather overstated emphasis on cultural imaginations over material infrastructures that characterizes some of the literature on publics (see Larkin 2008, 242–255), an emphasis itself arising out of a cultural constructivist impetus to correct the perceived technological determinism of earlier accounts of print culture (e.g., Eisenstein 1983). These two defamiliarizing perspectives are crucial to the understanding the specificity of the categories of Georgian print culture, for as I have already noted, the Georgian intelligentsia saw these two things as being central to their own abject historical predicament: the difficulties of creating a European print culture on the uneven terrain of Asia were in a sense equivalent to the way that infrastructure on the periphery of European modernity could not be presupposed and then forgotten in the same way it could be in the centers of European modernity.

The objective of this book is to build up a model of the cultural categories of Georgian print culture at the time of its emergence and consolidation, which affords a critical and comparative perspective on the implicit presuppositions of the Western model on which it is based. Accordingly, the organization of chapters is categorical rather than temporal or historical. The discussion begins with the most basic and defining category of the newspaper *Droeba*, correspondence from the readers which forms the bulk of the content of the newspaper. For most of the book, we follow a typical correspondent, a writer writing under the pseudonym Bavreli who was a special correspondent to the newly reconquered regions of Ottoman Georgia. Bavreli's predicaments of describing this new, as yet undescribed, landscape are of a piece with his predicaments as a new writer in a new print culture, at a time Georgian print culture as a self-sustaining and continuous presence was scarcely more than ten years old. Bavreli is a stranger in a strange land, writing about this strangeness to a newspaper that itself represents an innovation in Georgia. Consequently, his self-consciousness as a writer makes him a rich and perceptive commentator on Georgian print culture at precisely the time it was congealing at precisely the place and situation where it congealed—in the explosion of interest in these new lands, an event second in importance only to the end of serfdom a decade earlier as a defining moment of Georgian print culture.

Bavreli's self-consciousness about what he should write about, and how he should write it, give us an extensive source of indigenous meta-commentary about the categories of print culture at precisely the moment it was formed. His story forms the connecting narrative to which other narratives in the book are connected. His own self-conscious discussion of the genres, topics, and technologies of print culture give us a privileged indigenous viewpoint around which to organize the presentation of the categories of this print culture. The story is told not from the perspective of the leading figures of Georgian society but from the perspective of a marginal man, a literal "nobody" who is by that fact itself a hero of his times, an almost prototypical example of the emergent nonaristocratic intelligentsia.[5]

In the same way, the story is not told from the perspective of the center of Georgia, but from its oft-ignored spatial peripheries, from a strange yet familiar land, Ottoman Georgia, which has never been successfully integrated into Georgian mythic narratives of the nation. It is precisely the failure of this stranger in a strange land, Bavreli traveling in Ottoman Georgia, to integrate this *terra incognita* into the familiar terrain of the nation, which causes the defining crisis which leads to a redefinition of Georgia, and especially Georgian print culture, as being fundamentally "European" in opposition to its own internal "Orient."

Chapters 1 and 2 introduce the central themes and predicaments of Georgian intelligentsia self-definition by exploring in detail texts written about the northern boundaries of Georgia before and after the period of encounter with Ottoman Georgia. The texts form spatial, temporal, and generic "boundary works." In particular, Ilia Chavchavadze's manifesto *Letters of a Traveler* (1861–1871), discussed in chapter 1, sets the stage for all future writers, including Bavreli's writing about Ottoman Georgia. This text is a boundary work between aristocratic manuscript and intelligentsia print modes of circulation, between Russian state discourse of civilization and Georgian folk culture, between intertextual dialogs with aristocratic writers and intratextual dialogues between the intelligentsia and the people, and lastly, because it occurs on the very boundary of Russia and Georgia, Europe and Asia. The natural landscape the author traverses is appropriated by the author in a kind of Aesopianized version of Romantic descriptions of nature to engage with previous accounts of other travelers representative of other "geopoetic" discourses of the Caucasus and Georgia, Europe and Asia. In the following chapter, beginning with writers like Aleksandre Qazbegi and Urbneli writing about the same stretch of land in the 1880s, we see how the infrastructure of empire, the Georgian military road, increasingly takes the center stage away from the "romantic" aesthetically valorized natural landscape to produce a new "realist" vocabulary for geopoetic discourses about empire, but their writings also mark a new "turn to the people" of the pagan mountains of Georgia, and *away* from the unassimilable alienness of the Muslim Ottoman Georgians on the southern frontier.

The next chapters (from chapter 3 onward) turn from the northern boundary of Georgia to the southern boundary with Ottoman Georgia, and focus on writings in the newspaper *Droeba* from the period of Emancipation in the 1860s to the period of the reconquest of Ottoman Georgia at the end of the 1870s. This was the period of the formation of Georgian print culture, and with it intelligentsia understandings of themselves as a "public" in opposition to the illiterate "people," and as representing civilizing proxies for "Europe" in opposition to the "Tatarized" (Muslim) Oriental Georgians of Ottoman Georgia. In chapter 3, I introduce the genre which is the "hero" of what follows: correspondence. At the same time we meet our human "hero": a "nobody" whom we know only through his correspondence, S. Bavreli, a socially and spatially marginal person, who served as special correspondent for *Droeba* in Ottoman Georgia. The horizons of Georgian print mediated social imaginaries and imaginative geographies are explored by a series of striking moments from a single *Droeba* correspondent, the pseudonymous S. Bavreli, who is introduced here as a character who is a foil for well-known aristocratic intelligentsia writers like Chavchavadze in chapter 1. Bavreli is literally a nobody, unlike Chavchavadze, and his anxieties about writing reflect those of a new generation of intelligentsia writers who, unlike Chavchavadze, cannot depend on their aristocratic status to lend them authority as members of the intelligentsia. Bavreli becomes a constant companion through the first half of the book, as does the formative historical moment of the conquest of Ottoman Georgia, which becomes a moment when the genre of correspondence, and Georgian print culture in the newspaper *Droeba*, truly stabilizes. In this chapter, we begin to see the ways that correspondence from beyond the pale, Ottoman Georgia, stabilizes Georgian print culture as a specifically European culture of circulation.

The next chapter (4) revisits the contrast between aristocratic and intelligentsia modes of textual circulation, as well as Georgian aristocratic and intelligentsia ideals of service, respectively to the state and the people. The correspondence of a prominent aristocratic Georgian spy in preconquest Ottoman Georgia is compared to the correspondence of our "nobody," Bavreli, in the period immediately following the conquest. The use and abuse of Ottoman Georgian hospitality serves as an enabling condition both for the work of the aristocratic spy and our nobody correspondent, Bavreli. The same opposition, between aristocratic and intelligentsia publics and modes of publicity, is developed, again with reference to Ottoman Georgia, now returning to Tbilisi for a newspaper account written by an intelligentsia witness (Sergi Meskhi) of a public feast given by the Georgian aristocracy for representatives of the conquered Ottoman Georgian aristocracy. At the same time, we see the radical disconfirmation of both these fanciful aristocratic and intelligentsia theories by the *muxajirat* of Ottoman Georgians who fled their embrace on the eve of their repatriation for territories still controlled by the Ottomans in one of the many massive and catastrophic movements of Muslim populations of the Caucasus following Russian conquest in the modern period.

The next chapter (5) develops the emerging and deepening opposition between intelligentsia publics and the voice of the people, stressing the very different devices or technologies that the intelligentsia writer uses to inscribe their own voice within the world of print culture and transcribe the voice of the people. On the one hand, there is the whole semiotic technology of signature, and particularly pseudonyms, by which the intelligentsia author produces a writerly persona indigenous to print culture, contrasted with the various technologies by which the same writer transcribes the voice of the people as an anonymous and yet highly embodied voice, thus both bringing the voice of the people into print culture, all the while retaining its diagnostic alterity as a transcribed spoken *voice* within the world of print. The next chapter (6) develops the opposition between the voice of the intelligentsia and the people in terms of characteristic genres for these voices. Transcribed dialogs with peasants often contained within a single area of the newspaper called the *feuilleton* within which most correspondence appears, a space which later develops into a genre of the same name for a very different kind of dialog between intelligentsia. An implicit distinction emerges between "dialogue in the feuilleton," in which the dialogue between the intelligentsia and the people is represented within some other genre in this space on the page, and the "dialogue of the feuilleton," which happens as this space becomes a genre for the intimate dialogue between urban intelligentsia.

Chapter 7 moves from genres of representation to content, to the centrality of the act of *writing*, to the self-definition of intelligentsia like Bavreli, and the question, almost equivalent to the defining intelligentsia question of "What is to be done?": What do we write about? Writing, the defining activity of the intelligentsia, is brought up against its defining object, "life" (of the people). The kind of writing, defined as "realism" (Paperno 1988), with its privileging of real "life," with its strong materialism and empiricism, tended to avoid the categories of peasant life that were defined as unreal, specifically their fairy tales about sprites called *kajis*. The aesthetic and epistemic revalorization of these creatures from empty superstition in the 1870s opposed to "life" to figures expressive of peasant consciousness in the 1880s, real because part of folklore, is explored in this chapter.

The last chapter (8) deals with the geopoetics of Georgian intelligentsia travel and discourse about travel, as Georgian travelers define the trajectories of their mode of travel between Occidentalist, Orientalist, and localist imaginative geographies, thus reprising many themes introduced in the first chapter of the book. Part of the intimate self-critique of Georgian intelligentsia in this period is, despite certain marginal figures like Bavreli, a certain antipathy to travel that makes Georgians very unlike the imagined European. Bavreli, for example, follows Chavchavadze in continually grounding himself in, or comparing himself to, figures in the landscape that are his "fellow travelers," rivers like the Mtkvari, which, like him, travel but do not travel very far from home. He constantly contrasts himself with his more cosmopolitan fellow travelers, who do not show this intimate connection to the landscape. Thus, to discuss the geopoetics of Georgian travel is to discuss why so much of it doesn't seem to qualify as travel at all, even for Georgians at that time. But there are a few exceptions, and so this discourse of localism is complemented by a few clear examples of Georgian travel, Sergi

Meskhi's Occidentalist travel to Europe, the fad of archeological travel in the late nineteenth century, and of course, Bavreli's singular Orientalist voyages to Ottoman Georgia.

The first and last chapters, then, deal with travelers, borders, and the landscape of Georgia. Our first writer-traveler, Prince Ilia Chavchavadze, is easily the best known of all Georgian writers of this period. The second writer-traveler, the hero of the bulk of this book, S. Bavreli, is by contrast a true "native" of Georgian print culture, a "nobody" about whom we know little more than what he chose to write, in much the same way that, but for his writing, we would know as little about the "nobodies" about whom he wrote. As Shunsuke Nozawa points out for a parallel Japanese case, we can see here that Georgian print culture consisted of two related kinds of nobodies: nobody-writers like Bavreli, who enters a print culture as a pseudonymous "nobody-in-particular," a nobody in an almost literal sense of being a disembodied voice of a member of the "public"; and what Nozawa calls "real particular nobodies," the ordinary, insignificant, unnoticed, and nonnotable "people" which realist writers like Bavreli wrote about (compare Nozawa 2011, 5). Using the example of Bavreli, the book asks up to this point, "Under what historical conditions can a nobody writing about other nobodies come to be a central narrative form?" Naturally, in the process, we become interested in the private identity of our nobody anti-hero. In the final chapter, then, we turn to a detective story: Who was this Bavreli? Does it matter who he was? What do the paltry materials he left of his extra-public self tell us, if anything, about Georgian print culture in his period? Just as we see the Georgian notions of publicness and European identity can best be viewed from the boundaries, so it is a marginal writer like Bavreli from whom we learn the most about the beginnings of Georgian modernity.

I: LANGUAGES OF NATURE, CULTURE, AND CIVILIZATION: LETTERS OF A TRAVELER

KAZBEK, FROM THE POST STATION.   (from Freshfield 1869, facing p.185)

Figure 2

The situation of the post station (at Kazbek) has no beauty except when the great mountain is unveiled. Then the picture seen from the windows will not easily be forgotten. Again and again, it has been painted and photographed; it is met with in every book of travel, even in the shop windows of St. Petersburg. It is the keepsake view—the Jungfrau from Interlaken—of the Caucasus. (Freshfield 1896, 87)

The Dariel pass through the Caucasus today, as in the nineteenth century, provides the main viable route between Russia and Georgia, the Georgian military road. The journey from Vladikavkaz in modern North Ossetia into Georgia follows the Terek River, which flows north from Mount Kazbek (Georgian *Qaz[i]begi*, also *Mqinvari* "glacier") into Russia, while the southern flanks of the route follow the Aragvi River, flowing south toward Tbilisi (see map 1). This journey from Vladikavkaz to Tbilisi and vice versa is across some very well-traveled literary terrain for European, Russian, and Georgian Romantics (see for example Greenleaf 1991, 1994; Layton 1994, Ram and Shatirishvili 2004, Manning 2008), whose overlapping narratives in genres from fairy tale to travel account, lyric verse to adventure tale, gave the landscape a peculiar ambivalence where fact and fancy were intertwined, so much so that the Dariel gorge itself has sometimes been called "a fairy tale in twelve versts" (Graham 1911, 164). It is in this rugged and well-traversed piece of literary and geographical terrain that the noted Georgian writer Ilia Chavchavadze (1837–1907) positioned his travelogue-cum-literary manifesto, *Letters of a Traveler* (*Mgzavris Cerilebi* [composition begun in 1861, first published in 1871, and again in a fuller uncensored version in 1892]).[1]

Chavchavadze's *Letters of a Traveler* is perhaps the single most important piece of political writing of the Georgian generation of the 1860s, who called themselves *Terg-daleulebi* ("those who have drunk from the Terek River"). This term has potentially ambiguous reference in this text, denoting at once a member of the Russian-educated Georgian gentry intelligentsia represented by the narrator, who is *Terg-daleuli* because he has crossed ("drunk from") the Terek, the boundary between Russia and Georgia, in search of enlightenment, as well as denoting a member of the Georgian people, Lelt Ghunia, who as a Moxevian peasant, dwells beside the Terek River in Xevi, and could therefore implicitly be taken as a true *Terg-daleuli*.[2] The term *Terg-daleuli* itself undergoes a transformation and revalorization in the course of the text from the first sense to the second, as Chavchavadze becomes disenchanted with the promises of Russian civilization and discovers authentic culture instead among the Georgian folk. This transition is mirrored in the natural order in the changes in the character of the Terek River itself from the placid, servile Terek in the Russian plains at Vladikavkaz to the torrential, free Terek in the Caucasus mountains.

In this chapter, I am primarily interested in exploring the rhetorical opposition between *form* and *content* of Lelt Ghunia's speech, whose correct realistic representation Chavchavadze presents, in his coda, as being the *only* project of the text. I argue that Chavchavadze uses this opposition both to *naturalize* his own relationship to the peasant Lelt Ghunia as a member of the "intelligentsia" to the "people," creating an organic unity of language, a nation. At the same time, the lack of relationship between form and content in the disjointed dialogue of a drunken Russian officer he meets along the way has the opposite effect, emphasizing the immense gap between the pretenses of Russian civilization (form) and its actual effects in the lives of the Georgian people (content). In this manner, as the partner in two very different dialogues, Chavchavadze implicitly inserts himself between the Russian colonizing state and the colonized Georgian people as a mediating figure, as a *Terg-daleuli* in both the above senses, educated in Russia, Chavchavadze yet remains a Georgian, able to speak both languages and thus to bridge the gap between Russian civilization and Georgian folk culture.

It may seem odd that a Georgian movement for political and cultural reform would take its name (*Terg-daleuli*) from a river in the Caucasus mountains on the very border of Georgia (the Terek, Georgian *Tergi*), but here too Chavchavadze was locating himself in relation to an existing "geopoetic" tradition in which the political order was construed in terms of the natural order. In their discussion of the poetry of an earlier generation of Georgian Romanticism, Ram and Shatirishvili (2004) argue that Georgian gentry poets of an earlier generation used different "geopoetic" strategies to reduce the triadic opposition between Russia, Georgia, and the Caucasus into a dualist opposition expressive of their newfound and ambivalent position as a relatively privileged colonial class under Russian rule. A central tendency of such "geopoetics" is to elide the opposition between Russia and Georgia over and against the warlike and uncivilized tribes of the Caucasus (on which imaginings, see Layton 1997). In the text examined here however, Ilia Chavchavadze creates a defiant prose manifesto aimed at this earlier generation's geopoetics and geopolitics and proposes a new geopoetic strategy, eliding the opposition between Georgia and the Caucasus over and against Russian domination.[3] He does so first of all by appropriating the well-known image of the Terek River as a multivalent symbol of Caucasian freedom and savagery (Layton 1994), translating its untamed roar into a human voice expressing the woes of his motherland (thereby identifying the Caucasus with Georgia). Second, moving from nature to culture, he finds his exemplary Georgian speaker from among the territorially most marginal speakers of Georgian, the Moxevians, who dwell by the Terek in the Caucasus between Russia and Georgia. It is in their appropriated voice and dialect that the political ideology of *Terg-daleuli* gentry nationalism is delivered by proxy. *Terg-daleuli* mountaineer dialect paradoxically becomes the vehicle for *Terg-daleuli* gentry ideology.

In this respect, the text to be discussed here represents a radical change in the role of language and especially folk language as having an increasingly *constitutive* role in the imagining of larger social totalities, such as "nations" and "peoples," a change experienced both in Georgia and more generally throughout Europe in the nineteenth century. In this century, language increasingly came to be seen as a uniquely natural sign of social membership; hence a common linguistic heritage—however dialectically stratified—could suture together enlightened society and the unenlightened people. In contrast to older elites, in Georgia as elsewhere, these new elites increasingly resorted to language-based forms of legitimacy of social projects, seeing in these a kind of "authority of authenticity" (Gal and Woolard 2001). Like the texts of an earlier generation of Georgian Romantics (Ram and Shatirishvili 2004), this text places Georgia and the elites who spoke for it in a "geopoetic" context in which the crucial terms to which it is to be related are the Caucasus and Russia. Giving his reading of the aesthetics of this literary landscape, Chavchavadze engages his Romantic literary forebears in an explicitly *political* dialogue and offers a radical revision of the imaginative geography that separates Georgia from the Caucasus. Unlike these texts, however, in which intertextual relations are primarily with Russian antecedents, Ilia Chavchavadze engages both Georgian and Russian literary antecedents, as well as the voice of the "people" of whose voice Chavchavadze is the mere transcriber. Whereas travel accounts through the Caucasus by Romantics, Georgian and otherwise, represent it as a moving, but silent, landscape, Chavchavadze populates this landscape, positing a close, almost organic connection between the voice of nature in the form of the Terek River and the voice of the people in the form of Lelt Ghunia, a peasant dwelling by the Terek, thus at once humanizing the indigenous natural order (the Terek) and naturalizing the human order (Lelt Ghunia).

Author, Text, Context

Before addressing the main issue of this chapter—language as the basis for a national protest against Russian imperial civilization—a brief introduction of Ilia Chavchavadze, perhaps the most prominent and significant member of the generation of the 1860s, the *Terg-dauleulebi*, in Georgia, is in order. His multiple activities as writer, publicist, editor, and cultural reformer were instrumental in the development of Georgian print culture and the formulation of the ideological position of what may be called "gentry nationalism" (the term is Suny's [1988, 133–134]) in the late nineteenth century. His assassination in 1907 by parties unknown provided this group with a martyr, bringing this somewhat marginal nationalist ideology into closer alignment with more popular movements for social justice, thus helping to transform and combine the social and national movements in Georgia in the wake of the disappointment of failure of the "social movement" in Georgia during the 1905 revolution.[4] Known to Georgians simply as "Ilia," Chavchavadze was made an Orthodox saint in the last years of Soviet power, and to this day he remains the central authoritative figure for Georgian nationalism. Chavchavadze was also a key figure in articulating the relations between older nobility and the emergent intelligentsia in Georgia, for he belonged to both classes. A noble by birth, he attended university in the Faculty of Law in St. Petersburg from 1857 to 1861 and returned a member of the nascent Georgian intelligentsia, that is, as a true *terg-daleuli,* in the sense of one who crossed the Terek (the boundary of Russia and Georgia) to receive an education (on this sense of the term, see Suny 1988). Writing at a time when a Georgian print culture and a class of intelligentsia were emerging from the manuscript culture and court sociability of the nobility, he straddled both spheres as noble and writer of poetic manuscripts and printed prose. He engaged in debates with representatives of the older generation of the nobility like Grigol Orbeliani (1804–1883) on the proper form of literary Georgian, arguing for a style closer to that of the spoken norms of the folk (see below, chapter 4). Typical of the changes and contradictions of the period, these debates concerning the modernization and popularization of a Georgian print language and print culture were conducted in a typically classical and aristocratic form—a series of traditional exchanges of poetry in traditional meters, disseminated "domestically" by mouth or manuscript among members of the Georgian urban gentry, and only later publicized in print. The text, *Letters of a Traveler,* shares many of these ambiguities, since it circulated in various manuscript forms through aristocratic urban networks, encountering a face-to-face public over a period of ten years; it was eventually published for a potentially popular readership of anonymous contemporaries in full, uncensored and authoritative form thirty years later in 1892.

The text also witnesses other transformations as the Georgian aristocracy transformed itself into a Georgian intelligentsia. Just as the generation-defining poetic debate on literary style between Orbeliani and Chavchavadze revolved around the choice between an adherence to classicism (Orbeliani) and the need for a language that was popular, folk (Chavchavadze), so too we see in this text the first systematic attention to the description of a folk dialect in Georgian, the first application of the *narodnik* principles that were in the air in Russia (Chavchavadze had met the well-known Russian reformer Chernyshevsky in Russia) and now were applied to Georgia (with an extremely heavy admixture of apologetics for the preexisting feudal order, it should be noted, hence "gentry nationalism"). More generally, it was the first Georgian evidence of the trans-European turn to popular language-based forms of legitimation for elites. This turn to the people or folk (*xalxi*), of course, occurs on the eve of the Emancipation of the serfs in Georgia, and a transformation in the role of the Georgian nobility. Originally a rural agrarian estate depending on the serfs, the Georgian elite would become urban-educated class of bureaucrats, court officials, writers, and nascent *intelligenty* who in different ways would constitute themselves rhetorically as being in the service of "the people," in whose voice, and therefore, in whose language, they spoke. As a result, in this text, more than in any other of the period, the question of linguistic form takes on immediately political content.

Synopsis of the Text

Chavchavadze's *Letters of a Traveler* is a fairly short text divided into eight passages, narrating his journey from Vladikavkaz in modern-day Ossetia into Georgia across the Dariel pass. In the first section (I), which was heavily censored in the first printing of 1871, we encounter Chavchavadze in Vladikavkaz, taking leave of his traveling companion, a Frenchman. This authentic representative of Europe appears seemingly only to marvel at the backwardness of the Russian (postal) transportation system before he goes on his way. With a sideward glance at Russian artists' idealization of their own folk ("The reality is twice as repulsive as their pictures are beautiful"), he gives us an unflattering and detailed description of a Russian post cart driver (*yamshchik*), who is presented as being coarse, ugly, and stupid.

In the second passage (II), Chavchavadze leaves Vladikavkaz, and from this point the Terek River becomes his constant traveling companion. As he crosses a bridge over the Terek, he notes that it no longer resembles the madly rushing, "heroic-demonic Terek" found in the Caucasus and celebrated by Orbeliani, whose poem "Saghamo Gamosalmebisa" ("Night of Farewell" [1959 (1841), 58–9]) he cites twice in this passage. In the first of a series of allegorical meditations on the Terek, Chavchavadze identifies this change in the nature of the Terek from mountains to plains explicitly with both with the passivity of the Russian peasantry and co-optation of the Georgian gentry under Russian rule: "That destructive Terek! How two-faced it has been! See how deathly it is. Whenever it turns its back to us and its face to Russia, when it gets into the plains and the flat country, somehow that demonic, heroic voice ceases. . . . There it is as placid, as silent, as if it dwelt under the rod or had received a high official post." At the end of the section, he has reached the post station at Lars, where he reflects on the value of his four years of education in Petersburg, from which he is returning.

In the third section (III), Chavchavadze's random and confused reflections on what he has seen, suffered, and learned at home and abroad undergo what he describes as a "revolution," and he wonders whether these same four years away from his native land will make him a stranger to his land, unable to speak or understand its language and its complaints. His reverie is interrupted by a drunken Russian officer, who engages him in an unintentional mockery of enlightened discourse, first as an equal based on the fact that Chavchavadze is an emissary from civilization (Petersburg), and then when he finds that Chavchavadze is actually a Georgian, as a subaltern Oriental "local" in need of enlightenment. In the deranged conversation that ensues, Russia's pretenses to a civilizing mission are further deflated, as the drunken officer proves unable to define the terminology of civilization except in the most vulgar and debased terms.

The next two sections (IV–V) occur at the post station of Stepants-minda (also known as Kazbek), the first Georgian village along the route. Chavchavadze polemically engages with Orbeliani once more (IV) at sunset at Kazbek post station, citing another of Orbeliani's poems (*Sadghegrdzelo* "Toast" (1959 [1827–1870]), and covertly alluding to the description of nature contained in Orbeliani's "Night of Farewell," which takes place at the same spot. Here Chavchavadze makes another series of polemical, allegorical ruminations, this time on the opposition between Mount Kazbek and the rushing Terek River at its feet; he repudiates the gleaming inaccessibility of the mountain for the muddy raging torrents of the Terek, the former identified with idealism, death, and stasis, the latter identified with materialism, life, and above all, motion and circulation. At nightfall in section V, Chavchavadze has an epiphany with the

Terek River at its center—an epiphany which causes him to understand and identify with its voice. Here again, he allegorizes the silence and darkness of night as ignorance and lack of enlightenment, while the "unsilenced complaint" of the Terek in the darkness embodies human life awakened to the promise of a new day.

Departing Kazbek at dawn the next day, Ilia then has two conversations with Lelt Ghunia (VI–VII), who as a local mountaineer "Terek-drinker" peasant stands both in physical and mental counterpoint to the Russian post cart driver at Vladikavkaz: "In the end it appeared that he was an interested observer of that little land which fate had outlined around him and which she had appointed to vary his colorless life" (VI). Lelt Ghunia further clarifies the destruction actually wrought by Russian colonization in counterpoint to its putative civilizing mission presented in the dialogue at Lars (III), particularly dwelling on the corrosive effects of Russian rule on the (allegedly) once harmonious relations within and between estates. He concludes,

> This I want you to understand, that formerly if we gave our lives in service there were rewards, there were great gifts; we found our livelihood in glory and in bravery, a man did not live in vain. Now we find our livelihood in lying, immorality, breaking oaths, and in betraying one another. (VII)

Lastly, in the coda of the text (VIII), Chavchavadze explains that his sole purpose has been to dutifully record the ethnographic text found in the two preceding sections realistically. That is, his focus has been only on realistic verisimilitude to the form and not the factual veracity of Ghunia's speech:

> Whether my Moxevian spoke the truth or not I will not now inquire. And what business is it of mine? I merely mention in passing what I as a traveler heard from him. My one endeavor in this has been to give to his thoughts their own form and to his words his accent. If I have succeeded in this I have fulfilled my intention. (VIII)

For the remainder of this chapter, I will use roman numeral section headings (I–VIII) uniquely to identify passages from Ilia's text, whose relative location in the Dariel pass is indicated on the map (see map).

The Voice of the Intelligentsia and the Voice of the People

Chavchavadze presents Letters of a Traveler as a simple exercise in representational "realism," an absolutely neutral transcription of an ethnographic and linguistic reality, characteristic of the generation of the 1860s. Part of the central importance of the text then, is that it represents an important first *systematic* attempt at the faithful description of the dialect and political institutions of the Georgian "people."[5] This serious attention to correct representation of dialect form and ethnographic content is surely motivated by a new literary taste for "realism" (Paperno 1988). However, Chavchavadze's realism was strongly influenced by Russian understandings of realism as a kind of "civic aesthetics" (affirming the social role of literature) exemplified by writers like Chernyshevsky and shows a similar appreciation of the critical potential afforded by the aesthetic (Paperno 1988, 7). Also, like Chernyshevsky's realism, Chavchavadze's realism (like most other Russian and Georgian writers in the period) is a "social realism," an aesthetic of realism strongly tied to the "social question," describing the abject condition of the peasants in the Emancipation period (Frierson 1993). As with Russian social realism, the apparently neutral aesthetic perspective of realistic description becomes a rhetorical device allowing Chavchavadze to covertly critique the Russian colonial state, the obscurantism of whose civilizing pretenses is represented by a systematic failure of the forms of words to match their content. At the same time, while the form of Lelt Ghunia's transcribed conversation is humble *terg-daleuli* (Moxevian) dialect, the content of Lelt Ghunia's conversation is in effect the political program of the *terg-daleuli* intelligentsia. Hence, the opposition between *form* and *content* thematically central to the text becomes an organizing rhetorical opposition.

Presenting his work as an anonymous traveler's simple act of transcription of the voice of Lelt Ghunia, Chavchavadze makes his text pivot around this central identification—an elision which creates the "authority of authenticity" (Gal and Woolard 2001, 7) by which Chavchavadze identifies his own voice with the authentic voice of the *terg-daleuli* peasant, Lelt Ghunia. The text was composed in the 1860s (from 1861 to 1871) at the same time as the term intelligentsia was beginning to be used in Russian (and Georgian) society (Confino 1972, 117, Burbank 1996, 97). Not surprisingly, then, it replicates all the ambiguities which characterized the position of the imperial intelligentsia during the Great Reforms of the 1860s. This relation is made more complex, moreover, by Chavchavadze's position as a member of a *colonized* intelligentsia whose position reflects the peculiarities of the specificities of Georgian gentry intelligentsia under Russian colonialism.[6] As an intelligentsia manifesto, the text replicates the very "gulf between society and the people" that it seeks to mediate—that between a small educated reading public, mostly composed of gentry (the Georgian term *sazogadoeba* can mean aristocratic "society" or intelligentsia "public," compare Russian *obshchestvo*) and an often illiterate people, mostly composed of peasantry (Georgian *xalxi*, Russian *narod*) (Brooks 1978, 98, Todd 1986, 15ff; Gleason 1991, Frierson 1993). This "society" of the "fathers" gave birth to a (still mostly gentry) "intelligentsia" of the "sons" in the 1860s in fierce intergenerational debates that characterized "the reality of intelligentsia culture—an ongoing, hence self-contested, and self-refining culture based on personal and public statements about politics" (Burbank 1996, 107). As this intelligentsia culture was founded on opposition to autocracy and a notion of service to the "people," however imagined (Confino 1972, Gleason 1991, 20–1, Burbank 1996), so this text also opposes the discourses of the Russian colonizing state to those of the colonized Georgian people, using the ethnographic descriptions of the defunct political institutions of Georgian folk culture to critique the civilizing pretenses of the Russian state.

The dialogism of the text replicates all these well-known antinomies. In fact, the peculiarity of the text is the distinct form of the intertextual and intratextual strategies (Jenny 1976, 260; Bauman 2004) that Chavchavadze uses to mediate them, as well as the distinct strategic functions of these forms. An intertextual dialogue involving both overt citation and covert structural imitation or prior Russian and Georgian Romantic texts *addresses* the text to a purely literary public of Georgian intelligentsia. Rather than address these forebears directly, he addresses them indirectly through his own aesthetic discussion of the "already spoken about" landscape, largely through a radical rereading of the "voice" of the Terek River itself.

His radical rereadings of the natural landscape produces a literary filiation (Hubbard 1998), which locates this text within a retroactively imagined "intelligentsia tradition" (Confino 1972, Burbank 1996), thus performatively creating a literary genealogy for the text. Because Chavchavadze is a member of a colonial intelligentsia, this literary kinship is reckoned bilaterally, with both Russian and Georgian Romantic antecedents. At the same time, the text *reports* an actual dialogue with the actually existing folk who are not, it should be remembered, part of the audience of the text. The "people" are not yet a "public" (Gleason 1991).[7] Juxtaposition of the differing dialects of intelligentsia and folk in dialogue reveals the essential linguistic relatedness of intelligentsia and folk, their fraternal membership in a speech (if not literary) community of "Georgians." If the intertextual relationship creates vertical, generational, intertextual kinship of "fathers" and "sons" within Georgian gentry "society," the textual dialogic relationship creates horizontal linguistic kinship between educated Georgians and uneducated mountaineers as "brothers" (VII). This dialogue of intelligentsia and people is paired with and opposed to the dialogue with the drunken officer, who represents the Russian state and Russian civilization, and who claims to be a writer, an emissary from the world of Russian letters, and a notable inventor—in other words, an agent of civilizational progress. While the dialogue with the Georgian people associates high concepts of authentic Georgian traditions with the low forms of folk dialect, this dialogue instead reveals Russian civilization to be a farcical rendition of its European model, high concepts that are glossed with vulgar referents.

In all these dialogues, Chavchavadze's mediating position as *intelligent* is constructed as the almost invisible authorizing viewpoint that unites these dialogues into a single text, just as an *intelligent* is "entitled to speak for the good of the social whole" (Burbank 1996, 101). Serving both as a letter of introduction and a challenge to Georgian "society," it at once reproduces the pragmatic presuppositions of that discourse even as it seeks to transform them. All of these dialogues, in other words, build up a complex whole, an authorizing intelligentsia mythology, in which Chavchavadze underwrites his ability as *intelligent* to "speak for the people against the state" to an audience of other Georgian *intelligenty*.

The dialogue with Georgian Romanticism, in particular the figure of Grigol Orbeliani (1804–1883), a noted Georgian Romantic poet, noble and high-ranking tsarist official of the previous generation, is mostly overt. Chavchavadze achieves it through a series of pointed citations and barbed comments, but also by adopting the time and location (evening at Mount Kazbek) of Orbeliani's "Night of Farewell" for a series of allegorical ruminations on nature that occupy Chavchavadze in the middle of his text (IV–V). The intertextual dialogue with Russian Romanticism is by and large achieved covertly, by means of formal imitation.[8] Chavchavadze's title and genre recalls a much earlier account of the same journey by the Russian Romantic Aleksander Griboyedov (1795–1829), whose own "Travel Notes" about the same journey was composed in 1818 as a set of jottings and travel notes not intended for publication, but finally was published only a few years before in 1859, making it oddly contemporary (though whether the parallelisms between the texts reflect Chavchavadze's awareness of this text, or simply reflect the way the journey itself is divided into stages punctuated by postal stations, cannot be determined conclusively). Whereas Griboyedov, like many after him, is writing a private travel account of a journey from home into a strange, foreign land, Chavchavadze inverts the expectations produced by the title and genre, casting himself in the ironic role of an estranged "traveler" seeking to rediscover his homeland. This work is divided into eight separate "passages," and thus Chavchavadze's later travelogue formally echoes the structure of Griboyedov's work. He also disposes the passages of his journey (roman numerals I–VIII on Figure 3) spatially as a skewed icon of the passages of Griboyedov's journey (arabic numbers 1–8 on Figure 3). I note in passing that the divisions of each text reflect the "stages" of a journey.

The literary filiation with Griboyedov, a contemporary of Pushkin, places Chavchavadze in a covert genealogy with Russian Romanticism, just as his overt citation of Orbeliani places him in a genealogical relation to Georgian Romanticism. But more significantly, Griboyedov himself married Nino Chavchavadze (a distant relation of Ilia Chavchavadze), daughter of the Georgian noble and Romantic poet Aleksandre Chavchavadze. In the small circle of Georgian gentry who made up Georgian "society," literary relations and kinship relations were inseparable; if Orbeliani was addressed overtly as Chavchavadze's consanguineal literary kin, then Griboyedov could be reckoned covertly as his literary kin by marriage. By means of these intertextual allusions, Chavchavadze constructs a literary filiation as a "son" to two groups of wayward Romantic "fathers"—Georgian (Orbeliani) and Russian (Griboyedov). The dialogue with Russian and Georgian Romantics is done primarily through intertextuality of the landscape itself, an aestheticized landscape which more than any other was fraught with the political categories of colonial imaginative geography that Chavchavadze wishes to engage and revise.

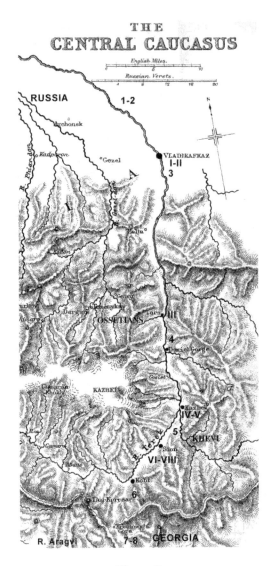

Figure 3

Stages of Two Literary Crossings of the Dariel Pass

I, II . . . VIII: Stages (chapters) in Chavchavadze's Journey
1, 2, . . . 8: Stages (chapters) in Griboyedov's Journey
(Adapted from map in Freshfield, 1869)

An Aesopian Discourse of Nature: Talking Politics through Aesthetics
Political engagement with Russian and Georgian Romantic imaginative geographies, which already reflected a strongly Orientalist essentializing mapping of geography to humanity (Layton 1992, 1994, 1997), occurred on the ground of aesthetics of the very natural landscape that Romanticism had invested with aesthetic or expressive value. Nature, then, assumes for Georgian discourse in this period a fundamentally political role. In an essentially "totemic" moment (Levi-Strauss 1963), expressive categories of aestheticized nature were mobilized as an *Aesopian discourse* of "talking politics." Perhaps this "Aesopian discourse," used in a tsarist literary context for veiled speech in the presence of the censor, was even more Aesopian than the ordinary Russian Aesopianism, for just as Aesop used tales of animals to speak in veiled terms of human society and politics, here the expressive categories of sublime nature, gloomy mountains, and raging rivers, are used totemically to produce an Aesopian language for political engagement with the inherited political-social-spatial imaginary of Romanticism. Russian and Georgian Romantics had ensured that aesthetics of the landscape, literary appropriations of nature, would be the point of departure for all further discourse about Georgia and the Caucasus. And nowhere was this imaginary found in such a concentrated and oft-described form as the passage to Georgia across the Dariel in the Caucasus, which was frequently compared to crossing of the Alps into Italy for the Grand Tour (Freshfield 1896, 87; on the Grand Tour which is the European object of comparison for the Dariel Crossing, see Chard 1999).

The crossing of watersheds is a transition from the uncivilized Caucasus to civilized, but Oriental, Georgia. In Russian Romantic Orientalist discourse, these two locales exhibit very different forms of alterity and suggesting very different colonial projects. As Layton (1992, 1994) argues, Georgia, though "civilized" and "Christian" was constructed by Russian Orientalism as a languid Oriental female, indeed, Georgia forms a classical Oriental counterpart to European Russia.[9] By contrast, the Caucasus was the exemplary locus of masculinity, full of masculine tribesmen to be fought and emulated, and not a few lovely mountaineer maids widely rumored "to be very well disposed toward travelers" (Pushkin [1835], 139; more generally see Layton 1994, 1997).

The two places, the Caucasus and Georgia are also opposed by being associated very different aesthetic categories, the masculine aesthetics of the sublime and the feminine aesthetics of the beautiful. Russian Romanticism adopted and adapted the European aesthetic opposition between the sublime and the beautiful as part of an imperial geopoetic strategy to appropriate these regions and realize their own coevality with Europeans (Layton 1994, Ram 2003). In Pan-European aesthetic discourse, the qualities diagnostic of the sublime, emphasizing grandeur, vastness, "wild, barren, savage and 'frowning' landscapes" are opposed to the qualities of beauty emphasizing "cultivated, fertile, gentle, and 'smiling' landscapes" (Chard 1999, 110). These aestheticized and expressive spatial qualities are in turn aligned with gendered qualities of person, "the sublime with the masculine and the beautiful with the feminine" (Chard 1999, 117–18). Thus, Russian Romantics like Pushkin and Griboyedov saw the masculine sublime primarily in the gloomy crags and defiles of the Caucasus Mountains (home of fierce, warlike people like the Chechens), opposed to the feminized, Orientalized aesthetics of the beautiful that typified the Georgian plains (Layton 1992).

Georgian Romantics, in turn, adopted the Russian aesthetics of the sublime and the beautiful to establish their own coevality with their Russian peers in the appropriation of this same terrain (Ram and Shatirishvili 2004, Manning 2008). With the generation of the 1860s, Chavchavadze in turn adopts this same aestheticized discourse of nature to create an Aesopian political engagement with both these groups of forebears, but radically revises and reverses the aesthetics of the landscape. By eliminating the opposition between "beautiful" feminine Georgia and the "sublime" masculine Caucasus, he erases this distinction and identifies Georgia with the masculine sublime by laying claim to the roar of the Terek and the landscape of Dariel, paving the way for a Georgian ethnographic and literary "turn to the mountains" in the 1880s (on which, see Le Galcher Baron 1993, Manning 2007, 2008).

Domesticating the Voice of the Terek

If earlier Georgian Romantics exulted over the natural beauty of the Caucasus, it was as often as not a nature alien to humanity and devoid of human voices. For example, Aleksandre Chavchavadze (1786–1846), whose poem "The Caucasus" (published in 1852), while strongly indebted to Russian Romantic antecedents (see Ram and Shatirishvili 2004 for an extended treatment), nevertheless differs from them pointedly in factor-

ing out all references to the human order often found in Russian render-
ings of the same landscape (the same tendency is true of Chavchavadze's
proximal interlocutor, Grigol Orbeliani):

> Absent in Ch'avch'avadze are any references to the hu-
> man inhabitants of the Northern Caucasus: we find
> deer and goats, but none of the evocations of fierce
> Circassians and Chechens that abound in the poems of
> Zhukovskii, Pushkin, and Lermontov. In the absence of
> ethnographic detail the Caucasus appears through most
> of Ch'avch'avadze's poem as a hypostasis of nature, both
> a part of the created world and the theurgic force behind
> its creation. Whether apocalyptic or occasionally pas-
> toral, the Caucasus are decidedly not human. (Ram and
> Shatirishvili 2004, 11)

It is very much as if Georgian Romantics had fully internalized Russian Romanticism's aesthetic appreciation for the landscape, but somehow balked at finding anything similar to appreciate in the people living
there.

Ilia Chavchavadze, in a sense reversing this tendency of earlier Georgian (but not Russian) Romanticism, humanizes this natural order (giving a human voice to the roar of the Terek) as a prologue to naturalizing
the human order (by naturalizing the human voice of the Terek-dwelling
peasant, Lelt Ghunia). In so doing, Chavchavadze radically revises the
geopoetics characteristic of these earlier Romantics, which as often as
not sought to align Georgia with Russia *against* the Caucasus, by creating
a novel geopoetics in which the Caucasus, in the form of the Terek River,
is identified with Georgia as opposed to Russia. In Griboyedov's text,
the frightening animal roar of the Terek in the first five passages marks
the terrain as being the uncivilized, dangerous, frightening Caucasus, a
land of war, strife, and uncivilized mountaineer tribes and bandits (see
in general, Layton 1994). The sixth passage marks the passage from the
uncivilized and frightening Caucasus symbolized by the roar of the Terek
to the pleasant and peaceful Georgia, symbolized by the Aragvi River,
"the morning song of the Georgians."[10]

Chavchavadze radically revises this imaginative geography by dis-
pensing with the Aragvi (which flows from these mountains into the

plains of Georgia) as a symbol of beautiful Georgia *as opposed to* the sublime Caucasus symbolized by the Terek. The Terek can now stand alone as a symbol of the Georgian Caucasus (the Xevi district beside the mouth waters of the Terek). By eliminating the ever-present inherited opposition between the Aragvi and the Terek—between the peaceful, feminine, civilized, and subdued Georgia and the warlike, masculine and free Caucasus—he brings Georgia into the Caucasus.[11]

Chavchavadze also proposes a radical rereading of the meaning of the roar of the Terek that figures in the texts of Orbeliani, Griboyedov, and others. The furious animal roar of the unbridled torrents of the Terek in the Caucasus is a long-standing Romantic symbol of mountaineer masculinity and freedom. The novelty of Chavchavadze's reading lies in how he appropriates the rebellious freedom of the Terek as part of the Georgian national tradition, representing an authentic Georgian culture which can be favorably compared to the pretended civilization of Russian rule, represented by the subdued flow of the Terek in the plains of Russia: "Happy Terek! You are at your best when you are restless. Stand still but a little while and do you not turn into a stinking pool and does not this fearsome roar of yours change to the croaking of frogs!" (IV)

The Terek is identified with freedom of motion and change, but not necessarily modernity or progress, for Chavchavadze's program cannot easily be understood as a progressive one. Rather, it is a somewhat jarringly eclectic combination: a celebration of mountaineer freedom and apologetic for the harmonious and mutually beneficial relations between estates that once—it is claimed—characterized Georgian feudalism. The motion and roar of the Terek in the mountains represents political self-determination and freedom of the (now defunct) autonomous community-based institutions of the mountaineer polity (*eroba*, what is more usually called the *temoba* by indigenous Moxevian writers like Aleksandre Qazbegi [1880, 164, 2]). But at the same time as he mourns the demise of the *eroba*, Lelt Ghunia extols the recognition of reciprocal obligations of service and reward and general harmonious relations between estates that once apparently existed between Georgian peasants and nobles. All this was lost, according to Lelt Ghunia, under the "empty peace" of the *Pax Russica*, which places the people economically at the mercy of usurious Armenian merchants and abrogates the system of reciprocal service and rewards between estates that once apparently made the Georgian people valorous. This changed social state of affairs, brought by the subjection of the Georgian people to Russian rule and co-optation of Georgian nobles like Orbeliani into Russian service, is again likened to the change of the natural order, witnessed in the domestication of the animal fury of the Terek as it moves into Russia. Chavchavadze notes that at Vladikavkaz, in the plains, the Terek flows "as placid, as silent, as if it dwelt under the rod or had received a high official post (*chini*)" (II); or as Lelt Ghunia would have it, the stagnant water of empty peace brought by Russia is for servile frogs, but free trout splash happily in the torrential Terek (VII).

The prior Georgian and Russian Romantic descriptions of this landscape with which Chavchavdze engages explicitly are notable for their rapturous communion with sublime nature (and Chavchavadze's is no exception), but in them, the noisy natural order (the terrifying wild animal roar of the Terek) is sometimes complemented by the complete silence of cultural order (mountaineer "Terek-drinkers"). In the poetry of Georgian Romantics like Aleksandre Chavchavadze or Grigol Oribeliani, if local inhabitants appear, they are largely of a piece with the natural order. For the Russian Romantic Griboyedov, the central and defining feature of the landscape is the inhuman "noise of the Terek." For Ilia Chavchavadze, by contrast, the phusiomorphic *noise* of the Terek by slow degrees is anthropomorphized into an articulate plaintive human *voice* which is ultimately identified with the fully human voice of the Terek-drinker, Lelt Ghunia.[12]

Chavchavadze humanizes the natural order via a subjective revelation that organizes the text, one which is mirrored in the natural order in the changes in the flow of the Terek as he ascends from Russian plains to Caucasian mountains. At first, a reluctant *Terg-daleuli* in the plains at Vladikavkaz, where the Terek flows lifeless and silent, he refuses to even look at, let alone drink from, the Terek, lest someone think him a *Terg-daleuli* (II). Ascending into the mountains, the Terek, ever more torrential, ever noisier, enters into communion with nature, finally coming to feel "a secret bond—a concord—between my thoughts and Terek's complaint" (V). Chavchavadze transforms the inchoate noise of the Terek into a human voice; first, the anthropomorphized voice of the river, whose complaint, the complaint of his motherland, he comes to understand (V); and then in the very real voice of the Georgian mountaineer who dwells by the Terek, whose dialect inflected voice Chavchavadze appropriates for his political message (VI–VII). The furious roar of the Terek in the mountains now appears explicitly as the voice of the free Caucasian mountaineers, who are, it needs to be added, also specifically *Georgian* mountaineers. Having humanized the voice of nature, the Terek, he now turns to naturalizing his relationship to the cultural order, giving voice to the Terek-dweller.

Form and Content: Languages of Culture and Civilization

This revisionist geopoetics of the natural order is paralleled on the linguistic plane in two lengthy dialogues which Chavchavadze has en route with representatives of the Russian state in the form of a drunken officer (III) and of the Georgian people in the form of Lelt Ghunia (VI–VII), a Georgian mountaineer peasant. The viability of a geopoetics that assimilates Georgia into Russia (characteristic of the older generation of Georgian Romantics) is called into question when the Russian officer reclassifies Chavchavadze from enlightened interlocutor to benighted local when he finds out Chavchavadze is actually a Georgian. At the same time, the parallel inherited geopoetic opposition between Caucasus and Georgia is elided when the mountaineer Lelt Ghunia and plains-dwelling Chavchavadze discover their common essential Georgianness underlying their accidental differences of dress and dialect.

Further developing this revisionist geopoetics, Chavchavadze uses the opposition between form and content in these two dialogues to show that Russian civilization is a form with at best debased content, while the traditional culture of the mountaineers, though expounded in the rather homely garb of folk dialect, is revealed to be authentic. He thus reverses the apparent value of form and content.

Chavchavadze continually defines and glosses terms to draw our attention to the opposition of form and content, but he works these devices differently in each dialogue, with different degrees of explicitness of framing (Bauman 2004) and with important rhetorical effects. The dialogue with Ghunia relies on implicit operations of glossing that allows recognition of natural similarities within the heteroglossia of dialect, and, moreover, recognition of Chavchavadze's kinship with Ghunia as Georgians. The linguistic relation is a fraternal kinship relation, therefore Chavchavadze is truly an "organic" intellectual. Using dialectal differences as a basis for the recognition of natural similarities, meanwhile, rhetorically resolves Chavchavadze's anxieties about whether Chavchavadze will understand his country's voice, the voice of Ghunia.

> But what shall I do if my country tells me her complaint,
> the secret causes of her sorrow, her hopes and despairs,
> and I, unaccustomed to her language, cannot understand
> her language, her speech? (III)

But just as quickly, he concludes that there exists a natural kinship connection between himself as patriot (*mamulishvili* lit. "child of the fatherland") and the fatherland (*mamuli*) itself, which would allow him both to understand the complaint of his fatherland and to make himself understood in turn:

> I decided that my country would receive me and acknowl-
> edge me because I am its blood and its flesh; I should
> understand its words and speech because a patriot [*mam-
> ulishvili*] hearkens to his fatherland [*mamuli*] not only
> with his ears, but with his heart too, which understands
> even the unspoken words; I will make them hearken to
> my words too, for a parent always listens to the words of
> his child. (III)

The dialogue with the Russian officer, by contrast, works with radical disjunctures between forms and meanings that are mediated only by his own explicit fiat, by which he seeks to make the difficulty of "scientific discourse" understandable to the unenlightened local, Chavchavadze. Again the problem is one of failure of recognition. When first he learns that Chavchavadze hails from St. Petersburg, he is full of great respect for an enlightened visitor from the pinnacle of civilization in these benighted parts. Upon learning that Chavchavadze is a *local*, "that is, a Georgian or an Armenian" (III), he imputes a radically opposed identity to him; he becomes full of contempt, and is merely glad that at least Chavchavadze is a Georgian and not a despised Armenian (a topic on which both he, Chavchavadze and Ghunia apparently all agree). Because it is revealed that Chavchavadze is *essentially* a benighted (Oriental) local and only *accidentally* resembles a (Western) visitor from a center of enlightenment, the Russian officer now assumes the role of an enlightener whose task is to explain and gloss the complex terminology of civilization for the backward Chavchavadze. Hence, where the first dialogue involves implicit recognition of essential identity underlying apparent difference of outward form, the second dialogue, premised on misrecognition of essential underlying difference despite appearances, involves explicit glossing operations that inadvertently reveal the obscurantism of the civilizing pretenses of the Russian state.

At issue are two very different views of form and content in language. One is a view of language, characteristic of Enlightenment thought (Taylor 1975, 14), where signs and their objects, form and content, are *externally* related (in that both sign and signified exist autonomously of the sign relation, and are therefore brought together arbitrarily by stipulative fiat), parodied by a *reductio ad absurdum* in the Russian officer's civilizing discourse (where French words are arbitrarily made to stand for discordant Russian realities). The other (characteristic of post-Enlightenment thought) is one where signifier and signified, form and content, are *internally* related, mutually constituting, organically interdependent, unable to exist apart. Here language is not merely an arbitrarily chosen means of reference about independently existing, objective states-of-affairs, but also expressive of, and therefore constitutive of interior, subjective essences (here, Georgianness). Such an "expressivist" view of language is essential, as Taylor points out, to any nationalism grounded in language (Taylor 1989, 415), and is certainly central to the discussion of the relation of form and content in Chavchavadze's dialogue with Lelt Ghunia. Hence, the two dialogues enact in their implied theories of language Enlightenment discourses of "civilization" as opposed to post-Enlightenment discourses of authentic indigenous "culture." Just as Chavchavadze brings himself into an organic relation with Lelt Ghunia on the basis of an expressive view of language and authentic culture, he pries Russia apart from European civilization by the arbitrariness and obscurantism by which Francophone civilizing discourses are accommodated to Russian realia, leaving Russia in a no-man's land between culture and civilization. In this process, he appears to revalorize the received term *Terg-daleuli* itself, from a term meaning "one who has received (false) enlightenment in Russia by crossing the Terek" to one meaning "one who has found (authentic) culture among the Georgians who dwell by the Terek."

Describing Dialect

Nowhere is the new concern for authenticity of representation of folk language more clear than in the dialogue with Lelt Ghunia (VI–VII), which resembles a folkloric text embedded within a larger prose narrative. The dialogue is a striking exercise in attempted literary realism: not merely a sprinkling of dialectics for flavor, it is possibly the first systematic, if distorted, representation of a nonstandard dialect of Georgian.[13] Lelt Ghunia's dialect is rendered in such a way that both its specificities of form are highlighted, but also its essential *Georgianness* is at the very same time retained. Dialectal difference within language is revealed to be a kind of accidental difference within a framework of essential similarity, differences of *form* of what are in effect the same *words,* so too differences of *dialect* of what are the same *language.* So too, the differences between the Moxevian peasant mountaineer Lelt Ghunia and the plains-dwelling gentry Chavchavadze become matters of outward form of dialect or dress that obscure an inner identity of Georgianness.

Chavchavadze begins their first dialogue (VI) by a number of failed gambits that make him resemble a Georgian noble of the previous generation, failing to recognize Ghunia's Georgianness underneath his mountaineer garb, failing to recognize the human poverty writ large in the entrancing natural beauty of the mountains. The remainder of the dialogue in VI allows Ghunia to correct these misapprehensions. In the following dialogues, the comparable terms of Chavchavadze and Ghunia's dialect are emphasized in brackets.

> 'Where [*sadauri*] do you come from?'
>
> 'Where [*sadável*]? From Gaibotani, here in the mountains on the banks of the Terek.'
>
> 'Are you Georgian or Ossetian [*osi*]?'
>
> 'Why would I be an Ossetian [*ovsí*]? I am a Georgian, a Moxevian.'
>
> 'Your home is in a good place.'
>
> 'It's not so bad [*gonjái*].* It suits our poverty.'
>
> 'Water and air like this are happiness itself.'
>
> 'Hm!' laughed the Moxevian.
>
> 'What are you laughing at [*icini*]?'
>
> 'I laugh [*vicíni*] at the laughable. An empty stomach cannot be filled with those.'

----

* *Gonjai—cudi* [*gonjai* –"bad"] (VI)

If the first dialogue concerns Chavchavadze's misrecognition of Ghunia as a possible non-Georgian mountaineer (an Ossetian), the second dialogue (VII) involves Ghunia's misrecognition of Chavchavadze as a Russian, as if echoing Chavchavadze's concern, that, as "one transplanted and reared in another soil" (III), he would not recognize his country, and his country would not recognize him.

The substance of the dialogue deals with the defunct ethnographic institutions of the Moxevians and the debasing effect of Russian political domination and Armenian economic domination on the Georgian people, both in the narrow sense (the *eroba* "(village) community," the traditional form of autonomous mountaineer polity) as well as broader sense (the Georgian *eri* "nation, folk, people").[14] As Ghunia explains the traditional ethnographic functions of an old monastery dedicated to the Holy Trinity to Chavchavadze, Chavchavadze demands clarification about one of them, the people's council (*erta sabch'o*), an important institution of the *eroba* (here translated "community"), at which point it is revealed that the institutions of the *eroba* no longer functions under Russian rule:[15]

'What in the world is a council [*sabch'o*]?'
'A council [*sabch'ói*]? There is a cell there, where justice was dispensed by judges. Whenever any serious affair arose in Xevi it was judged there. . . .When there took place in the community a great pursuit, any important affair, a big election, the community went there, chose as judges wise old men, men famed for their wisdom [*p'eit'róbit*]*, set them up in that cell to judge. Whatever these mediators then, in the name of the Trinity, having asked grace from God, speak and decide, none breaks, none infringes.'
'Have you been present at such a tribunal?'
'How should I have been present? I am telling you tales of former days.'
'Why is it now [*exla*] no longer as it was?'
. . .

'Nowadays [*ac'ína*]? . . . Where is the community [*eró-ba*]? We are under Russia. Now everything is destroyed, everything is changed.' (VII)[16]

----

*p'eit'robit—met'is gonebit saxelgantkmulni (p'eit'robit— "famed for great wisdom")

In both these dialogues, Chavchavadze uses the mechanisms of dialogue itself, specifically questions, answers, and repetitions to establish that differences of *form* overlay identities of *content*, an "outer clothing" of different dialect forms of what are *essentially* the same words. Using these devices, the translational equivalence of partially different dialectal word forms as "different ways of saying the same thing" is established *implicitly* in conversational question-and-answer pairs.

As can be seen from the examples above, Chavchavadze's questions are frequently met by a two-part reply from Ghunia. First, Ghunia repeats a single word from Chavchavadze's question as a question; for example, Chavchavadze: *sadauri?* ("where from?"), Ghunia: *sadável?* Chavchavadze: *osi?* ("Ossetian?"), Ghunia: *ovsí?* Chavchavadze: *sabch'o?* ("council?") Ghunia: *sabch'ói?* Chavchavadze: *exla?* ("now?") Ghunia: *ac'ína?* ("nowadays?"). This foregrounds the sundry differences of dialectal *form* (such as the pervasive marking of accentuation, for example) between otherwise equivalent *words*, as if striving to ascertain whether Ghunia's words *sadável* or *sabch'ói* "mean the same thing" (or "are the same words") as Chavchavadze's words *sadauri* or *sabch'o*. Then, Ghunia answers Chavchavadze's question in terms of its content, explaining where he is from or what a *sabch'o* is. The organization of the dialogue itself recursively divides off dialect form (the echo question) from content (the answer). At the same time, the first part of the response foregrounds differences of dialect form and acts as an implicit glossing operation establishing the underlying equivalences of words.

Whereas this device allows the common Georgianness of words to be recognized despite differences of "dialect," Chavchavadze establishes equivalence of meaning between different words through a separate textual device, the philological footnote. The text has six philological footnotes that offer glosses of Moxevian vocabulary (for example *gonjái* "bad" in the dialogue above glossed as standard Georgian *cudi* "bad"). These glosses are often presented denuded of other Moxevian formal peculiarities such as pervasive marking of accentuation, and thus as if they are part of the standard Georgian vocabulary. Thus there are two stages of "translation" of dialect into standard: a translation of form, by which an unfamiliar word in the text (e.g., *t'alávar*) is glossed in the footnote in a "citation form" denuded of distinctive dialectal features (e.g., *t'alavari*). This is followed by a translation of content, where this word is glossed by a standard Georgian word (*t'anisamosi* "clothing"). Thus, while the dialogic system discussed above uses the same words to present different dialect forms, this system highlights the *essential* identity of words across dialects, backgrounding *accidental* differences of dialectal form. The footnotes present Ghunia as if he were himself an ethnographic or philological text engaged in dialogue with his transcriber. If the dialogic glossing discussed above produces a precarious equality between their utterances and themselves as speakers of Georgian, the footnoting device reestablishes Ghunia as a philological text (speaking a nonstandard dialect) and Chavchavadze as a philologist (speaking the standard dialect).

As "dialect" is the outer garb of words, so too do their different styles of dress prevent Chavchavadze and Ghunia from recognizing their common Georgianness. On their first meeting, Chavchavadze mistakes Ghunia for an Ossetian, for which he receives a testy rebuke (VI).[17] In turn, before he reveals his true opinion of Russian civilization, the peasant Ghunia wants to know Chavchavadze's *mileti* (derived from the Ottoman term of ethno-religious classification, *millet*), assuming from his dress that he is a Russian (VII). "I am a Georgian, can't you recognize me?" is Chavchavadze's surprised response. "How would anyone recognize you?" Ghunia replies, "You don't dress like a Georgian. You resemble a Russian." Attempting to find a basis for mutual recognition that does not depend on such outward forms, Chavchavadze makes special pleading that Georgianness is not a matter of outward alienable *form* (dress), but a more essential trait, represented perhaps by language. Ghunia objects that "many speak the Georgian language, Armenians, Ossetians, Tatars, other *millets*" (VII). Chavchavadze concludes that perhaps Georgianness is not a matter of such relatively outward forms (dress, language), but still more inner essence, a matter "of the heart." Ghunia dubiously agrees, noting merely that clothing, at least, has the advantage of being visible. "Who can see into the heart?" he complains. For Chavchavadze, Georgianness is an essential content whose recognizability is not impaired by variation in outward form of dress or even language (though perhaps it should be reflected or expressed in it). Ghunia, in turn, argues that the outer form (dress) must express the inner content, or the outer form becomes the inner reality. "In Russian dress, a Georgian becomes a foreigner" (VII), just as the Terek changes its nature as it moves from Caucasian mountains to Russian plains (II).

Defining "Civilization"

The form of Lelt Ghunia's speech is as humble as that of the Russian officer's is "scientific" and elevated. But in terms of content, the reverse is the case. The historical predicament of Georgia is that the authentic culture of the folk has been displaced historically by the empty forms that Russian civilization has brought with it. Form and content are divorced in reality as well as discourse, a chiasmus of high terminology and vulgar referents of the Russian officer's speech is mirrored in the realities of Russian civilization.

The Russian officer is not the only representative of a civilized Europe in this text. In fact, Chavchavadze's first conversation at Vladikavkaz is with a French traveler, who, mocking the notorious Russian postal carts, appears merely to authoritatively demonstrate that Russians are *not* Europeans. "The whole of Russia travels like that? . . . Who in the world will ever catch up with them?" is his snide observation (I). This rhetorical separation of backward Russia from civilized Europe is continued in the speech of the drunken Russian officer (III). This dialogue has the quality of a "Through the Looking Glass" exposition of Russia's civilizing mission, presided over by a Russian analog of Humpty Dumpty, who glosses over the gap between form and content by fiat. The officer condescendingly notes that Chavchavadze, like most locals ("that is, Georgians or Armenians"), owing to his lack of enlightenment, does "not understand logical, orderly reasoning" and probably does not even know the meaning of terms like *civilizacia, associacia, arghumentacia, inteligencia, kassacia,* and *pilologia* (III). Since, of course, it is soon revealed that the officer himself does not know what these terms mean, it can be concluded that he chose them on the basis of their purely formal properties, that is, because they sound French and rhyme. Russian civilization is presented as an empty form, a Francophone jargon consisting of words that rhyme with *civilizacia*.

The scientific officer also engages in an explicit discourse of defini-

tional glossing, which seeks to bridge the imputed gap between his position as civilizing Russian and Chavchavadze's position as uncivilized
local, conceived as a linguistic barrier between "scientific language"
and "vulgar language," bridged by acts of "translation" that debase the
meanings of words. This glossing of "scientific" terminology (mostly of
European derivation) by "low" referents reveals the scientific officers
own lack of enlightenment, trading in high-minded abstractions for
low-minded vulgarities, revealing once again Russia's claims to civilization as being a fundamental vulgarization of the real thing, the empty
form of civilization as opposed to its reality. For the drunken Russian
officer, the pinnacle of civilization is Izler's Garden in St. Petersburg,
notable for its "fairies," a scientific term he is certain Chavchavadze will
not understand:

> 'Do you know what fairies are? That is a scientific word,
> perhaps you don't understand. If we translate it into
> the vulgar tongue that means that the garden is full of
> merry-eyed damsels. If you like you can take one by the
> arm, and, if you like, a second. See what enlightenment
> can do. Your women—as soon as they even see a man—
> they hide.' (III)

The scientific officer continues to help Chavchavadze understand
scientific discourse by this process of glossing, of translating scientific
language into the vulgar tongue: "It will be difficult for you to understand
scientific conversation, but I will translate scientific words here and there
into simple language and so thus make scientific conversation easy for
you" (III). He then proceeds, step by step, and numerous false starts,
tautologies, and asides, to gloss "enlightenment" for the unenlightened
Chavchavadze. In his asides, he inadvertently identifies the Russian imperial metropoles of Moscow and Petersburg with the colonial outposts
of Stavropol and Vladikavkaz, that is, cities not larger than Chavchavadze's own unenlightened Tbilisi, thereby undermining his assertions
of the self-evident superiority of metropole over colony. Let us follow the
culmination of his explanation:

> 'Now when we begin by saying that your country is not
> enlightened we must also say what enlightenment is. I

will explain this by an example; imagine a dark room—
have you imagined it or not?'

'I have imagined it.'

'No, perhaps you have left a window open somewhere,
close it too.'

'I have closed it', I said, and smiled.

'Very good. When you fasten the window you must let
down the blind.'

'I have let it down.'

'When you have let down the blind the room is dark-
ened, you can see nothing. Suddenly a candle is brought
and the room is illuminated. That is enlightenment. But
really, I tell you this cigarette is not bad. Is it from Petersburg?'

'No, I bought them in Vladikavkaz.'

'It's all the same. Now do you understand the meaning
of enlightenment?' (III)

Having defined enlightenment, the officer turns to measuring its progress among the locals. "How does civilization go among you?" the officer
asks. Just as the unit of measurement of enlightenment turns out to be
lumens for the Russian officer, the dry measure of civilization turns out
to be "generals." By "civilization" therefore, the scientific officer wishes
to know how many Georgian generals there are.[18] When Chavchavadze
answers "about twenty," the officer exclaims with disbelief, "This is great
civilization!" After considerable clarification of the "scientific" definition
of "general" (a matter ultimately having to do with mustaches and epau-
lettes), he quickly determines the mathematical constant for the rate of
growth of civilization in Georgia, measured as a constant in generals per
year: twenty Georgian generals, seventy years since Georgia has become a
Russian colony, yielding a constant rate of two generals every seven years.

As the conversation becomes increasingly deranged, the officer reveals an invention of his own devising that will give value to ordinary
flies (yes, flies), which will replace the complex and expensive machines
that are the engines of progress in European countries like France. As a
result of his invention, he cheerfully anticipates the beginnings of a bus-
tling commerce in flies, with the result that soon there will be "fly shops"
all across the empire. Such inventions in the aggregate, products of en-

lightened minds, which give value to worthless things, will lead to the establishment, perhaps, of an Izler's garden, symbol of enlightenment, in Chavchavadze's own backward town of Tbilisi, leading the elusive and standoffish women of Georgia to promenade boldly. Hence, Tbilisi will be transformed into a kind of paradise, the last term he tries to define for the unenlightened Chavchavadze: "Then the people will see their paradise, as the learned say, that is to put it simply . . . but what shall I say, paradise in the vulgar tongue is also paradise." (III)

Conclusion

Chavchavadze represents the core of the Russian civilizing discourse as a set of acts of translation and definition by which the officer attempts to mediate the putative divide between himself as enlightener and Chavchavadze as unenlightened local. The dialogue is the opposite of the dialogue with Ghunia. It is a parodic lampoon of the empty pretenses of the colonizing Russian state to a civilizing mission, confronted with a "realistic" ethnographic account of the predicament of the peasantry. The two dialogues, belonging to primary genres of parody and critical realism respectively, are juxtaposed without authorial comment. The processes of glossing found in each dialogue differ in degrees of explicitness of framing, the dialogue with Ghunia leading to implicit recognition of kinship of Georgians, the dialogue with the Russian a divorce of form and content sutured together by explicit fiat. The dialogue with Ghunia reveals lowly folk dialect to be a vehicle capable of bearing authentic culture, while the dialogue with the officer reveals the "scientific" Francophone language of the civilizer to be the empty jargon of a spurious civilization.[19]

By these various formal means, Chavchavadze constructs a complex genealogy for himself as *intelligent*, establishing an overt literary genealogy that addresses his text as a son's reply to a wayward generation of Georgian fathers who have abandoned the Georgian people for the Russian state (Orbeliani), and at the same time a covert sideward glance is made to the affinal relations of these same Georgians among Russian Romantics (Griboyedov). Distancing himself by opposing his kin within the literary community of Russified Georgian society, Chavchavadze turns to the people, establishing a naturalized fraternal kinship based on shared language within the speech community of Georgians (Lelt Ghunia), which he can use as a foil for the empty claims of the Francophone universe of discourse of Russian civilization represented by the Russian state. At the same time, he revalorizes the term by which his own generation of intelligentsia were already known, *terg-daleuli*, from a term which implies a Russophile geopoetics of assimilation of Georgia to Russia via enlightenment, to one which instead seeks to find authentic culture among the Terek-dwelling mountaineers of the Georgian Caucasus.

Chavchavadze's *Letters of a Traveler* is in many ways a watershed moment between the "Romanticism" of earlier generations and the "realism" of following ones. The "Romantic" allegorization of nature in this work transforms the landscape into a series of intertexts through which Chavchavadze can engage polemically with an entire series of Romantic predecessors, just as the "realist" transcription of the human voice of Lelt Ghunia makes this text the beginning of another intertextual series for Georgian intelligentsia to write about Georgia. Russian Romanticism had transformed the Dariel crossing into an intertextual space in which Russians could constitute themselves as Europeans (Greenleaf 1991, 1994). Georgian Romantics, in turn, by redescribing their own landscape in these borrowed European-Russian categories, established their own coevality with their Russian peers (Ram and Shatirishvili 2004, Manning 2008). Chavchavadze's appropriation of this Romantic discourse allows him to contest all the major themes and presuppositions of the Russian and Georgian Romantic imaginary of the Caucasus. In turn, Chavchavadze's *Letters of a Traveler* would spawn its own Georgian progeny. In the 1870s, his Aesopian discourse of nature (indebted to Romanticism), figured by the zoomorphic or theriomorphic, and then anthropomorphic Terek, and his realistic transcription of the voice of the Terek-drinker Lelt Ghunia on the northern boundaries of Georgia would provide a set of intertexts that could be transferred to the southern boundaries of Georgia, allowing correspondents like S. Bavreli a discursive framework for an internal Orientalist project of exploring the newly reconquered lands of "Ottoman Georgia." After the failure of this intelligentsia project of a rapprochement with the estranged "brothers" of Ottoman Georgia in the early 1880s, Chavchavadze's thematic focus on the mountaineers of Georgia as a privileged locality for pristine Georgianness of speech and custom would bring a harvest in the immense explosion of realist ethnographic and folkloric literature dealing with these regions Georgian press of the 1880s, beginning with the ethnographic and literary writings of the Moxevian writer Aleksandre Qazbegi.[20] While Bavreli's writings continue the hybrid aesthetics of Chavchavadze, continuing both the Romantic "Ae-sopian" discourse of nature (in the form of anthropomorphic rivers and "expressive" landscape) and the "realist" transcription of the voices of its people, the writings of later realists would firmly distinguish between the natural (material) and human orders, "life" would become exclusively a property of the people, and a realist description of "life" would turn reso-lutely away from even a fictional aesthetic anthropomorphism of nature. While the bulk of this book will explore the former moment, the internal Orientalist project of knowing the strange lands of first Western Georgia (in the 1860s–1870s) and then Ottoman Georgia (in the 1870s), we will skip ahead a moment in the narration to glance at the beginnings of this second discourse of "our mountaineers," a discourse which begins, once again, with a revisionist reading of the Dariel crossing.

II: Imperial and Colonial Sublime: The Aesthetics of Infrastructures

For travelers like Chavchavadze in the 1860s, still indebted to Romantic aesthetics of his interlocutors, the political antinomies of the geopoetics of the Dariel crossing through the Caucasus are figured primarily by natural features of the sublime landscape, Mount Kazbek and the Terek River (a Romantic discourse which I have called an "Aesopian discourse of nature"). By contrast, staunchly "realist" writers and ethnographers about the same region in the 1880s would have no patience for the hybrid, personified allegorical natural landscape of Romanticism; for these writers, the reality of the Russian state is always figured first and foremost by a cultural feature of the landscape, the Georgian military road, the single connection between the Russian Empire and Georgia through these mountains.[1] The aesthetic generational sea change from Romanticism to realism in this period can be summarized by the way natural features of the landscape (Mount Kazbek, the Terek River) cede their pride of place to cultural features of the landscape (the Russian road) in Georgian writings about the Dariel crossing. At the same time, we move from a veiled Aesopian critique of politics through the aesthetics of nature to a much more direct, unveiled critique of Russian imperial politics through the aesthetics of its hitherto invisible taken-for-granted infrastructure.

Because of the Russian road passing through it, the region of Xevi differs from other mountain regions in that it is *not* isolated either from the Russian state or the eyes of passing members of Georgian reading society. Being the *only* major passage between Russia and Georgia, it can be assumed that most members of the Georgian public will have encountered it at least once.[2] The paradox of Xevi is that it is the mountainous region that members of educated society will have the greatest firsthand familiarity with, and yet the greatest factual ignorance of, as Moxevian writer Aleksandre Qazbegi points out at the beginning of his ethnography of the region:

From every district of our country voices come and are printed in newspapers; every district is involved in our common life and is keeping us informed of its happiness and distress. Only one small part of our country, called 'Xevi', is missing from the harmony of this common life. It is indeed true, that from every corner comes correspondence after correspondence, article after article is printed, but about 'Xevi' you might see somewhere two lines or so written, because who cares about Xevi? Who knows about them, or to whom are they interesting, that they bother themselves for their sake? We are so unaware of the people who live in Xevi and their situation, that the greater part of reading society thinks that Xevi is part of Ossetia and its inhabitants are Ossetians. Such ignorance is very surprising about our Moxevians, who are pure Georgians and know no other language than Georgian, even though they are surrounded by people of other tribes.

This circumstance is all the more surprising, because Xevi is located by virtue of its own situation in such a place, where a great military road, which unites our land to the whole of Russia, goes straight through the middle of villages and therefore there hardly remains such a man who knows how to read and write, who, at least once, would not have passed through these places. . . . They have gone through, come back through yet again, Moxevians have many times taken different travelers back and forth in the mountains in the harsh winter, but these [travelers] quickly forgot the service and the help received from those in the mountains.[3]

Unlike more distant Georgian mountain regions like Svaneti and Xevsureti, the hand of the Russian state is omnipresent in Xevi. The historical experience, therefore, of the state is quite different viewed from Xevi than it is from elsewhere in the Georgian Caucasus. So far from being the sublime wilderness so oft-described by Romantic travelers, the landscape of the crossing is a "second nature," a nature completely transformed at the hands of the Russian state:

Whoever has gone or come through Xevi has without a doubt noticed these barren, skin and bone mountains, which tower in their immensity and are almost lost in the spaces of the sky. The greater part of these places once were covered with beautiful trees, giving Moxevians sufficient resources in life; but, ravaged by the boundless logging by the people and cut down for strategic reasons, they are now completely destroyed and instead of beautiful dense forests there remains only naked mountains.[4]

In Xevi, therefore, we find a privileged place to engage with the Russian state, both in terms of the cultural order of infrastructure, but also the way this order has transformed the indigenous cultural and natural order to become *part* of this infrastructure.

On the Road, Again: The Critical Aesthetics of Infrastructure
Romantic descriptions of the Dariel pass present an image of sublime nature, dominated by the Terek River, which serves as a natural figure for indigenous resistance. Against such a worthy sublime natural adversary, the victory of the cultural order of the Russian imperial mission can be figured as being equally sublime. By contrast, in "realist" period descriptions the cultural order, specifically the Russian military highway, is the dominant figure; the natural landscape is a "second nature" produced by strategic deforestation, in essence an extension of the infrastructure of the road itself. As the natural landscape has been transformed, so is the social landscape; while other Georgian mountaineer groups like the nearby Xevsurs tolerate occasional incursions of armed officials of the Russian state, the Moxevian social order has long since been completely transformed by Russian colonialism. Like most mountaineers, lacking any native aristocracy to speak of, Moxevians are alone of Georgian groups of their area in having a local lineage of Russian-appointed service nobles, the Qazbegi family, Aleksandre Qazbegi's own family (Le Galcher Baron 1993), and the (Ossetian and Georgian) peasants who live along the road have been drafted into innumerable forms of corvee labor associated with it, including serving an *jamshchiks* carrying post and travelers for hire along the road.

In Romantic descriptions, including to some extent that of Chavcha-vadze, the road is an often invisible infrastructural position from which the sublime natural landscape can be surveyed, but for the Moxevians and for the aesthetics of realist authors, the material reality of the Russian state and their own predicament is always figured first and foremost by the road itself. The Georgian military road, the construction of which was begun by General Ermolov at the behest of the tsar in the wake of their Russian annexation of Georgia in 1801, was only nominally finished in 1817. However, work continued on the road until 1863, at which point the bill stood at a staggering sum of four million pounds (in that period), the resulting road (at a period when such roads were otherwise nonexistent elsewhere in Russia and the Transcaucasus alike) was compared to the Simplon road in the Alps. The construction and maintenance of the strategically vital post road and attendant com-munications presented unique problems to the Russian imperial postal network (Bazilevich 1999[1927], 84–6), since it required not merely the building of infrastructure of the road and bridges and numerous postal stations, but also the pacification of the countryside (including stra-tegic deforestation) and military garrisons. Travel over this road took days with military escort (including cannons) in the period of Pushkin (1829). Travelers in this period often made use of the "opportunity" afforded by the military escort provided to the mail and joined their carriages to the mail convoy (Bazilevich 1999[1927], 86). By the time of Lermontov, however, the passage was (1840) already becoming a trivial affair, the technological improvements in the road and the mili-tary pacification of the countryside turning the passage through Dariel from a sublime crossing into an utterly prosaic one. As if to illustrate the aesthetic changes in the natural landscape wrought by infrastructural improvement, in the first paragraph of the first chapter of *A Hero of Our Time* (1840), Lermontov has his narrator *lose* his travel notes about the crossing (Lermontov 1983 [1840], 5). This fortunate misfortune allows him to dispense with "descriptions of mountains, meaningless excla-mations of rapture, depictions of scenery which convey nothing, and statistics which no one would ever read," noting merely that he "lunched at Kazbek, had tea at Lars, and was in Vladikavkaz in time for dinner."

British Georgianist Oliver Wardrop, in his account of the road in 1888, notes both the role of natural actors (the rivers which carved the passage the road would follow through the mountains) and state actors in producing the Georgian military road (Wardrop 1888, 34–6). Indeed Wardrop goes so far as to suggest that if Lermontov could dispense with a lengthy description of the Dariel passage, this was not merely a sign that the passage had become an utterly hackneyed literary trope, but that the passage itself had, by his time, become entirely unremarkable:

> The part which rivers have played in the history of civilization is well illustrated by this road. The Aragva, flowing southward from Grudaur [*sic*, Gudauri], and the Terek, running northward from it, have formed the highway along which countless crowds of Asiatics have penetrated into Europe. Between the two streams, there is a distance of some ten miles, forming a huge but not insurmountable barrier, the virtual removal of which did not take place until our own times. It was General Yermolov who, in 1824, succeeded in making the road practicable for troops of all kinds; but from the poet Puskhin's "Journey to Erzerum" (1829), we learn that there was still room for improvement. The traveler had to go with a convoy of 500 soldiers and a cannon, he dare not lag behind for fear of the mountaineers, provisions and lodgings were scarce and bad, the roads were impassable for carriages, the rate of speed was sometimes only ten miles a day. When we read Pushkin's account, and the one given by Lermontov, in "A Hero of Our Times," we can only ask ourselves, "What was the road like before Yermolov?"
>
> During the wars with Kasi-mullah and Shamil, it became indispensable to effect great improvements, and, at length, about five-and-twenty years ago, under the governorship of Prince Bariatinskii, the road was finished, and is now one of the finest in the world, besides being one of the highest—the Simplon is only 6147 feet above sea-level, while the Dariel road is nearly 2000 feet higher. The total distance from Tiflis to Vladikavkaz is 126 miles, and the distance can be done comfortably in less than twenty hours. During the summer 1150 horses are kept

in readiness at the stations, in the winter the number
is reduced by about 300. Two stage coaches start from
each end every day, but as they run during the night also,
much of the beauty of the scenery is lost by those who
avail themselves of this mode of conveyance; besides, it
is difficult to get an outside seat unless you book it a long
time in advance. It is far better to travel by troika, as you
are then free to stop when you like and as long as you
like, and you get an uninterrupted view of the country
through which you pass. (Wardrop 1888, 34–6)

By the time of Lermontov (1840) and certainly by the time of
Chavchavadze, the road and attendant infrastructure (such as post stations) has become almost invisible (on the invisibility of infrastructure,
see Star 1999, Robbins 2007, Larkin 2008, 245). The Russian road longer
battles with the Terek River as it did in the Romantic days of Griboyedov and Pushkin.[5] After the pacification of the mountaineers, too, this
military road is presented as being part of an essentially *economic* sphere
of circulation. Chavchavadze's travel letters made some references to
the economic predicaments of the Moxevian, and here the road is introduced as a possible solution to the economic hardship of the Moxevians
(and the Armenian shopkeeper the source of impoverishment, illustrating once again Chavchavadze's noted Armenophobia). Ghunia explains
to Chavchavadze the predicament represented by the road:

> 'This big road will give you help.'
> 'What difference does a road make! It's only of use
> to him who has things bought or made himself to carry
> and sell.'
> 'Then you do not hire yourself out?'
> 'Why would we not? Of course we do.'
> 'Then you get money from hire.'
> 'We get it. It doesn't stay in the pocket, though; a
> Moxevian mountaineer is the prey of the Armenian.
> There's no food and drink in the house; what we earn
> goes to the *dukan*. (VI)

But Chavchavadze's brief account of the economic role of the road in the impoverishment of those who dwelt by it was itself subject to revision in the realist writings of the 1880s. In a striking reprise of Chavchavadze's journey through Xevi in his *Letters of a Traveler,* Aleksandre Qazbegi (1880) invites us to follow a Moxevian peasant like Lelt Ghunia, who works by hire on the road, on a peasant's eye view of the same journey found in Chavchavadze's *Letters of a Traveler.* Like the road itself, the region of Xevi and the Moxevians themselves represent so much taken-for-granted, seen-but-unnoticed aspects of the landscape of the crossing that they have been, in a sense, like the road itself, relegated to the presupposed and invisible category of infrastructure (Star 1999). An important difference between the accounts is that Qazbegi shows us that economic poverty occurs at the hands of state agents, and not economic agents like the Armenians.

> Whoever looks at these places instantly notices, that there the land must not be rich with various plants and the inhabitants cannot only survive with only ploughing and sowing: therefore they must find some other means to keep themselves. Among other things, one of the means is to go between Vladikavkaz and Tbilisi for hire.
>
> Of course, this work, as a means for life, is a great mercy of god for Moxevians; but if you knew how many disasters accompany this labor you would be amazed, as to how in the world Moxevians go on hire and having lost energy they don't give up everything and banish themselves somewhere?!![6]

The problems faced by the Moxevian according to Qazbegi begin *before* any money is actually made by hire, whereas for Chavchavadze's Lelt Ghunia, the problem is what happens to the money *after* it is made. Seemingly a trivial point, but leading to very different objects of critique. Whereas Chavchavadze turns on his favorite enemies, the Armenians, Qazbegi covers the journey of the Moxevian to Tbilisi in some detail (just as he would do later in his recollections of life as a shepherd, Qazbegi was perhaps the only true Georgian *narodnik*, forsaking his family's tradition of service, he instead spent ten years of his life as a shepherd [Le Galcher Baron 1993]), finding corrupt and coercive agents of the Russian state, arbitrary imposts, fines and theft, in his way every step along the way. The result is that not only do cart drivers not make any money from the road in the first place, but they often even end up in debt! This is a very different image from that depicted by Chavchavadze: here the road enriches agents of the Russian state, not Armenian shop-keepers.

And certainly, it follows that since the state is omnipresent in the life of Xevi as well, an ethnographic picture of Xevi is impossible without the state, and indeed, an ethnography of Xevi is to a greater extent than anywhere else in the same breath an ethnography of the state. The intensity of contact between the Moxevians and the Russian state is guaranteed by their strategic location along the Georgian military road, not merely corruption of local Georgian go-betweens but also endless requirements of corvee labor, requisitions, bribes, and billeting of soldiers in the region, something not experienced, for example, in more out-of-the-way regions. It stands to reason, therefore, that Qazbegi's ethnography of the Moxevians (1880) should dwell for seven chapters on relations between the Moxevian peasant and the state, before he turns in a few final chapters to matters of "everyday life" that might be considered a few years later to be the province of "ethnography" proper. A comparison with the nearly contemporary ethnographic writings of mountain ethnographer Urbneli (a pseudonym of N. Xizanashvili [1940]) writing about the neighboring Xevsurs is instructive: Urbneli can concern himself almost exclusively with the indigenous forms of polity and everyday life of the Xevsurs, because the Russian state is still not the ubiquitous presence in everyday life there that it is in Xevi.

Part of the reason for this was that the Georgian military road infrastructure was a vital link in the Russian imperial postal network, a system which not only carried the post, but provided essentially all transportation and communication services (including passenger services and for most of the period, the telegraph as well) (Bazilevich 1999 [1927], Prigara 1981 [1941]). The corvee labor for Moxevian and Os-setian inhabitants of the Dariel region, for example, includes both road maintenance, billeting of soldiers, but also postal-carrying duties along this vital link in the Russian imperial postal network, explaining, perhaps, why as far south as Ardahan "Ossetian" is synonymous with "post rider" (*yamshchik*, postal carriers usually working as part of obligated service who could also carry passengers for a fee, as with Chavchavadze above). Because their homes are along this vital road, the Ossetians (and the Moxevians) become subsumed as human *parts* of the Caucasus postal infrastructure (for a discussion of the role of *yamshchik* in the Russian imperial post and the forms of exploitation they were subjected to, see Bazilevich 1999 [1927], 35–38; for the role of *yamshchiki* in providing transport for passengers via the postal network, see Bazilevich 1999 [1927], 45–61).

"Life" and the Road: From Anthropomorphic Nature to Anthropomophizing the State

How very different does the journey from Vladikavkaz to Tbilisi look when viewed not from the perspective of Chavchavadze but from the perspective of someone like Lelt Ghunia. This "deromanticization" and de-aestheticization of the journey, turning our attention from the sublime landscape (which itself turns out to be a second nature created through deforestation in tandem with the road) to the abject life of the inhabitants, typifies Qazbegi's writings, both his early ethnographies and the later short stories and novels for which he is most famous, but the critique of the colonial aesthetics of Dariel can be taken further. The typical traveler in Xevi, from Griboyedov to Chavchavadze, treats the landscape of Xevi as an aestheticized natural landscape, viewed from the neutral, almost invisible position of the road. But what if we were to turn this formulation on its head; what does the *road* look like when viewed from the landscape?

The mountain ethnographer Urbneli (N. Xizanashvili), known primarily for his ethnographic writings beginning in the 1880s about the neighboring Pshavs and Xevsurs (collected in Xizanashvili 1940), himself reprises the same literary aesthetic oppositions between Romanticism and realism in explicit form in a feuilleton of 1883 entitled "Notes of a Traveler." The aestheticized description of nature in Dariel, Urbneli supposes, will be familiar to all readers, and he argues that this aestheticized view created by Romanticized "descriptions of nature" prevent understanding the realities of "life":

> Everywhere and always there is the description of the beauty of nature. Our homeland attracts travelers more for the loveliness and beauty of its nature. . . . Take, for example, Russia's poets, Lermontov, Pushkin . . . it's all

the description of the beauty of nature and its inhabitants, it's all 'pure art' and rarely the truth and reality of
life. . . . This is why Europe looks at Georgia primarily
from an aesthetic perspective, and this is also why the
contents of our life remains uninvestigated, unknown to
others.[7]

The blame is laid on all, even Georgian poets "from the great to the
'microscopic'," have participated in the aesthetic alignment of Georgia
with "beauty" at the expense of understanding "life." But the "nature"
which is the object of Romanticism is not true nature; the Romanticized
appropriation of nature in the gorge is in itself a "second nature," identified with human artifice or "art" (*xelovneba*) and genres of "poetry"
(*poezia*), distinct from and inferior to the true "nature" that is the object
of realism, a positivist de-aestheticized nature which is identified with
descriptions of "life" (see below, chapter 7).

Thus far, Urbneli has somewhat predictably chosen the most aestheticized stretch of landscape in Georgia as a point of departure to
champion a realist aesthetics of utility and "life" against a Romantic
reduction of Georgia to (natural) "beauty" (a shorthand for all aesthetic
categories typical of Romanticism, including the sublime). He will not
be satisfied with a hybrid Aesopianism used by Chavchavadze to mo-
bilize Romantic aestheticized nature as a way of talking about society
and politics. Rather, he wants to draw attention away from the nonhuman world of nature (Romantic "beauty") as a veiled representation of
the human order and gaze directly on the human world with a realistic
aesthetics privileging human "life."

Having debunked the aesthetics of beauty which takes the traveler's
imagination away from social life to the natural landscape, his gaze is
free to return to the "life" of Xevi. He briefly entertains, and then dis-
misses, the idea that a traveler could find out about the "life" of Xevi
simply by learning the ethnographic lifeways of the local inhabitants:
"The identity of the inhabitants, their circumstances and fate we cannot
easily learn about. This would require a different kind of research and,
well, where would a traveler have time for that?" No, Urbneli's account
requires a double inversion of perspective, not merely moving from Romantic descriptions of nature to a realist description of "life," but also,
instead of looking at the landscape and locals from the perspective of

the travelers on the road, to look at the travelers on the road from the perspective of the locals. What does the road look like, and the beautiful carriages of the travelers on it, for example, from the perspective of a Moxevian peasant standing at the side of the road or working on it? The resulting aesthetic vision is one of jarring material contradiction:

> 'Do they give you money, boy?' I asked one Moxevian. 'Yes, but . . .' He fell silent, broke off his answer. And really—all this immense expense, all these beautiful buildings for travelers, elegant hotels and at the same time this shocking poverty of those dwelling by the Aragvi River and the Moxevians, of the inhabitants of this beautiful region, doesn't all this destroy the harmony of the soul and heart, doesn't it upset you? . . . Comedy and tragedy—with these two words is expressed the life of our mountain-dwellers.[8]

And what if we take our eyes off the sublime beauty of the landscape, and even take our eyes off the tragic and abject circumstances of the locals and consider the travelers themselves, what do we see?

> The road [itself] is different, roads are the veins and arteries of the state, as one old economist said. This, from one perspective, is correct. Yes, this Georgian military road too—is an artery of the Russian Empire and if you want to sense the strength and might of this empire, keep an eye on the travelers [along it]. Here military personnel are constantly moving, various *chinovniks* [bureaucrats]; rarely do we encounter an ordinary person, a merchant, a tradesman. Why? Because, in my opinion, that the whole life of Russia for the most part is based on military force and on bureaucracy.[9]

If the nature of the "life" of the local inhabitants is not visible to travelers from the road, then the nature of the "life" of the Russian Empire is certainly visible by considering the travelers on the road themselves. The circulation of the Russian road is not the civilizing circulation of *le doux commerce*, but the circulation of empire. Having banished anthropomorphic metaphors from the aesthetics of nature, Urbneli reintroduces them in the aesthetics of empire, using the mixed metaphor of circulation which conflates physiology with infrastructure (Schivelbusch 1977, 194–5). The Russian road is now an organic extension (veins and arteries) of an anthropomorphized empire; to sense the "life" and strength of this empire, one can test the pulse of its exposed artery in Dariel. Urbneli finishes his letter on the antitheses, aesthetic, economic, and political that present themselves in concentrated visible form in this narrow artery of empire, with a conversation with a fellow traveler on the road.

> 'Our entire life represents [a series of] antitheses,' I told one of my traveling companions—a doctor. 'You are a doctor and you try to save people from untimely death. So many officers, however, are born precisely [sc. to bring untimely death] to others. How much money goes on both state doctors and armies. The doctor has one task, the army has another. But they try to convince us that "they have one general task". What do you say to that?'
>
> 'You are still young. Then what power will subdue these savage people, if not the army?' The doctor answered me wrathfully. 'If not bureaucrats, then who will protect the law?' he added. I fell silent.[10]

As Urbneli points out, one of the key antitheses of Xevi is that while the ethnographic study of the "life" of the inhabitants along this road is difficult, the military road is probably the best place in the empire to apprehend the "life" of the Russian state. Though he does not call it that, since as a realist he is interested in a complete de-aestheticization of the heavily Romanticized landscape, we nevertheless see in Urbneli's account a version of the sublime transferred from the natural order to the human order, what could be called with some justice a rhetoric of the "imperial sublime."[11] But this is a sublime where the lyric subject does not seek identification with the imperial conqueror but with the terrified or prostrated imperial subject, and one where the objective locus of the sublime is not the greatness of sublime nature, but the sublime of the Russian state represented by the circulation on the Russian road itself.

Imperial and Colonial Sublime

In earlier Romantic articulations of the imperial sublime, the enraptured poet appropriates the sublime aesthetics of nature to frame, among many other possible things, a sublime reading of the empire, in part "as an attempt on the part of the Russian writer as lyric subject to establish a relationship (sometimes celebratory, sometimes mutedly critical) *with* the state" (Harsha Ram, personal communication). For Ram and Shatirishvili (2004, 13, see Ram 1998, 2003, Manning 2008 for other readings), "The Russian imperial sublime . . . involved two axes, a vertical axis provided in the "romantic period by the alpine landscape, and a horizontal axis created by the panoramic stretch of conquered territory that was viewed from a height by the enraptured lyric subject." Here, the imperial sublime projects the vastness of empire onto vertical and horizontal axes. The enraptured lyric subject of the imperial sublime often seeks identification with a greater power, imperial power embodied in the monarch, set in opposition to a largely dehumanized sublime nature, so that the rhetoric of the imperial sublime is one in which the empire attracts the sublime properties of the sublime nature it conquers.

The sublime nature of the Caucasus, embodied in different ways Mount Kazbek or the rushing, roaring Terek, represent for Russian travelers on the road the beauty and savagery of the Caucasus, and in the same breath, the "imperial sublime" of the vast and powerful Russian Empire that has conquered it. By contrast, for Urbneli, it is the Russian road itself, and specifically the nature of the traffic (state agents) on the road, that represents the "imperial sublime" of the Russian Empire, one viewed, however, not from the perspective of the conqueror but the conquered.

In this sense, Urbneli's confrontation with the Russian road bears a certain resemblance to what Larkin (2008) has termed "the colonial sublime," in which the colonizing power shows "the terrifying ability to remake landscapes and to force the natural world to conform to these technological projects by leveling mountains, flooding villages, and remaking cities; these were the ways in which the sublime was produced as a necessary spectacle of colonial rule" (Larkin 2008, 36). The colonial sublime is first of all a version of the technological sublime (Marx 1964, Nye 1990) which moves the prototypical object of the sublime from the sphere of nature to the sphere of culture and technology. Second, this is a sublime which, unlike the imperial sublime, does not so much emphasize the greatness of the sublime object as the abjection of the lyric subjects feel in the presence of such an object: "Here the sublime is experienced not so much through a sense of absolute greatness but through the overwhelming physical powerlessness individuals feel in the face of something overpowering and terrible" (Larkin 2008, 36). Unlike the imperial sublime, where the lyric subject seeks identification with the monarch surveying his vast dominion from a dizzying height, the colonial sublime interpellates the colonized subject, using technology both to incite awe and perhaps terror, but also to "proffer technology as a mode of development" so that the sublime aspect of technology will become domesticated and ultimately be taken for granted as part of colonial modernity (Larkin 2008, 36–7).

For Urbneli and Qazbegi, however, as critical realists, the "colonial sublime" of the Russian road contains only the first moment, the ability to incite awe and terror in the face of the power of the Russian state. The road lacks the second moment as a mode of civilizational or economic development for those living alongside it. Going far further than Chavchavadze in their critiques of Russian road, and by extension, the Russian Empire as an agent of civilizational progress for the colonized, particularly the mountain tribes of the Caucasus, they instead point up the ways in which the road remains almost exclusively an instrument of empire (see Jersild [1999, 510–11] for similar intelligentsia critiques of Russian technological projects elsewhere in the Caucasus).

The Russian road as an instantiation of the colonial sublime contains other semiotic vulnerabilities to intelligentsia critique as well, namely that, like all forms of the technological sublime, as Larkin points out, it quickly loses its sheen and becomes a taken-for-granted invisible infrastructural aspect of the landscape, or worse, it comes to be received in terms of the aesthetic category of the picturesque as being ruined, dilapidated, backward, and so on: "steamships render sailing ships slow, airplanes destroy steamboats' apparent speed, and jets make propeller planes anachronistic, nostalgic emblems of a previous era. . . . When [the] idea of the sublime is tied to the representation of colonial power it builds in a fragility that forever haunts its efforts" (Larkin 2008, 248). The Russian colonial sublime has the added vulnerability that these newer versions of the technological sublime are always already at hand somewhere else, Russian infrastructure will always suffer from invidious comparison with a European model; to compare the Dariel road across the Caucasus to the European Simplon road across the Alps seems like a compliment, taking the comparison of the natural sublime (Alps=Caucasus) to the technological sublime (Simplon=Dariel), but it is also a potential statement of backwardness, of derivativeness. As Harsha Ram (personal communication) notes, the difference between the imperial sublime, "which exists chiefly for the rulers and the ruling elite" and the colonial sublime is fundamentally temporal; "while the imperial sublime is related to the increasingly anachronistic ancient regime, the 'colonial sublime,' in using technology, is future-oriented. Ironically, it also becomes anachronistic, but through the inevitable obsolescence of technology."

The British colonial sublime discussed by Larkin takes advantage of a binary geopoetics so that the technological sublime can represent European civilization to the benighted colonies. However, in a ternary system in which Russian state both represents the colonized with respect to Europe and the colonizer with respect to the colonized people, the colonial sublime becomes even more unstable.[12] The voice of the local intelligentsia steps in here as elsewhere as a mediating figure: on the one hand, the intelligentsia is *already familiar* with these new *European* technologies and can readily compare the Russian version to its European or North American models that they have read about and find them wanting; on the other hand, the intelligentsia can stand with the state in contemplating the unenlightened "Oriental" peasantry's irrational animistic response to the technological sublime. Thus, even at the moment the railroad from Poti to Tbilisi is sparkling new (1872), an intelligentsia commentator finds that it is *already slow*, calculating its average speed as twenty to twenty-five versts an hour (about 21–26 km an hour, about the speed of a galloping horse). It is slow, then, not compared to anything else available in the Caucasus except perhaps the fabulous speed of a boat ride down the Choroxi River (on which below). It is slow compared to things one can read about in newspapers, for example, the "wondrous speed" of American and English railways, and "in Russia too, you can't find one railroad which still on average doesn't exceed 35–45 versts in an hour."[13] Having thus geopoetically divided this technological object into truly sublime Euro-American, not-so-sublime Russian, and not-at-all sublime Caucasus versions, the commentator is content to continue this strategy of damning with faint praise by noting that the local versions excel over the Russian versions in comfortable appointments of the interior, that a second-class cabin in the Caucasus is almost better than a first-class cabin in Russia.

The intelligentsia as mediating figure between colonizer and colonized, state and people, can simultaneously inhabit both sides of the colonial sublime, like the Georgian Romantics in their appropriation of the natural sublime (Ram and Shatirishvili 2004, Manning 2008). The Georgian intelligentsia, contemplating a new Russian railroad, can not only prove their coevality with European civilization by knowing what is, and what is not, a good candidate for awe, but also by adopting the stance of the colonial civilizers themselves in bemused contemplation of the imagined stupefaction and superstition of "our simple people" at these animated iron monsters (compare Bektas [2001], Larkin [2008, 40–43], on similar narratives imputing animism and credulity to Oriental or African audiences when faced with Western technological "wonders"):

> When the people do not understand the real explanation of a phenomenon or an object, then they try to explain it in their own peculiar way. Who knows what our simple people are saying about this railroad. Some say, 'some sort of evil spirit sits in this *mashina* [machine, the author is voicing the peasant's words] and it makes the wheels roll with its hands'; some say 'the *anglichans* [sc. the English] have captured a dragon and imprisoned it in the front room and it propels the train, and when it encounters difficulties, its shrieks and screams become more frequent.' And who knows what others say, how they explain the movement of the railroad![14]

The mediating intelligentsia position is also a critical position. Taking advantage of the semiotic vulnerability of the colonial sublime, which when working properly can at best aspire to becoming an invisible order of infrastructure, travelers like Chavchavadze, especially his imagined French fellow traveler, would seek to minimize or defang this "technological sublime" by focusing on more typically picturesque elements: stereotypically picturesque figures like antiquated post carts and draw attention away from the technological sublime to what one could call the dilapidated, backward, ruinous "technological picturesque."[15] By realigning the technological order of the Russian Empire with the technological picturesque as opposed to the technological sublime, such critiques could make powerful charges of Russian backwardness and consequent inability to embody civilization, which is then located elsewhere, in France or Britain.

And indeed, the infrastructure Russian postal system in the Dariel pass, upon which all travelers depend for transport, there as elsewhere provides a set of picturesque images of technological backwardness in the form of *yamshchiki* and Russian postal carts. On the technological level, since the *yam* or relay system upon which it was based always used local populations, local domesticated animals (horses, reindeers dogs, camels, etc.), and indigenous technological affordances (a picturesque assortment of carts, boats, sleds, and so forth) adapted to local conditions, the varied climates, landscapes, and conditions of the vast empire, it could not help but present itself as a picturesque assemblage of varied transport methods and technologies (Bazilevich 1999 [1927], 14, 67–88, 173). The passage through the Caucasus was certainly an exemplary picturesque spot within a network characterized by its technologically picturesque qualities (Bazilevich 1999 [1927], 84–88). Only in those portions of the network where steamship or train could be used could the system aspire to "technological sublime," and these links could always be found wanting by comparison with their American or European models and in any case could not displace the more "picturesque" local technologies of the relay system everywhere, particularly not in the Dariel passing (Bazilevich 1999 [1927], 172–189).

For example, Chavchavadze's *Letters of a Traveler* dwells on the Russian postal cart and *yamshchik*, primarily to allow him to critique Russia's pretensions to representing a civilizing colonial power (he brings in a Frenchman only to make fun of Russia's post carts!):

> When I had packed, that is, when I had put my little leather knapsack in the cart, I turned to bid farewell to my newly made French acquaintance.
>
> 'Who invented this vehicle?' He asked, pointing to the postcart on which the sleepy 'yamshchik' was stupidly dozing.
>
> 'The Russians', I answered.

'I imagine nobody is likely to dispute the honor with them. I pity you to be forced to addle your brain and shake up your stomach on a thing like that.'

'No harm done. If the whole of Russia travels like this, why should I complain?'

'They all travel like that? That's why they have gone so far! God give you a safe journey. As for me, I tell you frankly I would not risk my life by getting into it. Good bye! If we meet again some day I beg you to remember me.'

With these words he gave me his hand to bid farewell and grasped it firmly as only a European can.

I entered the postcart. (I)

Similarly, the Russian officer's delusional imagining of a Russian technological sublime in which *flies* become the engines of progress replacing the expensive machines of the French is introduced to underline the same opposition between the European technological sublime and the laughable Russian technological picturesque or even grotesque.

The French invent devilish sorts of things like that, but to buy their machines is dear, while my invention doesn't cost a farthing. What expense is there in catching two flies and putting them in a box? It is nothing. But now, see what will be the result of my invention: when it spreads perhaps there will be a trade in flies. There will thus be a new form of commerce in the land; some fine day you will go into your town and you will find a fly shop. That's not bad. How many hungry mouths may be filled by the help of flies! What are flies at present? Nothing. Of what use are they? None at all. Now you see of what great significance the labor and work of a learned and wise man is to the land. (III)

For critical writers about the Caucasus of the 1880s, like Qazbegi and Urbneli, the imperial sublime, as viewed from the perspective of the conquered, was one terrifying in its aspect and consequences and could not be so simply defanged by one laughing Frenchman or one laughable

Russian scientific officer. These "mountain writers" then, are somewhat exceptional compared to the rest of the Georgian intelligentsia in the fierceness of their critiques of the Russian civilizing mission, emphasizing the terrifying forceful aspect of the imperial sublime over the progressive potentialities of the colonial sublime in their assessment of the Russian road as a proxy for more general critiques of the savagery of the Russian military conquest of the "savage tribes" of the Caucasus (on which, see Layton 1994, 1997; Jersild 2002, Manning 2009). They thus emphasize one aspect of the more general ambivalent reception of the narrative of Russian colonial rule that characterized "native" intelligentsia elsewhere in the Caucasus, in which the savagery of Russian conquest of the Caucasus was complemented by its civilizing mission elsewhere (Khalid 1997, 1998; but see Jersild 1999 for native intelligentsia ambivalence about this aspect of the Russian civilizing mission as well).

> Many non-Russians in the Russian Empire were active members of imperial educated society (*obshchestvo*), and they often conceived of the colonial advance of Russia as part of the march of the progressive West and "civilization" itself into the backward lands of the East. Reformist empire builders who criticized the brutal wars and population transfers that marked the conquest of the southern border lands also emphasized the civilizing mission of the empire on its eastern frontier. (Jersild 1999, 503)

Conclusion: The Antinomies of Intelligentsia Discourse
"Our entire life represents antitheses," Urbneli tells his traveling companion. The antitheses that become visible in miniature form over this short stretch of land, in Dariel, are the same antitheses that haunt not only the Russian Empire, but the subaltern culture of circulation being created by the Georgian intelligentsia culture of circulation through this period.[16] Into each antithesis, Europe and Asia, civilization and savagery, the Russian Road and the Terek River, the state and the people, the intelligentsia inserts itself as a mediating voice. Beginning with Chavchavadze, the Georgian intelligentsia in the Dariel finds the

geographic object, Georgia, as a thing already spoken about, and so the Dariel pass becomes a privileged place as well as *topos* to engage all that was said before about Georgia as a whole. By the 1880s, this marginal area of Georgia in the Caucasus becomes the privileged place both to critique Russian imperial rule as well as to imagine a sublime ethnographic vision of Georgianness, the Georgians of the mountains, once considered savages, now imagined as surrogate selves whose freedoms make their communities an imagined "elsewhere" which Georgians can enjoy vicariously (again, following earlier Russian narratives of escape and vicarious identification with the mountaineer freedom of the Caucasus (Layton 1994, Ram 1999, Grant 2009, Manning 2009). By the 1890s, a reviewer of the works of Aleksandre Qazbegi could look back on his work as a new direction within Georgian realism characteristic of the 1880s, one which involved applying the principles of realism both to the ethnographic study of the life of Georgian mountain peoples (the topic with which Qazbegi began) and the simultaneous elaboration of the ethnographic life of these people in literary treatments (which Qazbegi turned his hands to after he finished his Mokhevian ethnographies).[17]

> This new direction is the study of our mountain people, their customs, *adats*, beliefs, ideals, poetry. This direction also has another side, that is, our poets and belletrists have turned the life of these people into themes for the practice of their own talents.[18]

To understand this "turn to the mountains" of the 1880s, we need to understand what happened in the decade between the publication of Chavchavadze's letters (1861–1871) and Aleksandre Qazbegi's first writings about the Moxevians (1880). The intervening period is the moment of the development and consolidation of a specifically Georgian print culture in 1860s–1870s in the newspaper *Droeba*. In this period, the mountains play a minor role; it is West Georgia and especially the newly conquered regions of Ottoman Georgia in the late 1870s that forms the critical borderlands in which the mediating voice of the intelligentsia forms itself. This period is defined by two main events: the emancipation of the serfs (announced for the empire in 1861, beginning in East Georgia in 1864, and continuing from 1865 to 1871 in West

Georgia) and the conquest of Ottoman Georgia (1878–9). Especially in the latter case, it might be argued that a radical disconfirmation of the happy fairytale reunification of the Georgian people, the disappointment of intelligentsia projects to mediate this divide between "Ottoman Georgia" and "European Georgia," evidenced first and foremost by the massive flight of Ottoman people from Russian rule (and their Georgian intelligentsia mediators), was what caused the subsequent immense boom of interest in the mountains of Georgia in the 1880s. The central intelligentsia project of the period to mediate between the lettered public of the intelligentsia and the unlettered voice of the people, that forms the core of Chavchavadze's text, encountered in the borderlands of Ottoman and European Georgia a transcribable, but unassimilable people and landscape. In Ottoman Georgia, Georgian intelligentsia moved from being "Orientals" in relation to Russia (as they are in *Letters of a Traveler*) to being "Europeans" in relation to the recently conquered population of "Ottoman Georgia." The recalcitrant realities of Ottoman Georgia which exploded the myths the intelligentsia had written for it made it a place unfit for the free play of the imagination, which then shifted into the mountains of Georgia, a place that Russian Romantics had already made into a fitting home for the imagination.

The story of an imagined Georgia which begins with Chavchavadze at the northern boundaries of Georgia in the Dariel pass ends at the southern boundaries not a decade later in the empty Ottoman town of Ardanuji with a correspondent writing under the pseudonym of S. Bavreli. After that, the Georgian imagination in the 1880s turns away from the southern borders back to the Caucasus. In between, the antinomies of this central text are reconstituted in the unfamiliar landscape of Ottoman Georgia. The next chapters tell that story, unfolding the categories of Georgian print culture as they emerge in this period in the context of this fateful encounter of European Georgia with its Oriental other.

KAZBEK, FROM THE SOUTH.

(from Freshfield 1869, facing p. 197)

Figure 4: Picturesque Technology and Sublime Nature on the Dariel Pass.

III: Correspondence: "Georgians, that is, readers of *Droeba*"

> In a specific issue of our respected newspaper of this year, one correspondent from Guria was writing with sadness, that 'the readers of "Droeba" don't even know, whether Guria is in Georgia, or not.' About this we cannot agree, for Guria has such a geographical location . . . that it is not possible that Georgians [*kartvelebma*], that is, readers of "Droeba", will not know about its existence.[1]

Taking my inspiration from this quote, I want to explore the specific role that regional *correspondence* in *Droeba* ("Times"), from the mid-1860s to the mid-1880s more or less the *only* Georgian newspaper,[2] had as part of a culture of circulation in forming a social imaginary, and what is not quite the same thing, an imagined geography of a nation that could only be apprehended through correspondence about its various regions, which appeared to be part of a single whole in part because they appeared next to each other in the pages of *Droeba*. Newspapers like *Droeba*, of course, represent a complex secondary genre, a heteroglot unity which is built up out of various primary genres, including telegrams, poems, announcements, stories, serialized novels, and so on that compose it (Bakhtin 1986, 612). However, unlike the comparable heteroglot unity of the novel, newspapers do not "absorb and digest" these primary genres. Within this heterogeneous assemblage of distinct primary genres, correspondence is one of those few genres (including the feuilleton, a term denoting a separate partitioned section of a newspaper where correspondence most often appears, and also somewhat later a kind of genre) which is most *at home* in a newspaper, and indeed, unlike a telegram, a poem, a story, or an announcement, *has no other home* than a newspaper. Correspondence was what made the news the news. Correspondence was the genre that allowed the representation of *simultaneity* of diverse regions of Georgia and allowed the pages of *Droeba* to become an accreting image of Georgia itself, including, for a short time, the expanded horizons of newly conquered Ottoman Georgia.

More than any other genre in the newspaper, except perhaps the closely related feuilleton, the genre of correspondence is the incorporated genre that seems to epitomize the "culture of circulation" represented by the newspaper *Droeba*. Here I will speak of "cultures of circulation" (Lee 2001, Lee and LiPuma 2002) in preference to terms like "public," "social imaginary," or "nation" because the former category identifies the dimensions of a material and semiotic process which can produce differing imaginaries of the latter type as product. A culture of circulation involves, but is not reducible to (1) the semiotic and material properties of circulatory objects, (2) the spatio-temporal dimensions of the "space-time" created by the actual circulation of those objects, and also (3) a reflexive awareness or imagination of that circulation (Lee 2001, 164). A culture of circulation is thus defined by the same (objective, spatio-temporal, and subjective) parameters as what Nancy Munn calls an intersubjective "space-time" (Munn 1986, 10–11), the main difference being that a culture of circulation may involve multiple space-times. For example, as Anderson's classic account of the newspaper shows (1991, 32–6), the juxtaposition of heterogeneous correspondence and other genres on a single dated issue of a newspaper like *Droeba*, and the subsequent circulation and nearly simultaneous consumption of this complex secondary genre produces a certain kind of intersubjective space-time of "Georgians, that is, readers of *Droeba*." However, as I will show presently, each of the individual primary genres from which this secondary unity is composed also represents a distinct kind of space-time. These distinct incorporated space-times are, in part, materially mediated not only by the properties of the circulatory objects, but just as importantly, by the properties of the easily forgotten infrastructures of circulation, after which some of these genres are named.

The neglect of the category of "infrastructure" in the model of "culture of circulation" shows us that this model has some blind spots that become obvious when it is applied to the uneven terrain of nineteenth-century Georgian print culture: the emphasis on circulation itself allows this literature to, perhaps accidentally, recapitulate a certain sort of liberal imagination of circulation that emphasizes and valorizes motion and mediation over obduracy, emphasizing abstract forms of semiotic value that emerge from circulation over the mere materiality of the infrastructure of circulation. In nineteenth-century liberal imaginaries, circulation, together with the related progressive valorization of new technologies that "annihilate space and time" (the heroic triad of railroad, steamship, telegraph that are the objects of the "technological sublime" (Marx 1964, Nye 1996), was also a directly normative moral category of civilizational progress). As Schivelbusch summarizes it: "The circulation concept serves as a key to unlock the open triumphs as well as the hidden anxieties of the nineteenth century. The formula is as simple as can be—whatever was part of circulation was regarded as healthy, progressive, constructive; all that was detached from circulation, on the other hand, appeared diseased, medieval, subversive, threatening" (Schivelbusch 1977, 195).

Needless to say, particularly for Georgian observers located on the boundaries of Europe and Asia, what was a temporal, epochal, or stadial opposition within European modernity between progressive ("modern") circulation and backward ("feudal") obduracy also served to differentiate the progressive temporality or historicity of Europe in contrast to the obdurate stasis and backwardness of Asia within an Orientalist imagined geography.

In a kind of "rhetoric of the circulatory sublime," the literature on cultures of circulation often draws our attention to the vast and awe-inspiring scales, horizons, and abstractions of circulation and away from the merely picturesque medium-scale networks of actants and material infrastructure that make circulation possible, or the uneven terrain of the geographies over which the circulation must occur. Statements like the following are typical: "Circulation is a central dimension of contemporary global processes, involving the velocity, scale, and form of movement of ideas, persons, commodities, and images, in ways that disturb virtually all existing cartographies of culture, place and identity" (Lee 2001, 164).

By contrast, Georgian observers could only participate in the technological or circulatory sublime from afar, for they found their own culture of circulation mired materially in a rather more picturesque infrastructural assemblage that again defined their condition as one of Oriental backwardness in opposition to the progressive cultures of circulation of Europe that served as their aspirational models. As Brian Larkin (personal communication) notes, in contrast to Western theorists who prefer to focus on the sublime rather than picturesque aspects of technologies of circulation, Georgian commentators seem to define

themselves as being in a state of abjection by continuously drawing attention to

> the 'comparative' nature of these technologies . . . 'com-
> parative' in that they cannot simply exist in and of them-
> selves but are always compared to other infrastructures
> elsewhere, which seems to lead to a form of abjection.
> There is a way that all the technologies that—according
> to a certain literature—should bring peoples and ter-
> ritories into tighter connection are here present but do
> the opposite. The road goes through the villages of Xevi
> but isolates them. The presence of print means there
> are newspapers which seem only to confirm one's isola-
> tion from the news. Technologies, by virtue of constant
> comparison to better, faster, livelier such technologies
> concurrently existing elsewhere, seem not to connect
> but to confirm one's expulsion and isolation from this
> world they are supposed to represent. Abjection—the
> sense of being cast aside—seems an apt description of
> their situation. (Brian Larkin, personal communication)

In a sense, the state of abjection expressed by Georgian correspondents when comparing the "picturesque" state of local infrastructure
to their "sublime" Western models, or even the curious isolating effect that such sublime imperial technologies of communication have
in actual fact, finds its most direct expression in another comparison
of technologies: the opposition between the telegram (a technological
channel most clearly identified with the space-time of empire) and local
postal correspondence (a technological channel used by correspondents
of *Droeba* to describe the localities *between* telegraph stations).

Channel, Genre, Space-time: Postal Correspondence and the Telegram
The name of the newspaper *Droeba* of course translates as "Times"—appropriately, because this newspaper is not only an assemblage of different primary genres, but also different circulatory space-times that
these different genres mediate. The specificity of "correspondence" is
best illustrated by contrast with the more celebrated genre of the "tele-

gram" usually found on the same page, the telegrams occupying, along with announcements of theatrical events or other items relevant to the urban reader, the upper left-hand column under the masthead, followed by an editorial section or a section entitled "Georgia." Postal correspondence, by contrast, usually occupied the bottom half of the page, in a space separated by a black bar designated, as it is elsewhere in Europe, the *feuilleton*.

Figure 5: Front page of Droeba, July 20, 1879.

Local announcements and telegrams occupy the space in the upper left under the masthead section (top); postal correspondence is usually found in the feuilleton (*Peluoni*) section which occupies a space divided by a bar on the lower half of the page.

Initially, both postal correspondence and telegrams have in common that they are genres defined more by infrastructural *technologies* or *channels* of circulation than their internal form or content: postal correspondence by definition comes in the form of letters carried by the postal network, while telegrams came to *Droeba* through the Caucasus telegraph network, created at the initiative of Prince Grigol Orbeliani in 1863 which by the late 1860s linked Tbilisi via Russia to Europe and via Persia to the East to India (Huurdeman 2003, 109). It is easy to overdraw the opposition between these two channels, and imagine that the telegraph, a new technology associated with the miraculous new force of electricity, represented a qualitatively new immaterial technology in contrast to the technologically picturesque assemblage of a diverse human and nonhuman actors, including Ossetian post riders and postal carts traveling over bad roads, that constituted the postal network of correspondence (on which generally, see Bazilevich 1999 [1927]). However, in Russian Georgia, these two networks expanded in tandem and shared the same fates, the telegraph depended crucially on the very same actors and almost simultaneously expanding infrastructures of the shipping, rail, and postal network that made correspondence possible (Karbelashvili 1991, 279), and the post and the telegraph (always potentially linked at individual stations) were officially united into a single system in 1884 (Bazilevich 1999[1927], 153):

> Now, it is easy to overemphasize the revolutionary consequences of the telegraph. It is not an infrequent to be driving along an interstate highway and to become aware that the highway is paralled by a river, a canal, a railway track, or telegraph and telephone wires. In that instant, one may realize that each of these improvements in transportation or communications merely worked a modification on what preceded it. The telegraph twisted and altered but did not displace patterns of connection formed by natural geography, by the river and primitive foot and horse paths and later by the wooden turnpike and canal. (Carey 1989, 156)

In line with this general tendency to overemphasize the differences between the technologically sublime and the technologically picturesque channels, telegraph and postal, one might think too that the telegraph, relative to written letters, was an instantaneous mode of transmission, a perfect example of the "annihilation of space and time" that was the mantra of the period. Factually, however, since each telegraph had to be relayed from station to station, "transit" telegrams traveling through the Caucasus from Europe to India, which represented 63 percent of all telegraphic correspondence passing through the Caucasus on the Siemens Indo-European Telegraph in the year 1880, could take six to seven days on the average (Karbelashvili 1991, 278, 280). A survey of the datelines similarly shows that telegrams printed in *Droeba* from Vienna or Berlin would take two to three days to arrive in Tbilisi. Thus, though telegrams were certainly much faster than the post, neither was even close to instantaneous or "immediate"; they traveled along the same paths and were relayed between stations, fresh horses and riders or new telegraph operators relaying them all along the way. Thus, the telegram and postal correspondence had in common the printing of their time of origin just as they printed their spatial point of origin; any sense of simultaneity in homogeneous empty time was produced by calibrating these different space-times to the same printed and dated page of *Droeba* (subsequently distributed through the same postal network that brought in correspondence) and the (relative) simultaneity of the rituals of their consumption (as Anderson [1991] has famously argued), and certainly not the simultaneity of their transmission.

Both telegrams and written correspondence are not merely technological or infrastructural channels, but each quickly develops into a *medium* in two senses distinguished by Lisa Gitelman (cited in Jenkins 2006, 13–14). That is, both are initially identified with a medium in the sense of being a technological channel ("a technology that enables communication"), but both quickly develop into a medium in a second sense as a "set of associated protocols or cultural practices that have grown up around that technology." Clearly, Gitelman's definition somewhat problematically recapitulates a dualism in which media are sociotechnical hybrids, which can be divided into technical/technological and social/cultural elements, where the latter accrete around the former. Following Spitulnik (2000), I will refer to Gitelman's first definition of medium as a *channel*, and the second sense of medium as a *genre* (in something like Bakhtin's sense [1986, 60–102], however, these are specifically *not* "speech genres").

While both genres (both of which, after all, are named after *channels* of circulation and not *content*) are centrally defined in terms of categories of circulation and in terms of space-time and technological manner of circulation, they form polar opposites in other ways. Obviously, technological constraints make the content of the telegram "telegraphic" compared to the fulsome prosiness of the postal correspondence of the period. Compared to local correspondence, the telegram makes a comparatively minor contribution to the "news" in *Droeba*. Partly this is a sign of the kinds of space-times the telegraph is poised to mediate: telegrams move between imperial metropole and colony, traversing the space between imperial metropole and colony or frontline position of the army without registering the space in between. In fact, most of the messages transmitted on the Caucasus telegraph in 1880 were not even between Russian metropole and Caucasian colony, but between Britain and India. As Carey emphasizes, the space-time mediated by the telegraph is initially at least an imperial one: "It was the cable and the telegraph . . . that turned colonialism into imperialism: a system in which the center of an empire could dictate rather than merely respond to the margin" (1989, 164). In this sense, the telegraph is comparable to Urbneli's observation about the human traffic along Dariel road: telegrams and travelling bureaucrats alike belong to the order of, and are in the service of, empire. However, telegrams are unlike bureaucrats, in that they are usually in the service of some *other* empire. The cosmopolitan messages of the telegram are voices of state agents, interstate chatter, and the chatter between imperial metropole and periphery conveyed by the mediation of telegraph engineers in an array of relay stations. The local voices of the people living in the gaps between these stations are carried through the mediating intervention of intelligentsia correspondents traveling in the spaces between these points. While the telegraph and the railway connected distant spaces, abolishing space and time between them, postal correspondence proliferated in the "abject" residual spaces in between those distant telegraph and railway stations.

Strangers and Strange Lands:
Social Imaginaries and Imaginative Geographies
What I want to argue is that the kinds of imagined communities cre-

ated by the circulation of *Droeba*, and writ large in each performative act of correspondence, are twofold. On the one hand, correspondence addressed to other readers of *Droeba* creates a reflexive image of a *social imaginary*, a "public." Central to such a public is the presupposition of a reflexive understanding based on a sense of empathy, reciprocity, and interchangeability of perspectives and between strangers (Warner 2002). On the other hand, correspondence also presupposes a divide between a benighted locality and locals ("the people") described in a quasi-ethnographic voice emphasizing alterity and backwardness, and this imagined nonlocalized deterritorialized space in which that correspondence is being read ("the public"), a kind of *imaginative geography* typified by Orientalist discourse (Said 1978). Correspondence simultaneously performatively creates two kinds of imagined communities: a community of anonymous *strangers* who are addressed (an Occidentalist social imaginary), and a *strange land* whose strange denizens are described (an Orientalist imaginative geography).

A social imaginary is a reflexive "we-imaginary," that is, a social imaginary is how "we" imagine "ourselves," without explicit acknowledgment of the alterity against which such imaginings inevitably define themselves. In contrast, Said (1978), along with Asad (1973, 2003) and Coombe (1996), remind us that such imaginings require imaginative geographies, imaginings of alterity against which such imaginings of identity implicitly or explicitly define themselves (see also Hastings and Manning 2004). The literature on social imaginaries shows us that these are constituted at least in part by reflexive reciprocities of perspectives between stranger contemporaries mediated by circulatory objects, they are thus "cultures of circulation" (Lee 2001, Lee and LiPuma 2002), while from the literature on imaginative geographies, it is clear that the horizons of possibility of this commerce of perspectives is defined against an alterity of those strangers who are truly strange, with whom this reciprocity cannot happen. In the case of Georgia, the former defines a "public" of intelligentsia who can readily imagine the response of their interlocutor, the latter defines a "people" who are so estranged from the intelligentsia and so locked in the particularity of their locality that their minds can be known only indirectly through conversations described with painstaking realism. Thus, the culture of circulation of Georgia is defined at the intersection of different kinds of strangers, the liberal or "occidentalist stranger" of the intelligentsia public, who is an anonymous stranger but who is not by that very strange, and the unknown inhabitants of the strange land of the countryside, of West Georgia, of Ottoman Georgia, "orientalist strangers" whom the intelligentsia must "get to know" ethnographically (in a movement that parallels and is derived from the Russian intelligentsia "going to the people" movement [Frierson 1993]).

Strangers

First, social imaginaries. Unlike Orientalist imaginative geographies, social imaginaries always seem to be considered as reflexive self-imaginings; they are tellingly what "we" (Western moderns) think about "ourselves" (Taylor 2002, 106). They are seemingly always given strongly Occidentalist genealogies in Western liberalism. For example, Lee and LiPuma recently (2002) recharacterized Charles Taylor's three main, modern social imaginaries (publics, nation-states, and markets) as "cultures of circulation." They propose that the normative core of all three social imaginaries is that they "presuppose a *self-reflexive structure of circulation* built around *some reciprocal social action*, whether that action be reading, in the case of the public sphere and nationalism, or buying and selling, as in the case of the market" (Lee and LiPuma 2002, 193). Lee and LiPuma locate the prototype for these forms of "creative social self-reflexivity" in the reciprocity of performative acts of promising and agreeing embedded in social contracts. As with Warner and Taylor, then, Lee and LiPuma tell a story of liberal modernities that grow out of the fundamental historical narrative of liberalism itself, characterized succinctly by Henry Maine as a continuous, progressive movement "from status to contract" as a basis for social relations (Kockelman 2007). Lee and LiPuma are certainly correct in identifying certain kinds of reciprocity of perspectives with strangers as foundational to the theorization of modern social imaginaries, for example, Anderson's well-known characterizations of the emergent reciprocity of perspectives and emergent sense of contemporaneity of fellow newspaper readers, or his characterization of the imaginary transposability and reciprocity of perspectives between the career movements of bureaucratic fellow travelers within the space of the state (Anderson 1991, 55–6). The point is that these Occidentalist *strangers* with whom we create these reciprocities of perspectives are not *strange*; they are imagined as being people like ourselves, with whom reciprocal social action, reciprocity of perspectives, is possible (Warner 2002, 83).

This fundamentally liberal narrative of reciprocity of perspectives and abstract equivalency between strangers is certainly one constitutive element of the print culture of *Droeba*, the founding editors of which, after all, considered themselves to be liberals. This sense of absolute transposability of perspectives between an enlightened public is particularly constituted of the emergent notion of intelligentsia publics, particularly of the intimate familiar discourse "amongst ourselves" of the intelligentsia dialogue of the feuilleton discussed below in chapter 6, and also of the highly presupposing esoteric public of underground and bohemian discourse found in Aesopian language and the playful use of pseudonyms in chapter 5. But it coexists uneasily with a conservative naturalizing, essentializing narrative of mutual face-to-face recognition based on essential status attributes like Georgianness that is at the core of Georgian gentry nationalist thought (exhibited in the dialogue of Chavchavadze and Ghunia in chapter 1, which collapses in the face of empirical nonrecognition of Ottoman Georgians of their common Georgianness on the eve of the conquest of Ottoman Georgia discussed in the next chapter). It also deserves comparison with the narrative of "going to the people," of "getting to know them" through their transcribed voice that recognizes instead a basic alterity, a great divide, between the perspectives of the enlightened intelligentsia and the predicament of the unenlightened people which can be overcome through getting to know them through realist portrayal of dialogue and ethnographic description of the material conditions of their "life" (discussed in chapters 5–7).

At the same time, *Droeba* correspondence is a frankly Occidentalist discourse which explicitly opposes itself to and comments on an Orientalist imaginary of spatial and social difference or alterity, against which one might argue (although he does not) Taylor's social imaginaries also necessarily define themselves. Taylor's frankly Eurocentric discussion of modernity is always bounded by entities he calls "civilizations" (van de Veer 2001, 160), while he graciously accedes to Chakrabarty's call to "provincialize Europe" (2000), he defines his own project as being delimited by the Modern West (2004, 195–6). The only major alterity which his singular "social imaginary of the Modern West" is defined is a small group of "premodern social imaginaries," which, upon inspection, also appear to be in one way or another part of this same transhistorical civilizational unity (a motley group of Indo-European tribes and Greek philosophers [Taylor 2002, 94–95]). While Taylor's genealogy of modern social imaginaries, then, is like many other genealogies of modernity in which modernity is defined only in relation to, and develops out of, its own European historical antecedents, (variously ancient, medieval) "anti-modernities" which enter the argument only to establish the novelty of modernity itself. However, as van de Veer notes for British modernity, comparisons with the societies of the colonized were crucial elements in defining the society European metropole as being uniquely modern or civilized (van de Veer 2001, 5). Thus, in Europe, as in Georgia, the discourse of modern social imaginaries was forged just as much on the ground of representations of the Orientalist other as it was on the Occidentalist self.

Strange Lands

This brings us to imaginative geographies. Beyond the pale of this somewhat triumphalist rehearsal of liberal self-understandings of Western modernity, we are in the territory covered by Said's discussion of "imaginative geographies" in Orientalist discourse (1978, see also the important discussion in Asad 2003, chapter 5, with reference to the Russian Empire, see for example Layton 1986, 1994; Jersild 1999, 2002, Khalid 2000). In sharp contrast to the rather self-involved literature on social imaginaries, the literature on Orientalism instead emphasizes the historically crucial role played by "imaginative geographies" of difference and alterity in modern social imaginaries. Such imaginative geographies are cartographies of essentialized forms of social and spatial difference that *preclude* precisely such operations of interchangeability and reciprocity of perspectives that constitute modern social imaginaries. Social imaginaries, it seems, focus on abstract socially and spatially horizontal spaces, reciprocity of perspectives, circulation; Orientalist imaginative geographies describe rather more uneven obdurate material spaces of alterity recalcitrant to circulation, empathy, or reason.

Despite their apparent differences, both Occidentalist social imaginaries and Orientalist imaginative geographies have much in common. Both literatures focus on the constitutive function of imaginations of spatio-temporal horizons of circulation; both are powerfully mediated by the circulation of texts or discourse, and in both discourses, strangers proliferate. But there are two kinds of strangers: the liberal Occidentalist strangers of a social imaginary are not *strange*; they are familiar enough for us to imagine them from the inside out. From their own interior subjective perspective, they read, write, and think as we do. The Orientalist strangers of an imaginative geography are strange indeed; they can only be imagined from an exterior objective perspective, from the outside in, in terms of the embodied alterity of voice and appearance. The stranger of the liberal social imaginary is the work of a kind of *via negativa* of abstracting away from the positive, embodied properties of the self to create a universal subjectivity created solely by participation in discourse (Warner 2002, 56), while the stranger of an imaginative geography, "foreign, alien, misplaced" (Warner 2002, 57), universalizes the Oriental other by endowing this other with ever-more essentialized and embodied attributes of alterity, who becomes ever more trapped within social closures of traditional tribalism or religious fanaticism (e.g., Said 1978, 108–9, Asad 2003, chapter 5). The liberal Occidentalist stranger is, so to speak, characterized entirely in terms of the language of contract; the Orientalist stranger is characterized entirely in the language of status.

Warner implicitly contrasts the disembodied stranger without positive content of the social imaginary in opposition to the "marvelously exotic" stranger in terms of what Fabian (1983) calls *allochrony*, the former is the modern stranger inhabiting a modern social imaginary, the latter is a "stranger in the ancient sense." However, even as modern social imaginaries produce strangers in the first sense within the magic circle of the public, they also produce strangers in the second sense, both in a negative sense—those excluded from participation within a modern public—but also in a positive sense, by virtue of the essentialized allochronic others mapped to spatial and cultural alterity produced in Orientalist imaginative geographies. Orientalist strangers described in imaginative geographies are circulated in the same print cultures that produce Occidentalist strangers by address. Occidentalist strangers are imagined as contemporaries; the Orientalist ones imagined as being allochronic, belonging to another time: "Orientalism . . . views the Orient as something whose existence is not only displayed but has remained fixed in time and place for the West" (Said 1978, 100).

The liberal stranger is a rather abstract creature, composed largely of "abstract modes of being as rights-bearing personhood, species-being, and sexuality" (Warner 2002, 57) which are conferred upon them by the equally abstract way they are summoned into being simply by being addressed in print. This very abstraction produces a tendency to universalize this kind of subject, "misrecognizing the indefinite scope of their expansive address as universality" (Warner 2002, 88). The way the strangers without positive content of liberal publics present themselves as embodiments of universal humanity stands in contrast, again, to the embodied parochialism and particularity that social imaginaries implicitly (by exclusion of address) and Orientalist imaginative geographies explicitly deny to their objects of representation (Said 1978, 108; note that Warner specifically identifies counter-publics as being publics with these same properties). To borrow an insightful distinction from Shunsuke Nozawa (2011, 5), one might say that the universalized disembodied liberal stranger represents a kind of "nobody-in-particular," while Orientalist strangers, always embodied, always mired in abject particularity and irrelevance, are instead "real, particular nobodies."

A commonplace critique of the implied universality of the literature on publics is to point to the exclusions generated by the very presuppositions of the discourse, a homogeneous equality of liberal strangers achieved only at the price of myriad exclusions (of the working class, of women, of children . . . the list goes on) (e.g., van de Veer 2001, 17). As Warner puts it:

> The magic by which discourse conjures a public into being, however, remains imperfect because of how much it must presuppose. And because many of the defining elements in the self-understanding of publics are to some extent always contradicted by practice, the sorcerer must continually cast spells against the darkness. A public seems to be self-organized by discourse, but in fact requires preexisting forms and channels of circulation. It appears to be open to indefinite strangers, but in fact selects participants by criteria of shared social space (though not necessarily territorial space), habitus, topical concerns, intergeneric references and circulating intelligible forms (including idiolects or speech genres). (Warner 2002, 75)

The exclusions internal to a Western public, the ring of outer darkness against which the sorcery of publics must cast its universalizing spells, are paralleled by the way a Western liberal public, implicitly or explicitly, defines its *own* strangers as an embodiment of universal humanity against the excluded strangers of Orientalist alterity. Just as the universalizing discourse of the liberal stranger *must* produce excluded others within the magic circle of the public, so such Occidentalist social imaginaries, promoted to bounded "civilizations," cannot help but produce strange lands of excluded Orientalist alterity (see the discussion in Asad 2003, chapter 5).

Strangers and Even Stranger Lands: The Public and the People/Europe and Asia

It is significant that Warner uses the metaphor of darkness to describe the zones outside the illuminated space of publics. "Darkness" (a word with the attendant meanings of "unenlightened, ignorant" in both Russian and Georgian) was precisely the dominant characteristic attributed to the unenlightened "people" in Georgian and Russian intelligentsia discourse. My critique of these blind spots of the literature on publics and social imaginaries is partly to explain an empirical divide within the constitution of Georgian print culture which gives it its specificity. For example, the division between strangers I have noted, between those that are summoned into being by address within a social imaginary and those summoned into being by representation within an imaginative geography, reflects a crucial division between "the public" and "the people" within European Georgia, between those included and those excluded from public address, between those who can represent themselves and those whose picturesque particularity of language means they must be represented. When this social division is translated to a broader geographic canvas with the Russian conquest of Ottoman Georgia, it becomes the distinction between the public of European Georgia and the transcriptions by European Georgian correspondents of the strange voices of the people of Ottoman Georgia. Georgian print culture, unlike the Western print cultures that have assumed a privileged place in the literature on social imaginaries and publics, could not afford to pass over unmentioned its exclusion of the Oriental other, a social imaginary could not be imagined that was not also situated within an Orientalist imaginative geography. Georgians, who were positioned, as they saw it, on the borderline of European modernity and civilization, could not imagine themselves as a social imaginary (a public, a nation, a site of European modernity) without constant reference to the lack, the absence of civilizational progress which was due to the stubborn obduracy of the space of Asia. Europe was imagined first and foremost in categories of *circulation* (time, motion, history), and Asia was imagined as an obstinate spatial category of stasis and dilapidated infrastructure.

Correspondence to *Droeba* figured the predicament of Georgia, in which the "public" (a sublime social imaginary) was separated from "the people" (situated within a picturesque imaginative geography of alterity), in much the same way as "Europe" was separated from "Asia." The term I translate as "public," *sazogadoeba* (an abstract noun from *sazogado*, meaning "[of] general [interest], public"), I will also translate as "audience," "society," or "enlightened society" or "aristocratic society," because it is a term which can have all these meanings, and, in fact, it is the changing meanings of this term in relation to the opposed term, *xalxi* "the people, the folk," that we are interested in. Thus, correspondence in *Droeba* was imagined along both a horizontal spatial dimension, but it also was imagined along a vertical social dimension (compare Ram 2003, Ram and Shatirishvili 2004 for the horizontal and vertical dimensions of the "Imperial Sublime"). By contrast, an Andersonian model of print culture, or Taylor's or Warner's conception of a public, is at least *imagined* as a complete transposability and reciprocity of perspectives between writers and readers and those written about, "the people" and "the public" are imagined to be the same.

By contrast, the social imaginary latent in correspondence to *Droeba* is one deeply divided between an aristocratic reading "public" and an illiterate mass of peasantry who form the imagined "people": here "the people" are not yet "the public." This opposition is most salient in the genre of correspondence, in which members of literate "society" or "the public" wrote about the illiterate "folk" or "people" of their respective regions. Thus, returning to the quote that gives me my title, members of enlightened society or "the public" were "Georgians," while the folk, the people, composed of illiterate peasants were primarily Gurians, Mingrelians, and so forth. It is this division between writers and those written about, readers and those read about, the public and the people, the intelligentsia and the folk, that makes *Droeba* correspondence tend toward the folkloric, the ethnographic, view of its object. Unlike the Andersonian model of an imagined community (1991), *Droeba* assumed the presence of a reciprocity of perspectives between writers and readers (the public), but an absence of any such intersubjective communion between the readers of *Droeba* and the people they were reading about. Under such conditions, one might well expect someone to define "Georgians, that is, readers of *Droeba*" in contrast to "Gurians," mere members of a locality.

Within Russian Georgia, the genre of correspondence was what positioned the intelligentsia, "Georgians, that is, readers of *Droeba*," in opposition to the illiterate and Georgian folk of each locality, such as "Gurians," as a literate "public" to illiterate "people," as a universal sublime "view from nowhere" to a particular, highly parochial and localized picturesque quasi-ethnographic object, constructing an intelligentsia "authority of anonymity" in opposition to a folkloric "authority of authenticity" (Gal and Woolard 2001, 7). But in the aftermath of the Russo-Ottoman War (1877–1878), the epistemic presuppositions of the genre of correspondence worked homologously to position Russian Georgia as literate, civilized "Europe" in relation to the Ottoman Georgia as illiterate, backward "Asia." For *Droeba*, and for Georgian print culture as a whole, it was correspondence about Ottoman Georgia that produced the most striking images of Georgian reflexive awareness of the culture of circulation that *Droeba* was creating in European Georgia. The culture of circulation of *Droeba*, of European Georgia, became visible only in its absence, in correspondence to *Droeba* from the circulatory no-man's-land of Ottoman Georgia. If the circulation of *Droeba* helped define the public in opposition to the people on a vertical dimension within European Georgia, on a horizontal dimension the circulation of *Droeba* helped align Georgia with Europe in opposition with Ottoman Georgia (Asia).

To illustrate how the reconquest of Ottoman Georgia was crucial to this imagination, I will explore a couple of moments in which the newspaper's circulation is explicitly reflexively imagined. As I will show, the empirical horizons of circulation of *Droeba* are aligned, in the imagination, to absolute cosmological limits of alterity: heaven and earth, dreams and waking life, and in particular the horizons of an Orientalist imaginative geography whose opposed poles are Europe and Asia.

Imagined Horizons of Circulation:
Daily News and Nightly Dreams in Ardanuji

Throughout the years 1878–1880, the period immediately after the Russian conquest of "Ottoman Georgia," the reading public of the Georgian newspaper *Droeba* gleaned much of what it was ever to learn of many of these newly conquered, but anciently Georgian lands, from a single correspondent writing under the pseudonym S. Bavreli ("One from Bavra").[3] From now on, Bavreli will be our constant traveling companion, and we join him in the middle of his travels, in a letter with the dateline December 24, 1878—Ardanuji. The letter begins on a plaintive note, comparing on the remoteness, distance, of this town in Ottoman Georgia (Ardanuji) to the world of his readers as being equivalent to the cosmological distance between the world of the living and the afterlife, "that world" (*saikio*), where "news" becomes as precious as revelations about the afterlife.

> For a while now your world compared to our world has become like the afterlife [*saikio* 'that world']. . . And for us, information about the afterlife has gotten very precious, it becomes that much more precious because of the lack of a postal service. After a flood in the Ardanuj-Chai and Choroxi river valleys, wheeled carts no longer pass, nor is walking possible now. There isn't a pigeon post among us, and if there was one, it still wouldn't even be any use to us, because the pigeons who had gone to 'that world' wouldn't come back: they would like life there [*ikauroba*] too much and would never again look back towards poor Ardanuji. We sit here, exiled, disconsolate.[4]

For more than a year up to this point, Bavreli has been in motion, exploring and chronicling with excitement these "new lands" of Ottoman Georgia for the newspaper *Droeba*. Now everything has ground to a halt, himself included. Bavreli wants to go home, or at least, *hear some news* about home. But there is no news; he finds himself writing, but not reading, news. And starved of the news, he becomes ever more reflexively aware of the precarious materiality and temporality of the world of circulation of "the news." Rather than writing news for the newspaper *there* about life *here*, he craves news of "that world," the world of the readers; moreover, he craves news that is *new*, like freshly baked bread. Bavreli complains that he only receives news of "that world" once a month in the forms of delayed papers brought by an Ossetian post rider, "but what's the difference? Does freshly baked bread and stale bread have the same taste?"[5]

Part of the irony is this: Bavreli is a special correspondent to *Droeba* to report on long-lost Georgian lands that had been reunited with Georgia by the Russian army. But the result has been far different. Places like Ardanuji, so far from being united with Georgia, now seem to be in another universe: Tbilisi, the center of European Georgia, seems as far from Ardanuji as heaven from earth. Bavreli has discovered the edge of his circulatory universe in Ardanuji and has stepped outside it into limbo. Circulation has ground to a halt here; Bavreli never really noticed until this moment the lively universe of circulation that characterized his old life in Georgia, with newspapers, news, information, until he came to rest, finally, in the frontier town of Ardanuji. He wonders, too, if he should take up his pen and write the news of what is happening locally, that is, news of "this world" back to *Droeba*; he wonders if it would ever reach its public, or whether it would end up in the corner of some Ossetian postal-rider's hut.[6]

But there is no news *here*, either. The town of Ardanuji too is dead, after the war. The people themselves, so far from being delighted with being reunited with their long-lost brothers in Russian Georgia, have fled or are fleeing Russian rule (another form of circulation, the mass emigration of Ottoman Georgians, fleeing to Ottoman lands). Bavreli is left sitting in an emptied-out town in an emptied-out world. Worst of all, he and his traveling companion in a freshly minted ghost town are *bored*, starved of news and books, with nothing left to read but the Quran.[7]

In this informational vacuum, in the absence of letters, books, and newspapers, and when even the book that stands emblematically for their position in the Orient, the Quran, fails them, they build a new informational economy, where the daily news consists of reporting their nightly dreams. Hence, the strange title of this correspondence letter: "News of a New World (Seen in Dreams and Awake)." Bavreli and his fellow travelers are so bored that each morning, in the absence of real news, they tell each other their *dreams*. Just as real news about Tbilisi has become news about a fantastic "afterlife," and just as scarce, so their own local informational economy has replaced the real with the imagined, news with dreams. He tells one such dream in detail:

> Sometimes we are so bored by that, too, that we tell each other different stories and dreams. Once my companion woke me up early in the morning and said:
>
> "Get up! Get up! I have a dream to tell you!"
>
> "Mm, te-ll-me!" I agreed and with what strength, what might I had, I began to stretch like a sleepy cat.
>
> "You know, man, what I dreamed? It was war again. In the currently occupied cities there was again that happiness, again that playing of music, again that clanking of spurs and swords and that . . ."
>
> "Then?"
>
> "Then I dreamed that a writer had taken as a bribe a cask of cream, or yogurt, I don't remember exactly. A local general found out about this incident. He summoned this unfortunate; he made him bring this cask full of yogurt. A little yogurt remained at the bottom and they placed this cream or yogurt cask on the head of this poor man and then they placed him at the gates as a clown!"
>
> "Ha ha ha! What a funny dream! Then you don't remember who this young man was?"
>
> "I remember, I dreamed that he was some Mingrelian. I have never had such a lucid clear dream!"
>
> "Hmmm, he was apparently a Georgian because they found out about his theft so quickly!!"[8]

This is the end of the letter, the author ending only that "This dream remained unexplained. Reader, I entrust its interpretation to you . . ."

Perhaps the specific meaning of the dream will forever elude us, but the dream illustrates some of the tensions of the print culture of the period with the plight of this writer, just as the figure of the double emptiness of the Ottoman Georgian ghost town of Ardanuji illustrates a no-man's-land which lacks both the Ottoman life of its past and the vibrant print culture of Russian Georgia. There is no news here: nothing to write about, and nothing to read about, either. The fact that their informational economies now consist of narrating *dreams* rather than reading the *news* reminds us that a culture of circulation, while it must be imagined, can never consist entirely of the stuff of imagination (dreams), but is mediated by circulatory objects with material and semiotic properties (dated copies of *Droeba*, which, like bread, can go stale) as well as spatio-temporal dimensions of circulation (depending on the distance and quality of roads between Tbilisi and Ardanuji, as well as the contingent mediation of the Ossetian post-rider and the corner of his hut, where things like letters and newspapers may well end up). The narrating of dreams points to the absence of *Droeba* itself, and to the material dimension of circulation, the infrastructures it presupposes, become visible only in their absence, including viable roads, bridges, Ossetian post-riders, all of which make it impossible for anything but a stale copy of *Droeba* to arrive in Ardanuji (Just as the normative presupposability of these things in places like Europe makes it quite possible to imagine a fresh copy of *Droeba* arriving in Paris, as we will see below). The point is that a social imaginary like a print public is underwritten by the material infrastructures underlying a culture of circulation, and these material presuppositions are imagined as being unevenly mapped onto an Orientalist imaginative geography, so that they are presupposable in Tbilisi or Europe but not in Ardanuji or Asia more generally (compare Larkin 2008, 242–4 for Nigeria). A social imaginary, stripped of its materiality, is just an act of imagination, very much like the narrating of dreams in the absence of the news.

The narrating of dreams is also an epistemic device. The device of the dream, of course, changes a factual narration (prefaced by the complementizer *rom* "that" used for factive complements, statements assumed to be true) to a nonfactual one (prefaced by irrealis *vitom* "as if," used to introduce statements not assumed to be true), and, like the quoted speech of Lelt Ghunia, this allows a criticism to be lodged by an author who does not have to take full responsibility for what is said. Telling a story critical of the tsarist state as a *dream*, and then refusing to give an interpretation, all this is typical of the "Aesopian" language of tsarist intelligentsia, a form of language which indexes the presence of the censor as being constitutive of a peculiar sort of publicness of texts:

> Chernyshevsky's reference to 'guessing what has been left unsaid' implicitly points to something *he* has left

unsaid, but expects to be widely understood, that this very work, which was written through a censor—in fact, more than one, since Chernyshevsky composed in prison—contains meanings beyond its apparent meanings. Using 'Aesopian language,' the Russian phrase for this kind of hidden political allegory, Chernyshevsky's text invites an esoteric, as well as exoteric, reading. *What is To Be Done?*, therefore, relies on yet another kind of double encoding, this one with the censor as dupe and the readers—or more accurately, some readers—as partners in deceit. In short reading becomes a form of complicity, which is to say, a political act. (Morson 1981, 102)

The veiled Aesopian nature of the speech, leaving the moral to be drawn by the reader, reminds us that the censor is present as one of the addressees, or rather, stands in between the writer and the readership. Aesopian language, like other esoteric genres, such as biblical parables, Gnostic gospels, and even inside jokes, interpellates different kinds of readers, creating an exoteric discourse limited to what is said (for the ordinary reader, including, hopefully, the censor), and an esoteric discourse of what can be inferred (by the clever reader). The implied presence of the supervisory power of the state in the person of the shadowy censor creates a specific kind of "public" address and a kind of layered "public" which differs considerably from the rather explicitly normative model of self-organized publics assumed by Taylor (2002) or Warner (2002), so much so that Taylor (2002, 112) refers to such publics that are not self-organized as "faked." But rather than make such an all-or-nothing, frankly reductive, normative division between real (Western) publics (which remain an ideal type in the West, an aspirational teleological goal of what Taylor characterizes as a "long march") and "fake" (Eastern or otherwise despotic, authoritarian) publics (which are empty simulacra of publics, adopted only because the outward form of the public, like "democracy," has become hegemonic), it seems more productive to analytically explore how the practices constitutive of publics change under conditions when publics are not entirely self-organized.

The differences turn out to be far-reaching. In such publics, the censor as the addressee is in an important way constitutive of public address. Here, too, public address itself divides its audience, in the manner of a parable, between an exoteric public (including the censor) and an esoteric public. Places of publication, too, are arranged into a hierarchy based on this principle of state supervision which constitutes publicness: out of the way places, like the town of Poti, in which state supervision in the form of the censor is less, or foreign places, are frequently resorted to in order to publish things that could never be published in Tbilisi. Whole spheres of textual circulation are defined along analogous lines, for example, between openly published texts and *samizdats* or publications of a literary underground (Morson 1981, 103, Komaromi 2004). Even, as we shall see, different functions of pseudonyms can be located within such a model of the public, the existence of secrets (pseudonyms, Aesopian discourse) in place of complete transparency helps produce a specific kind of figure of the author (compare Buurma 2007, 23–4).

What does the dream really mean? The dream or fable is about writers and generals, and this is significant, for Georgians figured prominently on the conquered landscape of Ottoman Georgia among the ranks of both aristocratic generals and intelligentsia writers. Or rather, the conquest of Ottoman Georgia was an event in which both the Russian Empire and Georgian society figured, and individual Georgians figured ambiguously now as representatives of the Russian Empire, now as representatives of Georgian society. As we will see below, the period saw heated debates within Georgian aristocracy as to which was a better model for aristocratic public service: a public career as a general or as a journalist. In the dream there is an anonymous writer, a Mingrelian, or perhaps, a Georgian, because Mingrelians are crafty and would not have been caught. He is punished for a petty crime in a humiliating fashion, in the time of war, by a general who might be Russian or Georgian, but is certainly from the side of the conquerors. The relationships between two portions of "society," the society of the conquerors, in Ottoman Georgia, are depicted in highly unequal terms, as is the ambiguous story of crime and punishment. For Ottoman Georgia was conquered by the Russian sword (with many Georgian generals and soldiers, too, of course), but it was Georgian writers, like Bavreli, who came in their wake to conquer it with the pen. The Russian army added this region materially to the Russian Empire, the Georgian writers in turn came to try to return morally this region to Georgia. What all this has to do with whether the cask was full of cream, or yogurt, is unclear, but the lines of opposition between imperial (Russian? Georgian?) generals and local (Georgian?

Mingrelian?) writers like the pacifist Bavreli are clear enough.

And what of the writer? After all, Bavreli asks the dreamer whether he knew who the writer was. All we know is that he was from Georgia, a Mingrelian, or, as Bavreli deduces because he was not so clever at stealing, a Georgian. Here was have an anonymous writer in a dream narrated by a writer, S. Bavreli, about whom we know almost as little. Bavreli means "one from Bavra," a town on the current border of Georgia and Armenia, which, at that time, was on the border between European and Ottoman Georgia. Beyond that, from his writings, we know he is a pacifist from humble peasant origins, and little else. Unlike Chavchavadze, whose public career as a writer builds on his public status as a noble, Bavreli is a nobody, writing is all he has, and his writings are all we know, or need to know, about him. At a time when Georgian "society" was transforming itself from a "society" defined by the face-to-face sociability of known, indeed well-known, members of aristocratic families, into one defined by the abstract stranger sociability of a society defined by the meeting of writers and readers on the pages of *Droeba*, Bavreli's own anonymity, like the anonymity of the writer in the dream, stands as a figure of the times.

Imagined Horizons of Circulation: Reading Droeba in a Café in Paris
Why was the military and literary reconquest of Ottoman Georgia so crucial to imagining a Georgian print culture? The period of the conquest of Ottoman Georgia (1877–8) introduced a vast territorial change in the boundaries of both the Russian Empire and Georgia, which would be followed over the next half a decade by a vast population movement (more than two hundred thousand souls) as Ottoman Georgians fled to the territories still controlled by the sultan. In this period Georgian imperial elites attempted to imagine a greater Georgia through largely a priori gentry nationalist discourse of essentialized, naturalized Georgianness that required only mutual recognition, such as that articulated by Chavchavadze in relation to Lelt Ghunia. This a priori discourse of mutual recognition received a severe, indeed conclusive, empirical rebuke when the Ottoman Georgians themselves refused to acknowledge their Georgianness or live under the same imperial roof with their erstwhile brothers. This was referred to the inability of the category of Georgianness as a basis for reciprocal recognition to overcome the imagined

division between enlightened Europe and Oriental fanaticism, further entrenching Russian Georgia's self-perception on the European side of the great divide over and against benighted Asia of Ottoman Georgia.

These changes in the definition of "Georgia" and "Georgians" within the imperial context occurred during the same period that the definition of the term "society" (*sazogadoeba*) was itself changing. In this period, the term moves from a notion of "aristocratic society" based on the face-to-face and manuscript circulation of known consociates among an urbanizing Georgian aristocracy to a notion of society as a public, based on the print mediated circulatory universe of intelligentsia stranger-contemporaries, writers to and readers of *Droeba*. The pages of *Droeba* contained members of both definitions of society, princes turned writers like Akaki Tsereteli writing under their name and hereditary title, and socially peripheral writers of obscure origins, literal "nobodies" writing under pseudonyms like S. Bavreli.

The spatial periphery of the newly widened circulatory universe of "Georgia" would be scouted out by correspondents and writers inhabiting the social periphery of "society." The "new lands" of erstwhile Ottoman Georgia would be scouted out by new men like Bavreli, himself already a man from the Georgian borderlands (Bavra) and socially peripheral (of peasant origin), he has, in effect, traveled beyond the pale of the circulatory horizons of *Droeba*, and hence, beyond *Georgia*, at precisely the *Ottoman Georgian* town of Ardanuji. In effect, Georgia is figured in *Droeba* as being divided between the European Georgia (where one can buy and read *Droeba*) and Asiatic Georgia (a place where intrepid correspondents write stories to *Droeba* from, but where they cannot get a fresh copy).

More generally, the figure of the newspaper, with its internal circulatory divide of readers (circulation) and writers (correspondence), can figure the divide between Europe and Asia, Russian and Ottoman Georgia. This is best exemplified by 1873 *Droeba* serial (*Feuilleton/Peltoni*), titled "a picture from the life of Ottoman Georgia." With a title such as this, we might well expect some sort of travel account, a set of pictures of the life of Ottoman Georgia by a passing Georgian traveler, someone like Bavreli. Instead, our mise-en-scène is a picture of a Georgian reading *Droeba*, the same paper we are reading, in a "local *qavaxana* [coffeehouse, café]."[9] Another man, sitting at a nearby table, begins to look at the distinctively alphabetized pages of *Droeba*, and in a short time surprises the reader by asking him, in the purest Georgian, if he is

Georgian. It turns out they are both Georgians, the *Droeba* reader from Russian Georgia, the other from Ottoman Georgia. The "picture of the life of Ottoman Georgia," then, is a secondhand narration of the plight of Ottoman Georgians, but we do not know where this narration occurs. This we are not told until we look at the signature line at the end of the article. The "local *qavaxana*," where the writer is reading a fresh copy of *Droeba*, which given that the Georgian word *qavaxana* is based on a Turkish word, we might imagine to be somewhere either in Georgia or the Ottoman Empire, is in fact better rendered as a "local café," because it is *in Paris*.

The significance of this letter resides more in the setting for the story than in the story itself. A whole imaginative geography is summed up precisely by imagining this chance encounter between strangers who happen to be Georgians as happening when the writer is reading *Droeba* in a Parisian café. First, the figure of the paper, *Droeba*. Just as it is the correspondence in the pages of *Droeba* that allow Georgians, that is, readers of *Droeba*, to be introduced to new lands like Ottoman Georgia, so too, in this little Parisian café scene, it is precisely the pages of *Droeba*, the distinctive Georgian alphabet on the page that allows these two strangers, expatriates from two very different Georgias, to recognize one another as Georgians. The thoroughly modern notion of a stranger-sociability mediated by the circulation of the newspaper *Droeba*, an imagined public of contemporaries, is like the equally modern stranger-sociability characteristic of a café (and, indeed, the earlier Ottoman coffeehouse which is the model for the European coffeehouse and café [Ellis 2008] and which gives the Georgian language a word, *qavaxana*, that can be used both for Ottoman coffeehouses and Parisian cafés), where strangers can be face-to-face consociates and yet remain strangers (compare Cody 2009, 2011 for comparable images of teashop sociability in Tamil newspapers). This is, in fact, this sort of stranger sociability, a stranger who is not *strange*, that is frequently argued to be foundational for modern social imaginaries, markets, nations, and publics. But of course, where is such modern stranger-sociability best instantiated? In Europe, of course. And where in Europe but in Paris? And where in Paris but in a café?

Apparently, Georgians in this period will not balk at the idea that one can sit down in a café in Paris and read a copy of *Droeba* that has "recently arrived." How different a place, then, is Paris, capital of Europe, from Ardanuji, in Ottoman Georgia, in Asia? And what better place for two

strangers from the two separated halves of Georgia, Russian and Ottoman, the former not quite Europe, the latter not quite Asia, to meet and
recognize each other as Georgians? What place is more unimaginably
distant from the everyday experience of either kind of Georgian, and at
the same time large enough and cosmopolitan enough for their coinci-
dental meeting to be believable in the first place, than in a Parisian café?

Imagined Horizons of Circulation:
Wanderings in an Airship in Ottoman Georgia

At the end of his travels, Bavreli moved away from his serial travel accounts to try to find a way to sum up, to grasp "at a glance," the changes
in a wide territory that could not, by definition, be grasped at once. How
to produce a synthetic image of simultaneous changes happening here
and there, how to imagine panoramically a whole culture of circulation
of things and persons? What point of view could be adequate? For this
would be required a point of view that would allow the projection of
nearly simultaneous images, something that would replace the seriality of the technology of the newspaper, the serialized feuilleton, which
can only represent Ottoman Georgia as a *series* of particular scenes and
situations, with an imagined technology that would allow him to represent Ottoman Georgia as a whole, at once (on the 'seriality' of the
newspaper compared to the 'simultaneity' he had emphasized in his
earlier work [Anderson 1991], see Anderson 1998). To do this, Bavreli
ended his series of letters with a most peculiar one, an imaginary letter,
sent from the distant Ottoman Georgian town of Artvini on September
20, published in Tbilisi on October 8, 1879, titled "Wanderings in an
airship [aerostat] in Ottoman Georgia." Using the literary device of an
imagined technological device (an airship) allowed him to sum up his
experiences, an image of panopticality and simultaneity, to produce an
overview of something that could only be grasped seriatim in a series of
travel letters:

> I got bored, gentlemen, with uneven wanderings on the
> poor earth, sometimes on foot, sometimes on horse-
> back, sometimes on horseback and foot! I decided that
> I would fly! Flying, of course, is better than walking,
> especially in these newly unified countries, where a

man aspires with a beating heart to know every place and understand everything: what is happening where, what the news and what movement is where, and where at every step you encounter immense cliffs, mountains, gorges sided by bottomless chasms . . . But, how to fly? For humans at this time there is only one means of flight—the airship [aerostat]—. . . My airship is free: it enters where it wants, it goes where it desires. . . . and where it goes, no one can see it, nor can they find out about it. The reason for my desire to fly is: to be everywhere, to know good and bad; to criticize bad, to praise and take pleasure in good.[10]

The imaginary device of the airship (the term he uses, *aerostat*, embraces all craft which stay aloft using aerostatic buoyancy, including balloons; however, the aerostat imagined by Bavreli can be piloted at will *and* is invisible, making it more of a fantastic Jules Verne science-fiction craft) stands in contrast to his own real wanderings as correspondent, in which he must slowly make his way through the obdurate terrain, the terrible roads, of real Ottoman Georgia. In a sense, too, his image of an airship is like the newspaper in which it is contained, like a heraldic *myse en abyme*, an image of what newspaper correspondence can achieve in terms of assembling a whole which is a condensed image of a larger whole. In terms of geography, he can represent the whole of the Transcaucasus a glance by its natural geographic boundaries. Bavreli uses the airship as an epistemic narrative device to present a series of snapshots for comparison of what was presented seriatim in his own travel writings over the last two years, a comprehensive simultaneous image of "Ottoman Georgia" at a glance. But he is particularly concerned with using this image to draw attention to something that might be lost in the endless particularity of letters of travel: the singular fact that a vast and simultaneous movement of population is occurring in all these regions, the Georgian Muslims, the Tatars, are leaving:

A big winter has passed . . . now it is spring. . . . there have been many minor events, so they passed, now so they became so bitter, that I could not be present to write them down and now it is not worth sharing them with you. Some however I present to you for a taste:

In Ardanuji district there is no activity at all. They announced a long time ago to the people that they would be given the right to emigrate; many are happy, many not, many are going the following spring, many are staying, the rich are going, the poor are staying.

I directed my airship to Batumi. Along the road we meet many Tatar [Georgian Muslim] peasants and their women, who with bent waists loyally help their slow husbands; they reap with sickles. . . .

In the district of Artvini too there are no sweet tidings. Some of the inhabitants are also ready to emigrate; only this false hope, that Artvini will remain with the Tatars, hinders them; spring after next their caravans too will be placed on the road. . . .

Here is Ajaria, too. The roads are lined with those who are emigrating. They leave their homes, their lands, and those places, where they grew up in their adolescence, which are precious to them; they flee, God knows where? . . .

The smell of wine and debauchery comes: it seems that it is Batumi now. Here comes a ship and it will take away our brothers away forever, take them far away. . . .[11]

From the synthetic perspective of his imaginary airship, Bavreli can discern new forms of motion. Two forms of circulation, of motion of things and people, side by side; the conquest of Ottoman Georgia, which led to confident predictions of recognition and reconciliation, now leads to one of the largest single emigrations in Georgian history, a vast emptying-out of many of the lands of Ottoman Georgia of Ottoman Georgians; and the only way to grasp this vast movement of peoples is by the correspondence in the newspaper Droeba, writings of pseudonymous travelers like Bavreli who presented their findings of their travels to Tbilisi society, the scandalous fact that there was neither going to be recognition, nor reconciliation, only the lands would remain. For Bavreli, the only figure adequate to make this point of the *simultaneous* movement of so many people *from* Ottoman Georgia, and make it nearly *simultaneously* to all the Georgians everywhere, was the imaginary technological figure of the airship, which as a narrative device allows him to review the changes in Ottoman Georgia since 1877, and also, as a kind of technological figure for the new representational technology and genres and emerging culture of circulation of the period, including the postal system upon which his and all other "correspondence" depended, and especially personified in the newspaper *Droeba* "Times," which from 1866 to 1885 was in effect *the* Georgian newspaper.

To return to the chapter title, then, "Georgians, that is, readers of *Droeba*," Georgianness, in one sense, then refers to a notion of "the people," as when one says that, for example, "Gurians, Mingrelians, and Imeretians are all Georgians," but here it rather more connotes a persistent opposition, that is, between the readers and writers of *Droeba*, "society," who from their literally sublime height can see the whole of Georgia as in Bavreli's airship, and the "low" people, trapped in their various picturesque localities, who are represented in the pages of *Droeba*, but are not a public of *Droeba*. This correspondence itself to *Droeba* persistently reenacts this second divide between "educated reading society," the public, the correspondents, and the object of correspondence, soon to become objects of folkloric and ethnographic interest, the picturesque "people" of Georgia. The former, like Bavreli in his airship, imagine themselves to be able to see the whole, see the people, everywhere, via correspondence, and like Bavreli's airship, they themselves are everywhere and yet nowhere, they are invisible themselves (compare Roinashvili's strikingly similar image of a Georgian reading a newspaper in mid-air in figure 1 above).

IV: SPIES AND JOURNALISTS:
ARISTOCRATIC AND INTELLIGENTSIA PUBLICS

Bavreli's dream about the general and the writer reminds us that throughout the period of its publication (1866–1885), the newspaper *Droeba* remains a house divided as an expression of two uneasily coexisting notions of "society" (*sazogadoeba*). Both conceptions of society are united, perhaps, in dividing enlightened "readers of *Droeba*" from the illiterate people (*xalxi*) of Georgia, but otherwise they are quite different. One of them is basically an urban aristocratic model of society, which treats the new culture of circulation of the newspaper as being an *extension*, or *augmentation*, of the face-to-face publics of the urban aristocracy centering on the viceroy's court in Tbilisi. This urban aristocratic society found its publicness as much on face-to-face ritual displays of commensality and hospitality between known contemporaries, particularly feasts called supras, as it does on circulation of texts.[1] The other is "society" in the sense of a emergent intelligentsia public (*sazogadoeba* derived from the sense of the adjective *sazogado* as "of general, public interest"), a new culture of circulation in which one's public voice would be sharply divided from one's embodied status attributes or any face-to-face "society," in which a new kind of disembodied voice, of a new kind of person, a nonaristocratic Georgian writer, a *complete stranger, a nobody*, like Bavreli, was at home.

As I will show in this chapter, the differences between these two understandings of "society," often latent in the capital, Tbilisi, where many important aristocrats were also writers, can be seen more clearly on the periphery in Ottoman Georgia. In Tbilisi, after all, Georgian generals and journalists might mingle together at a face-to-face society function like a supra (ritual feast), but in Ottoman Georgia, the anonymity of the imperial spy and the professional journalist, and the local hospitality their work depends on, are very different. In both these different understandings of society, the category of hospitality plays a crucial role as a kind of *infrastructure* of circulation alongside, for example, roads.[2] Hospitality in different forms both directly enacts the "representative publicness" of aristocratic society as a culture of circulation and also serves as a seen-but-unnoticed infrastructure to the circulation of strangers in strange lands that also makes liberal print culture possible.

At the same time, the aristocratic model of society, which privileges embodied ritual forms of publicity (often embedded in aristocratic acts of largesse and hospitality like the supra by which the host encompasses the guest (on moral discourse of the supra see Kotthoff 1995, Mars and Altman 1991, on the ways that hospitality creates hierarchy see Meneley 1996, Valeri 2001)) over disembodied, relatively egalitarian, textual ones, received its greatest test on the eve of the reunification with Ottoman Georgia. In 1878, Georgian aristocratic society celebrated the reunification of the long-lost Georgians with a society supra in Tbilisi to which representatives of Ottoman society were invited as guests. At this society supra, which was simultaneously reported in the press, the toasts expressed a notion that the reconciliation of the two Georgias would be as simple as recognition "at a glance" in this ritual context. In the coming months, however, this aristocratic ritual model of publicity and its theory of Georgianness as a largely secular set of signs of shared "nationality" that permitted mutual recognition at a glance would be dashed to smithereens by the shocking fact of nonrecognition displayed by the *muxajirat*, the massive flight of Ottoman Georgians from the conquered territories. This same shocking event thus contributed both to changing models of publicness and changing models of the nation: aristocratic models of society and publicity (the supra) could no more encompass Ottoman Georgia than secular models of Georgianness articulated in toasts at the supra.

The opposition between the two notions of society displays the contrast between what Habermas calls "representative publicness" (Habermas 1991, 5–14), in which a specific group within the social whole, say, the aristocracy, seems to embody in their very persons the property of publicness and displays it before an audience, as in a ritual feast or in a theater, and a "bourgeois" notion of disembodied publicness mediated entirely by the circulation of texts. It is noteworthy that the newly urbanized Georgian aristocracy found their most typical and distinctive "public" genres in the domain of theater, including both European-style theatrical performances and *tableaux vivants*; the world of Georgian European-style urban theater was born in domestic interiors of urban aristocratic households with aristocratic actors and retained this aristocratic character when the performances moved to public theaters (for example, Grishashvili 1963, 197, [who contrasts this "high" European mode of theater with existing popular urban traditions of "Oriental" street theater and puppet theater], Saqvarelidze 1956, compare Habermas 1991, 14).

Aristocratic urban "society" is thus based on the ability of the aristocracy to embody publicness in their own persons, and it therefore stands to reason that they would privilege and monopolize genres of embodied public performance (feasts, rituals, and theater, which, after are all related forms, see Valeri 2001, 9–10) over disembodied texts favored by the intelligentsia. In effect, Georgian theatrical publics grow out of, and remediate, the representative publicness of the Georgian urban aristocracy and the ritual of the viceroy's court. The two senses of society also reveal elites with very different teleologies and senses of social totality in which they located those teleologies, founded on very different notions of "service," as well, imperial service defining society as an imperial court society or an aristocratic service estate, versus a sense of service "to the people" defining a journalistic public defined on the pages of *Droeba*. Yet for all these differences, throughout the period in question, these two forms of society participated in each other's forms of publicness: society supras were publicized in the press, and many of the figures of nineteenth-century print culture belonged to society in both senses, writers who were also aristocrats. The categorical opposition between the two forms of society or publicness is complicated by the continuities and proliferation of hybrid forms on the ground.

The defining generational debate about the nature, composition, and social function of "society" of the same period did not take place on the pages of *Droeba*, rather, it took the form of a poetic exchange conducted largely outside the domain of public print culture, being exchanged as manuscripts and only latterly published, *within the Georgian aristocracy*. As Ilia Chavchavadze characterized it, the literature of the older generation of aristocracy was a "domestic" (*shinauri*) literature: "I call it 'domestic' because it was born among intimates [*shinaurobashi*] and so circulated within a small circle of intimates [*shinauroba*], because at that time neither journals and newspapers existed, nor was there a custom of printing separate books" (Chavchavadze 1977 [1892], 172). From its form and circulation, Chavchavadze deduces its content, which had nothing universal (*saqoveltao*) to say to a general public; consisting primarily of lyric poetry based on European models, its content was primarily expressive of the individual poet's vagaries of affect rather than any sort of progressive social thought (1977 [1892], 172). According to Chavchavadze, its only progressive quality was formal, the gradual adoption of European forms and the spurning of inherited Persian poetic forms (1977[1892], 175).[3] Just as pseudonymous writers like Bavreli were the model members of the republic of print, the model for aristocratic courtly society was the poet, the preferred mode of circulation was the manuscript copied and transmitted by hand between known consociates. In fact, it was precisely this contrast, between plebeian journalists and aristocratic poets, that seemed to typify the generational opposition for the older generation of aristocrats. However, this was a debate about journalism to which plebeian journalists were not invited.

The well-known, generation-defining debate between the "fathers" and "sons" of the 1860s–1870s began when Prince Ilia Chavchavadze circulated, in manuscript form, a series of satirical kenning sketches (titled *Gamocanebi* "Riddles" [Chavchavadze 1977 (1871), 88–91]) satirizing members of the nobility. Prince Grigol Orbeliani, a prominent aristocrat, service noble, general, and poet of the older generation, responded to this provocation with a poem titled "Answer to the Sons" (*Pasuxi Shvilta* Orbeliani 1959 [1874, 67–72]), thus framing the debate as a debate between different generations of the Georgian aristocracy. This debate happened in the early 1870s, around the same time as Chavchavadze was writing polemical engagements with Orbeliani and others in *Letters of a Traveler* (1871). In his poem, Orbeliani chastised Chavchavadze in particular and the younger generation of Georgian aristocrats in general for turning away from the deeds that characterized the older generation of nobility, service in the sense of specifically military service as generals in the Russian army, just as they had turned away from the classical language. Angered by the way that Chavchavadze had satirized Georgian nobles who had fought for the fatherland (*mamuli*) as generals in the mountains of Daghestan, he characterizes the new generation's notion of service to the fatherland with sarcastic dismissal:

St'ambit mohpinon sc'avla	With the press, they will
mamulsa!	spread learning in the
Aghchndnen mc'erlebi,	fatherland! There have
Zhurnalist'ebi	appeared writers, journalists.

(Orbeliani 1959 [1874], 72)

Chavchavadze, adopting the same meter as his opponent in his "Answer to the Answer" (*Pasuxis Pasuxi*, Chavchavadze 1977 [1872], 97–101) not only defended his use of an (ever so slightly) more popular, less classical version of the Georgian language, but more importantly, agreed to this characterization of the distinction between the two generations of nobility in terms of their different notions of service and relations to the state. In Chavchavadze's characterization of the opposition, the older generation was characterized by its position on the table of ranks in the Russian service nobility, *chini*, the younger by a lack of such a relation to the state. He begins his reply as follows:

Chven uchinoni	Us who lack rank
Chven uchinoni	Us who lack rank
Tkven, chinianta, buzad	You, who have rank, think are
ggonivart . . .	flies . . .

(Chavchavadze 1977 [1872]: 97)

For Orbeliani, turning away from poetry and classical versions of the Georgian language to journalism and the language of the press was in a sense equivalent to turning away from the life of heroic service to the state as a general to the life of a mere journalist. For Orbeliani, this was equivalent to leaving the aristocratic ideals of expression behind entirely; hence the parallelism between moving from general to journalist is also a debate about the proper form and language of poetry.

Since the ranks of journalists include both aristocrats (Chavchavadze) and nonaristocrats (Sergi Mesxi, editor of *Droeba* for most of the period from 1869 to 1882), what began as a debate *within the aristocracy* (conducted in an entirely aristocratic form and forum of exchanges of poetry in manuscript form) over the proper form of aristocratic service (and the appropriate form of the Georgian language) became immediately a debate over aristocratic and emergent intelligentsia notions of publicness. It was, however, a debate in which only aristocrats were welcome to, or able to, participate. Ilia Chavchavadze, as a wayward son within the aristocracy, would never sustain the level of hostility of criticism from Orbeliani that journalists like Mesxi, who were non-aristocratic in origin, would. Indeed, Orbeliani and Chavchavadze, for all their savage sparring, remained lifelong friends in the manner that aristocrats will. Nonaristocrats like Mesxi are neither addressed by these poems nor able to reply, since they do not command the poetic register and most importantly, simply because they are not aristocrats. They are spoken of savagely in the way that one might speak of someone who cannot talk back. Elsewhere, Orbeliani even more savagely attacks the nonaristocratic outsider Mesxi, criticizing the language of *Droeba* (in a satirical poem entitled "for the ten-year jubilee of *Droeba*" [Orbeliani 1959 (1876), 75]) as "the language of the bazaar, of an Armenian." Ironically enough, this urban "language of the bazaar" that Orbeliani disdains in his public persona is precisely the language that Orbeliani would adopt in his private cycle of "oriental" urban *muxambazi* poetry (Ram 2007, Manning 2004, 2009c, Manning and Shatirishvili 2011).

Spies and Journalists in Ottoman Georgia

This poetic debate encapsulates many of the key oppositions of the period, over the nature of publics and the genres and kinds of language used to address them, but also the specific novel ways that Georgian aristocrats saw themselves in service to the public (generals versus journalists, service to the state versus service to "the people"). Most importantly, it shows the way that what begins as an *internal* opposition *within* aristocratic "society" (Orbeliani versus Chavchavadze, "father" versus "son") had by now become an *external* opposition between aristocratic "society" (Orbeliani) and an emergent nonaristocratic intelligentsia "public" (Mesxi). These emergent differences emerge most clearly a few years later on the ground of the newly conquered territories of Ottoman Georgia. We need only go back to Bavreli's Aesopian dream about the general and the writer to see how very different the terms of engagement between servants of the state (generals) and servants of the people (writers, journalists), the former imagined as a cosmopolitan imperial category consisting indifferently of Russians or

Georgians, the latter a clearly "local" category imagined as being either Georgian or Mingrelian, were on the ground in recently conquered Ottoman Georgia.

The generational schism between Orbeliani and Chavchavadze, between the general and the writer of Bavreli's dream, is echoed in two travel accounts from Ottoman Georgia during the same period, one by Giorgi Qazbegi (1839–1921), a near relation of the writer Aleksandre Qazbegi and a Georgian officer serving as an imperial spy prior to the 1877–1878 war, the other by S. Bavreli himself, serving as a correspondent to the Georgian press, immediately after the war. While the two authors share more or less the same itinerary and, as Georgians of their period, similar interests in the Georgian ruins that dot the landscape and the Georgianness of the people preserved in customs and language, it is the contrasts between them and the conditions of their travel that illustrate all the generational tensions discussed above, the tensions that are the hidden theme of Bavreli's dream.

The first difference, of course, is that Qazbegi is a spy in the service of the Russian state, writing in Russian, surveying the countryside and mapping the roads of an enemy country in anticipation of a future war; while Bavreli is a correspondent for *Droeba*, writing in Georgian to a Georgian public, traveling these same roads after the Russian victory. We are reminded that like most colonial print cultures, Georgian print culture is a subaltern print culture, a younger brother of Russian imperial print culture, always finding its object already spoken about by its older brother. While Bavreli is a non-noble writer, Qazbegi is a service noble from a Georgian noble family created ex nihilo by the Russian state. Bavreli's only patron is the editor of *Droeba*, Qazbegis's entire career is the result of personalistic patronage of the imperial viceroy, like most imperial bureaucrats crossing the Dariel pass, a frequent guest in the Qazbegi house. Bavreli hides his identity from his own public under a pseudonym, but speaks openly of himself and his mission to his hosts in Ottoman Georgia; Qazbegi is a Russian imperial spy, hiding his identity and mission from his hosts in Ottoman Georgia, but publishing his story (in Russsian) under his own name. Bavreli is writing about the disastrous effects of the conquest of Ottoman Georgia, Qazbegi is planning it. Both are anonymous travelers, but the anonymity of the journalist before a public and the anonymity of the spy working on behalf of the state are very different ways of being "nobody-in-particular."

But the most striking differences between the two are the conditions, and pretexts, upon which they take these voyages, and the way that their respective statuses changes the way they travel and what kind of hospitality they receive from their hosts (which both writers assiduously chronicle). Giorgi Qazbegi was in many ways a typical exemplar of Orbeliani's model of Georgian aristocratic service to the Russian Empire. The entire Qazbegi family, from their noble title to their surname, was a creature of the Russian colonial state, every bit as much as the Georgian military road they presided over. The same is true of the individual career of Giorgi Qazbegi. Given an education at the behest of the Viceroy Vorontsov (a frequent guest at the Qazbegi household, which, after all, was in the Dariel pass, the only practical route between Russia and Georgia), Giorgi quickly rose through the ranks of the imperial army (Xarazi 1995, 7–8). In the early 1870s, the generals of the Russian army determined that, given the difficulty of sending spies into the disputed territories between Russia and the Ottoman Empire, they might avail themselves of local help and decided to send Georgian service nobles who were closely related to the leaders of Ottoman Georgia, using the ties of hospitality and kinship as a cover for a spying and scouting mission. The general they chose was Grigol Gurieli (1812–1891), who was a relative of the Ximshiashvilis, the ruling aristocratic dynasty of Ottoman Georgian provinces Ajaria and Shavsheti. Since Gurieli did not have the requisite geographical training for the mission, they sent Qazbegi, who had specialized training in the requisite areas, ostensibly as a minor aide in Gurieli's camp (Xarazi 1995, 8–9).

Qazbegi's recounting of his travels are remarkably disingenuous, casting his espionage as being disinterested scientific description whose final public is not the Russian state, but European science into which the Russian state's interests are uneasily elided: "Europe knows nothing about many of the places seen by me in this area," Qazbegi says, and when he says "Europe," he means more specifically "European science," which "knows less about some places . . . in Turkish Georgia, than Inner Africa" (Qazbegi 1995 [1875], 29). Amazingly, given that he is, in fact, an *imperial spy*, he represents the apparently completely accurate Ottoman suspicions of the intentions of scientific travelers like himself as being a signal of their own irrationality and backwardness:

Travel in Asian Turkey is not only dangerous, especially in places along the Russian border, and at the same time for Russians. Our neighbor imagines a threat in everything. For that reason a myriad hindrances lay ahead of the traveler's every step, every question, and especially every attempt to write down or draw something. The interests of science are incomprehensible not only to the people, but to the government of Turkey, as well. For that reason the open and systematic collection of materials to describe the country is for the time being impossible. The only outcome is the write down everything seen and heard from memory, or, in the best circumstances writing down incomplete accounts of impressions. (Qazbegi 1995 [1875], 29)

Their suspicions, in the case of Qazbegi, were of course, completely correct. Sherif Ximshiashvili, one of their hosts, eventually became suspicious about this scribbling aide de camp and sent Qazbegi packing, *with profuse apologies*, even after such a gross violation of the norms of hospitality by his guests (Xarazi 1995, 9)! The conditions of possibility for Qazbegi's spy work was entirely based his systematic abuse of hospitality, on aristocratic linkages of kinship and obligations of hospitality between Georgian service nobles (Gurieli) and the local Ottoman equivalents in the service of the sultan (the Ximshiashvilis).

Perhaps appropriately, given the bad faith in which he accepts this hospitality, Qazbegi experiences their hospitality as a tedious burden; he dutifully describes the Oriental hospitality upon which his mission depends but finds tiresome drinking coffee *a la turca* four to five times a day in the company of Begs in Sxalta (Qazbegi 1995 [1875], 39), or ten times a day in *qavaxanas* the town of Artvin (Qazbegi 1995 [1875], 111). Qazbegi is most comfortable neither in European-style guest-houses of Begs nor Oriental *qavaxanas*, but rather, in a space in nature's bosom where, for once, they can escape the "hospitality turned into a dogma" (Qazbegi 1995 [1875], 61) that characterizes both the Orient and the Caucasus, and instead of drinking coffee *a la turca*, instead drink Muscovite tea from a samovar:

At the Duz-Gurji stop our caravan spent an enjoyable

night. We felt for the first time after Abastumani that we were not guests, our Tula samovar hosted us with Muscovite tea as if we were at home, after which we slept under gigantic beech trees. To memorialize our stay for future travelers we cut several Russian and Georgian characters in these trees. (Qazbegi 1995 [1875], 137)

Qazbegi, in short, is a bit of an ungracious guest; he receives the best hospitality available in the region under false pretexts, and complains about it anyway. By contrast, while Bavreli, as a nonnoble, must sometimes spend the night in the hut of a mountain Kurd or a *qavaxana* on the banks of the Choroxi, he is much less churlish about the hospitality he is given, on which his travels ultimately depend. Like Qazbegi, Bavreli's main worry is that he will be mistaken for an agent of the Russian Empire, the only difference is that Qazbegi is in fact such an agent, and Bavreli is not:

> The contemporary inhabitants too are very hospitable. When I first entered the village, they looked at me as being somehow untrustworthy,—they thought I was a 'Urusi' and asked each other in Tatar (they thought I couldn't understand):
>   —What does this Giaor want? He's not a constable [*iasauli*], is he? He's not demanding *soxra*, is he?
>   When they found out, that I was none of those and that I knew the language, too, then with great respect they asked me to stay one or two days. I refused. They brought me a good meal, which consisted of sweets . . .[4]

Of all the forms of hospitality offered him by his aristocratic hosts, Qazbegi is most thankful for their maintenance of the roads (Qazbegi 1995 [1875], 47). Certainly, all travelers are thankful for this form of generalized hospitality, but Qazbegi, the imperial spy planning a conquest, is particularly so. He is as generous as he is detailed in his discussion of the (as yet unfinished) hard surface Batumi road (a description which fills a number of pages: Qazbegi 1995 [1875], 104–108). A sample:

From the village of Batsa itself the surface [of the road]
is mortar mixed with lime, but for the first four versts
[a little more than 4 kilometres] clay predominates. It
presents to us all different kinds of colors—from yel-
low to violet. The road's width is from 2 to 2 ½ *sazhen*
[4–5 metres]. . . . Although the existing road is only an
embankment for the future paved road, which perhaps
in its finished form will present itself to us as one of the
best constructions of European roads.
(Qazbegi 1995 [1875], 106)

While all travelers like a good road, Qazbegi seems to truly love
roads. This is not really surprising; he has an almost hereditary affinity
for roads. His entire family owes their noble status and wealth to that
singular road connecting Russia to Georgia, the Georgian military road
through the Dariel pass. The Qazbegi family and the Georgian military
highway were created at the same time, their destiny intertwined.

The only features of the nonhuman landscape Qazbegi lavishes
more pages of description on than Ottoman roads are the ruins of
Georgian churches (e.g., Qazbegi 1995[1875], 41–43; 78–81; 87–89;
100–103; 143–147). Roads and ruins form a nonhuman material dyad
emblematic of his own disemic perspective from which he surveys
these lands as a Russian imperial spy and a Georgian national. The
cosmopolitan figure of the road stands for progress, civilization, the
future, and commerce (which he both commends in the abstract but
also sees as being alien to the Georgian character, Georgians are not
traders, and the local Georgians have not betrayed their Georgianness
at least in that respect [Qazbegi 1995 (1875), 38]) and planned future
conquest; the national figure of the Georgian ruin (always a church)
stands instead for his own sense of national specificity, belonging,
rootedness, but it is also a sign for the past that these lands once belonged to the Georgian nation and provide an excuse for reconquest to
its imperial protector, Orthodox Russia (on the compatibility between
imperial cosmopolitanism and notions of national specificity in the
context of the period, see Jersild 2002, 60). Both these nonhuman
orders stand for different temporal orders (European roads [future],
Georgian ruins [past]) opposed to the human order of the Ottoman
ethnographic present.

His explicit comparison of the Batumi road with the absolute standard, European roads, reminds us that for Qazbegi, roads stand to Europe and progress as roadlessness and stasis to Asia. Pages later, as he is wrapping up his description of the Batumi paved road, he pauses to consider its world-historical significance for the region of Livan:

> While discussing the Batumi paved road, we must mention that, in our opinion, this road creates a new epoch in the history of Turkish Georgia. From the beginning of the century in Livan the lack of roads for wheeled transport and as well as the character of the landscape itself conditioned the centuries-long stasis of the described territory. As is known, wheels bring with them civilization and trade, while without the wheel there will be neither the one nor the other. Without the Batumi road for trade, the wealth of Livan, Shavsheti and Artvini would become dead capital and the influence of Europe, which has enlightened many corners of Asia, would remain beyond the stone walls encircling Turkish Georgia. We have talked for a long time about the necessity of breaching of these walls and opening the gates of this country for trade. [He goes to describe the benefits for trade that would follow such a 'breaching' of the walls]. It is possible this [Batumi] road will even be turned into a transit highway between Europe and Persia. (Qazbegi 1995 [1875], 107–8)

Even as he praises the European engineering of the Batumi road, he criticizes the shortsightedness of Ottoman rule for not building or maintaining key roads, strangling commerce and leaving Ottoman Georgia (particularly those road regions that are on the marchlands with the Russian Empire) in a stasis characteristic of Asia. The "stone walls" he speaks of here are figurative, but it is striking how quickly he moves from praise for the really existing Ottoman-built road system as a sign of progress and history and its benefits for commerce to comparing Ottoman rule to a set of "stone walls" that prevent commerce, enlightenment, and can only be taken down by (Russian) conquest.

Qazbegi sets up a complex and ambivalent representation of Ottoman rule as being on the one hand "European," symbolized by the very concretely material "European" paved Batumi road (and by the guest-houses furnished in European style furnished by local Begs), and on the other hand "Oriental," for which he constructs an opposed purely metaphoric set of "stone walls." But his praise for the impersonal hospitality of good roads reminds us that the hospitality upon which all travel depends takes different forms, ranging from those embedded in personal networks of kinship or friendship (either aristocratic kinship or the fictive kinship institution of the *konaghi/kunak* relationship, a long-distance relation both of asymmetric patronage in some locality, as well as reciprocal hospitality and friendship found throughout the Caucasus [Bagby 2002, 132–133]), to those expressed materially in architectures or infrastructures of hospitality addressed to indefinite strangers like the *qavaxana*, the coffeehouse which is also an inn (which is, after all, the model for the putatively specifically modern and specifically European stranger-sociability of the English coffeehouse or Parisian café [Ellis 2008], on coffeehouses as infrastructures, see Elyachar 2010, 454), to the completely impersonal hospitality addressed "to whom it may concern" of the roads.[5]

The Cosmology of Pavement:
Sociotechnical Infrastructures and Social Imaginaries

The Batumi road, then, belongs to multiple cosmological orders: (1) opposed to Georgian ruins, as the Ottoman present to the Georgian past; (2) as a "European" road opposed to the metaphoric "stone walls" of Livan, it stands as a symbol of progressive European circulatory civilization to the stasis and obduracy of Asia; (3) the maintenance of the road by the local beg is of a piece with the other forms of hospitality offered by the begs to guests of appropriate status (from European-styled guesthouses to Oriental meals), (4) but at the same time, like associated networks of *qavaxanas*, it is an infrastructure of hospitality that is addressed to indefinite strangers, irrespective of their status, one which makes possible the travels and correspondence of aristocratic spies and plebeian journalists alike. Commenting on the state of the roads, then, is central, rather than peripheral, to the reflexivity that constitutes the public of a newspaper like *Droeba*, because it reminds the reader that the ever-thematized, ever-topical deficits of the material infrastructure in a country painfully aware of its own backwardness compared to the normative and teleological aspirational model of historical and civilizational progress, Europe.

In contrast, contemporary theoretical discussions of cultures of circulation and publics frequently proceed without any discussion of infrastructures of circulation, leading to an almost entirely dematerialized and deterritorialized notion of publicity. Taylor, for example, divides publics very strongly into an embodied face-to-face, spatialized or "topical" public (the word "public" is often in scare quotes for Taylor [1995] when applied to spatial face-to-face assemblies) and a despatialized, dematerialized, transcendent, nonlocal "metatopical" public (Taylor 1995, 263). Between these two extremes of the absolutely face-to-face and the sublime horizons of metatopical circulation, the middle ground of mediating material architectures and infrastructures, road networks, and city streets, *qavaxanas*, and cafés, is completely erased. Within such a sociocentric paradigm in which publicness is essentially a property of discourse, and which strongly divides discursive publics into those which consist of face-to-face consociates and those that consist of imagined contemporaries, there is simply no way to conceptualize publicness as a property of material spaces (architectures of stranger sociability of various scales, from cafés to cities [Kaviraj 1997]), nor is there any way to conceptualize the relationship between the deterritorialized stranger of the text and the stranger in the café or on the city streets.

It is true that certain respectable "public spaces" like coffeehouses make cameos in this literature (famously for Habermas [1991, 30–3, 42], but also Taylor [2002, 113]), though almost always in a subsidiary role, providing models for despatialized, dematerialized publics, it is not clear what role they play in the maintenance of publics once they are established other than providing a "satisfying homology" between despatialized and spatialized publics (Laurier and Philo 2007, 263, but see Cody 2009, 2011a for more complex real and imagined interplays between despatialized and spatialized publics, newspapers and teashops). Thus, public places like the coffeehouse belong to the public sphere only because of their resemblance or kinship to the true model of disembodied publicness of the public sphere. Other places we habitually (and apparently mistakenly) call "public," like the city street, are quite the opposite of publicness. For Habermas, the city street where strangers can aggregate to form unruly masses, contains all the violent, coercive forms of embodiment that are muted in the coffeehouse and not present at all in the disembodied public sphere, as Montag (2000) has argued (see also Manning 2007b):

> [F]or Habermas, the street is an unruly territory, a place of violent conflict consistently descending into the use of force to back up demands, and as such it departs from the hypothesized peaceful spaces of the public sphere wherein the only force is that of the superior argument most thoroughly reasoned out for all present to hear, understand and [logically] accept. 'To speak from the street', Montag (2000, 141) glosses, 'is to speak from outside the public sphere'; it is 'in no way an alternative public sphere', for 'it is precisely not a sphere of rational critique or even discussion at all'. The street and the public sphere are therefore fundamentally separate, even opposed, and ideally should be kept apart and devoid of mixing. (Laurier and Philo 2007, 266)

Thus, the spatial or material dimension of publicness can be recognized only to the extent that it provides "satisfying homologies" with, or is a part of the material circulation of, the privileged, dematerialized, discursive model of publicness. The literature on publics thus aggressively rewrites the everyday meaning of the term "public" itself in normative terms, excising from it most of the spatial practices by which publicness is actually enacted (hence, the use of scare quotes around the term in some of Taylor's writings when it is applied to "topical" spaces; see also Kaviraj 1997):

> [For Habermas] the public sphere often appear[s] as a highly 'literary' endeavour, but the reader is told little about the routines of bourgeois men moving around the townscape, walking or going by carriage, meeting, sitting down together, gesturing, laughing, sighing, lifting food or drink to their mouths, talking to waiting staff, and so on. The reader might imagine these practices, the conduct of which cannot but be central to the accom-

plishment of anything resembling a public sphere, but they remain stubbornly absent from Habermas's own text. (Laurier and Philo 2007, 268)

Another reason for this dematerializing neglect of infrastructures is certainly the desire to avoid any form of technological determinism so characteristic of earlier accounts of print culture. Warner's earlier work begins with a strongly social constructionist approach to print culture (1990, chapter 1), which, while certainly a valid counterpoint at that time to the received wisdom of technical determinism, nevertheless seems to have the sole effect of continuing this dematerialization of print culture, silencing the voices of nonhuman actors. Warner's elegant argument seeks to elide the crude ontological opposition in technological determinist positions between material technologies and their symbolic, cultural, and political mediations but in the process seems to reduce the obduracy of materiality into the seamless web of cultural intentions. But as Larkin reminds us (2008, 248–50), the material mediation of objects, technologies, and infrastructures always presents itself as an excess (or lack) of sensuous and causal properties bundled in the material object beyond those mobilized in cultural intentions (Keane 2003). Unlike a symmetric account of infrastructures, such as that offered by Larkin and others, social constructivism fails to allow the "natural world or the device in question . . . to have a voice of their own in the explanation, what is generally captured under the notion of 'obduracy'" (Law 1987, 131).

The strangeness of a new media like a newspaper is one of new vistas and new forms of communication between purely social (human) actors it affords, and this is usually taken to be more interesting than the nonhuman strangeness of infrastructure, which is an "embedded strangeness, a second-order one, that of the forgotten, the background, the frozen in place" (Star 1999, 379). Demoted from sufficient condition to a mere presupposition, for writers on publics like Warner or Taylor, infrastructure simply drops to an aside, a footnote, something fundamentally boring (Star 1999) to be skipped over (or absorbed) in pursuit of something fundamentally more interesting.

[T]here are clearly infrastructural conditions to the rise of the public sphere. There had to be printed materials, circulating from a plurality of independent sources, for there to be the bases of what could be seen as a common discussion. As is often said, the modern public sphere relied on 'print capitalism' to get going. But, as Warner shows, printing itself, and even print capitalism, didn't provide a sufficient condition. The printed words had to be taken up in the right cultural contexts, where the essential common understandings could arise. (Taylor 1995, 262)

Social constructivism, in this case, appears to be in the service of demoting technological infrastructure to an irrelevant aside, a necessary, but not sufficient, condition; in the process, print culture becomes implausibly deracinated, dematerialized, idealized, the sensuous and material excesses that artifacts have beyond those qualities are foregrounded and rendered meaningful by social construction are ignored, and can be ignored because their material obduracy, their excesses or lacks that can causally destabilize these constructions, have themselves been domesticated (Keane 2003, Larkin 2008, 248–50). For that to happen, the infrastructure has to be in such good working order that it does not become thematized, but rather, like the form of buried cables and pipes of our cities, the infrastructure of circulation falls out of sight. Such is the aspirational goal of the Georgian intelligentsia, but their common understandings of their plight were formed primarily by talking about the abjection of their material predicament, their backwardness relative to places where infrastructure could be presupposed, and hence, talking about these technical, material conditions were essential to generating these "essential common understandings."

Thus, for theorists of Western publics to talk about roads, or infrastructure in general, seems fundamentally boring, to do so for Taylor or Warner is to miss the point of the generative cultural understandings and the new forms of sociability emergent in metatopical spaces. But infrastructure is only really infrastructure if it works well enough to become boring, to be presupposed, unseen and forgotten. As Star puts it more generally:

People commonly envision infrastructure as a system of substrates—railroad lines, pipes and plumbing, electrical power plants, and wires. It is by definition invisible, part of the background for other kinds of work. It is ready-to-hand. This image holds up well enough for many purposes—turn on the faucet for a drink of water and you use a vast infrastructure of plumbing and water regulation without usually thinking much about it. The image becomes more complicated when one begins to investigate large-scale technical systems in the making, or to examine the situations of those who are *not* served by a particular infrastructure. For a railroad engineer, the rails are not infrastructure but topic . . . One person's infrastructure is another's topic, or difficulty. (Star 1999, 380)

Thus, for Georgian publics to talk about roads and infrastructure is to talk about the common predicament; it is the very essence of the reflexive discourse constitutive of publics. As we have already seen and will see again in chapter 8, travel writing for Georgians is as often as not defined by writing about the infrastructure as it is by writing about the landscape. The infrastructural difficulties of the postal network of Ottoman Georgia are always topical for Bavreli, who, as a traveling correspondent, must first of all find a way to travel. Like all travelers in Georgia, he confronts an infrastructural system of travel which, first and foremost, as Urbneli points out for the Georgian military highway, is in the service of state agents and not especially designed for civilians such as himself, although passenger transport is in fact one of the secondary purposes of the Russian postal network (Bazilevich 1999 [1927], 45–6). When he is not lucky enough to find a traveling Russian bureaucrat to hitch a ride with, he has essentially four options, either a post wagon, an official's wagon, or gain an official travel letter from a district officer and travel from station to station on a regular run. His other option is to rent horses privately, which is the best means of travel, but also the most expensive. Bavreli's problem is that the post network, with regular runs, has not been extended to Ardahan. Having been refused the first two options and there being no room in the wagon of the third, he is delighted to find a couple of horses to rent cheaply. The problem, he later discovers, is that he only had them so cheaply because one of them was completely blind—and the other had sight in only one eye![6]

The ability to travel is only one consideration for a correspondent; correspondence always requires an act of faith in anonymous contemporaries, specifically faith that the letter deposited in the mail will arrive in the editorial office of *Droeba* in Tbilisi and not in the corner of an Ossetian postal rider's hut, as Bavreli ruefully notes. But these agents of the postal network are not imaginary beings: as Bavreli travels, he frequently has Ossetian riders as his travel companions, and at a couple points, he pauses to describe the picturesque misery of Ossetian postal stations in Ottoman Georgia.[7] Bavreli also takes great interest in the problems of road building in Ottoman Georgia, where, he complains, the construction of the planned road between Ardahan and Batumi has been held up by a battle between the engineers and the planners. It is already 1880, and Bavreli has been wandering in the locality for more than two years, and still they have not arranged a simple postal service between Artvin and Ardanuji.[8] He illustrates the human costs of infrastructural failures with two pictures:

> A man, who has halfway become an old man from longing to see his wife and child after two years absence [one suspects he is talking about himself], receives a letter, and this is a registered [*zakaznoi*] letter too, after two months and it has been opened too! In this letter is written, perhaps, his family's secrets. First fifteen strangers have read it and *then* the addressee gets to read it. That's great!
>
> Another example: A young doctor, who had made a promise to marry a woman, fate has driven into the wilderness. The doctor writes letters and the woman writes letters too; the letters neither reach the one nor the other. After six months a telegram arrives for the doctor, in which is written:
>
> 'I waited and waited a long time for you, but I haven't received from you a single letter, nor any words of comfort, and now I belong to another.'[9]

Georgian print culture could not presuppose a working, and therefore invisible, infrastructure: the obduracy, and consequent thematization, of the infrastructure, then, like that of the landscape, is always part of, has a voice in, the resultant imaginary. In this sense, the intelligentsia social imaginary of Georgian print culture bears comparison *mutatis mutandis* to what Kelty has recently called, with respect to "geeks" in new digital publics of the Internet, a "recursive social imaginary," a social imaginary that is as concerned reflexively with the sociotechnical conditions of possibility of address as address itself: "If, as Warner suggests, publics are constituted solely through the self-referential and self-organizing system of address, then . . . the particular sociotechnical constitution of the means of address may also be the proper subject of a public" (Kelty 2005, 200). Kelty's "geek" recursive publics are similar to Georgian intelligentsia publics to that extent, that they focalize the sociotechnical or infrastructural conditions of possibility of address in a way that the publics considered by Warner do not, because they need not. Georgian intelligentsia publics, like Kelty's geek publics, have a social imaginary which includes nonhuman as well as human actors, explicitly foregrounding both technical and social forms of mediation. For Georgian intelligentsia, discussion of the infrastructure that affords or resists their mode of publicness is directly equivalent to diagnosing the more general problems of backwardness and the intelligentsia predicament: what is to be done? Understanding this sense of infrastructural obduracy focalized in "Oriental" places like Ardanuji compared to the "European" apex of civilizational progress, Paris, is indeed an essential part of understanding the sense of backwardness *here*, and progress *there* that gave the Georgian intelligentsia their mission. Bavreli's quasi-magical aerostat is, after all, not so much an image adequate to visualize the *sublime* aspirational aspects of the culture of circulation as to express the *picturesque* abject ones, specifically the unrealizable fantasy of an exhausted traveler who is sick of walking on bad roads through hill and dale.

Hospitality and Representative Publicity: A Feast in Tbilisi
If before the conquest, the noble Qazbegi was a guest among the nobility of Ottoman Georgia, after the conquest, Tbilisian nobility could finally repay that debt of hospitality. The Ottoman Georgian nobles would now be brought to Tbilisi as guests, and Georgians would learn about those newly conquered peoples by inviting them, in turn, to a specifically Georgian style of feast called a supra. Like the smaller meals

enjoyed by Qazbegi and Bavreli, these larger ritual events carried with them their own specific kinds of food and drink (in the case of the supra, somewhat problematically for the Ottoman Georgian guests, drinking of wine or champagne), and along with them their own epistemic presuppositions and imagined performative efficacies.

The Georgian ritual of the supra (feast) was also the event where the Georgian aristocracy most clearly represented their initial theory of how the reconciliation of the divided halves of Georgia would happen. At the beginning, the "problem" of reuniting the estranged Ottoman Georgians seemed like it could be solved in a single, simple ritual, at the level of aristocratic *sazogadoeba*, "society," an event that would, in turn, be duly reported before the public of *Droeba*. After all, what better way to express the integration of these estranged "brothers" than a traditional ritual, a Georgian *supra*, a traditional Georgian feast involving complex rituals of toasting and drinking wine, itself expressive of commensality and solidarity? ". . . In order that, if nothing else, together, to affirm to them [the Ottoman Georgians] from the beginning at a public/society [*sazogado*] supra, by brotherly breaking of bread, their own sympathy and love."[10]

This ritual event was held in Tbilisi in November 1878, attended by members of Georgian society, both gentry and literary, to which were invited a deputation of some sixteen representatives of Ottoman Georgian "society" (various Begs as well as religious representatives of the *millets* of Ottoman Georgia, it appears).[11] Sergi Mesxi, the editor of *Droeba,* followed the visit of this deputation in his "daily" (*dghiuri*) column from mid-November 1978 forward with eager anticipation: "This is the first coming into the old capital Tbilisi of our quondam brothers (*modzmeebi*) and of representatives of people distanced from us by the passing of time."[12]

Part of the value of bringing these "brothers" and "representatives of the people" together *physically* with their coeval members of Georgian imperial society was an epistemic one. The face-to-face relationship of ritual conviviality between guests and hosts that would allow them to confirm, *at a glance,* to each other that these were still *Georgians,* despite this distance in religion, state and time, nothing "real" had really changed about them, neither appearance, language, custom, nor anything else:

It is more than two hundred years that they have been separated from us; they have changed their religion, they have [been] subjected to another foreign state, different laws and rules. But one look is sufficient, for a man to discern in them even now the old, real Georgian. The same appearance, the same language, customs and everything else.[13]

But this rhetoric of "recognition at a glance" was largely an *a priori* one, one that had become almost a dogma by the time of this feast. We have already seen how in 1874 a writer to *Droeba* imagined such a recognition happening at a glance between these erstwhile brothers in a Parisian café. Three years before this feast, the same editor, Sergi Mesxi, had already stated the problem in these same terms, down to reports of "secret Christianity" (an important dogma about Ottoman Georgians was that they were still practicing Christianity secretly among the ruins of old churches), before the Ottoman-Russian War (1877–1878) in an appeal he issued for more information about Ottoman Georgia in the wake of the publication, in Russian, of Qazbegi's account of Ottoman Georgia in 1875:

> Centuries have passed since the Ottoman has seized these lands, during which time the Ottoman has been trying to make local Georgians become Tatars. But, look at the endurance of the Georgian tribe,—aside from religion, they haven't changed anything at all; and even this they were forced to change only by coercion and different Ottoman tricks. Their mother tongue, the character of the people, their customs, even their superstitions and everyday life are traditional, Georgian . . . In a word, the entire people of Ottoman Georgian even now have the character of the Georgian people, they have the soul of the Georgian people. They have the appearance of a real Georgian, the customs and life of Georgia; the people, although it is a long time that they have become Muslims, but even now they apparently go about in the ruins of local Georgian churches and bring sacrifices as an expression of belief.[14]

Apparently, then, the common Georgianness of the Ottoman Georgians was so well-established that there would be little to do in this ritual event other than do the sort of work that is normal at a Georgian supra, namely, to recognize this brotherhood by saying toasts to glasses of wine, or in this case at a more official "European"-style supra, champagne.

The difference between this aristocratic supra and others of its kind was that this ritual was being reported to a larger audience of the Georgian reading public on the pages of *Droeba*. This was a *sazogado* supra, which we can translate either as "society supra" (in the sense of "aristocratic society") or "public supra." It was a moment in which two very different kinds of publicity were commingled. First, there was what Habermas calls "representative publicness," the way that a distinguished part of the social whole comes to represent the social whole itself in a quasi-ritual or theatrical manner, in this case the courtly "society" of Georgian aristocracy, themselves embodied or represented publicness before the other estates (Habermas 1991). This notion of publicness embodied in representative estates, "society," allows publicness to be literally incarnated in the persons of the participants of a single ritual, a supra (see also Valeri 2001 on the publics of aristocratic feasting). The second notion of publicness is not this quasi-ritual sense of representiveness, but a new kind of representation in the press, the second sense of "society" in this period, that is, society as a modern print public, not a face-to-face theatrical public as in ritual, but an imagined relationship between contemporaries reading a newspaper story about a feast. It would appear, initially, that these two forms of publicity, the aristocratic and the intelligentsia notions of publicness, were articulated as "society feast" to "report about a feast to reading society." However, if this feast did not manage to create lasting reconciliations between Russian and Ottoman Georgian aristocratic societies, it was the beginning of signs of a reconciliation between the society of Georgian aristocrats and the society of Georgian intelligentsia writers.

Since this was to be a quasi-*representative* reconciliation of the "societies" of the two halves of Georgia, the list of those invited would be significant. The guest list includes the most distinguished nobles of Ottoman Georgia, along with representatives of various *millets*, thus employing a sort of Ottoman notion of representativeness. But Mesxi is clearly more interested in delineating the representative publicness of the hosts. The hosts, representatives of Georgian urban *sazogadoeba*, therefore almost all of whom were nobles, were divided into (1) representatives of nobility proper, the unmarked case, (2) representatives of service nobility, specifically generals, and (3) representatives of literature (most of whom were *also* nobles): "Everyone, who in this our capital city is distinguished or prominent by their own intellect, genealogy and rank."[15] Sergi Mesxi, (the nonnoble editor of *Droeba*, invited to write about, but not speak at, this supra) does not give an exhaustive list of names, but first lists those higher nobility who need no further qualification, beginning with Grigol Orbeliani, followed by generals, and lastly, "the representatives of Georgian literature were nearly all there, with the exception of Prince Ilia Chavchavadze, who was not in the city at the time." While membership in society as depicted in this ritual moment is shown to be defined at the intersection of several overlapping definitions (rank, genealogy, talent), this hybrid whole remains dominated by hereditary Georgian nobility, who are listed first, followed by the service nobles and lastly the writers. Moreover, even the writers are mostly nobles. Similarly, their opposed numbers among the Ottomans list nobles proper first, followed by named representatives of different Ottoman *millets*. This overlapping definition of society as a whole is carried over into many of the individual members, Grigol Orbeliani is all three, and Akaki Tsereteli is a writer and a noble.

The kind of publicness, then, is representative publicness in Habermas's sense, "society" is incarnated by the presence of representatives of its most distinguished members of each kind. The order of introduction in the newspaper (which introduces the pedigreed nobles first, the writers last) as well as the *degree of* participation in the ritual (who performs the key ritual role of speaking a toast, versus who is merely an audience or correspondent for the press), underline the way in which this "society" remains aristocratic in focus. All those who speak at the supra are noble, whether or not they are representatives, for example, of nobility proper or literature. Many of the literary representatives do not have noble rank, but Akaki Tsereteli, as one who is both a representative of literature and has rank, is the representative from that group who actually speaks. Within the context of ritual representative publicity, the new form of publicness represented by the writer is only represented by riding on the aristocratic coattails of aristocratic rank.

This being a Georgian supra (feast), the speeches given (all but one reproduced in full in the pages of *Droeba*) took the form of supra toasts. At a contemporary supra ritual, not only is the content of the toast significant, but also the order in which toasts are given. The toasts at a supra are a "social network made manifest" in Mars and Altman's felicitous phrase (1991), a ritual mapping of the social universe of those gathered and a recognition of their social ties and mutual obligations. At this feast, too, the toasts produce a diagram of a social universe, here a simplified diagram of the Russian Empire itself, and the place of Georgia nestled within its bosom, which is the space in which the guests and the hosts both find themselves.

Speaker	**Theme of Toast**
1. Grigol Orbeliani	*to the tsar*
2. Husein-Beg Bezhan-Oghli (Guest)	*to the viceroy* (Host)
3. Aleksandre Zubalashvili	*to the people of Russia*
4. Dimitri Qipiani (Host)	*to our long-lost brothers* (Guest)
5. Akaki Tsereteli	*to the ancestors*

Beginning with the tsar indicates that the feast is a "public" one. Toasting first the tsar, then the viceroy, establishes a motion from the center of empire to the center of the periphery, Tbilisi, the court of the tsar to the court of the viceroy. Since the empire is a gift not merely from the tsar, next there are thanks given by the Georgians to the "people of Russia," the focal population of the empire (see Grant 2009). The first three toasts, then, establish an "imperial" framework and map out an ontology of imperial representative publicness, an imaginative geography in which the hosts and the guests, Georgians in general, both are now contained after the Russian victory of 1878. The next two toasts, firmly contained within this imaginative geography of empire, first recognize the common Georgianness of the hosts and guests, and lastly the common cause of their commonalities, the ancestors. The overall order of the toasting then acts as a diagram of an imperial imaginary of Georgian nationality, in which the Georgian nation is firmly and happily ensconced within a broader Russian Empire (just as each individual face-to-face or print public within the empire is established ultimately with reference to the representative publicness of the tsar) in which "Georgian nativism was easily compatible with empire" (Jersild 2002, 151):

> The 'national question,' however, remained on the distant horizon. Educated society in the borderlands throughout the nineteenth century was thinking through the problem of empire, and the question of cultural 'originality' was compatible with—indeed, fostered by—imperial rule. (Jersild 2002, 152)

If the order of the toasting created a way in which the theme of reuniting Georgia was placed within an imperial bedrock, then the list of speakers, too, produced its own arguments about reconciliation at the level of "society." Each toast was given by representatives of different groups to be constitutive of Georgian aristocratic "society." The two ranking nobles of each deputation were paired off for the first two toasts: Grigol Orbeliani, speaking first both as the highest ranking bearer of rank, also as the most distinguished holder of hereditary noble rank; Husein-Beg Bezhan-Oghli, speaking as the ranking representative of the coordinate Ottoman Georgian "society." Next, two more prominent nobles, Aleksandre Zubalov (Zubalashvili) and so on (a general, presumably speaking for the service nobility) and Dmitri Qipiani, who was speaking primarily as host but also was known at the time as the key representative of the Georgian hereditary landed nobility (see Suny 1988, 97–101), and finally Akaki Tsereteli, though a noble, speaking as a representative of the writers (*mcerloba*). The aristocracy is its various levels is constituted into a unitary speaking subject (consisting of rank, nobility and talent, although all are nobility), and also seeks to traverse the divide between "Russian" and "Ottoman" Georgian "society."

In content, too, each toast in some sense also stands as a kind of characterization of the sorts of presuppositions that animated later investigators of Ottoman Georgia, but also the way in which Georgian society performatively attempted to integrate their opposite members at the level of educated society. The first toast, to the tsar, for example, by the representative of the older generation, Orbeliani, presents their present happiness as an *effect* of a distal *cause*, the tsar. The typical sentimental history of Georgia's past suffering is given an imperial salvation:

Gentlemen! What does our meeting here today betoken? Why are we happy? What are we toasting? This meeting represents the happy sight, when the children of one mother, separated by black fate, lost to one another for a long time,—suddenly, unexpectedly meet, recognize one another, and embrace other another with heartfelt love. We too were also such children of Georgia, lost to one another over a period of centuries; we suffered much from enemies, we went through many ravagings, but still we did not forget our separated brothers. We kept our eyes, our hearts on you, gentlemen, and we wished for the day when the sun of unification would rise on us! (*In the audience* [*sazogadoeba*] *is heard lively applause*). And lo, God also heard us, and today among us we see our separated brothers and happily we thank God and we entreat him that this our unification be indestructible forever! . . . And from today forward in both happiness and sadness we must be together, like the sons of one mother, Georgia.

But, gentlemen, who is other than God, the cause of our being so blessed? The all-merciful great Emperor, the restorer and protector of ancient Iveria [Georgia]! And the blessing of God be spread to his glorious crowned head many and many times, joyfully of his great empire. Gentlemen! God bless our great Emperor . . . Hurrah? (*After these words a long Hurrah went on uninterrupted for some time in the audience* [*sazogadoeba*]).[16]

After a toast to the viceroy by the Ottoman guest, whose text we do not know, nor do we know what he drank, the next toast by Lord A. Zubalov (Zubalashvili) had a similar structure, again expressing happiness that the "gulf" between the two groups of Georgians, "Russian and Ottoman Georgia," had been eliminated, "now, like it or not, we are our own," a larger unity once again expressed in the microcosm by the fact "we are gathered together at a supra and we toast the destruction of the divide between us, our brotherly gathering 'in the old way, in our way.'"[17] Again, this happy occasion in the present locality was attributed to a distant imperial cause, the Russian people.

The most interesting toast, the crowning and final toast of the evening, was that of the representative of literature, Akaki Tsereteli. The preceding toasts had on the one hand, expressed joy at the return of "our lost brothers" "children of the same mother, Georgia" and so on, but they had attributed and toasted in each case an effective cause which was located outside of Georgia, the empire, first the tsar, then the viceroy, then the Russian people, then a toast, from the host of the supra, Qipiani, to the guests. The crowning and final toast of the supra, the only one addressed to *Georgians*, Tsereteli's was also the longest. This was a toast to the ancestors, who are represented in rather more nationalist terms as being ultimate *cause* of the happiness felt, Georgianness being an *effect* of their accumulated work, the will (*anderdzi*, "will" in the sense of "last will and testament") of the ancestors. Noting that this supra, unlike any other, had a unique property of unblemished happiness that all felt, Tsereteli begins by asking what explains this quality of unrelieved happiness:

> And to what must we attribute this [sc. quality of un-blemished happiness]? Although each of us also feels it well, but I must nevertheless say, that its cause is the renewal of our unity and brotherly connection with our brothers who have been estranged from us by the pass-ing of time, whose representatives are seated here. Yes, gentlemen, today we can go to the graves of our ances-tors and cry out to them, that we have not yet broken their last will and testament! And what, gentlemen, was that last will and testament?

The last will (including both elements of will and items left to pos-terity) of the ancestor resides in their accumulated works, language and nationality, which they both bequeath to their descendants and entrust to them:

> The first, that is, language, they have so richly adorned and have given to its such a taste also, that not yet have we been able to forget it and not only us, but those brothers of ours as well, who in the course of several

centuries have been separated from us, even they have retained the mother tongue for sweetly speaking.

The second of these, *eroba*, nationality, is much more vaguely explained. It again is the product of the work and sacrifice of the ancestors, representing a communal debt of the present to the past. Like language, *eroba* is conceptualized as a set of *signs*. These signs have been imprinted by the ancestors on the Georgian both *externally* and *internally*, and the content of these signs are simply that they visibly indicate belonging to a nation (*eri*).

> The second, that is, nationality (*eroba*), they have so richly worked out and have in such a way imprinted it on the Georgian as a property as both external and internal signs of belonging to a nation (*eris*), that even today a Georgian at a single glance can be recognized. Our brothers also have retained exactly such signs; to prove this let us no longer go far, it is sufficient, that right here, at this supra, that we look back and forth at each other.[18]

Eroba, nationality, then, is a *set of signs* that indicate membership in the *eri*, which in turn is constituted by the set of such sign-bearing Georgians. This nationalist toast (not necessarily incompatible with the explicitly imperialist ones that preceded it) provides the epistemic framework of Georgianness necessary to explain how reconciliation between the two Georgias could happen here and now at a supra: this set of signs includes *visible external* signs of belonging, so that a Georgian can be known even today, "at a glance," here, at this supra, without need to send anyone anywhere to prove it.

Such was the *a priori* discourse of Georgianness on the eve of the repatriation of Ottoman Georgia, before anyone had actually bothered to go to Ottoman Georgia and see if any of this was actually true. Partially, this was because it would be unnecessary, as Akaki Tsereteli maintained, they could already *see* that in the context of the supra itself.

The Crisis of the Muxajirat: *The Shock of Nonrecognition*
In retrospect, four years later, it became clear that the society discourse of "recognition at a glance" was among other things an epistemological failure, as one "Voice from Mohammedan Georgia" explained in 1882:

> [At the end of the war] both writers as well as more gen-
> erally our entire enlightened society met the union of
> this region with great enthusiasm. At that time, wher-
> ever you would look, everyone was talking about it; 'We
> have found our long lost brothers; they are damaged by
> the war, let us give them aid, let us raise schools, let us
> help them in intellectual progress and in other matters
> of prosperity.' Many such things were said then among
> us and yet not one person asked this—in what condi-
> tion did we find 'our brothers'? . . .
>
> It is true, many things were being written from this
> region, many things were said about local administra-
> tion and its actions, but the people themselves, their
> intellectual and moral aspects, their specific charac-
> teristics, their soul, character and customs and beliefs
> either no one at all has touched upon, or if someone did,
> they did so in passing and this too they so represented
> to the reader, as it really is not. . . . I also said this into
> order to demonstrate this idea, that our society does
> not know these people at all and when it puts its hand
> to write about them, error follows upon error. . . .
>
> [S]ociety . . . has not represented these people [sc.
> Ottoman Georgians], as they really are, it has a view of
> them that is completely contrary to the truth; it looks at
> them with the same eyes that it looks at other Georgian
> tribes, but unfortunately historical causes and develop-
> ment of time has so disfigured these people in mind
> and morals, that only their language and external ap-
> pearance have remained Georgian,—all the rest, which
> constitutes the specific characteristics of Georgians and
> by which they are differentiated from other neighbor-
> ing peoples has been smashed to smithereens and ex-
> tinguished.[19]

The epistemological discourse of the supra, cast in the sentimental form of toasts which present *a priori* truths about which no debate is possible, represented the project of reuniting the two Georgias as a simple matter of mutual recognition which could be accomplished "at a glance" at the level of aristocratic society. But, as was already becoming clear on the same pages of *Droeba* from correspondents traveling in Ottoman Georgia, the project of reuniting the two Georgias was destined to fail somewhat catastrophically at the popular level. The problem was that far from recognizing their Georgian brothers at a glance, instead the Ottoman Georgians fled *en masse*. As Pelkmans notes, the flight of the Ottoman Georgians radically disconfirmed the superficial thesis of "recognition at a glance" proposed by Grigol Orbeliani at the supra, and in a private letter of 1879, he (like most other Georgian writers) wrote with shock "[The Ottoman Georgians] run away from us, as if they are running from the plague! Is it possible that the single explanation for this is fanaticism?" (Cited in Pelkmans 2006, 98.) Faced with such a shocking disconfirmation of their views, Georgian writers frequently cited Ottoman "fanaticism" stirred up by Ottoman *mollahs* and spies to explain the failure of recognition and reunification between European and Oriental Georgia in Orientalist terms, but the shock also pointed up failures in Georgian society, including the ritually mediated model of representative publicity on which it was based. Each and every presupposition of the supra in Tbilisi in 1878 received a categorical disconfirmation in the unfolding events of the subsequent year: the specifically aristocratic model of society based on ritual and representative forms of publicity, the model of reconciliation by "recognition at a glance" in the ritual context of the supra, and lastly, the widely shared quasi-secular model of a common Georgianness based on signs of nationality and language, which served as a semiotic ground for such recognition at a glance that would allow happy reconciliation to happen at the level of society in the context of a single ritual.

Years later, in 1893, it was clear that the family of Georgians remained, and would remain divided, and that, moreover, the work of reuniting the two halves of Georgia could not have been accomplished at the level of *sazogadoeba*, "society" (rather than among the "people"), by a simple act of recognition at a single feast in Tbilisi, even if it was a very big one. Much more work by Georgian society would have been required, involving a whole different model of "society," involving not feasts in Tbilisi but an active "going to the people," and this work was not done. In this year, Il. Alxanishvili concluded a multipart description of a portion of Ottoman Georgia (the first one published in years) with the following pessimistic assessment that placed the blame not on the fanaticism of the Ottoman Georgians, but the indifference of Georgian society:

> So that I no longer annoy the reader with talk, I will end my notes of a traveler and, though with such a description in passing it is hard to draw for the reader a complete picture of local nature and customs, but I yet have one thing to ask. What moral dependence do the Georgians left behind on local ruins have on the remainder of the Georgians? None. What has our leading society done to take care that they have moral influence and become closer on these newly found brothers (relations)? Nothing. . . . A new period has begun. It is now 65 years, that we have united the Georgians of these two districts, thanks to the sword of Russia [these regions were conquered earlier in the Russo-Ottoman war of 1828–9], first to the *gubernia* of Kutaisi and now that of Tbilisi, then what have we done in these 65 years? Have we drawn local Georgians in some way (to ourselves)? Not at all.[20]

Both in 1878 and in 1893, the active agent is assumed to be "society," but the nature and sphere of activity of that society has changed considerably. In 1878, the attempt to suture the two kinds of Georgians into one nation is approached as a simple matter of convening their two representative aristocratic "societies" together in a traditional act of commensality, a supra. Aristocratic "society," Russian Georgian and Ottoman Georgian, appear to be transparent representatives of their respective "people."

It is interesting to note that while Habermas (1991, 5–15) posits very little in the way of a bridge between aristocratic and bourgeois senses of publicness (the former embodied as a status attribute, the latter created by the disembodied circulation of texts), treating the transition between them as an unmediated historical chasm (Kaviraj 1997, 95 note 12), in the Georgian case, we can see clearly intelligentsia notions of print publicness propagating through the social networks of the aristocracy, little by little converting representative publicness into print publicness (which accords well with the Georgian intelligentsia narrative that gives the intelligentsia aristocratic origins, cf., the commonplace definition of the intelligentsia as an "aristocracy of the soul"). As in Russian Georgia, so in Ottoman Georgia, the development of popular literacy and print publics was felt to depend on the exemplary representative publicness of aristocratic society.[21] Just as the incorporation of the people of Ottoman Georgia into Russian Georgia would happen through aristocratic representatives at a feast, so the spread of print publics, the propagation of literacy among the people of Ottoman Georgia was to happen through the incorporation of the *begs* of Ottoman Georgia into Russian Georgian print culture, and propagation of literacy from "society" to the "people" as in Russian Georgia. To this end, the editor of *Droeba*, Sergi Mesxi, sent *seven exemplars* of the newspaper *Droeba*, along with a larger number of small books, to the *begs* [local nobles] of Ottoman Georgia, the newspapers to be read by the *begs* and the books to be "circulated among the people." One might easily compare the number of newspapers sent to Ottoman Georgia in 1878 with the number of Ottoman guests brought to Tbilisi for the feast the same year, very likely the recipients and the guests were the same or related people.

Within this aristocratic model of the propagation of literacy, however, is also nestled the emerging categories of a new discourse of publicness, of the duties of writers to the people. Of course, Mesxi admits, seven copies of a newspaper and books whose numbers apparently were no more than a hundred is nothing much. What is important, according to Mesxi, is the *desire* they show, a "desire to read Georgian and get to know [*gacnoba*] our life [*qopa-cxovreba*]": "Today the *begs* have this desire, tomorrow it can be aroused among the people."[22] Here aristocratic "recognition (*gacnoba*) at a glance" (representative, embodied, publicness) is replaced with an intelligentsia conceptualization of the purpose of writing as "getting to know" (*gacnoba*) the "life" (*qopa-cxovreba*) of the people. In a sense, then, the tasks presented by Ottoman Georgia were much of a piece, even a model test case, for the general tasks of the Georgian writer with respect to the Georgian people, that is, the creation of a popular literature, popular (*saxalxo*) both in the sense of "folklore," collection of oral folk texts, and also "for the people," the propagation of literacy, all for the purpose of *gacnoba* (getting to know) each other:

> As far as the propagation of popular (*saxalxo*) literature,—this, of course, is dependent on time. People need to appear among us, who will collect in Ajaria, Kobuleti, Shavsheti, and other re-united regions their compositions of folk (*saxalxo*) poetry, their fairy tales (*zghap'rebi*), legends, historical and other traditions, folk poems (*saxalxo leksebi*) and so on and this will help them both as a means for the propagation of literacy and help us get to know them, too.[23]

By 1893, the nature of society and its duties to the people have indeed been expanded along these lines, and from this perspective, Alxanishvili's assessment is that society in this new sense has failed its new people.

What is interesting about Alxanishvili's account is his treatment of the failure of reconciliation as a failure of society to go to the people, to create moral linkages with them. At the same time, then, the reconciliation of the estranged halves of Georgia can be read as a failure to build an infrastructure of hospitality, a failure of circulation, whether of mutual hospitality or other forms of exchange. The rather meager hospitality offered by Georgian society to their new Ottoman brothers, essentially, amounted to that one single feast in Tbilisi in 1878. As Alxanishvili notes, stresses, nothing comparable happened at the level of the people, and after decades such meager ritual hospitality could not compete with the massive existing networks of horizontal ties of hospitality (*konaghi/kunak* relationships) maintained by the Ottoman Georgians who remained within the boundaries of Russia to their friends and hosts in Ottoman lands. In place of a single ritual act of commensality, here were many comings and goings, presumably solidified by equivalent acts of commensality, into the relation of the *konaghi/kunak*, commerce, in short, a whole popular *culture of circulation* of persons that drew the Ottoman Georgians who remained closer to the Ottomans than to their Georgian "kin":

Imagine, that even now the Javaxetian Georgian still has turned his face more toward the Ottoman, than to us. They arrange comings and goings, friendship, commerce trade and every moral dependence more to Ottomans and especially again to them. It is hard to find that [Javaxetian] Georgian, who has even gone to Chobis Xeoba and begun with Kartlian Georgians some sort of relationship, friendship, or commerce. The same Georgians have Ottoman *konaghis* (hosts, protectors) almost as far as Arzrum and arrange among each other friendship and trade.[24]

However, the single greatest shock for Georgians was the shock of non-recognition, as the Ottoman Georgians began to leave in droves for the Ottoman Empire. Variations on the term *muxajirat* (as Georgian and Russian sources would call it [Georgian *muxajiroba*, Russian *muxajirstvo*]) are used for all the mass migrations of Muslim populations from the Caucasus (Circassia, Abxazia, Ottoman Georgia). The term appears to be based on the Arabic form *muhajirat* ("emigrants"), a term which specifically locates the migration within a Muslim narrative of *hijrah* from non-Muslim to Muslim lands, modeled on the original *hijrah* from Mecca to Medina. More problematically, the term implies that these were voluntary migrations, which is hotly debated at both the popular and academic levels. The Ottoman Georgian *muxajirat* was a large mass population movement (of perhaps over two hundred thousand souls) even in a period known for many deportations and emigrations of extremely large Muslim populations from Russian rule (Jersild 2002). For comparison, the earlier emigrations following the end of the Circassian wars from 1864 onward, which effectively depopulated the coastal regions of Circassia, involved upward of two hundred thousand in the first year, and a total of perhaps four hundred thousand Circassians and two hundred thousand Ajarians and Abxazians.[25] The happiness of the feast quickly was confronted with the sadness that there would, in effect, be no homecoming and no reconciliation. This shock and disillusionment was largely not affected by the decision of large numbers of Ottoman Georgians to return between 1881 and 1882 (Pelkmans 2006, 99).

Again and again, Georgian intelligentsia run after the fleeing peasants of Ottoman Georgia to ask them why they are fleeing, only to meet
a stolid reticence based on a lack of mutual recognition as Georgians
(see also the reported conversations and discussion in Pelkmans 2006,
98–100):

> I was happy, thinking "Now I will see and get to know
> our newly repatriated Georgians!" But soon a certain
> event wiped away these signs of happiness from my
> heart. The event—regarding the emigration of the Ajar-
> ians. The pitiable people were lined up and with loaded
> horses, they were hastening off somewhere or another.
> —Hello! I told them, but with such disgust, with
> downturned faces they glanced at me, that a man would
> have said, that they are angry at me for something.
> — Where have you gone, brother! Why do you not
> say anything to me, I am a *Gurji* [Georgian in Ottoman
> dialect]. . .
> — How were we to know, that you are a *Gurji*? The
> bad Armenians have learnt *Gurjian (Gurjuli)*, and tell us
> that 'We are *Gurji*'! . . .
> —But they did not give me an answer to my ques-
> tion. My conversationalist however whispered: Hurry,
> let's go, to Trapizon a long road awaits us. The moment
> I heard "Trapizon" I asked:
> —What do you want in Trapizon?
> —Well what are we to do? We can't stomach Rus-
> sians [*Urusebi*]. We have been told that that they will
> treat us badly, show our women roubles and invite them
> out to do bad things. We can't tolerate that.[26]

The lack of mutual recognition, of course, emerges from the lack of
a shared semiotic ground for such recognition based on a secular model
of shared language and nationality. What Georgians discovered in the
shock of each event of nonrecognition was something that had already
been long reported by travelers before this point. Tsereteli's model of
Georgianness, which afforded "recognition at a glance" at the supra in
1878, was an essentially secular one, which treated nationality as a se-

ries of outward and inward signs, therefore particularly foregrounding language as a basis of recognition, and passed over the elephant in the room, religious difference, in silence. This model however obviously did not persuade Ottoman Georgians (a fact that was usually explained by their "fanaticism" partially inherent, partially stirred up by Ottoman agents), and importantly, it also did not actually correspond to the discourse of other actors, notably these same Georgians themselves, when they discussed Ottoman Georgians.

The "fanaticism" of Ottoman Georgians, evidenced by their obsessive referral of identity to religious difference (according to impatient Georgians) and refusal to recognize any secular basis for commonality with those they called *Gurjis*, such as language, was already a matter of record long before 1878 (Pelkmans 2006, 99–100). Indeed, it is an index of wishful thinking and selective reading of earlier accounts that Georgians managed to be surprised at all by the catastrophic disconfirmation of their discourse of the nation. Bakradze, in an oft-cited account, had already noted in 1873 that "the word 'Georgian' (*kartveli*) is unknown to the Ajarians and they call themselves only 'Ajarians,' but they call their language 'Gurji' language." This lack of recognition that Gurji was not only a language but a secular basis for mutual recognition of being "one people" (*xalxi*), is blamed on the obfuscating influence of Islam:

> it is impossible not to take notice that the consciousness of the Ajarians about their national origin is extremely confused by the influence of Islam: their perspective on this question, like so many others, flows from the viewpoint of religion, and if you try to persuade some of them that religion is one thing and national origin another, and that the unity of our language is the best proof, that both we and the Ajarians are a single people. For their own part, they were telling me 'at some point our ancestors were Gurjis, but after Islam arrived among us. . . . Even though we speak Gurjian.' (Bakradze 1987 [1878], 45–6)

The official rhetoric of liberal intelligentsia discourse opposed religious identity to linguistic or "national" identity and was explicitly opposed to Orthodox Christian proselytization (see Moshtashari 2001 for the ambivalent position of the Russian Orthodox authorities about the prospect of converting "ex-Christian" Muslim populations in various parts of the Caucasus).[27] However, Christian Georgian discourse was as ambivalent about Ottoman Georgians, as Ottoman Georgians were about Gurjis. First of all, despite the apparent secularism of discourse which sought to ignore differences of religion, this apparent secularism was systematically undermined in several ways.

First of all, at the ritual of 1878 itself, Georgian Christians treated certain aspects of their day-to-day ritual practices, like drinking wine at a supra to purely secular toasts, as being thoroughly secular ritual enactments of Georgian identity, which they accordingly expected their Muslim guests to engage in as Georgians. We do not know what the representative of the Ottomans said or drank at the supra (I have heard rumors he drank water, for example), but the fact that the very *form* (not to mention the substance) of the ritual of reconciliation would be predicated on such a fundamental misrecognition is symptomatic of the whole problem (that this "alcohol test" of loyalty is a continuing form of misrecognition, one of many leading to explicit or implicit exclusion of Ajarian Muslims from Georgian national identity is discussed at length by Pelkmans 2006, 127–9).

But just as Christian Georgians underestimated the religious presuppositions of their own secularism, they tended to impute secret Christian identities to the Ottomans. At the beginning of a long series of articles on "Ottoman Georgia" in the newly launched literary gazette *Iveria* 1877, even a conservative writer like (editor) Ilia Chavchavadze (mostly remembered for formulating Georgian nationality as being defined by shared "land, language and religion"), apparently converted to a secular nationalist position emphasizing "unity of history" over other factors (including religion and language) in the formation of national identity (see Pelkmans 2006, 99). However, throughout this same series of articles, Ottoman Georgians are continuously represented as "secret Christians," that is, practicing Christianity in secret among the ruins of old churches. Ottoman Georgians, like other Georgian Muslims, were claimed to have only superficially converted to Islam, a fact which was linked to their allegedly having been converted by force.[28] Such a discourse of the "secret Christianity" and "superficial Islam" (both of which became widespread in subsequent Georgian nationalist discourses from the socialist period onward [see Pelkmans 2006, 108, 120]) allowed Georgians to have their cake and eat it too; they could engage in a secular public discourse in which they ignored religious differences and privately engage in the fantasy that their Muslim brothers really weren't very Muslim after all and were actually secretly Christians.[29]

Like the rest of the discourse of mutual "recognition at a glance," Georgian secular discourse was itself superficial. Georgians created a fantasy in which language and "nationality" (eroba) would create mutual recognition and reconciliation on purely secular grounds, and at the very same time, often in the same breath, imagined that the religious difference between themselves and the Ottomans was probably only skin deep, a surface glaze of Islam under which hid a secret Christian, a product of an imagined history of coercive conversion associated with Islam. As a result of the contradictions and antinomies of this putatively secular discourse of nationality which was inherited and crystallized under socialism and post-socialism, erstwhile Ottoman Georgians in regions like Ajaria remain afflicted with irresolvable dilemmas because they were "partly included and partly excluded from the Georgian national imagery. In this imagery, Ajarian Muslims were not complete 'others' but were rather 'incomplete selves'; they were simultaneously brother and potential enemy" (Pelkmans 2006, 140). Ironically, this "incomplete self," it might be argued, was produced by the sincere attempt to create a secular basis for national identity, in which both the concept of nationality and individual Ottoman Georgians alike were "emptied" of religious content. However, the difference that was repressed continuously returned: under socialism, for example, largely Christian Georgian cadres used official atheism primarily to physically repress Islamic difference even as socialist history of the region erased Islam as being a superficial symptom of a tragic history of violent, coercive, and backward Ottoman or Islamic rule, having no organic relation to national identity (Pelkmans 2006, 106–9). In the postsocialist period, with the resurgence of Orthodoxy as an integral part of Georgian nationalism, this secular socialist discourse treating Islam as a side effect of a tragic history of violence and coercion, thereby effectively erasing Islam, was retooled and integrated into an explicitly Christian narrative of the nation, producing further dilemmas for Ajarian Muslims (see Pelkmans 2006, 91–168).

Even worse, Georgian secular discourse was careful to separate religious from secular identity only in careful speech on special occasions: while Georgians were careful to speak of "Georgians who have become Muslim" when emphasizing the opposition between secular and religious identity, in informal contexts these were simply Tatars, lumped together indifferently with all the other Muslims of the Russian Empire. In other words, Georgians spoke of the inhabitants of Ottoman Georgia not in terms of secular nationality or language, but in confessional terms of Ottoman *millet*. Their public secular discourse of national identity, adopted specifically to deal with the Ottoman case, was systematically belied by an informal private discourse privileging religious alterity.

Bavreli, for example, for most purposes uses the term "Tatar" in distinction to "Georgian"; he does not refer to Ottoman Georgians as "Georgians" (*kartveli*) in general but as Tatars (as opposed to Armenians and "French" [*prangi*, Georgian Catholics]). If Bavreli wishes to indicate that the Tatars in question are in some sense Georgians, he usually calls them "Tatars like us" or "our kind of Tatars" (*chveneburi tatrebi*).[30] Usually, however, he uses the term *Tatari* to mean "Ottoman Georgian" and *Kartveli* to mean "Christian Georgian":

> From the very first glance you can tell the local Armenians from the Tatars, although there is no difference in clothing. The Armenians are mobile, active, the Tatars gentle and slow in their movements, and along with that have peaceful faces. You already know about the clothing of Tatar women. Many of them wear Georgian style dresses; if a miracle happened and you were to see somewhere a Tatar woman in a Georgian dress, you wouldn't be able to tell whether she was a Georgian [*kartveli*] woman or a Tatar one. Especially among the Begs there are such, which represent a real Kartlian [*kartlis*] Aznauri. If you saw the deputy from Ardanuji, Emin-Afendi, well, how could you distinguish him from a Georgian [*kartveli*]?[31]

Sometimes, he finds that the opposition between "Tatar" and "Georgian" is recursive and can reside within a single individual, perhaps as accident (clothing) to essence (features): "I asked a young Tatar, whose white *chalma* said, 'I am a Tatar,' but whose black eye brows, face beautiful to see, and large nose were to the contrary: 'No, I am a Georgian.'"[32]

When Georgians spoke officially in the liberal secular mode about the Ottoman Georgians, they indicated their recognition of their common nationality as Georgians irrespective of religious difference by the careful use of phrases such as *Gamahmadianebuli Kartvelebi* "Georgians who have become Muslim," which carefully separates religious and secular (national) identity. However, as Ottoman Georgian complained (their voices dutifully transcribed by Georgian intelligentsia) such careful phrases separating religious from secular (national) identity (this Ottoman uses the phrase *musulmani Gurji*) is belied by the frequent colloquial use of terms like "Turk" and "Tatar" to describe them:

> Although in terms of religion we are indeed nowadays Muslim Georgians (*Musulmani Gurjebi*), nevertheless in terms of descent we are Georgians (*Kartvelni*) and not Ottomans or Turks who have come in. . . . Everyone calls us 'Turk' and Georgians (*Kartvelebi*) loathe us most of all.[33]

All pieties expressed at supras aside, Georgian commentators agree that this is the general stereotype, explaining that, among other things, it works the other way around too, that the term "Georgian" for Ottomans (Ajarians, in this case) includes all "Christians" regardless of ethnicity or type.

> Previously some Armenian priest signing himself 'Meghushi' wrote 'the Ajarians hate Georgians.' First of all he should have understood this: Who are they [The Ajarians] calling 'Georgians' [*Kartvelebs*]? Georgian and Christian are synonyms. Georgia [*Sakartvelo*] and Christianity are for them one and the same thing.[34]

The failure of discourses of "nation" to disentangle themselves from "religion" was quite general all through these territories. Bavreli, like most commentators, essentially uses an Ottoman *millet* classification— classification by confessional community—so that each community he describes contains Armenians and Tatars, and also *Prangi* (literally "French," Georgian Catholics). However, here too, attempts were made to recruit these "French" to the category of secularized Georgianness. In 1876, Sergi Mesxi issued an editorial in *Droeba* in response to a local correspondence from Axalcixe that a local Armenian priest was trying to convince the Georgian Catholics that they were Armenians and not Georgians, trying hard to spread the Armenian language among such Georgians "who in their own time were not Armenians and who also consider themselves to be real Georgians."[35] Mesxi points here to the more general failure of this secular project:

> The complete entanglement that exists among us between religion, people (*xalxi*), nation (*nacia*) is astonishing; we haven't been able to separate religion and nation from each other: If a Georgian, due to whatever circumstances, let us say, has accepted the Catholic religion, this person no longer considers themselves Georgian, but 'French' ('*Prangi*'), as if the change of religion changed their Georgianness (nationality).[36]

The most assiduous chronicler of the depopulation of Ottoman Georgia was Bavreli, who, at the end of his travels, in his imagined survey in an aerostat, asked finally whose fault was it that this much anticipated recognition *did not happen*. Having taken for granted that the matter would take care of itself, that recognition would happen at a glance, did the Georgians attempt to *circulate* themselves among the Ottoman Georgians? No. Bavreli anticipates Alxanishvili by a generation, chiding the Georgian intelligentsia for the failure on the ground of the very thing that the supra promised to have done at the ritual level and perform an act of recognition that would lead to reconciliation of "our long-lost brothers." He blames the Georgian intelligentsia, the Georgian aristocracy, the imposition of Russian imperial taxation, and (of course) Ottoman Georgian Muslim fanaticism:

> Well how did the Georgians [*Kartvelebi*] make them [Ottoman Georgians] see, that they were brothers [*modzmeebi*] of the Ajarians? In this case too our youth were unable to fulfill their own duty: their "Ohs" and "Ahs"

were for naught! . . . last year I said, that we should make every effort that there be appointed in Ajaria and other places Georgians of good conscience; but our wish went for nothing; it is true, there were and are Georgians, but they are few and without effect, they too are under the influence of others and circumstances. . . . It didn't happen, we could not make them love us, for various reasons.[37]

In one of his very last published writings, Bavreli again takes his imaginary aerostat out of storage to give us one last look at Ottoman Georgia as a whole. By 1891, Ottoman Georgia has well and truly been forgotten by Georgian society; there is nothing written from the region and the region has few Georgian visitors:

Lo, it has now been ten or eleven years, that nothing has been written from Muslim Georgia in Georgian newspapers. . . . In the passing of a tenth of a century what have we, Georgians, done in this newly-conquered region? The answer is very short: nothing, except this, that some Georgians, either for reasons of work or for scientific purposes, have visited the district of Artvin and reminded the local Mohamedanized Georgians that 'Your ancestors were Georgians' and nothing much more, and with that the matter ends.[38]

According to Bavreli, a "wall of fanaticism raised by historical circumstances stands between us and them." But more than anything else, behind the repetition of tired banalities about ancient kinship, we sense that Georgians are bored or tired of Ottoman Georgia. The relationship looks very similar from the Ottoman Georgian perspective, who patiently agree in turn "*Baili* [Yes], we are *Gurjis*," but one third of them have long since left for Ottoman lands, and the rest of them are looking for a means to do so.

The only Georgians who visit this land are here because their work takes them there (making them like the chinovnik who Bavreli travels with early on, for whom each post or place he travels is just another "somewhere" in the empire), and those who are there for scientific purposes (like Alxanishvili, writing just a few years later). The modality of scientific interest in Ottoman Georgia is not the Georgianness of the people (who, it is stipulated, are Georgians, but there is no ethnographic interest in reassembling the ruins of their Georgianness) but a specifically archaeological interest in the Georgian ruins of Ottoman Georgia.[39] As we will see below, the monuments dotting the landscape provided a more durable set of outward signs of Georgianness, including language, in the form of Georgian inscriptions in ruined churches, than the people living among these ruins. The Georgianness of Ottoman Georgia belongs to the order of ruins and archaeological knowledge, the people are, and will remain strangers, hurrying off to a strange land. The moral of the story would be that the *lands* were Georgian, but not the *people*. To find living representatives of this secular semiotic model of Georgianness appropriate to ethnographic and folkloric description, Georgian writers in the 1880s would turn away from ruins of Georgianness in this region to the mountain dwellers on the northern borders of Georgia, "pagan" Georgians who were, if not Orthodox, at least were reassuringly not Muslims either (Manning 2006, 2007, 2008).

V: Writers and Speakers: Pseudonymous Intelligentsia and Anonymous People

> Without a faith—justified or not—in self-organized publics, organically linked to our activity in their very existence, capable of being addressed, and capable of action, we would be nothing but the peasants of capital. (Warner 2002, 52)

Warner casually uses the word "peasant" to describe one (under the conditions of modern global capitalism) who cannot imagine a self-organized public. The Georgian intelligentsia would surely have agreed: the word "peasant" denoted precisely the sort of person who was not a member of the public. In the post-Emancipation social imaginary, the unenlightened people (*xalxi*, identified with the rural peasantry) and enlightened society or public (*sazogadoeba*, the urbanizing aristocracy and intelligentsia) were imagined as almost diametrical opposites. It was precisely this gap between "the people" and "the public" that the intelligentsia saw as their historic role to overcome through projects like the spread of literacy, but generally speaking, in the meantime, the voices of the people could only enter the public and be known by acts of transcription. Until such time as the invidious distinction between the people (the rural peasantry) and the public (the urban intelligentsia) could be abolished by propagation of literacy, the intelligentsia could come to know (*gacnoba*) the estranged people by describing their lives and by transcribing their voices.

Warner's offhand comment seizes on "peasants" as a term for the benighted denizens of an imaginary Orientalist or capitalist "anti-public" which stands in handy opposition to the enlightened "people" of a liberal Occidentalist public. But by doing so, Warner, inadvertently perhaps, illustrates a basic structural difference between how Western publics and what we could call Eastern European "intelligentsia publics" are imagined, allowing us a critical vantage point for more precisely characterizing the differences between the Western liberal model of public and its abject Eastern other. Central to understanding these differences will be devices of inscription (pseudonyms), by which the intelligentsia constitute themselves as members of a "public" understood to consist not so much of Andersonian readers as *writers,* and devices of transcription, by which the intelligentsia constitute "the people" as peasants, those who cannot be addressed by public discourse and can only speak in print through a mediating act of transcription.

The peasant was indeed a very rare guest among the correspondents to *Droeba.* Around the same period that Ilia Chavchavadze finally completed his *Letters of a Traveler* (1871), we find an unusual letter to *Droeba* entitled "the rules of burying the dead in Imereti."[1] There is nothing particularly unusual about the title or content of the letter, which is an utterly commonplace attack on a "harmful and impoverishing custom" typical of the backwardness of West Georgia, specifically the crippling expenses related to funeral feasts. Letters describing such "harmful and impoverishing customs" form a mainstay of local correspondence to *Droeba* throughout the period. Rather, it is the authorship of the letter that makes it unusual. The author signs himself "A temporarily obligated peasant from Kulashi" (*erti kulasheli valdebuli glexi*) and introduces himself deferentially to the *Lord Editor* [*upalo redaktoro,* the correct form of address for an editor] as at best a marginal participant of print culture:

> I hope, Lord Editor, that you will not scorn printing an article received from a peasant man in your respected newspaper.[2]

The peasant writer seems familiar enough with the norms of print culture to know that he, as a peasant, is an outsider. Certainly, the print culture of *Droeba* assumes a certain kind of person as the normal writer and reader, centering on a male urban member of the aristocracy or emergent intelligentsia. Letters from peasants or women are rare enough to elicit special editorial comment or special treatment throughout the period. For example, female writers, like peasants, are a relative rarity, and thus tend to elicit special editorial comment. To a letter written in 1869 in a somewhat archaic and stilted style from Germany, the editor appends a half-apologetic, patronizing footnote:

> *) This article is a response to our own article and as the reader can see, belongs to a woman's pen, with which

she represents to us her own ideas, which she has gotten from reading our article. We hope that our public will be satisfied with this article and will encourage our women, who increasingly pursue reading (more than men), to occasionally inform 'Droeba' of their own ideas. . . . – Editors[3]

What is strange about the letter from the peasant of 1872 is, first of all, how familiar this peasant outsider is with the conventions of print culture correspondence, including the proper way to address an editor, or the use of a pseudonym, so much so that he deferentially anticipates a possible objection to printing a letter from an outsider like himself.

To show how familiar this peasant is with the norms of print culture, let us look at another letter from a peasant describing the grievances of the mountain-dwelling Xevsurs. This peasant writer signs himself with what appears to be his real name, Imeda Kistauri of the village Ghuli, and writes in (or is transcribed in) an extremely strong Xevsur dialect with little or no sign of familiarity with standard Georgian, spoken or written. He does not even appear to be aware that there is a difference as addressees between the public of *Droeba* and the state! Unlike the other peasant letter writer, Imeda Kistauri lacks any self-consciousness about his own marginality, and also seems to be ignorant in every last detail of any of the conventions or devices of literate correspondence. Unlike "the peasant from Kulashi," Imeda Kistauri of Ghuli neither uses a pseudonym for himself, nor does he know how to properly address the editor (whom he addresses as *Mr. Newspaperman* [*batono megazete*]). The letter is so clearly alien to the print culture of *Droeba* that the editor makes no attempt to adapt it to the conventions of print, instead signaling its otherness with a footnote stating, "*) We print this with language unchanged."[4]

The peasant from Kulashi, who is clearly not the complete outsider that Imeda Kistauri is, anticipates a further question about the identity of the author. Or rather, since this is a letter from a peasant, two questions: Who is the author, the "peasant from Kulashi," and since peasants are by definition illiterate, who is the *writer*?

Perhaps, you would wonder: who is this 'Peasant from Kulashi' and who is the writer of the article? That is true, I neither know how to write nor to read, but I am having someone who knows writing write with my words.[5]

This peasant is aware that the identity of "peasant" implies that the role of author must be divided into a speaker and a transcriber. If the answer to the first question ("who is the speaker?") is "a peasant," the answer to the follow-up question ("who is the transcriber?") is, of course, "an aristocrat." If peasants are all illiterate, it follows that writers are primarily aristocrats, and transcription is not innocent of relations of power between the aristocratic writer and the peasant speaker, particularly for a newly emancipated serf who is still temporarily obligated to his former lord. Here, for example, having explained the conditions of possibility of this letter as an act of transcription, the peasant correspondent goes on to describe the suffering caused even among the wealthy aristocrats by the crippling costs of funeral customs, the rapacity of village priests, and so on. But just as he is about to describe the even greater suffering caused by these harmful and expensive customs among the impoverished peasantry, his narrative cuts short, because his transcriber, himself a nobleman, has apparently become angry at the words he is transcribing, critical as they are of his own estate, flung his pen down, and stormed off:

> With great contentment I would have told you about these things, but my secretary is of high rank, and . . . flung the pen from his hand and told me angrily: 'It is indeed not a lie what they say about peasants: "If you seat a peasant by your side, he demands to be treated like an in-law,"' he stopped writing and left me angrily, until I should find [someone else] accept this and when I have found one, then I will describe to you. . . .[6]

While the peasant from Kulashi is initially quite forthcoming about how his letter was transcribed, at the end of the letter, we are not at all clear how this moment of scribal rebellion was itself transcribed. Just as we begin to wonder about this, we also begin to wonder how what purports to be a transcription of the speech of an illiterate peasant comes to be accompanied by such writerly devices as *footnotes* (including footnotes that gloss terms unfamiliar to the reader of *Droeba*, along with those that contain other local knowledge), more or less as Chavchavadze used footnotes to render the dialogue with Ghunia as a folkloric text.[7] At this point, we may well wonder if the we should be asking not "Who is the speaking peasant, and who is the writer?," but rather, "Who is the writer hiding under the guise of transcription of the voice of a peasant?"

As the peasant from Kulashi notes, transcription makes authorial identity into a nonidentity, the question of authorial identity becomes two separate questions. Since the peasant uses an obvious pseudonym ("Peasant from Kulashi") rather than a proper name (like Imeda Kistauri), there is the question raised by any obvious pseudonym: Who is this Peasant from Kulashi? And since he *is* a peasant from Kulashi and can, by definition, only be the creator of the spoken words, a second question arises of how these words came to be written: Who is the writer transcribing them onto the page? These two kinds of questions, one relating to the authorial figure created by technologies of *inscription*, by literary devices like the pseudonym "Peasant from Kulashi," and the other to the authorial figure created by technologies of *transcription* that turn "living" speaking voices into words on a page, then, form the material for this chapter.[8] Both technologies create an opposition between an embodied, flesh-and-blood self-identical speaking subject, what I will call, following Goffman, a "natural figure," a figure which "stands for itself" (Goffman 1974: 524–5), bundled with all manner of individuating particularities, linguistic and material, verbal, bodily, and sartorial, embodied status attributes, what we might call "qualities of presence," and a disembodied "printed figure" with considerably diminished qualities of presence (and virtually all of a linguistic order) (Goffman 1974, 529).

However, while both of these devices create a gap between a natural and a textual figure, the pseudonym emphasizes this gap; transcription seeks to minimize it (I am borrowing here from the conceptualization of intertextual gaps presented by Bauman 2004). Pseudonyms create an anonymous universe of liberal strangers, unencumbered by their embodied status attributes, while transcriptions create a universe of Orientalist strangers; its technologies are designed to convey the embodied *strangeness* of the voice of the other. The device of the pseudonym produces a disembodied figure of a writer, an intelligentsia member of a public. It functions, for the most part, to establish and maintain a gap between the natural figure and the printed figure which in fact constitutes the writer *as a writer*; the authentic presence of the embodied natural figure is effaced and replaced by a printed figure that makes no pretense of being a natural figure, the writer begins where the speaker ends. If anything, what is displayed by the pseudonym, like the theatrical mask, is the nonidentity of *author* and *actor*, what Goffman calls a "staged figure" (Goffman 1974, 523–4), only here it is a print version of a staged figure.

The device of transcription also creates a printed figure, but more specifically what Goffman calls a "cited figure," a figure within quotation marks (Goffman 1974, 529). Here too there is a nonidentity between the writer and the speaker: the former a mere transcriber, the latter the author and principal of the words. The transcribed speaker is almost always an illiterate peasant (as a transcribed voice) and the technologies of transcription are devoted, for the most part, to reestablishing the qualities of presence of embodied speech in the spoken transcript. These two figures also demarcate different imagined spheres of circulation (written and oral, print and folklore, intelligentsia and folk) and different forms of authority, what can be called, following Gal and Woolard (2001, 7) an "authority of anonymity" and an "authority of authenticity."

These two spheres of textual circulation (print and oral, intelligentsia and peasant) are comparable to the classic "spheres of exchange" in anthropological literature (Kopytoff 1986), in that they are imagined as existing in pure isolation from one another. The anonymous "voice" of the peasant (belonging to the folkloric sphere of a pure oral tradition) can only enter print culture through the translating mediation of the intelligentsia, either by transcription, or as we will see below, through dialogue. At the same time, even as they transcribe the voice of the peasant into the sphere of print culture, the intelligentsia transcribers of folklore devote considerable work to both render the voice of the peasant as a paradoxically anonymous and yet embodied voice, and at the same time purify this voice of any signs of contact with intelligentsia print culture or the differentiated individuality of intelligentsia writers. In so doing, the very act of transcription presupposes the absolute separation of the spheres of circulation that it mediates.

Both of these strategies, of inscription and transcription, importantly, involve the obligatory mediating presence of a writer and help figure the writer's relationship to the rest of the social whole. The pseudonym, we will see, figures the writer in changing relationships to "society," the "public," and the "state." The act of transcription, too, requires a writer (a member of "society") to serve as a transcriber for a speaker (a member of "the people"). Therefore, each act of transcription is in itself a figure for changing understandings of the relationship of service between enlightened society and the unenlightened people. In the case of the "Peasant from Kulashi," who, let us remember, is a "temporarily obligated" peasant, that is, one who has received his freedom but is still indentured monetarily to his erstwhile master (Suny 1988, 106), we can see the seigneurial dependency of the voice of the peasantry on their transcribers, their aristocratic masters (this "temporary dependency" continued in Georgia until virtually the eve of the Russian revolution [Jones 2005, 26]). In the case of the free peasant Lelt Ghunia and Chavchavadze, the transcription figures a new role of post-Emancipation intelligentsia writers in relation to the people, in which transcription becomes a way to close the immense gap between "society" and the "the people," helping the former to "get to know" (*gacnoba*) the latter, but also becoming a kind of service of the intelligentsia to the people. At the same time, the taste for transcription of the voice of the peasantry reflects the hegemony of the aesthetic of social realism that characterized the movement of "going to the people" in both Russia and Georgia in this period (Paperno 1988, Frierson 1993). At the same time, as we have already seen, transcription of the speaking voice of the people also allowed intelligentsia writers an alternative way to position themselves with respect to the state and their publics.

In the world of performing objects, the pseudonym most resembles a mask, obscuring the natural figure of the self and presenting a staged figure of the theatrical role or persona. In the case of transcription, the writer hides in plain view; there are two figures on the stage, quoter and quoted, like a ventriloquist with a dummy or a puppeteer and his puppets. The orthographic alterations and augmentations forming the technologies of transcription (including not only additional letters but also those diacritics, like accentuation, that do not transcribe semantically distinctive features but seem *only* to indicate the alterity of the "spoken" qualities of voice to the written word) find their homology in vocal technology like a swazzle to disguise their natural voice.[9] Using an orthographic version of such a device, writers like Chavchavadze could ground their criticisms in the "authority of authenticity," disavowing any responsibility for the contents of what they transcribe, and at the same time, presenting themselves as humble scribes of the voice of the people: "I merely write down what I, as a traveler, heard from him [Lelt Ghunia], in passing."

Pseudonyms: Public Names

Benedict Anderson's remarkable discussion of the ritual of reading the daily newspaper shows how the semiotic and material properties of the newspaper as print commodity, the simultaneous montage on a single dated page of an unbounded heterogeneity of places and voices, reflect and help mediate the homologous properties of the circulation of this same commodity, particularly the equally simultaneous ritual consumption of the newspaper commodity, so that these two in tandem help produce modern social imaginaries, space-times founded on a sense of contemporaneity. Importantly, Anderson's analysis of the newspaper of print commodity is based on the basic premise that the imaginary it creates is based on a specific kind of imagined reciprocity of perspectives: "almost precisely simultaneous consumption" (Anderson 1991, 35), one that is confirmed by day-to-day observation of consociates as well as reciprocities of perspectives with imagined contemporaries: "the newspaper reader, observing exact replicas of his own paper being consumed by his subway, barbershop, or residential neighbors, is continually reassured that the imagined world is visibly rooted in everyday life" (Anderson 1991, 35–6). Anderson seems to take a modern newspaper as his point of reference, where the readers might well imagine a transposability of perspectives, but only with *other readers*, *consumers* of the same print commodity.

Warner's influential accounts of publics follows Anderson in focusing on the way the public text constitutes itself by the way it interpellates the reader/consumer, a public "exists *by virtue of being addressed*" (Warner 2002, 50, I thank Alejandro Paz for making this observation). Publicness is, in this view, constituted by a specific kind of Bakhtinian "addressivity," a "typical conception of the addressee" (in this case as a peculiar unbounded one) which defines it as a genre (Bakhtin 1986, 95). But with Bakhtin, I also want to insist that this "public addressivity" of *Droeba* depends in part on its *responsibility*, that is, the way it interpellates an addressee as also a potential respondent, it includes "*the possibility of responding to it*" (Bakhtin 1986, 76).

A nineteenth-century newspaper like *Droeba* in general differs from the twentieth-century one imagined by Anderson in particular in that there was also a lively perspectival commerce between *readers* and *writers*, whose model is the genre of correspondence. Unlike a modern newspaper staffed by professional journalists (where "letters to the editor" form a minor section within the whole), a nineteenth-century newspaper like *Droeba* is much more likely to be composed more or less entirely of occasional amateur correspondence from the readership, particularly the *feuilleton* section of the newspaper, forming the lower section of the page, which at least in the *Droeba* period is composed largely of occasional correspondence. All of Bavreli's correspondence, as well as much of the other material I consider in this book, were placed in this special, heterogeneous section of the newspaper. As we will see in the next chapter, the feuilleton moves from being an exemplary space of heterogeneity within an already heterogeneous whole to being a genre in its own right and these external relations of heterogeneity have become internalized as a constitutive feature of the genre. At the same time, the perspectival dialogues between writers and readers that form the external set of relations of newspaper correspondence become internal relations in the feuilleton, formed as an imagined familiar dialogue between the feuilletonist (who increasingly becomes a pseudonymous "star" or celebrity author) and the readership. But the main contrast to bear in mind is that the public, Georgians, that is, readers of *Droeba*, were also by and large imagined as potential *writers to* Droeba—correspondents.

Readers of *Droeba* entered the public not only by virtue of being addressed, but in part by responding, by writing, by correspondence. *How* they did this, specifically how they *signed* their correspondence, in part helped constitute the public they addressed as being of a specific sort. Each different way of signing oneself, what I will call strategies of inscription, produce a different "printed figure" for the writer and projects a different imagining of "society." There are four general strategies of inscription I will discuss: (1) the use of anonymity or pseudonyms to produce a kind of "principle of negativity," which secures the autonomy of the public as a domain of textual circulation from the embodied status attributes of writers; (2) the use of signature using real names or noms de plume to produce a public, which is an extension or augmentation of aristocratic or urban face-to-face publics; (3) the use of pseudonyms as a kind of nom de guerre, protecting the author from state supervision and creating a literary underground; and (4) the use of pseudonyms as a kind of cryptonym, a kind of joking or kenning "anti-name" to produce a secret society of a literary bohemia.

The Via Negativa of Democratic Anonymity

First of all, there is something like a novel sense of "society" as a "public" consisting of liberal strangers in roughly Michael Warner's sense. A writer writing to such a public of fellow writers would write under a pseudonym or pseudonyms, in part to separate the "society" of letters from the "society" of known contemporaries, in particular society in the sense of "urban aristocratic society." Writers of this kind have as their model S. Bavreli, about whom we know nothing more than what they choose to tell us. A pseudonym like Bavreli ("one from Bavra," a very common kind of pseudonym in the Georgian press, to use one's first initial plus a toponymic pseudonym), then plays a number of important roles in creating a specific kind of authorial figure, one specifically involving a moment of *anonymity,* creating an opposition between the personal embodied properties of a person and the impersonal character of public discourse. The opposition so created echoes a fundamental principle of liberalism that arguments should be evaluated independently of the persons who make them. This rupture between embodied "natural figure" and disembodied "printed figure" (the terms are Goffman's 1974, 523–4), represented by the pseudonym, is captured by Warner under a "principle of negativity" (Warner 1990, 48–9). According to this principle, the autonomy of public discourse is constituted in part by the way that persons are stripped of their embodied status attributes and enter public discourse as an anonymous or pseudonymous voice of a text (Remer 2000, 78–9). Aristotelian appeals to *ethos* (namely, persuasion based on the properties of the person who makes the argument rather than the properties of the argument itself) are supposedly thereby rendered impossible (Remer 2000, 82). Warner's "principle of negativity" makes anonymity, the rupture between the person and the text, the negation or absence of the person of the author, central to the pragmatics of pseudonymity and constitutive of the publicness of the text.

In Warner's earlier work on publics (1990), this particular kind of anonymity is located within the very specific (American) historical conditions of notions of "republican virtue," a kind of positive *ethos* that is produced *precisely by negation of one's private identity* (*negativity*) and by positing an illimitable audience (*supervision*) produces a sense (*ethos*, a kind of positive property of the fictive persona) in which the discourse is that of a virtuous public citizen and not a private person, a "voice from nowhere," in effect:

> The difference between the private, interested person and the citizen of the public sphere appears both as a condition of political validity and an expression of the character of print. We have already seen that the illimitable readership of print discourse becomes important as the correlative of public supervision; here the apparent absence of a personal author in printed language has become important as the correlative of the principle of negativity . . . [A] distinct preference for fictitious personae . . . expresses the general principle of negativity in representational politics. (Warner 1990, 43)

Obviously, the pragmatics of pseudonyms ("fictitious personae") cannot, in fact, be entirely reduced to anonymity, the absence of a personal author in printed language (see also Buurma 2007, Coleman 2012, Knuttila 2011, Nozawa 2012 for logics of anonymity often specifically opposed to pseudonymity in different nineteenth-century print and contemporary virtual cultures). For example, a nom de plume, which might well be regarded as a kind of pseudonym, involves assuming an identity as a writer without necessarily entailing anonymity at the same time. As Donath (1998) notes for uncannily similar contemporary use of anonymity and pseudonymity to manage online/offline identity relations:

> It is useful to distinguish between pseudonymity and pure anonymity. In the virtual world, many degrees of identification are possible. Full anonymity is one extreme of a continuum that runs from the totally anonymous to the thoroughly named. A pseudonym, though it may be untraceable to a real-world person, may have a well-established reputation in the virtual domain; a pseudonymous message may thus come with a wealth of contextual information about the sender. A

purely anonymous message, on the other hand, stands alone. (Donath 1998: 21)

Even if anonymity does not exhaust the pragmatic potentiality of pseudonyms, Warner is certainly correct that the pragmatics of most pseudonyms presuppose a foundational moment of anonymity, in the sense of the negation of the embodied, personal author, the production of a stranger. For some authors, it is the anonymity of the pseudonym that allows them to speak in print publics, where they might never speak in face-to-face publics.

Aristocratic Titles and Noms de Plume: The Via Positiva of Aristocratic Society

Competing with this anonymous or pseudonymous sense of "society" as an autonomous public defined entirely by the circulation of texts, as a negation of embodied status, is one in which the society of print is treated as an augmentation or extension of embodied status, specifically an aristocratic or urban "society," a society of known, potentially even famed, consociates (for a parallel opposition between autonomy and augmentation as relations between online and offline worlds, see Boellstorff 2008; for the comparison, see Manning 2009b). Writers from the gentry or nobility, like the princes Ilia Chavchavadze or Akaki Tsereteli, for example, did not need to represent themselves as pseudonymous correspondents from peripheral regions. Usually, they inserted themselves into the "society" in the sense of print public from their position in face-to-face "society" in the aristocratic sense. By signing their own name, often accompanied by their title, they created an intertextual linkage between those two senses of "society," between the spatially localizable, "topical" face-to-face society of the supra, the theater, the opera, the viceroy's court, the city street, and the "metatopical" "society" in the sense of the public of *Droeba* (for these distinctions see, for example, Warner 2002, Taylor 2002). In the case of service nobles and holy orders, their representative publicity itself prevented them from descending in literary polemics *without* the use of pseudonyms (Mikadze 1998, 11–13), so that Grigol Orbeliani, the highest-ranking Georgian service noble of the period, used pseudonyms to protect this official representative publicity from the tarnish of his poetic or polemical print publicity personae (Mikadze 1998, 12–3).

Nonservice noble aristocratic authors who did not have this sort of conflict of interest might also use pseudonyms, but for them, there would always be a specific *stylistic* or contextual reason for making use of such a device, having nothing to do specifically with negation of their embodied status. For example, Akaki Tsereteli, the noble who represented and spoke for the "writers" at the supra for the Ottoman Georgian guests of 1878, relatively rarely had recourse to pseudonyms compared even to other nobles like Ilia Chavchavadze (Grishashvili 1987, 8). When he did, he always had specific reasons for doing so. Like many young authors, uncertain of how their works will be received and not wanting to live forever under a "spoiled" literary identity, he used a pseudonym (*s__li*) for his literary debut in 1858 (Mikadze 1984, 10). On other occasions, when a certain censor named Isarlov forbade him to publish a certain poem, he published it in an out-of-the-way place (Poti, a common gambit) under the pseudonym Luka Isarlov (Mikadze 1984, 22). Since Tsereteli was not a service noble, he did not, like nobles occupying highly public positions within the state apparatus, have to have frequent recourse to a pseudonym in order to publish at all (Mikadze 1984, 12–14).

But most of the time, he would sign his works with some version of his actual name, ranging from his full name and title *T. Ak. Tsereteli* (in a letter from 1869), where the *T* stands for *tavadi* "prince," to just his first name (*Akaki* in 1875). The first name signature, which he adopts later, so far from being a pseudonym, designed to obscure his identity within a society in which there were many people named Akaki, instead presupposed that his writerly voice was so familiar to his reading public that there was no need for further specification. Like Ilia Chavchavadze, Vazha Pshavela, Galaktion Tabidze, and other well-known writers of the socialist canon, he is referred to by his first name today, even in scholarly works (Mikadze 1984, 29–30). Hence, signature moves from delineating one's position *primarily* in terms of one's position in terms of *status within extra-literary aristocratic "society"* (noble title) to one *primarily* in terms of one's achieved *status within literary society* (fame, familiarity to the "public"), one's first name becomes, in effect, a nom de plume, and even indexes the tone of familiarity, even intimacy, of the literary world found in the dialogue of the *feuilloton*. But the basic strategy is one in which the way one signs oneself in the world of the press extends or augments, rather than negates, one's embodied personal status attributes.

Cryptonyms: Underground and Bohemian Identities

While Warner's (1990) influential account of the eighteenth-century republic of letters certainly had no pretense of being a general account of publics everywhere, the categories developed for this singular historical episode, like the principle of negativity, or the idea that publics in general must be self-organized, autonomous from state supervision, can be mistaken for cryptonormative universal categories that publics everywhere must satisfy in order to be properly qualified as publics (for example, in Taylor 2002, Warner 2002). But so far from being a universal attribute of public discourse as such, it appears that some of these categories may have been contested, and partial, ideologies of publicness even within their own historical context. Gary Remer has argued that Warner's "principle of negativity" privileges a specific and interested (antifederalist) ideology of the press, by treating pseudonymy as being essentially a form of anonymity, an attempt to eliminate Aristotelian appeals to *ethos*, the rhetorical "presence" of the embodied person in their public arguments. By contrast, Remer shows that the competing Federalist ideology, which seeks to use pseudonyms to provide disembodied texts with characterological forms of ethos (e.g., classical pseudonyms redolent of Republican virtue like Agrippa, Atticus, Cato, etc.), or alternatively, to find out the true embodied identities of the authors behind the disembodied texts, were just as prevalent a cultural logic constitutive of the formation of the eighteenth-century American press (Remer 2000, 78–84).

What emerges from this discussion is that the use of pseudonyms (like the features of a public defined by Warner [2002]) can be related to, and must be understood in terms of, different historically specific and politically positioned imaginaries of the public, and we should probably add that there is no real evidence that these social imaginaries have any internal tendencies to move in certain directions; it may be a "long march," but there is no evidence that this long march is going anywhere, and therefore, that anyone is going to "get there" ahead of anyone else, *pace* Taylor's rather unrepentantly Eurocentric, Hegelian, and normative model of historical progress. While the pragmatic goals to which pseudonyms of various kinds can be put, other than merely establishing anonymity, are probably endless and many of them quite generically applicable to many forms of print or virtual culture (and Mikadze [1984] for example devotes no less than twenty pages to listing the possibilities in Georgian tsarist period discourse; see also Grishashvili [1987] and Mikadze [1998] for discussions of the remarkable profusion of forms and functions of Georgian pseudonyms), I wish to argue that there remain certain uses of pseudonyms that index the specificities of the tsarist public sphere as social imaginary. I want to focus on two, the *underground* pseudonym and the *bohemian* pseudonym. The use of the pseudonym to constitute a secret discourse among intelligentsia away from state supervision we can collect under the term "underground." The often related use of playful pseudonyms that are sometimes kennings of one's true name (cryptograms or cryptonyms) that creates an esoteric discourse among intelligentsia we can call a "bohemia." Indeed, Ioseb Grishashvili, the Georgian author responsible for creating a folklorized modernist social mythology of "Old Tbilisi" as a "literary Bohemia" (Grishashvili 1963[1927], was also both a prodigious user of pseudonyms [having over one hundred personae] as well as a connoisseur and expert on Georgian cryptograms and pseudonyms [Grishashvili 1969, 1987] (on Old Tbilisi, see Manning 2004, 2009, Manning and Shatirishvili 2011). Both of these are related in a sense as being directly or indirectly by-products (like "Aesopian language" discussed above) of state supervision.

The most striking difference between the kind of "self-organized" Western liberal public that Taylor and Warner take as their ideal and a tsarist public is the normalized existence, in a tsarist public, of state supervision, censors, and repression. That is, these things also exist in Western print publics, but there, they are always treated as a pathological deviation from the normal state of publics, whereas in tsarist and socialist print culture, they are treated as normal, even constitutive, aspects of publicness. This presence of state supervision produces one very obvious difference in the function of pseudonyms, where pseudonyms become, in certain periods, actual secrets, the sphere of circulation they define being called an "underground." Here the pseudonym is not so much addressed to finding a place for the author in a public still dominated by aristocratic society, but addressed to the third party of any public communication, the state, and the censor. The one case where we find an aristocratic author like Akaki Tsereteli use a pseudonym, for example, is when he is avoiding a censor, publishing his work under a pseudonym in an out-of-the-way location.

The pseudonym Akakai Tsereteli chooses is the name of the censor himself. This brings us to a second related use of the pseudonym *not merely* to evade the censor, but as a sort of *inside joke* at the expense of the censor and those members of the public who are not in on the joke. The intelligentsia self-definition as members of an underground, during periods of state repression in particular, by use of a pseudonym is clear enough, but this same state supervision induces changes in writing and public address that produces a more subtle, related use of pseudonyms to define a kind of "bohemia" at other times. The presence of the censor intervening between the writer and the public means that writing itself will not be quite the same relation to a public as in Warner's example, and neither, consequently, will pseudonyms. Part of the value of the censor is that it constitutes the publicness of writing in a very specific way: the figure of the censors makes the publicness of writing independent of ever actually *reaching* a public, a self-valuable, heroic, and untrammeled expression of personal creativity, even unrecognized genius.[10]

Such conditions of state supervision give rise to their own characteristic, perhaps pathological, forms of writing (including Aesopian language, for example): one of these, Boym argues, is the social pathology of *graphomania*: "Graphomania . . . is a literary disease, an uncontrollable obsession to write and be a writer" (Boym 1994, 168). Graphomania, which is characterized, among other things, by a "feverish plagiarism, genius-envy, and a sadomasochistic relationship with the reader" (ibid.), is also a form of writing that in a sense is constituted in a relationship with a censor (Boym 1994, 172). The presence of the censor, after all, encourages the writer to think of the act of writing as being a self-sufficient act of self-expression, of "aesthetic emancipation" (Boym 1994, 173), the defiant act of an unrecognized genius. Graphomania also leads to a proliferation of pseudonymous personae: "Graphomania complicates the relationship between author and character, between the author and his multiple personae and pseudonyms, the fictional and semifictional selves that incarnate Romantic geniuses and graphomaniacs" (Boym 1994, 173–4).

As Boym argues, an important symptom of graphomania is the proliferation of pseudonymous personae in writing that is so supervised. Therefore, an important aspect of intelligentsia self-definition is the use of pseudonyms as joking personas, producing a set of pseudonyms as decodable *anti-names*, paralleling Halliday's discussion of subcultural "anti-languages." In the Georgian press, for example, most writers tend to adopt a serious and stable pseudonym as their main authorial persona, by which one creates an intertextual relation of authority, but graphomaniac writers, particularly for humorous or satirical writings, tend to accrete an almost limitless series of alternative joking occasional pseudonyms (Mikadze 1984, 25, Grishashvili 1987, Mikadze 1998), similar to what are called "alts" ("alternate personae") in contemporary online role-playing games (Boellstorff 2008, Manning 2009b). Noted Georgian modernist writer (and folklorist of the urban "Bohemia" of Tbilisi) Ioseb Grishashvili (also a pseudonym) himself used over one hundred pseudonyms (Lortkipanidze 1987, 5-6), many of them variations of (es) (me) ar(a) var "this is not me"—direct metapragmatic statements of nonidentity. Such a profusion of pseudonyms was not unusual, Grishashvili recollected that in the prerevolutionary period

> Coworkers at humor publications made use of the most pseudonyms. I. Evdoshvili had ten pseudonyms, Axosp'ireli—15 more, Eshmak'i and Taguna ([Pseudonyms of] N. K'alandadze and Sh. Sharashidze, [respectively]—GM), who knows how many! And that's how it had to be. After 1905, when the reaction got stronger, pseudonyms were necessary (Grishashvili 1987, 8)

Many such pseudonyms are far from being erasures of one's natural figure but are wordplays on the person's actual name. Like the lexicon of an anti-language, these pseudonyms are based on the ordinary name and become puzzles or riddles, *cryptograms* or *cryptonyms* in which the natural figure of the author is concealed (Grishashvili 1987). Indeed, many of the same formal processes Halliday identified in the conversion of an ordinary lexicon into an anti-language (Halliday 1976, 576–7) are found in the process of producing cryptonyms out of ordinary names. For example, riddling forms used in anti-languages often involve simple inversion of sounds or letters, and this is true too of cryptonyms as play forms (Mikadze 1984, 28–9, Mikadze 1998, 22–25): whole name, e.g., Aleksandre Toidze—*A. Edziot* (1888, dz is a single letter in Georgian); Ivane Tsilosani—*Enavi Inasolits* (1914); of part of the name, the folklorist Tedo Razikashvili (Vazha Pshavela's brother)—*R. Odet* (1905); Mose Janashvili—*Esom* (1886–1896), as well as other kinds of kennings, virtually every imaginable variation from simple initials, to simple initials spelled out using the names of characters as in the Russian or Georgian alphabet (examples 1–2 below), to various other formal operations of substitution and deletion of the beginning, end or middle of the name (examples 3–4 below), were possible. Additional variations were made possible by using a Latin alphabet or indicating the initials using a numerological puzzle ("904" indicates the initials "Sh. D." [Shalva Dadiani] because conventionally the 900 is the numerical value of the letter *S* and 4 is the value of the letter *D* in the Georgian alphabet [Mikadze 1984, 45]).

An excellent example of the coincidence of pseudonymy as play language and actual play languages is given by the example of a certain Samson Qipiani, who, in weekly feuilleton entitled "A Letter from Witchland" (*Cerili Kudianetidam*) appropriately disguised his first name using a playful children's anti-language called *kajuri* (named after a kind of sprite, a kaji [on which, see chapter 7] who is noted for doing everything backwards). In *kajuri*, one inserts a syllabified consonant, either [ts'] or as here [p] after every open syllable (CV becomes CVpV, where C stands for a consonant and V for a vowel) or after every nasal in the syllable coda (CVN becomes CVpVNp, where N is a nasal [m, n]). Hence, *Samsoni* ("Samson") becomes *sapampsoponipi* (*Sa(pa)m(p)so(po)ni(pi)*) (example 5 below).

Examples

Name	Pseudonym	Process	Source
(1) Mixeil Bebutashvili	*embe*	initials M B as prounounced in Russian	*Droeba* 1881
(2) Ilia Peradze	*in da pari*	initials pronounced in Georgan plus "and"	*Iveria* 1895
(3) Andro Dolidze	*doli*	*doli (dze)*	*Mogzauri* 1910
(4) K'ondrat'i Gvasalia	*alia*	*(gvas) alia*	*Cnobis Purceli* 189?
(5) Samson Qipiani	*Sapampsoponipi*	*Sa(pa)m(p)so(po)ni(pi)*	*Iveria* 1887 (p. 34)

The list of formal operations attested almost exhausts the logical formal possibilities. The point is that these are not secrets any more than "Pig Latin" or *kajuri* are viable secret codes; they are riddles, puzzles, playful inside jokes that, like Aesopian discourse, separate those who know from those who don't, those can solve them and those who can't, or simply reflexively index by their form their own playful intent (cf., Mikadze 1984, 46). As Halliday argues with respect to anti-languages, the very "looking glass form" of anti-languages as inversions of normal language produces an indexical icon of anti-societies that view themselves as inversions of normal society. The anti-language, then, is not merely a referential "set" (to secrecy, hiding the meaning of everyday words by inverting their form, appropriate to avoid state supervision), nor yet a "set" to the form of language (verbal art, poetics, verbal play, play languages, exemplifying the sheer fun of making up new anti-words and kennings and testing creativity), but indeed is an image of the social totality that produces them, a "set" to the social totality (Halliday 1976). In effect, adopting a pseudonym expresses a writer's intention to address a public, a cryptonym serves to divide this public into an exoteric public including both the censor and ordinary people, and a bohemian counter public, a urban literary bohemia (Grishashvili 1963 [1927]) which is akin to Halliday's "anti-society" of criminals (and in later Georgian urban life, these two would merge; see Manning 2009c). The riddling quality of these names could hardly serve functions of secrecy, but they do produce a kind of esoteric discourse within public discourse, in which members of the aristocratic/intelligentsia "society" could recognize each other's playful selves. Writers like Warner are fascinated by the potentially limitless, indeed infinite, potential reach of public address: "The meaning of public utterance . . . is established by the very fact that their exchange can be read and participated in by any number of unknown and *in principle unknowable* others" (Warner 1990, 40–1). But it must be remembered how very finite, even microscopic, Georgian print culture was and is, compared, for example, to its defining model, Russian print culture or French print culture, and how self-aware it was of this finitude.

In fact, this very sense of finitude is also registered in the use of pseudonyms. To produce a sense of an infinite public address of limitless strangers in the cramped world of known contemporaries, Georgian print culture resorted to the semiotic technology of the pseudonym.

Pseudonyms could serve to give an impression of wider boundaries or greater population to this imagined print culture than actually existed. A prolific single author, or an editor who wishes his journal to appear to have many contributors, might write many articles under different names to produce a sense of a broad base of correspondence and diversity of perspectives (Mikadze 1984, 10). Writers' circles like the Georgian bohemian poets of the 1920s wished that their circle could have contained a woman poet, but, alas, they knew no women poets, so Paolo Iashvili made one up and wrote poems under her name (Mikadze 1984, 11). In fact, if women writers occasionally made use of male pseudonyms to overcome the difficulties of reception their gender presented them as writers (Mikadze 1998, 13), an even larger number of Georgian men wrote under female pseudonyms for various reasons (Grishashvili 1987, 13).

The sense that Georgian print culture was not only finite, but anything *but* cosmopolitan also played a role in pseudonymy. Writers especially of non-Georgian origin might wish to present themselves via pseudonym as Georgian, this part of a more common process that included proper names and surnames as well (Beglar Aghamov as Beglar Axosp'ireli, Bughdan Evangulov as B. Davitashvili, etc. [Mikadze 1984, 15]). At the same time, writers wishing to produce a sense of cosmopolitan alterity and authority within such a small, perhaps stiflingly small, national print discourse, might instead posit themselves as a voice of Russian or European origin, sometimes rendered in a Cyrillic or Latin alphabet, as appropriate, connecting the author's voice with international or cosmopolitan political programs (Mikadze 1984, 16). Such Occidentalizing tendencies could be matched by a rarer Orientalizing tendency restricted to bohemian authors of the 1910s–1920s, who sometimes adopted pseudonyms of "Oriental" origins (Mikadze 1984, 16–17) (Ioseb Imedashvili—*Ali Oghli* [1913], Ioseb Grishashvili—*Rashid Vardanoghli* [1923], Davit K'asradze—*Ali Azizi* [in Batumi newspapers], and so on).

Under such circumstances, too, these others were *never* "in principle unknowable," and the guesswork of trying to locate the real person behind the pseudonym in closely linked networks of known social others in a small country and even smaller urban intelligentsia society could easily become a game of mutual self-recognition. Georgian literature was born, as Chavchavadze argues "*shinaurobashi*," among closed circles of intimates: producing a public of strangers out of this familiar discourse between intimates required a certain work of *estrangement* (as Warner puts it [2002, 81]), perhaps a greater work than we suppose, pseudonyms on this level were an important technology of estrangement, working to produce an infinite "universe" of stranger contemporaries (Mikadze's [1998] book is after all titled *In the Universe of Georgian Pseudonyms*) out of an extremely finite "village" of known consociates. At the same time, this public of strangers, which is always already divided between an exoteric public discourse and an esoteric bohemian discourse, always verges on recreating a literature *shinaurobashi* ('domestic, between intimates') on a new level, precisely this tendency is indexed by the use of kenning cryptonyms, and later, by the "intimate stranger" voicing of the urban feuilleton. It is a form of elitist, esoteric, bohemian social closure very like the social closure of aristocratic networks within print culture, very different from the principle of "supervisory publicness" in a Western republic of letters. More characteristic of a later, already self-aware and self-obsessed intelligentsia of the late 1890s and early twentieth century, this understanding opposes the avant-garde intelligentsia as *underground* to the state, and as urban *bohemia* to the rural people. But most of all, we see from the pseudonymy of the graphomaniac and the celebrity writer, especially the serialized feuilletonist, all of whom "branded" their popular weekly columns by the use of pseudonyms, that if pseudonyms strip the author of their old, embodied identity, this is not merely a shedding of an old identity; it is an act of rebaptism that transforms a mere scribbler into a well-known *writer*. To be a writer, then, is defined first and foremost by having at least one, and perhaps many, pseudonyms. As with monastics and soviet mafia, to enter this world, one must be rebaptized as a stranger.

Transcribing the People

If the creation of a liberal public required an act of "unknowing," turning a finite list of known urban contemporaries into an infinite universe of strangers, the intelligentsia's relation with the people was figured by the opposite imperative of "getting to know" the strange people and lands of rural Georgia. In the wake of emancipation in Georgia, as in Russia, the perception of a vast gulf between the unenlightened "people" and enlightened "society" occasioned a "sense of moral responsibility and guilt toward, and a perception of a dreadful separation from, the vast majority of the population. . . . Most of the authors who went to the countryside were seeking redemption through rapprochement with the peasantry" (Frierson 1993, 9). For Georgians, in the post-Emancipation period of the 1860s up to the Russo-Ottoman War (1877–8), it seemed imperative that members of society should become reacquainted with, "get to know" (*gacnoba*), the people. In the wake of the Russian victories and the capture of Ottoman Georgia, this motive would be displaced from the people of European Georgia to the even more estranged people of Ottoman Georgia.

"Getting to know" the people would not only involve the traversing the vast social divide between oral and literate cultures of the unenlightened "people" and enlightened "society," but it would also involve concrete movement in space, because the peasantry mostly lived in villages, and "society" now lived primarily in cities. Luckily, however, unlike Russian "society" who perhaps had to travel some great distance to the countryside, perhaps to a village they had never seen before, in the case of Georgian society, the distance to be traversed to get to know the people was short, and it was an excursion they made from the city every summer in any case:

> Summer has come and the society (*sazogadoeba*) of our cities is going out to the village. How many could have gained much utility along with pleasure! Whoever has learning and a sharp mind, how much bad and good would he observe in the village, how much that is new would he become aware of and see, he would get to know [*gacnoba*] the life of the people![11]

So begins the inaugural in 1871 call for the collection of folklore by correspondence in the pages of *Droeba*. The author, Petre Umikashvili, argues that the annual return of urban society to the village is more than an opportunity to escape the stifling heat of the city and rest, but it is also an opportunity to "get to know" the people; for example, by the collection of folkloric materials, materials for creation of a specifically Georgian print culture, published books of folklore. This already-existing form of yearly urban-rural transhumancy is for Umikashvili not only an opportunity for the collection of oral materials from among the people to be published, it is also a moment in which these published materials, in the form of printed books, can be returned to the people. Hence, his answer to the question, "How must we spread Georgian books among the people?" published the next year is envisioned as happening in precisely parallel terms:

> Lo, summer has come and now all of us are spreading ourselves out here and there in villages and cities: couldn't we writers get books on credit and take them to villages to sell among our relatives? . . . Taking this matter forward is something we all can do, whoever we are, whether we live part time in the village, or permanently.[12]

Circulation of texts, in a country as small as Georgia, far from being imagined as being infinite or limitless, is in fact imagined as being much of a piece with the embodied circulation of the writers themselves. In fact, the yearly circulation of urban society among the rural people is precisely the motor that drives the circulation of texts, it is the mechanism by which the voice of the rural people can enter the urban public world of print discourse (via folkloric transcription), so that the public can get to know the people, and it is also the mechanism by which printed texts, and literacy more generally, can be propagated among the people, so that the people can become a public.

The project is to "get to know" (*gacnoba*) the people, and Umikashvili suggests that the best way to get to know the people is by *transcription*, that is, by collecting "folk stories, songs, *shairi*, tales, riddles, charms, proverbs," because "the people's beliefs, thoughts, suffering, happiness, hope—are expressed and dispersed in the poems and stories of the people."[13] He argues not only that this is easy to do, it is something that, for example, students could do, "because they all live in villages in the summer anyway and have lots of free time, too";[14] it is also something that Georgians *should* do, because the "living words of the people" form better materials for the work of historians than "rotten, ancient tomes." Furthermore, there is the existing example that "in Europe distinguished and famous writers have gone from village to village, have written and published" and in Russia too since 1815.[15]

Transcription, I have argued, occurs in and mediates not only a social imaginary divided between an illiterate people and a literate society and their corresponding spheres of textual circulation, but also an imaginative geography divided between a people rooted in the village and a mobile society that circulates between the city and the village. The voice to be transcribed is defined in terms of these categories, and the theory of transcription both presupposes and polices the boundaries of these categories: one must transcribe "generally what the people (*xalxi*), that is the peasant people (*glexi xalxi*), the people of the village (*soplis xalxi*), sing." Transcription will turn this pure stream of oral folk circulation into written correspondence, bring the voice of the people into the public, and eventually bring it back to the same people as part of a campaign to spread literacy. But in the moment of transcription itself the stream of folk, oral speech must be kept pure and segregated from the stream of print circulation, of writers and urban people. Umikashvili's methodological strictures are particularly concerned with establishing the folkloric pedigrees of texts and avoiding hybrids, something he regards to be particularly important "in this period of mixed up language" (*enis areul-dareuloba*).[16] He complains that up until now, only a handful of authentic folkloric texts have been published, and existing chrestomathies mix up "folk" ("peasant, village") with "city" songs, which are either "compositions of some writer" (as opposed to the "people" who presumably represent an anonymous, collective author which does not "write" but "sings") or represent the work of an urban guild worker (not "a peasant"), and in general circulate only in the social milieu of the city.[17]

Here, in the specification of what constitutes "the people," we see a series of exclusions that seek to constitute the folk and the folk sphere of circulation as being the diametric opposite of the sphere of circulation of the transcriber, a metapragmatic specification of *kinds of author*, the authorial identity of the transcriber and the transcribed, the intelligentsia society and the people, which is constituted in transcription (transcriber, transcribed) and in correspondence (city, village). The author of intelligentsia urban print culture is an individual who writes with a pseudonymous signature; the speaker of rural folk culture is collective and speaks anonymously.

Such a definition of the parameters of "folk" (*xalxuri*) circulation becomes standard for Georgian folklore throughout the socialist period. The twentieth-century linguist and folklorist Akaki Shanidze, cofounder of Tbilisi State University and of the academic discipline of Kartvelology, including Georgian philology and folklore studies (on whom, see Cherchi and Manning 2002) in general followed Umikashvili and his European predecessors in defining folklore as a mode of textual circulation that differed in every respect from print culture, from authorship to mode of circulation to kind of public. The only difference between Umikashvili writing in 1871 and Shanidze writing in 1931 is that, following the October Revolution, the rural peasantry is also considered to be proletarian. Since the mode of transmission is communal and the poetry is mutable, questions of attribution and authorship are irrelevant:[18]

> When I say "folk poetry", I mean such poetry as was born, developed and circulates among the working people of the village, among the peasantry, in that social circle, which is at work and labor and mostly ignorant of reading and writing. This is that poetry, which spreads usually by oral transmission from one man to another and from the older generation to the younger. Its preserver and defender is the memory of many persons and this is the reason that its form and content is mutable. . . . (Shanidze 1931, 5)

Purism of pedigree of this authentic voice must be attended by purity of form, preserved by a strict proceduralism in transcription. Umikashvili is quite strict (both to the writer *and* the peasant): "You *must make the peasant say,* and you must write it completely, thus unchanged, as the peasant says it: not one letter must be changed" [emphasis added].[19] Umikashvili allows that this method is really only applicable to poems, which can be transcribed by line-by-line repetition; stories, by contrast, have to be gotten in one take, and in effect, *recomposed* rather than transcribed. Here Umikashvili simply allows that "after hearing the whole thing once you can write it, you should, of course, preserve the language of the people, the proper names and whatever poems there are here and there within in."[20]

Not merely must the transcription preserve the distinctive *form* of the speech of the peasant, using devices like special supplements to the orthography or footnotes (2–3), but peasant speech is always contextualized in an itemized list of indexical features of context that must accompany the transcription (1, 4–6), including features that pay special attention to the changes the text undergoes in the process of circulation (1), or which seek to identify whether the source of the poem is in fact "folk" (*saxalxo*) or whether it entered folk circulation from books or from the repertoires of minstrels (4–5). In all these considerations, maintaining a pure, unmixed pedigree of the oral text from the moment of oral composition (1, 4–6) to the moment of written transcription (1–3) is paramount to segregate authentic examples of "folk" (*saxalxo*) circulation from other parallel forms of circulation, written or oral, but also constitutes folk circulation as being about form, rather than referential content, a matter of performances, rather than circulating texts. It emerges that that oral circulation of texts is the very antithesis of print circulation.

(1) *Repetition:* While the technology of print propagates printed texts as identical copies, oral texts are ever changing in the process of circulation, losing or gaining a word or two there, or otherwise changing their form, hence "However many times a man encounters one and the same song, poem, fairytale, he must write it down."

(2) *Form:* "every letter (*aso*) must be written as the peasant pronounces it," a formal device which separates the spoken transcription from the written text, in particular, by expanding the kinds of letters which are used in transcriptions beyond those used normally.

(3) *Footnotes:* "The meaning of words that the transcriber does not understand, he should ask and make for them a footnote," a device we have seen with both Chavchavadze and others; the footnote in particular establishes a hierarchical relationship between the order of transcribed voice and the order of the commentator, in a manner homologous to the way the editorial footnote subsumes and subordinates the text of the writer.

While these features attend to the form of the text, the next features attend more to locating the text within a field of circulation and performance, again with a view to ensuring that it belongs to a sphere of "folk" (*saxalxo*) circulation. (4) *Place:* "In what village did the transcription occur, from what village did the speaker learn it, or did he learn it at the house of a lord?" This latter question is important, because such poems are not folk, if they were "learnt from books in the house of the master." Nowhere does Umikashvili ask that we write down the name of the speaker, all one needs to know is *where*, not *who*, because the folk author is anonymous and collective. (5) *Source:* Just as Christian prayers become "folk" to the extent that they have been refashioned in some way, so too the repertoires of traveling minstrels can eventually enter the folk repertoire, become folk (*saxalxo*) "in the end." But until this happens, a sharp demarcation of minstrel's works and folk works must be maintained, just as the repertoire of the city must not be mixed up with that of the village: always ask with respect to any work whether "that poem (*leksi*) was composed or not by the speaker, or heard from a minstrel or from a peasant." (6) *Contexts of performance:* "Always ask what context each poem is sung in, which ones are sung working," and so on. (7) Lastly, for those poems written in languages or dialects that are unintelligible to a Georgian (Mingrelian, Svan, Ingilo), a Georgian translation must be provided.[21]

In a penetrating analysis of different ideologies of transcription that inform discourses of language endangerment and preservation, Robert Moore (2006) has recently noted the way that writing is positioned as mediating across an almost metaphysical divide between oblivion and status as a "language": "[T]he act of writing [is situated] precisely astraddle that line, endowing writing with the power to move (a) language, word by painstakingly transcribed word, from one side of that metaphysical divide to the other." Certainly Georgian folklorists like Umikashvili saw in the act of transcription a power to mediate metaphysically the divide between these two spheres of circulation, but transcription also constituted and policed the boundaries of the spheres of circulation it mediated.

The objective of transcription is to reduce a living text "as if in amber," but at the same time, an attempt to animate an inanimate written text, to confer qualities of life and movement, of living speech, to something that must now circulate under the conditions of print culture. Seeking to mediate a metaphysical divide between living speech and print, transcription reproduces the difference in a new form. The order of transcription implies an ontological opposition between embodied peasant speech, which is always laden with a surplus of form beyond what can be transcribed, and is always contextualized by surplus of indexicality when compared with the disembodied, decontextualized writing of intelligentsia, which, propagated in self-identical form in print, is always entextualized, maximally independent from context. The speech of the peasant is not only distinctive and different in its embodied form, which must somehow be conveyed in writing, but while circulation of a newspaper like *Droeba* is unbounded in space and time, peasant circulation is ever changing and always shot through with indexical relations to its context. Writerly works are sharply entextualized texts, that is, formally, sharply bounded, decontextualized texts, able to be circulated in more or less the same form on the pages of *Droeba*, peasant speech is always part of a local, highly contextualized *hic et nunc*, performance (for these distinctions see for example Bauman 2004). The speech of the folk becomes writing through the service of the writer, and hence, the voice of the folk, like Lelt Ghunia, is always in quotation marks.

VI: DIALOGIC GENRES: CONVERSATIONS AND FEUILLETONS

> Whether my Moxevian spoke the truth or not I will not
> now enquire. And what business is it of mine? I merely
> mention in passing what I as a traveler heard from him.
> My one endeavor in this has been to give to his thoughts
> their own form (*peri*) and to his words his accent (*k'ilo*). If
> I have succeeded in this I have fulfilled my intention. My
> Moxevian told me much more, but for various reasons it
> would not do to write down all his conversation. . . . I will
> only say that in his own words he made me a sharer in
> his heart's woe. (Chavchavadze, *Letters of a Traveler*, VIII)

While Georgian Romantics sometimes represent the landscape of the Caucasus as a hypostasis of nature, a "natural world seemingly uninhabited by humans" (Ram and Shatirishvili 2004, 13), devoid in particular of human voices, by the 1870s the landscape described by Georgian travelers would seem incomplete without realistic transcriptions of the speech of the inhabitants, usually in the form of dialogues with the traveler himself. Practices of realistic transcription of peasant speech constitutive of the authenticity of folkloric texts (Umikashvili 1871) were also deployed by Chavchavadze that same year in his *Letters of a Traveler* (1871) to constitute the authenticity of these "dialogs with a peasant." Where Umikashvili locates the collection of folklore by transcription within a broader epistemic imperative to "get to know" the people, the genre of "dialogs with a peasant" *displays* this imperative in action. The people, after all, were not yet a public; the only way they could be addressed by the intelligentsia was in face-to-face dialogue, and the only way they could speak their minds to the intelligentsia was to have these conversations transcribed and printed in turn.

If *quoted dialogues* often taking the form of realistic portrayals of the speech of peasants formed a primary genre incorporated within the complex, heterogeneous assemblage of such genres of the secondary genre of the newspaper, it is also the case that the newspaper itself represents, as a whole, represents a kind of *quoting dialogue* between intelligentsia writers/readers of *Droeba* (I borrow this distinction from Inoue 2006, 111). *Droeba*, after all, is primarily composed of heterogeneous correspondence written by its readers. This correspondence is particularly found in the *feuilleton* section of the newspaper, forming the lower section of the page, which at least in the *Droeba* period is composed largely of occasional correspondence. All of Bavreli's correspondence, as well as much of the other material I consider in this book, including virtually *all* the examples of reported dialogues with peasants, was placed in this special, heterogeneous section of the newspaper. As we will see below in more detail, following a tendency that had long been observed in Russia (Morson 1981, 15–17, Dianina 2003ab), the feuilleton moves from denoting merely an exemplary space of heterogeneity (a specially demarcated bottom portion of a page) within an already heterogeneous whole (a newspaper) to denoting a genre in its own right, a genre in which these external relations of heterogeneity are becoming internalized and dialogized as a constitutive generic feature of the genre. So too, the perspectival dialogues between writers and readers that form the external set of relations of the newspaper become internal relations in the feuilleton, dialogized as an imagined familiar dialogue between the feuilletonist and the readership within the familiar space of the city.

What I will show in this chapter is how these two dialogic genres, dialogue and feuilleton, come to be emblematic respectively of the way the emergent intelligentsia both imagined its relation to the people as a problematic divide to be overcome by "getting to know" the people in dialogue, and the way the intelligentsia came to imagine the print public of *Droeba* as a kind of intimate dialogue between people already well-acquainted. The opposition between (transcribed) dialogue (with peasants) and feuilleton, I will argue, illustrates a shift from the "extroversion" of the intelligentsia in 1860s–1870s to the "introversion" of urban intelligentsia of the 1880–1890s. This external opposition between genres, I will show, is mirrored by the development of the feuilleton itself from a space on the printed page where dialogues with peasants can be represented ("the conversation *in* the feuilleton"), among a great many other things, to a genre in its own right dedicated to familiar, intimate dialogues between the urban intelligentsia ("the conversation *of* the feuilleton"). This parallels the way that transcription produces a serious, realistic, and embodied image of the peasant speaker that is opposed to the almost fantastic, playful disembodied image of the intelligentsia feuilletonist created by practices of pseudonymy.

Within the category of dialogues with peasants (transcribed "conversations in the feuilleton"), we will see how different possible ways of framing the relation between intelligentsia and peasant in conversation are explored: on the one hand, a transcriptive realism we have seen above which emphasizes and essentializes the alterity between the peasant and intelligentsia even as it seeks to bring these different voices together in dialogue; on the other hand, a liberal model of dialogue which instead emphasizes the substance of arguments over form and treats the status differences between peasants and aristocrats as an extrinsic historical predicament that prevents egalitarian dialogue in the present tense. The development of the feuilleton into a genre devoted to imagined dialogues between the feuilletonist and the readership (which happens relatively late in Georgia) instead draws our attention away from peasants in their villages to a self-conscious print public which is also a self-consciously urban intelligentsia. The focus of print culture in Georgia moves thus from dialogues with Orientalist strangers to dialogues with Occidentalist strangers, from the village to the city, from the peasant other to the intelligentsia self.

The very genres used to represent these two relations (both the opposition between transcription and inscription, dialogue and feuilleton) come to structure them in turn, producing finally a kind of unresolved and unresolvable contradiction between representations of the people and the public (or "society"), which are linked together by a notion of complementarity and service, but divided discursively. The sort of social totality I have been calling an "intelligentsia public" is very different from Western publics described by, for example, Taylor and Warner, which derive much of their potential for agency because they are identified with a kind of social totality (which is also understood to be sovereign in the ideal case), so much so that in English, "*the* public" is more or less understood to be the same as "*the* people" (whatever that described intentionally, which varies according to the variety of modern political imaginaries):

> *The* public is a kind of social totality. Its most common sense is that of the people in general It might be the people organized as the nation, the commonwealth,

the city, the state, or some other community. It might be very general, as in Christendom or humanity. But in each case the public, as a people, is thought to include everyone within the field in question (Warner 2002, 49).

Warner connects the way that "partial publics" can become "the public" and thence function as a proxy for "the people" to the fact that publics are self-organized and that they are indeed publics of discourse.

[T]he modern sense of the public as the social totality in fact derives much of its character from the way we understand the partial publics of discourse, like the public of this essay, as self-organized. The way *the* public functions in the public sphere—as *the people*—is only possible because it is really *a* public of discourse. (Warner 2002, 51–52)

Both Western and tsarist publics make necessary discursive reference to "the people"; what is different is how the categories of discourse and the people are related and integrated into an imagined social totality.

In Western publics, there is a conflation of discursive category of potentially unlimited address (a public) with a universal category of discourse (the public) and thence to a social totality (the people). Warner argues that some publics are more likely to be conflated with "the public" because of their own universalistic claims to discussing "the people": "Some publics . . . are more likely than others to stand in for *the* public, to frame their address as the universal discussion of the people" (Warner 2002: 82). Warner seems to equivocate here between what kind of universal discursive category "the people" are, whether they are what is *addressed* by such a public address, or whether they are what is *discussed* by such a public address. In either case, "the people" and "the public" are more or less understood to be different names for what amounts to the same referent, and that sense of referential identity is how they are constructed as being the same object.

Here is the difference: the intelligentsia public is, after all, universal like a Western public because it discusses "the people" (the object of the question "What is to be done?") in genres like ethnographic sketches or realistic descriptions of the voice of the people in dialogue. But at the same time, the "public" that is addressed, in the familiar dialogue of the feuilleton, is not imagined to include "the people" (though it is imagined to be in the service of the "people"). It is here that we find portrayals of the society of writers themselves, often playful, satirical, and always familiar or intimate. Thus, representations of the people and the public are found in different dialogic genres with opposed epistemic frameworks: realism versus satire, dialogue as an external relationship between utterances of different embodied speakers versus dialogism, dialogue as an internal relationship between writer and reader. The net result is what Herzfeld has called a "disemic" vision of a social totality divided between genres of official self-display and genres of intimate self-recognition (Herzfeld 1989, 1997), between an official representation of the national self, the people, embodied in the peasant other, captured in ethnography, realistic descriptions of dialogue and folklore, and a familiar, intimate, smiling, satirical representation of the intelligentsia self.

This disemic opposition carries over into an opposition between two kinds of conversations found in the *feuilleton*: the reported, quoted dialogue with the peasant, the framed "conversation *in* the feuilleton," and the reporting, quoting dialogue with the reader, the framing "conversation *of* the feuilleton" (Morson 1981, 20). The former "conversation *in* the feuilleton" converts the peasant not, as perhaps intended, into a dialogic partner whose voice participates in the public debate, but rather into a framed, quoted voice, a kind of set of official representations of the people, what Frierson compares to an iconostasis (1993, 6, 194), that is the matter of intelligentsia debate, but not a participant. Rather, it is the containing genre, the "conversation *of* the feuilleton" between the writer and the readership, which can be about anything, that provides the reflexive meta-position for imagining the social totality of this particular variety of print public, the standpoint that Bavreli searched for by using the fantastic figure of the new technology of flight, the aerostat, a position which allowed him to survey the people invisibly from a dizzying height.

In Georgia, as in Russia, the attempt to "close the gap between educated society and the peasantry through personal experience and shared knowledge of the village was thus a reassertion of the polarity of Russian society [sc. between 'society' and 'the people']" (Frierson 1993, 194). Like an iconostasis, Frierson argues, these images of the peasant reproduced a division like that in a church between the sanctuary and the nave, the village and the world of educated Russians, but failed to produce the desired secular equivalent of the cosmological mediation provided by an iconostasis, to mediate this divide and join these two into a single social totality (which was the goal of the Georgian discourse of "getting to know" the peasant and its Russian equivalents). If the realistic ethnographic sketch is an idealizing *iconostasis* of the peasant, then the feuilleton is more like a caricature or cartoon—a smiling, parodic voice. In fact, the urban figure of the graphomaniac writer with pretensions to literary fame, the feuilletonist, whose writings obey not the realist strictures of knowledge or truth of ethnographic, but hiding behind a pseudonym which is both a protective mask and a literary celebrity, are smiling lampoons and satires.

Boundary Work:
Conversation in the Feuilleton and Conversation of the Feuilleton

The 1870s was a time in which the impulse to "get to know" the recently emancipated people of Georgia, or later in the decade, the recently reconquered people of Ottoman Georgia, was reflected emblematically in the reportive realism of the "conversation *in* the feuilleton." By contrast, the late 1880s and 1890s was a period in which, as the feuilleton itself moved from being a space in the newspaper characterized by an endless heterogeneity of genres to being a genre of heterogeneity in its own right, this extroverted impulse for knowledge of the peasant other became instead an introspective "conversation *of* the feuilleton," a dialogue between and about the urban intelligentsia.

These two genres of conversation and definitions of *feuilleton* coexisted in *feuilleton* section of *Droeba* throughout the period of the 1880s. The first example I have found of a "boundary work," a work that stands both on the boundary between these two different epistemes (reportive realism and familiar satire) and epistemic objects (peasantry, intelligentsia), these two kinds of dialogue and two different senses of *feuilleton*, dates from 1880. By "boundary work," I mean a work that stands on the boundary of these two (admittedly exaggerated) periodizations, but also a work in which "it is uncertain which of two mutually exclusive sets of conventions governs a work . . . [where] it is possible to read the work according to different hermeneutic procedures and hence, all other things being equal, derive two contradictory interpretations" (Morson

1981, 48). This work, found in the feuilleton section of *Droeba*, 1880, number 246, at the bottom of the page separated by a black cutoff bar and labeled "Droeba Feuilleton, 21 November," and at the same time contains the word "Feuilleton" in its own title as a description of the genre: "Ajarian Feuilleton." This feuilleton is a "boundary work," a work that is a feuilleton in both the spatial and generic sense, as well as one that can be read both as a realistic, transcribed dialogue with the people and an imagined dialogue with the public, illustrating the two kinds of conversation I am talking about here, one quoted, one quoting.

In this feuilleton, the feuilletonist, writing, as feuilletonists always do, under a pseudonym (*Ucnauridze* "Stranger-son"), reports a conversation with an Ajarian Muslim Georgian. Unlike the usual member of the intelligentsia of the period, who runs chasing after a group of peasants in eagerness to know their minds and set down their words redolent with rusticity on paper, this one represents himself as minding his own business, resting under a tree, enjoying a peaceful moment of communion with nature, only to be *rudely* interrupted by the approach of an old Ottoman peasant. With mild irritation to have his reverie with nature interrupted, he reluctantly invites the peasant to take a seat beside him. When the narrator asks him what news (using the Georgian *ambavi*) he has, the Ottoman peasant complains that he, rather, should be asking the narrator for news (repeating the Georgian word *ambavi* and then substituting the Turkish word *xambari*):

> —What will you tell me, grandfather, news? What news is there among you?
> —News [*ambavi*]? You will know the *xambari* [Turkish, 'News', Georgian *ambavi*], who tells us anything, or the truth, in such godforsaken places? You read the newspapers of the world and you know everything . . . I came to you to find out the news [*xabrebi*], what is the news [*ambavi*] in the world. How goes the affairs of our Padishah, does anyone threaten him with *qavla* (*omi* ['war'])?[1]

The peasant seems to know about the universe of circulation that is denied him. This is the first sign that this is a "boundary work," a boundary condition that seems to be emblematized by the use the Georgian word *ambavi* "news" in insistent juxtaposition with the Turk-

ish synonym *xambari*. The feuilletonist responds that the peasant need
no longer detain himself with worry over his former ruler, and the talk
between them turns to whether the peasant intends *muxajirat* (emigration), again ostentatiously deploying a non-Georgian word, and if so,
why?[2] The conversation goes in this fashion, exemplifying an aesthetic
of transcriptive realism, with both of them liberally littering their speech
with Ottomanisms (almost all of which have some sort of specifically
Muslim religious referent, drawing attention not only to alterity of language but alterity of religion as well between the interlocutors), each
parenthetically glossed in Georgian.[3]

As in many such dialogues, the feuilletonist (reluctantly) assumes
the mantle of enlightener, using various arguments to try and persuade
the peasant that he should not engage in *muxajirat*. Finally, in an effort
to overcome the deference implied by the way the peasant addressed
him as *aznauro* "lord," the feuilletonist explains the new idea of egali-
tarianism, explaining, too, that he is no more than a peasant himself:

> —No no, Lord (*aznauro*), for that we have a separate
> *emri* (*brdzaneba* ['command']) from Allah, that we must
> be on the land of the Padishah.
> —Do not call me 'Lord', I am the child of a peasant
> like you, call me by my name.
> —What for, is lord a bad word? We call anyone 'lord',
> who is a great man, or respected.
> —No, grandfather, among us now it isn't like that,
> among us a lord and respected is that one, who eats
> bread won with his own sweat.
> —Hahaha! He laughed with a pained smile, if it were
> that way, we would all be lords, I don't only sweat, I wa-
> ter my fields with sweat and in this way I barely bring
> enough cornmeal bread for my *oghlu-shighi* (*col-shvili*
> ['wife and children']).[4]

In the typical manner of a transcription of an aggrieved "voice of the
people," the peasant is allowed a litany of sorrowful complaint, and the
writer finally, perhaps impatiently, asks him, "If you don't let anyone
know about your sorrow, how can anyone help you? Who knows anything about what pains you?" But this is where the conversation *in the*

feuilleton becomes instead a conversation *of* the feuilleton. Because as the peasant announced when we met with him first, "Why ask me the news? You are the one who can read newspapers, I was going to ask you that!," so too, the peasant points out, that it would be difficult to imagine anyone in the writer's public who *did not know* about their problems, "Even the frogs in the water know about our affairs and if someone wanted to help, they couldn't find out?!" No, the peasant concludes, everyone (he means "of you, the readers") knows the problem, it is just that that no one cares. The intelligentsia dialogue with the peasant, both as speaker and listener, is over: "But today they won't let us speak and there are no godly men who listen to our sorrow."[5]

This peasant seems somehow to know how much the readers know already, and the voice of the peasant moves from being a quoted voice of a conversation *in* the feuilleton to being the framing voice of the conversation *of* the feuilleton. This peasant is indeed well-informed and well-read, because, after all, the feuilleton section of *Droeba*, particularly in 1880 up to this point, was filled with reported conversations with Ottoman peasants, or otherwise reported the plight and flight of Ottoman, and specifically Ajarian, peasants.[6] This particular feuilleton is the most reflexive of these, elevating the quoted voice of the peasant to a commentary on these quoting voices, using the device of the intelligentsia dialogue with the Ottoman peasant, in effect, to comment on the *imminent demise* of the dialogue with the Ottoman peasant. It is at this point, when the peasant's accusing gaze moves out of the quoted diegetic space and looks the reader full in the face, that the feuilletonist's description of this peasant's complaint is cut short, this time not because of a recalcitrant aristocratic scribe, but with a nod to the other party of their conversation, the censor: "Aside from this the old man spoke to me about many other things, whose description I will leave off because they wouldn't be printed"[7]

On one level, this dialogue is almost an exact replication of the genre established by Chavchavadze in *Letters of a Traveler*. The parallelism of the coda of this dialogue (with a nod to the censor) with a peasant with the coda of Chavchavadze's *Letters of a Traveler* (quoted above) is striking. There, as here, there is, of course, a thorough-going commitment to realistic depiction not only of the referential content ("thoughts" and "words") but also the specificity of form attendant to each ("thoughts" take on formal specificity (*peri* "color, form") as words of dialect (mediated by the technology of footnotes, or here, as bracketed glosses), so words in turn take on a further degree of specificity through distinctive accent (k'ilo) (mediated by technologies of transcription).

There, as here, exists a hierarchical organization of faculties (Warner 2002, 89) in which rational-critical discourse is identified with the voice of the intelligentsia while the voice of the peasant is typified as a sorrowful voice of complaint, an emotional appeal to *pathos* (contrasted with the rational "enlightener" voice of the intelligentsia). The intelligentsia is interpellated by this peasant voice of complaint as, in some sense, servants of the people, people who hear the plaintive cry of the people, and who *merely* transcribe this inchoate, affect laden complaint for the public (and of course, *implicitly* translate it into a political program of action). The partners in dialogue (intelligentsia, peasant) are also parts of the social totality, which have distinct and complementary faculties (reason, woe) associated with them, resulting in a vertically organized Durkheimian "organic" solidarity of dissimilars with complementary functions, as opposed to the "mechanical" solidarity between fundamentally similar parts forming a "deep, horizontal comradeship" that is typical of the social totalities of a Western public (Anderson 1991, 7). There, as here, even this apparently neutral, objective, realistic transcription of the plight of the peasant cannot be completed, because the censor (the state) is also a party to this discourse.

But at the same time, where Chavchavadze was made into a "sharer in woe," this feuilleton is less addressed to sharing the woe of the peasant with the reader, but rather, since the readers will already know about this woe, accusing them of indifference. The end of dialogue with the peasant reflexively, metapragmatically announces the end of *all* dialogues with peasants. At the same time, as a "boundary work" (in more than one sense) it can be read as, and illustrates, two kinds of dialogue: a represented, quoted dialogue between the feuilletonist and the Ottoman peasant, and a representing, quoting dialogue, between the feuilletonist and his readers, a possibility which the writers draws attention to by titling his contribution "Ajarian *Feuilleton.*" The former dialogue represents an act of turning toward the people, a dialogue of introduction (*gacnoba*), the second dialogue represents this as, in fact, a turning away from the people, a dialogue of farewell. What begins as an apparent exercise in realism, "getting to know" the Ottoman people, ends as a muted satirical critique of the intelligentsia, part of a dialogue with the readers of *Droeba*, accusing them of indifference to "getting to know" the peasant (illustrated, indeed, by the indifference, even mild irritation, of the narrator that he is forced to interrupt his reverie with nature to have this dialogue at all).

Liberal Dialogues:
Arguments about Equality and the Equality of Arguments
While Chavchavadze's *Letters of a Traveler* (1871) was perhaps the most influential model of realism applied to dialogue with a peasant, it was not, in fact, the first time either the device of travel letters, nor the device of dialogue between a member of the proto-intelligentsia and a member of the peasantry, had been used in this way. In the second year of *Droeba* (1867), on the very eve of the belated and drawn-out emancipation of the peasants in West Georgia (1865–1871), another writer had used the device of traveler letters and dialogue to explore these issues. The author of this letter was the Western-educated liberal writer Giorgi Tsereteli (writing anonymously), Georgia's "first professional journalist" and editor of many radical Georgian newspapers, including the founding editor of *Droeba* itself from 1866 to 1869 (Jones 2005, 39). Tsereteli was a member of the "second generation" (*meore dasi*) of *terg-daleuli* intelligentsia (following a genealogy proposed by Tsereteli himself) (Jones 2005, 37–8), referring to themselves as the *axali axalgazrdoba* ("the New Youth), which broke with the more conservative "first generation" *terg-daleuli* gentry nationalists like Chavchavadze in the Emancipation period (Suny 1988, 131, see Jones 2005 for Tsereteli's changing political position across multiple generations of Georgian politics).

The place of travel for these "travel letters" was West Georgia, including Imereti, Svaneti, and Mingrelia, and the author, unlike Chavchavadze, is not traveling a familiar terrain densely populated with the voices of other writers, however, he is traveling a terrain populated with the voices of nobles and peasants, with much to talk about. However, unlike the speech of Lelt Ghunia, which is so overwhelmingly clothed in "qualities of presence" that at times it becomes impossible to decipher, here the peasant speech, at least in its outward form, is no more or less intelligible with its Imeretian dialectisms than that of their noble interlocutors. The emphasis is not on the difficulty produced by formal alterity or authenticity of their speech, nor even on their voice as an inchoate affect-laden cry of woe and sorrow, but rather, an almost Habermasian concern for the referential content of arguments, what arguments can be made, and what arguments cannot be made, under what conditions, the difficulty of achieving egalitarian dialogue when the partners in the dialogue are not equals.

The world reported in these letters, written on the eve of the end of seugneurial Georgia, is one in which status differences between peasant and aristocrat registered in outward embodied signs, especially clothing, are of the foremost importance. Clothing also forms an important topic of conversation between Chavchavadze and Ghunia, there Ghunia prefers *Georgian* clothing to European clothing as an "outer" "visible" sign of "inner" "invisible" Georgianness: "In Russian dress a Georgian becomes a foreigner." For the narrator here, however, European clothing is preferable to Georgian clothing, preferable precisely because it displays at a glance the difference between noble and peasant. The political differences between Chavchavadze and Tsereteli can be seen in the semiotic value of European clothing: for Chavchavadze the semiotic value of clothing is located in the national question and demarcates national difference (Russian/Georgian), while for Tsereteli it is located in the social question and demarcates status difference (noble/peasant). Our author, an impoverished son of the gentry, is dressed badly: "I was dressed in a soiled white *choxa* [a distinctive Caucasian coat] of worsted wool." His filthy white *choxa*, like the fact that his mount is an old donkey, shows that he is gentry on the skids, potentially mistaken for a peasant. As for his companions, he briefly describes their much more respectable dress, with an apology to the reader as to why such picayune details are important:

> Gigoliki was dressed in European clothing, and Chikoliki was wearing a red-collared *Sartuki* [Russian-style shirt]. Don't you wonder that I am talking about such trivial matters as these!—but inasmuch as they evaluate the man by his clothing here, for that reason it is not possible that I would not have said anything about it; all the more, because my poor clothing, as one from a lineage of boaster aristocrats, made me undergo considerable humiliation. In this region if someone is dressed in a European fashion, they will immediately conclude, 'this one must be without a doubt someone high-ranking.'[8]

Clothing determines how you will be treated, in particular, what kind of hospitality you will receive as a traveler. If you are dressed well, particularly if you are dressed in European style, you will be recognized as a person of importance, shown respect and housed with a good host, "But if you are dressed in our fashion, simply [*ubralod*] and they recognize you as a simple person [*ubralo* in the sense of 'of low estate']," then God help you, they will claim no one is in and send you on your way to some other house: "In such circumstances, it is no wonder, that European clothing has great significance . . ."[9]

He is treated no better, or even worse, by some of his noble traveling companions on this account. Even one of his traveling companions, an Imeretian nobleman with the pseudonym Kudabzika (a nickname derived from a term which basically means a "stuck up but on the skids" member of the gentry), who is riding a somewhat ratty horse, in principle no better than this own mount, is unhappy to be riding next to him, even though he knows him to be of aristocratic descent. He says nothing, because he knows our author is a noble like himself dressed as a peasant, but our writer can read his thoughts and recognizes his irritation and distaste to be seen riding next to someone dressed like a peasant.[10] In fact, very little of what transpires between him and Kudabzika is registered in terms of actual speech, but is rather, like the "conversation *of* the feuilleton," an imagined, imputed dialogue based on intimate familiarity (very similar to the sort of intimate familiarity that Warner sees between the intimate strangers of a Western public). Our writer, based on his own intimate knowledge via membership in Imeretian nobility, comfortably populates Kudabzika's mind with insults unspoken, just as our writer records his own imagined retorts and other redressive actions that would be possible if he were dressed properly. Kudabzika cannot speak his insults directly and cannot call the writer a "peasant" (based on his dress) as he would like, because he knows the writer to be an aristocrat like himself. The writer, on the contrary, feels the implied insults as an aristocrat but cannot reply or take umbrage openly, because he *is* dressed as a peasant. The discord between their appearances is the occasion for their imagined dialogue, their shared status as aristocrats is both what permits it to be imagined and what prevents it from being openly articulated in words. Their conversation is a silent one of imagined slights and imagined retorts.

How different then, are the many open conversations they have with the peasants. The first conversation begins as an attempt by an aristocratic guest to repay the peasant host's hospitality in food with words, specifically information about the coming emancipation. During their conversation that evening (before dinner) we learn, among other things, that Chikoliki, the leader of this band of travelers, is a blowhard who likes to talk about, indeed praise, the ideas and works of European authors he has never read, but has only read *about* in Russian journals and gazettes, and all this in extremely stilted and pedantic language. Summarizing at some length both Chikoliki's posturing and the more general malaise he represents, namely, the false sense of enlightenment and knowledge that comes from reading not the European authors themselves, but only reading a brief review of that author in a Russian gazette, represents a good half of this long letter. Having concluded that while perhaps in the future genuine knowledge and (European) enlightenment will arrive in Georgia, he contents himself with the observation that "For the time being, we are all Chikolikis."[11]

But the fact that Chikoliki is a blowhard who likes to hear himself talk about things he knows of only secondhand is indeed an important part of the context for the first after-dinner conversation. Chikoliki likes to talk, and after being served a tasty meal, he wants to pay the host back in kind, "if not in deeds, at least in words." This was an area in which Chikoliki excelled: particularly inasmuch as he knew that the question of emancipation was very much of interest to the locals, and it was something about which they hungered for information: "They awaited the arrival of these changes impatiently, as a small child awaits Easter." Chikoliki, then, desirous of repaying his host's hospitality with words, "for this reason he began to talk about the emancipation of the peasants," announcing to the brother of his host that this would happen within the space of a year.

The attempt at egalitarian conversation, seeking to achieve reciprocity between guest and host by imparting useful information, cannot overcome the traditions of deference between aristocrat and serf. This man, Merekipe, is obviously pleased by this news but strains to hide his involuntary smile from his guests, and eventually with some effort controls himself, managing to replace the involuntary smile with a grimace of pain. Instead of expressing joy, he begins to complain that the end of serfdom will be a disaster. To each of Chikoliki's arguments that it will improve the lot of the peasantry, he instead foretells a story of gloom and doom. His reaction, of course, is partially because he wants more information and partially out of deference to his guest, whom he knows to be of aristocratic background: "He began to oppose Chikoliki on this matter because he wanted him to tell him more news, and at the same time he also knew, that Chikoliki was one of the masters and he was buttering him up."[12] Finally, having met Chikoliki's confident predictions with one prophecy of doom and gloom after another, he concludes that at least "a man who has a good lord at least is protected from his enemies": "with these words he pretended to announce his grief at the end of serfdom; but it appeared from his happy face, that if Chikoliki and Zigoliki had not been there, he would have danced in the (Cossack style) lekur-bukna style." Somehow this mutual attempt at deference and ingratiation between guest and host, aristocrat and serf, ends up in a disagreement. Meanwhile, inspired by the topic, as if to illustrate the decisive role of status, two other peasants at the other end of the table manage to have an egalitarian conversational disagreement as to whether the replacement of direct seigneurial rule with the rule of government officials will be beneficial or disastrous, a conversation in which they take diametrically opposed positions and which *also* descends rapidly into name-calling.

Chikoliki's conversational foray, significantly, is part of an attempt to achieve reciprocity with his generous peasant host, his host having assuaged their hunger with good food, he hopes to assuage the peasant's hunger for good news. In this respect, Chikoliki is unlike other aristocratic guests of his time, for like one-sided conversations, so too one-sided hospitality is characteristic of the relationship between aristocratic guest and peasant host in pre-emancipation Western Georgia. Precisely this historical lack of reciprocity confronts them as a practical and actual problem in the next village, the village of Zubi. Zubi is a village that belonged to the D___ni family (almost certainly the major noble lineage Dadiani), who had apparently also been frequent, and rapacious, guests of the villagers:

> [The lord D__ni] would come usually with forty, sometimes sixty, mounted men and a horde of people of this size would stay for two weeks or even a month. It was clear on the face of the Xelosani [village headman],

how much an occasion for happiness was the coming of D__ni. . . . The xelosani of Zubi loved his merciful lord, much as a goat loves a wolf. It is not to be wondered that he was none too happy about our own guesthood, for he expected from us the same sort of mercy, as from his own lord.[13]

The hostility to these potentially rapacious aristocratic guests only changes when a smiling Chikoliki promises that he will repay their hospitality in turn "then the xelosani cheered up and swiftly found us everything we needed."

The theme of status inequality being registered in inequality of hospitality and conversation appears later, in the final letter, when a local member of the aristocracy (Bakura) meets his equal, a man, Giorgi the Svan, from the one area of Georgia that had always been "free": upper or "free Svaneti." The Svans are a high mountain-dwelling group speaking a language related to, but not mutually unintelligible with, Georgian, and within the next decade of *Droeba* Svans will quickly become a byword of obstinate backwardness and cultural alterity (a tendency found to this day in Georgia, where Svans are the protagonists of all jokes involving backwardness, barbarousness, and stupidity). This essentializing tendency to present Svans in terms of natural alterity is to some extent already present here in this piece, as Tsereteli likens the natural temperament of the Svans to the expressive properties of Enguri River, on whose banks in the laps of the mountains the Svans have settled the communes of "Free Svaneti": "The Svans are of the same sort of angry and savage nature, as the roaring Enguri River itself."[14] Like the rest of his people, Giorgi the Svan is a free, proud man, but also perhaps more than a little "savage" (*veluri*) in looks and in personal habits (if the meat runs out, he sits down to eat the bones).

He openly shows his dislike for a young and equally proud local aristocrat named Bakura. Bakura is a listless young man of prodigious drinking capacity, one of those aristocrats who, though he has plenty of wine and food awaiting him at home, always manages to sniff out which peasant house is entertaining a guest, and as a matter of aristocratic privilege, always enlists himself as a sort of lieutenant host on the guest list: "perhaps he felt in his heart that the ill-mannered peasants cannot hold up their end in a proper conversation with a respectable guest, 'therefore my presence there is required, that my courteous guest will not become bored.'"[15] Giorgi, as a proud, free Svan takes an instant dislike to this arrogant young noble leech, Bakura, and because he wishes to convey this distaste, he seats himself next to Bakura at the table, which he knows Bakura will not like, and hopes to enrage him with words.

> 'Alas, the lords really made a mistake when they freed the peasants. Now you have to hoe and do everything by hand yourselves.' These words were like thorns in the heart of Lord Bakura. He glared at Giorgi the Svan, looked to the side, spread out his hands and fiercely cried out: 'Look now at this goiter-afflicted Svan [Svans are conventionally associated with this affliction because of salt shortage]! Who asked your opinion about the emancipation of the peasants? . . .'
>
> —Yes yes!—Giorgi the Svan is a very freedom-loving man—Chikoliki cried out with a smile—He feels pain in his heart for the peasants, since he himself is free in his own land.
>
> —That torn choxa and those muddy feet don't seem like freedom. Everyone has that kind of freedom. He is not free, our peasants are better than a goitrous Svan.
>
> —Yeah, just because you are a lord [*aznauri*], how are you better. In my country I am an *mdivanbegi* [chief judge].
>
> —Yes, Yes. I have him as my *mdivanbegi*. Chikoliki cried out, pleased with himself.
>
> —If you were among us, if you were guilty of some offense, I would make you leave off that nobility of yours, I would catch you and lead you along in chains to the police captain—Giorgi the Svan told Bakura, laughing at him.[16]

This conversation does not get into the substance of the issue at hand, the emancipation of the serfs; that conversation can only happen between aristocratic peers secluded in the garden afterward. This is a conversation about the very possibility of a conversation between a lord and a peasant, albeit a free one, about this, or anything else. It all ends badly, Bakura storms off, and after Kudabzika's further attempt to have a conversation between peers with him about the emancipation in the courtyard, the whole thing ends in mutual name-calling, threats of violence, and nearly comes to blows. At the end, the peasant Giorgi is pleased he has gotten rid of the hateful aristocratic guest, but the visiting aristocrats decide it is time to high-tail it out of the village entirely, which is where this set of travel letters ends.

Taken as a whole, the point of each of these conversations is didactic; they are in effect a set of sophistic displays, represented by realistic conversations, designed to lay out the various arguments, pro and con, for different positions. They are not as much *dialogues* as *dissoi logoi*, a Greek sophistic practice, exemplified for example in Thucydides's *History*, in which for any given position two possible different opposing antinomic arguments are laid out. These are *interested* positions, so these arguments are associated with the sort of person (and attendant status attributes) who would make them in which kinds of contexts. Status inequalities or equality between conversational partners in turn become the metapragmatic theme of arguments, not because, as in Chavchavadze's *Letters*, they are registered in the *form* of the utterances, but because they are politically structuring conditions of the very possibility of dialogue: a peasant might not make the argument they wanted out of deference to an aristocratic guest, or might begin such an argument in order to please someone else or irritate someone. Because of the way they unravel and turn into fights, these conversations also remind us of what a precarious accomplishment is the newly won equality between lord and peasant, whether in matters of reciprocity between host and guest or in conversation. Attempts by Chikoliki to please his peasant host by news of emancipation run up against an impenetrable wall of seigneurial deference, while Bakura's aggressive and angry reaction to Giorgi the Svan's nettlesome remarks about the consequences of emancipation for the aristocracy remind us that such deferential behavior in the first conversation is not merely some habit of mind, but born in part out of fear of noble retribution. Conversation is represented in terms of its precariousness, in relation to deference and hospitality as well as in relation to the danger that it might descend into violence, even between status equals, let alone between lords and peasants, both those about to be freed, and those who have always been free.

The differences of representation of dialogue in Tsereteli's *Travel Letters* and Chavchavadze's *Letters of a Traveler*, composed independently in the same period, strikingly diagrams the political opposition between the liberalism of Tsereteli and the "new youth" and the sort of "Merrie Georgia" gentry nationalism of Chavchavadze and the *Tergdaleuli* movement (Suny 1988, 129, see also Jones 2005, 38–39).[17] In Chavchavadze's *Letters of a Traveler,* there is a clear opposition between the folklorized speech of Lelt Ghunia and his modest transcriber, Ilia Chavchavadze. In Tsereteli's *Travel Letters,* there is essentially no difference between the speech of nobles, peasants, or indeed, the style of the narrator: Imeretian dialect prevails in the speech of all and sundry, and the device of the footnote is used as much to gloss the narrative text as noble or peasant dialogue. The differences between estates are not so much indexed in their embodied voice as in their embodied status (clothing, for example) that prevents them from being equal conversational partners. Unlike the realism of portrayal of the alterity of peasant speech in Chavchavadze's *Letters of a Traveler,* there is here no essentialized division between the embodied speech of the peasant, with nonstandard form and crawling with diacritics emblematic of its status as transcribed speech, and virtually identical voice/writing of the narrator, which both converses with, and comments upon, this subsumed folkloric voice of the peasant. In this sense, the dialogism of these letters might well be called a kind of "liberal" narrative of dialogue, in which status difference between aristocrat and peasant affects not the *form* of the utterance, but rather, the referential *content,* the political *conditions of possibility of enunciation.* In a similar way, clothing is not important because it expresses *national specificity of form* (as it is for Ghunia), but because it constitutes a visible sign of a social status that is an enabling condition for participation in such dialogue as an equal.

In a sense, the model of conversation in Tsereteli's *Travel Letters* is a familiar one within Western discourse, from Renaissance humanism to Habermas, in which conversation is treated as a model of political deliberation (Remer 2000, 2008). Tsereteli's conversations show, for example, the importance of freedom and equality of the participants in conversation (conversations are only possible between peers; between nonpeers, they become distorted). They also show the importance of the absence of coercion, not merely that of actual threats and violence, but also *ethos* (the status differential between aristocrat and peasant) but also *pathos* (strong emotions, particularly anger which leads to violence). Where deliberation does occur between peers (for example, between Kudabzika and the Bakura), the author attempts to present the arguments as being rationally motivated in terms of interests and not passions, though the fact of disagreement then leads to violent altercations (see Remer 2000, 2008). The historical predicament Tsereteli illustrates is one where the ideal model of conversation as deliberation can be enacted nowhere because of the pervasive distortions of extrinsic factors (*ethos, pathos*) that typify the historical "given conditions." At the same time, he preserves an essentially liberal model of conversation in which *ethos* or *pathos* are extrinsic, coercive, and distorting historical contextual factors which prevent the essential features of conversation as free, unconstrained, rational deliberation (about the end of serfdom) between free and equal, interested individuals from being realized.

By contrast, the model of "conversations with the peasant" of Chavchavadze's *Letters of a Traveler* and after does not serve as a model of rational, free, and egalitarian liberal political deliberation *a la* Habermas (on which, see Remer 2000, 2008). Nor again does it reflect a model of publics that are imagined as being in effect an intertextual enactment of such a dialogue (on the misrecognition involved in pervasive metaphors of publics as "conversation," see Warner [2002, 62–3, 68, 82–3] for an insightful critique). One important difference is the distinct role of *ethos* and especially *pathos*, which forms play an organic constitutive role in Chavchavadze's "conservative" dialogues (the rational intelligentsia becomes a "sharer in woe") and an extrinsic, distorting role in "liberal dialogues." In the former there is a linkage of the *pathos* of the people to intelligentsia action, which is very different from deliberative models of conversation, as Remer argues:

> Even if you argue that decisions should be arrived at rationally, the impetus to act on your decision usually involves pathos. Accordingly, because political debate was destined to conclude in action, classical rhetoricians included the passions in deliberative oratory. Theorists of deliberative democracy, however, escape the link between emotions and action by de-emphasizing the role of action. Political debate, they imply, is about discussion, but this discussion need not culminate in activity. (Remer 2008, 192)

Thus, the political moment of affect-laden conversations with peasants is predicated on an essential division and complementarity between the fully embodied, affect-laden urgency of the appeal of the peasant (containing both rhetorical appeals to *ethos* and *pathos* that are anathema to any liberal model of conversation, see Remer 2000, 2008), and the rational transcribing voice of the intelligentsia, who comes to understand the life and plight of the peasant and is moved to act. The way a hierarchical complementarity is established between popular affect (the transcribed voice of the peasant) and public reason (the transcribing voice of the intelligentsia) which are brought together in dialogue and within a single social totality in print should be contrasted with the way the same hierarchy of faculties between rational-critical faculties (elevated to universal attributes of humanity that allows discourse characterized by these properties to be treated as public or general) and (personal, private, or particular) embodied-affective ones, constitutes instead the opposition between Western publics and counterpublics (Warner 2002, 83–84, 89).

The orientation is not to dialogue as being self-valuable expression (as in models of conversational political deliberation (Remer 2000, 2008)) and publics that are imagined on the model of such dialogues (Taylor 2002, Warner 2002), but contains a certain urgency, an orientation toward action, toward "What is to be done?" The discursive complementarity between the aggrieved voice of the peasant and the rational intelligentsia much more closely resembles, for example, the way that the affect-laden *pathos* of feminine practices of ritual wailing in the Caucasus act unofficially as a kind of spur to action in men's political deliberations in politics of blood vengeance (for comparable oppositions in Ancient and Modern Greece, see, for example, Loraux 1986, 1998, Holst-Warhaft 1992, chapters 3–4, Seremaṭakis 1991, chapter 7).[18]

Conservative Dialogues:
Realistic Dialogue and the Alterity of the Voice of the Peasant

By contrast, after 1871, with the example of Chavchavadze's dialogues with Lelt Ghunia before them, and the strict injunctions of Umikashvili to transcribe the speech of the peasant precisely and authentically, representing the outer tradition garb of speech, the *form and color of peasant speech*, becomes as obligatory as representing the *thoughts* and *words*. The peasant was to be known through dialogues, indeed, the very process of "getting to know" (*gacnoba*) the peasant in general was best displayed by dialogues illustrating a specific instance of getting to know a peasant (usually beginning from a mutual exchange of greetings), in which the process of mutual recognition (including initial *mis*recognition) is often dramatized. In this period of the hegemony of an aesthetics and episteme of realism (which applied, of course, disproportionately to the representation of "the people" [see Frierson 1993]), represented dialogues needed to reproduce as much as possible the authentic embodied properties of peasant speech just as much as a folkloric text. Here Georgian writers (like their Japanese equivalents discussed by Inoue) "faced the stylistic question of how to entextualize linguistic excess, the sheer physicality and materiality of the human voice" (Inoue 2006, 85). This representation of this "linguistic excess" required development of a whole typographic technology of representation of the indexical, nonreferential material surplus of embodied speech, and borrowed heavily from the methodological strictures in folklore laid out by Umikashvili (1871) or the concrete example of the textual practices of Chavchavadze (1871).

The imperative for realistic portrayal of this linguistic excess, transcriptive realism, in some cases, ran up against the problem of unintelligibility, particularly among the even more unfamiliar peasants of Ottoman Georgia. Voloshinov comments with respect to the new taste for a "pictorial style" in representation of speech in nineteenth-century realism that the nonreferential indexical aspects of authentic character speech could render the referential content almost unintelligible, a tendency we certainly see in Chavchavadze's obsessive transcription of Ghunia's speech, where, as in the speech of Gogol's characters "character's speech sometimes loses almost all its referential meaning and becomes decor instead, on a par with clothing, appearance, furnishings, etc." (Voloshinov 1986, 121). This was a typical dilemma: one writer who reproduces many such conversations with Ottoman Georgian peasants, but without attending to the form of their dialect, begins his transcription of such a dialogue (which, of course, begins at the very beginning, with an exchange of greetings) with a note apologizing for and explaining their absence; the distance between their speech and his readers is simply too great to be represented.

*) I beg the pardon from the reader, if I cannot report what the local people said in that dialect, the dialect [*kilo*] they were speaking, that is, the *ma iulur* dialect. They mix in a lot of Imeretian and Tatar words in their speech.[19]

Bavreli is generally quite assiduous in attempting to represent the speech of Ottoman populations. Since the lexical differences that need to be glossed are so many, he dispenses with the cumbersome device of footnotes used by Chavchavadze and simply inserts the Georgian gloss in parentheses (. . .) after each unfamiliar word (a device also used by Tsereteli to gloss Imeretisms in dialogue and narrative alike). For example, in one of a series of utterly banal conversations in a village where they stop at a *qavaxana* for the evening on their boat ride down the Choroxi, he talks to two boys who are playing. It seems the only purpose of the conversation is to show the alterity of their speech:

—What is it that you have in your hands?
  —*aia-oxia* (*shvild-isari* [a bow and arrows])
  —What do you want it for?
  —*qushi unda movk'la* (*prinveli unda movk'la* [I want to kill birds])[20]

Bavreli's writings are littered with transcriptions of Tatar, Russian, Ossetian, Armenian, and Kurdish speech, partially attesting to his own multilingual repertoire. Bavreli's nearly endless transcriptions of diverse forms of Ottoman speech answer to demand for realism, answered by the painstaking and frequent representation of dialogue, as part of a desire to "get to know the peasant" to overcome the imagined gap between literate society and the illiterate folk in the early 1870s in both Russia and Georgia (Paperno 1988, Frierson 1993), and the even greater gap between Russian and Ottoman Georgians at the end of the decade. In sharp contrast to the stance Tsereteli in the 1860s, who presumes a stance of existing familiarity and freely imputes hidden motives, left unsaid but perhaps expressed in nonverbal ways, to aristocratic and peasant others, the peasant is presumed to be unfamiliar and can be known only by the words actually spoken. Such realism based on external description of speech can reinforce the pervasive sense of unknowable alterity of the other. As Layton comments in her discussion of Tolstoy's realistic representations of mountain tribesmen, in revolt against the way that his Romantic predecessors like Marlinskii freely populated their "fiery tribal surrogates" with familiar knowable internal states, the description of Tolstoy confines itself to external facticity (including a new attention to the realistic description of tribesman speech using devices like pidgin Russian and interpreters): "The tribesman's mind remains *terra incognita* for the author . . ." (Layton 1994, 248)

The realistic transcriptions of peasant voices, but particularly in the case of Ottoman speech, increasingly emphasize the alterity of that speech, and by extension, the alterity of the speakers. In the process of realistic transcription of form, the clear transcription of the open challenge to the aristocratic order represented by the articulate free peasant Giorgi the Svan in the 1860s becomes concealed behind an almost Aesopian language of realism of form in the speech of Lelt Ghunia. As Inoue comments with respect to the transcription of schoolgirl speech in early modern Japan "reducing the cultural significance of [schoolgirl] speech to its nonreferential aspect denies and repressed her *referential* voice, her will to mean and signify something in a rational manner. This is precisely a way of turning her speech into a 'fable'—she is speaking, but she does not know what she is saying. . . . Alterity is, thus, tamed and contained not by being silenced but on the contrary by being allowed to be loquacious" (Inoue 2006, 54). In turn, the peasant finds in the voice of his intelligentsia dialogic partner a voice that is constructed as having all the opposite properties, a spoken voice essentially identical to the written voice of the narrator, a metalinguistic, reporting, quoting voice (representating a hegemonic "authority of anonymity") rather than a linguistic, reported, quoted voice (representing a subaltern "authority of authenticity"). Inoue's discussion of a homologous process in Japanese modernity is worth comparing:

> In more concrete terms, the new narrating voice functioned at the metalinguistic level to signal that whatever it narrates, reports, describes, represents and states is true, real, serious and credible, and that it speaks not from a particular individual's point of view, but from the point of view of the modern rational and national (male) citizen—an omniscient point of view that purports not

to be a point of view at all. This metalinguistic function
was facilitated by formal (and diacritic) devices that
separate the narrating voice and the narrated—whether
it be people, events or things. Translating and appropriating the Western realist novel required . . . writers
to develop subordinated linguistic space in the form
of dialogue and reported speech. This is a formal space
where *alterity* is constructed, highlighted, and neatly
kept apart from the self. (Inoue 2006, 92)

However, in the post-Emancipation period in Georgia, the device of
realistic dialogue in this case is also motivated by a certain basic *narodnik*
impetus (on which, more generally, see Paperno 1988, Frierson 1993,
38–47); it both constructs and highlights the alterity of the dialogic
other, but it also represents a "going to the people," an attempt to overcome this alterity *in dialogue*. While the narrator does not usually adopt
native garb in clothing or in speech (though in conversations with the
even more "other" Ottoman Georgians, both Bavreli and other authors
freely adopt or use Ottomanisms in their speech, indexing, along with
their translations, their own multilingualism that enables their mediating role), the very act of placing themselves within the dialogue with the
peasant allows the egalitarian writer to step down from their Parnassian
metalinguistic heights and slum with the peasant in dialogue, moving
from being the quoting footnoting voice of the folklorist to being one of
the quoted (albeit not footnoted) voices in a dialogue. The peasant and
the writer do not speak in the same voice, but the copresence of these
different voices in the present tense of dialogue at least illustrates that
they share the same time and space of Georgian modernity, an egalitarian move which serves to more strikingly illustrate their material
inequality within that order.[21]

Strictly Entre Nous:
The Familiar Dialogue of the Intelligentsia Feuilleton

While the simultaneous consumption of the modern newspaper as print
commodity, the "one-day best seller," imagined by Anderson expresses
the sense of contemporaneity and reciprocity of perspectives between
readers (Anderson 1991, 35), a newspaper like *Droeba* was the expres-

sion of a public of readers who were also writers; most of the content of *Droeba* ultimately is written by its readers in the form of correspondence from different localities. Correspondence, both produced and consumed by the public, which forms the bulk of the newspaper and its characteristic genre, is a figure for the space-time of the newspaper's circulation, the way a newspaper assembles reports from distinct and possibly distant localities into a single space-time of contemporaneous newspaper consumers. But it is also a figure for the way the public of the newspaper is produced by readers in different localities who are also writers, whose writings always dialogic in that they anticipate a response from the other readers. Thus, the newspaper *Droeba* was a dialogic form as a whole, expressing a dialogue between readers who were also writers, a kind of dialogism typified initially by the genre of correspondence.

Anderson's classic account also emphasizes the way a newspaper as a genre creates an indexical icon of a homogeneous space-time of circulation by indifferently juxtaposing reports about distant contemporaneous events on a single page, the "imagined linkage" between them mediated temporally by calendrical coincidence of the events and spatially by the circulation of the newspaper within the space of a market (Anderson 1991, 33). But my focus on the centrality of correspondence to *Droeba* suggests that the space-time of circulation of such a newspaper is not internally homogeneous, and the space-times of *Droeba* are in part imagined on the basis of the uneven ground of the problematic material infrastructures, the channels, that mediate them. The newspaper is not only a kind of purely sociological assemblage of human voices, letters, and other correspondence; the genres of the newspaper also point to a sociotechnical assemblage of the various human and nonhuman, social, and technological actants (Latour 1992, 2005) that are combined into the "blackbox" of the finished product.

Infrastructures or channels of communication external to the newspaper become names for genres internal to the newspaper, each corresponding to a specific and distinct imagined space-time of circulation. I have already discussed two examples of this, correspondence and telegram. Correspondence, even if it was not specifically *about* roads and roadlessness (and this latter category was always topical), reminded the reader by its very existence of a spotty infrastructural network of the postal network, roads, and railways, as well as Ossetian postal riders and trains, from which it takes its name. Partly by virtue of the reflexivity of correspondence about its own infrastructural conditions of possibility, correspondence moves from denoting, in effect, a material infrastructural *channel* (answering the question of how this piece of writing arrived to be printed) to being treated as a characteristic *genre* of the newspaper, typically named as such and allocated its own specific space on the newspaper page, which points to an imagined local circulatory space-time of rural localities connected by this infrastructure. So too, the "telegram," usually printed on the upper left-hand side of the front page (see figure 5 above), is another genre named after an infrastructural channel which affords the imagining of still broader imperial and cosmopolitan space-times of circulation beyond the horizons of the local sphere mediated by correspondence.

Alongside these two space-times of circulation, the local or national (correspondence) and cosmopolitan (telegram), we find other genres in the heterogeneous assemblage of the newspaper pointing to other space-times of circulation. Announcements and advertisements for theatrical evenings in Tbilisi, occupying the same space on the printed page as telegrams, reminds us that the anonymous public of *Droeba* is also a largely urban aristocratic society (the other sense of *sazogadoeba*), anonymous contemporaries who are always potentially known face-to-face consociates in the infrastructure of public sociability represented by the city and it theaters, cafés, and streets. Needless to say, this usually invisible world of the readers of *Droeba* is imagined in implicit or explicit contrast to the largely rural world mediated by correspondence. This is the world, after all, that Bavreli imagines as being equivalent to "that world" (the afterlife) when he is mired in the infrastructural limbo of Ardanuji.

The genre most characteristic of the space-time of the city, in contrast to the largely rural space-time of correspondence, is the *feuilleton*, a term whose changing meaning in this period illustrates a parallel transition from infrastructure to genre, channel to message similar to that found with correspondence. Originally, the feuilleton might be regarded as belonging rather more to the material, infrastructural order of the channel, it simply denotes a space in the newspaper dedicated to the heterogeneity of correspondence to the newspaper. The feuilleton quickly develops from a space for messages of heterogeneous genres to being a genre in its own right, a genre that is internally characterized by heterogenelty. In the *space* of the feuilleton, therefore, among all the various genres that might appear (including novels, poems, and other genres), two distinct *genres* pointing to different imagined space-times of circulation jostle with each other from the 1870s to 1890s. The earlier of these, characteristic of the 1870s, is the genre of correspondence, a genre associated with the imagined space-time of rural Georgia, whose object is transcription or description of the rural people ("conversations *in* the feuilleton"). The later of these, characteristic of the 1880s to 1890s, is the *genre* of the *feuilleton*, a genre pointing to the emerging sense of a space-time of the city, a heterogeneous genre devoted to an equally heterogeneous object, whose object is an intimate dialogue between the urban intelligentsia ("conversations *of* the feuilleton").

As in Russia, the feuilleton originally designated a space at the bottom of the page, below a cutoff line, where virtually any sort of correspondence, in any genre, might be printed (Dianina 2003b, 254–5). From here, it became a genre unto itself, characterized by an internalized heterogeneity and satirical, "smiling voice," "predicated on a certain social intimacy between author and reader" (Dianina 2003a, 204), registering a familiar dialogic rapport within the intelligentsia:

> Originally a journalistic miscellany in which disconnected items of the city's cultural life were presented, the feuilleton gradually became tied together by the loose and whimsical transitions of a digressive persona wandering from topic to topic—and sometimes, in the conventional role of flaneur, from place to place as well. The genre's subject matter was characteristically broad—so broad, indeed, that the problematic unity of the feuilleton because a theme for both feuilletonist and their critics (who sometimes attacked feuilletons in feuilletons). 'It is not necessary to explain what a feuilleton is,' observed one author . . . (1843) 'Everyone knows what it is. A feuilleton is everything: theatrical reviews, stories, anecdotes, the chatter of drawing rooms, all kinds of odds and ends, a table laid with every type of excellent little things' . . . As this heterogeneous list implies, almost the only topics excluded from the feuilleton were political ones forbidden by the censor—and so 'Aesopian' hints at the censorship came to have a place

in this genre's testing of its ill-defined limits. (Morson
1981, 16)

All of these developments happened much earlier in Russia than in
Georgia. The question arises: Why does this kind of intimate discourse,
which could have been borrowed from the Russian example from the
very start, seem to begin so late in Georgian newspapers? The feuilleton
is, after all, an *urban* genre, in it is expressed the imagined community
of the city, and thus, in order to understand its development, we need
to look to the city of Tbilisi itself. Because the possibility of imagining
an *intimate* conversation with a readership emerges when the proper
historical "given conditions" have been achieved locally, that is, when a
generation of readers have "grown old together" to form a reading community, when a city like Tbilisi and the intelligentsia has developed a
large and sophisticated enough reading society and enough social events
and locales beyond the life of the courtly circles to merit a flaneuresque
appreciation. Certainly, this was a period in which Tbilisi was growing
by leaps and bounds, its population growing from 78, 500 in the 1880s
to 160,000 by 1897 (the population of Kutaisi in the Kutaisi *guberniia*
[West Georgia] was at this time only 32, 492, Batumi 28, 512). By the
end of the century, almost a quarter of the Tiflis *guberniia* (East Georgia)
lived in Tbilisi itself, while in "backward" West Georgia only about 9 percent of the population lived in cities (Jones 2005, 13). It was precisely
in this period that Tbilisi developed into the home of a self-conscious
urban intelligentsia, which evolved its own specific urban mythology
and urban genres of self-representation including the feuilleton (Manning and Shatirishvili 2011).

Of course, "given conditions" do not translate into social imaginaries
automatically, there must be not only circulation, but also a reflexive
imagining of that circulation. And who would be more qualified to imagine the development of the conditions of possibility of the urban discourse of the feuilleton than a feuilletonist? In a feuilleton on "Georgian
literature [our enemies and friends],"[22] the well-known feuilletonist
Sano begins by asking his readers to recall the Georgian print culture of
the 1870s, when universe of discourse of Georgian society (*sazogadoeba*)
was much smaller. This was a period when the readership was still in its
"apprenticeship," and dialogues happened between different writers in
the press, as well as between readers in anticipation of the next install-

ment of writerly dialogue, but the conditions did not yet exist for the internal dialogue between the feuilletonist and his implied reader that typifies the feuilleton:

> Maybe you remember, reader, what sort of tenden-
> cies afflicted Georgian literature 10–15 years ago.
> Then Georgian society had one newspaper and two
> journals. . . . Then the greatest number and best read-
> ers were apprentices. These [apprentices] kept a careful
> eye on everything which 'Droeba', 'Mnatobi' or 'Krebuli'
> printed. I too, your most obedient servant, was one such
> apprentice-reader. From week to week the discussions
> of Georgian students were all about what Mr. Nikoladze
> wrote in response to Mr. Purceladze and we spent our
> time trying to guess 'Well, now, how will Mr. Purceladze
> respond to Mr. Nikoladze?'[23]

Certainly, one major change in the period is that as Georgian print culture expanded and these apprentice readers grew up, there was more to talk about each week than these political debates between two well-known firebrands. Eventually, these external dialogues between actual "apprentice" readers discussing the contents of the press could mature to become internal dialogues between the feuilletonist and the imagined reader.

At the same time, on a broader imperial level, we are seeing the same transition here between the ethnographic period of interest in the peasant and the people in which the emerging intelligentsia defined itself in terms of its exoteric, official narrative of "What is to be done?" (in the 1870s to early 1880s, the period of *Droeba*) to the self-absorption of self-defined, esoteric bohemian discourse of the urban intelligentsia of the 1890s:

> When 'pathological pessimism over the *muzhik* [peas-
> ant]' had possessed educated society in the late 1880s,
> the question, Who is the Russian peasant?, was replaced
> in serious journals by the question, What is the intel-
> ligentsia? Attention shifted from the peasantry as the
> key to Russian culture and development to the educated,

critically thinking elements of society as the decisive actors. Articles on the intelligentsia became as prominent
as articles on the peasantry had been a decade earlier.
(Frierson 1993, 189)

If the genre of "correspondence" is the one that typified the impulse
to "get to know" the peasant, then the genre of feuilleton was that most
fitted for the intelligentsia to define themselves. With the feuilleton as
genre, the focus of interest moves from the village to the city, from the
people to enlightened society, from getting to know the social other to
an intimate discourse *entre nous*. The feuilleton was a collagelike genre
that was essentially defined by describing the heterogeneity of a specifically *urban* context: the feuilletonist, like the correspondent, was a per-
ambulatory figure, but his perambulations took place within the space
of the city streets rather than on the ruinous roads of rural Georgia:

> To deliver the most recent tidbits of news to his reader-
> ship, the feuilletonist would run all over the city, hunt-
> ing for mass gatherings and sites of entertainment, and
> then represent his findings in a manner that was moving
> and engaging. The resultant column, appearing regularly
> in the pages of the contemporary journal or newspaper,
> would offer a slice of urban culture: a collage of every-
> thing that has occurred in the area and that deserved
> mention, however passing. The feuilleton, in short, was
> 'everything: theater reviews, novellas, anecdotes, the
> chatter of drawing rooms—a true medley of all sorts of
> things, a table laid with every kind of glittering trinket.'
> (Dianina 2003a, 187)

The average feuilletonist of the Iveria period (beginning in 1885), for
example, someone like Sano, whose column is labeled *kartvelta shoris*
"between Georgians," spends most of his time talking about the discourse of newspapers (since now there is more than one newspaper), as
above, or its sociospatial equivalent, the city and its typical inhabitant,
the intelligentsia. Another feuilletonist, digressing (as feuilletonists
always do, a feuilleton consisting of a series of digressions) to con
sider newspaper correspondence of past years, notes that much of it,

amounting to little more than gossipy personal attacks carried out in public, lacked the "general/public" (*sazogado*) significance that made it appropriate to be published before society (*sazogadoeba*). Note the fluid way the feuilletonist imagines real and imagined conversations among the readers.

> There was a time, when, in letters of correspondence sent from cities and villages, we would rarely read about any themes, other than those [devoted to] finding fault with, reprimanding, censuring and completely destroying someone. 'He committed this or that crime', you read it and you did not believe it; 'What is there here appropriate for a newspaper, what general (*sazogado*) significance does it have?' you asked yourself and you asked others.[24]

Feuilletonists are a form of life that could only evolve in close proximity to newspapers and cities. Even if the purview of the feuilletonist leaves the city, they may find themselves in some other city, and again, surveying the local intelligentsia, and not, for example, the local peasantry.[25] The city forms the milieu and the purview of the feuilleton, just as the village forms the typical milieu and purview of correspondence. Where correspondence seeks to get to know the peasant other, the feuilleton seeks to define the urban intelligentsia self. While certainly no dearth of serious feuilletons were written under titles like "What Is the Intelligentsia?" it was perhaps more characteristic of the intimate satirical register of self-recognition of the feuilleton to approach the question of intelligentsia self-definition by satirically exploring pathological or defective versions of the type, such as the "useless intelligentsia" (*laqe* translated here as "useless" also has connotations of stupidity):

<Droeba's> Feuilleton, 17 Oct.
WEEKLY FEUILLETON
. . . If you, Mr. Reader, were not born on the moon and have arisen on our native land, —of course, for better or worse, you must be familiar with that small portion of the intelligentsia, which among ourselves [*shinaobashi*] are called 'useless intelligentsia.'[26]

To external appearances, of course, the useless intelligentsia seem to be normal representatives of humanity, dressed respectably, even fashionably, in European clothing. No, to diagnose this person's problem, one must inspect this "man" more closely. Upon further inspection, his nature is found to be a monstrous hybrid, as if a series of different satirical literary personages from Russian and Georgian literature were mixed in a pot, boiled, and spiced with a generous helping of aristocratic arrogance (the term used is *k'udabzik'a*, a kind of arrogance whose personification is Kudabzika above) in custom and comportment. But the mongrel literary genealogy of the "useless intelligent" is due to the conditions under which he was conceived, a bastard love child of Europe and Asia, his hybridity instantiates as an unresolved contradiction the very oppositions Orientalist imaginative geography (Europe, Asia; progress, stasis; civilization, barbarism) which it is the historic role of the intelligentsia in general to overcome (bringing Georgia out of Asia into Europe).

> From one side this [mixture] too is not surprising: the circumstances of his birth were such that it would have to have without a doubt resulted in such a creature. The civilization of Europe flirted with the ignorance of Asia, made eyes at her, smiled at her devilishly, lept at her and in the end seduced her completely to boot and from this illegal marriage was born this strange being, which . . . resembles neither its mother nor its father. It has an external appearance that is European, if not completely, at least to the extent that at first glance you can't detect anything [wrong with him]: he doesn't gobble raw meat, he doesn't try to eat the glasses, and so on; but as far as other internal, essential qualities of the European [are concerned],—throw him back and go on your way.[27]

Since the essential property that characterizes a European is the property of being civilized, naturally, the opposite of Europeanness would be exemplified by characteristic acts of savagery, like eating raw meat or mistaking utensils for food. While this creature resembles a European only in exteriorities, more or less by not giving himself away with such acts of savagery, he does not resemble a "real Asian" either. Here, the concrete object of comparison, the "real Asian," is *also*, like the "imbecile intelligentsia" itself (and unlike the real European), a figure found locally in, and typifying, the urban context of Tbilisi, a (Azerbaijani) Tatar, a mutton-pilaf maker (a typically Asian—that is, Azerbaijani—as opposed to Georgian, food), in the bazaar of Tatar Square in Tbilisi, whose virtues are those of one locked in the stasis of tradition, specifically, because he knows his place and respects the authority of "society":

> A Tatar, maker of mutton-pilaf, somewhere in Tatar Square, stands higher than this [useless intelligent] in this case. For one, the fact that this Tatar makes mutton-pilaf, which, they say, is apparently pretty good-tasting, and in this respect he is bringing some small amount of utility both to himself and to others. Secondly, the same Tatar is at least intelligent enough that he cannot dare to blather publicly about those topics which do not concern mutton-pilaf and therefore exceed his knowledge and competence, he [knows he] cannot call white 'black' and cannot make black white. He cannot dare to show contempt for that which demands respect, nor respect that which demands contempt. He cannot dare to do this because he respects first of all [enlightened] society and secondly himself for his own part considers respect for both of these as a duty.
>
> Such is a true Asian.[28]

The "useless intelligentsia" then lacks both the sympathetic respect for authority and tradition characterizing the true Asian or the enlightenment of a true European. But this character, surely, is an externalization and personification of the anxieties and internal disemia which characterizes the rest of the urban intelligentsia, which, after all, explicitly sees its civilizing role to overcome all the oppositions subtended by the imaginary geographic opposition between Europe and Asia (civilization; barbarism; progress, stasis; universality, national specificity, etc.). The "useless intelligentsia," the hybrid unintended product of the unchaperoned flirtation of European civilization and Asian backwardness, is the reverse image of this civilizing role. The useless *intelligent manqué* instead is a disemic figuration of fake enlightenment as a mere superficial imitation of external European appearances combined with a loss of national specificity, resulting in a rootless being that belongs neither to Europe nor Asia, but has the deficiencies of both. He combines the aristocratic arrogance of Kudabzika, the superficial empty enlightenment of Chikoliki, and the lack of respect for traditions and authority of a Nihilist. Through caricatured images like the "useless intelligentsia" in the feuilleton, the intelligentsia could explore, *shinaobashi* (*entre nous*, intimately, between ourselves, domestically) the repressed anxieties and doubts of the "real intelligentsia" about their own hybridity, their latent but repressed Oriental backwardness, and their incomplete assimilation of European civilization, and thus their own adequacy to their mediating role in the civilizing process.

The voice of the feuilleton belongs with other characteristics of this disemic intelligentsia discourse, specifically belonging not to the official extroverted register of respectable self-presentation, but belonging to the intimate register of self-recognition, it is a discourse that happens *shinaobashi*, that is, "indoors, at home, among one's own; domestically, internally." (Recall that Chavchavadze characterized the aristocratic manuscript circulation of lyric poetry of the earlier aristocratic writers as a literature that circulated *shinaurobashi* "among intimates, domestically"; the discourse of the feuilleton refashions this real intimacy between aristocratic consociates as an imagined intimacy *shinaobashi* between intelligentsia contemporaries within print culture.) The feuilletonist posits an intimacy between himself and the readers, but he is a stranger, albeit an intimate one: the feuilleton almost always is published anonymously (that is, pseudonymously [Mikadze 1984, 6]). The development of the authorial persona specific to this genre is strongly associated with the proliferation of pseudonymous personae, each feuilleton, becoming, in effect, an extension of the author's pseudonymous persona, which becomes in effect a kind of literary celebrity: "Although most feuilletons, particularly in the newspapers, were published anonymously, the personality of the author, with his individual literary background and ideological perspective, was blended into the potpourri of the narrative to such an extent that it made this inherently journalistic form of writing almost border on fiction" (Dianina 2003a, 194). In the same period, the device of the pseudonym, obligatory for a feuilletonist, becomes like Aesopian language, a way of enacting a disemic divide within the public between an exoteric public of official self-display and an esoteric public of intimate self-recognition. The same disemic tendency to move from extroverted "getting to know the people" to introverted "getting to know oneself" is exhibited in the opposition between the dialogue with the peasant, characteristic of the 1870s, and the imagined dialogue with the reader in the *feuilleton* of the 1880s. For the intelligentsia do constitute themselves by the socialist period with respect to the people in a quasi-disemic manner, between an *exoteric*, official nationalist narrative in which the intelligentsia form an organic unity with the folk within the nation, and an *esoteric* bohemian narrative in which the intelligentsia are sharply segregated from the folk, as I have argued elsewhere, there is

> a central contradiction within the cultural ideologies of the intelligentsia between an 'exoteric' national narrative unifying the urban intelligentsia and rural folk and an 'esoteric' 'bohemian' narrative that kept these categories residentially and functionally distinct. . . . The intelligentsia imagined itself as being in a symbiotic relation to the people in ideal terms (from which it was separated in practical terms), and in practical terms it existed in a symbiotic relation to the state (from which it distantiated itself in ideal terms) (Manning 2009c).

The opposition between the reported dialogue with a peasant (usually within a letter which is itself in the *feuilleton* space of the journal) and the imagined conversation with the reader of the *feuilleton* genre parallels the disemic opposition between the official nationalist narrative in which the intelligentsia seeks to overcome the social divide with the peasant, and the unofficial bohemian narrative of intimate self-recognition of the urban intelligentsia.

VII: Writing and Life: Fact and Fairy Tale

For realist Georgian writers of the generation of the 1860s, the question, "What shall I write?" seemed almost as important and consequential a question as the more general question defining the intelligentsia in this period: "What is to be done?" The generation-defining imperative of the aesthetic of "realism," combined with the social imperative to engage with the changing "life" of these new times, left Georgian writers with many practical questions about what to write about. As in Russia (Paperno 1988, 8) the question, "What was realism?"—the question of the relation between literature and reality, and the function of literature in real life, meant that a large part of this writing would involve writing *about* writing, or literary criticism (*kritika* [Paperno 1988, 10–12]). As we will see in this chapter, writing about writing (*kritika*) also necessarily involved writing about what did, and did not, constitute "reality," or as it was called in shorthand, "life." While it was clear that the current material conditions of the "life" of the people formed the nucleus of the "real," it was not immediately clear what to do with the harmful customs and especially superstitious beliefs of the people in fantastic creatures called *chinkas* and kajis: did these represent the "traces" of a past life to be passed over in silence or expunged, or did these beliefs, too, represent part of the present ethnographic "life" of the people to be described alongside their material conditions? As I will show in this chapter, paradoxically, the changing treatment of fantastic creatures like chinkas [*ch'ink'a*] and kajis [*kaji*] provide a powerful bellwether of changes in the way the intelligentsia viewed the defining object of realism, the "life" of the peasantry, from a largely materialistic rationalizing naturalism in the 1860s (which preferred to ignore or expunge these beliefs) to the explicitly "ethnographic" reading of realism of the 1880s (which tended to treat all customs and superstitions as being equally worthy of description as part of the "life" of the peasants). Intelligentsia quandaries about the definition of realism, then, can be illuminated best by looking at how elements of the folk fantastic fared under changing versions of this aesthetic and epistemic program. Throughout the period, the realism of the intelligentsia is haunted by peasant narratives of the fantastic, which initially represent the absolute excluded other of realism, and yet finally are included within its purview.

Our hero, Bavreli, is a typical member of this generation in that he is extremely self-conscious as writer, unable to begin writing without writing *about* writing. Even at the very moment of the end of the war, Bavreli is not as caught up in the happiness and celebration of the armistice as his anxieties about how to write about it:

> From Ardahan (*Droeba* Correspondence)
>
> —Hurray! Armistice, Hurray!—With this cry one of my comrades, with a bursting heart, came dashing in to me, when I was sitting and thinking about what a newspaper editor would like and what would please a reader . . . When an inexperienced man like myself takes up a pen and wants to write something, he does not know what to write about. He thinks anxiously: should he write about private [*kerjo*] life, or about public [*sazogado*] life? . . . If I say something about public [*sazogado*] life, we ought to know its parts; for this knowledge a man must have eye-glasses, that he can discern these well. Unfortunately I do not have those eye-glasses.[1]

Because Bavreli is anxious and uncertain about what constitutes "public" writing (defined not by address but by topics of general concern), Bavreli begins with the trivial details of his own situated position, his own "private" experience. He describes the recent spring weather in Ardahan, which has been bad, rainy, before that, unpredictable, now cold, now hot. He turns to the sad conditions of the local houses in which they stay, the way they leak so much "that when we sleep, you would think we were lying on the shores of a lake or the banks of a river somewhere, and as we toss and turn, we have to be careful that we don't fall into the lake. . . . Now, thank God and Praise Allah, we are saved . . . !"[2]

Having illustrated his private suffering, the "public" question again arises: the announcement of the armistice. Bavreli is skeptical as to whether the announced armistice is real or just a rumor. One day, an officer comes to him and asks him if the war is truly over, and Bavreli convinces him that he may have dreamed it. But it was not a dream;

finally, the news arrives at the front in Ardahan via telegram. Amid the general explosion of celebration, Bavreli defines himself as a writer precisely by sitting to the side and writing, while everyone else celebrates:

> Here today we received a telegram! A sweet voice, a pleasant voice, a voice of peace and armistice! Officers enraptured with this voice go from street to street with music and and are joyful. Shouts of 'hurray' and the pop of champagne bottles cause the very angels in the heavens to tremble . . .
>
> While I was writing this, another acquaintance came in to see me—a man of an extremely joking and mirthful character. He was a Georgian.
>
> —What are you writing? He asked me.
> —What I see around me today—about the armistice.
> —So, are you happy?
> —Of course! Don't be silly! The whole world is happy and I am not?
> —. . . . .[3]

We will never know what his witty comrade told him, because it bears the marks of the censors. Censors, in this period, made their presence visible, presumably because they acted on the manuscript that was already laid out to be printed, so the effaced text in the form of a series of dots (. . . . .) reminds the reader of the presence of an absence, and also the presence of state supervision. At the same time, in this scene we see another emergent typifying feature of the writer, the almost self-conscious asceticism, of sitting apart from life in order to write about it, that would later become one stereotype about the intelligentsia, the idea (expressed, of course, in the absolutely paradigmatic context for such an idea, by the feuilletonist Sano in a feuilleton about the intelligentsia) that "the intelligentsia . . . must withdraw itself from life" as well as from the social circles of nobility, of the priesthood, or the bureaucracy.[4]

If self-consciousness, metaawareness of writing as a socially meaningful, constitutive act defines the new self-segregating class of "writers," then *kritika*, self-conscious acts of writing about writing (usually taking the form of a feuilleton), would eventually define these writers as *intel-*

ligentsia. By the late 1880s, Ilia Chavchavadze would refer the absence of *kritika* in Georgia not, as some proposed, to the absence of writing worthy of *kritika*, that is, *literatura* (Chavchavadze 1977[1887], 132), but to the weakness of the "so-called intelligentsia" and specifically, to their weakly developed sense of reflexivity ("the faculty of talking about themselves, looking at themselves" [*unari tvitmsjelobisa, tvitmxedvelobisa*]) (Chavchavadze 1977 [1887], 135). Thus, it was not merely the act of writing that constituted oneself as a writer/member of the intelligentsia, nor the act of *kritika*, writing about writing, that constitutes an intelligentsia, but the reflexivity, the capacity for self-awareness and self-criticism, implied by that act (Paperno 1988, 10–12).

Kritika, writing about writing, especially in the genre of the feuilleton, is the most explicit form of the reflexive intertextuality that constitutes the emergent intelligentsia, but every individual intelligentsia text also constitutes itself reflexively, in part by addressing itself to literary forebears by strategies of intertextuality. Chavchavadze's travel letters made the densely populated literary landscape of the Dariel crossing into a new point of departure for Georgian literary appropriations of their landscape. This particular reading of the landscape based on allegorical personifications of mountains and especially rivers became almost an obligatory motif so that other writers, even if writing about other regions, still felt the need to pay homage to Mount Kazbek and the Terek (map 2). For example, the mountaineer poet Vazha Pshavela (1861–1915) would obliquely cite the opposition between the Terek and Mount Kazbek [*Mqinvari*] in *Letters of a Traveler* as his point of departure for an ethnographic dialogue with a Xevsur mountaineer named Torghva: "Many have said something about *Mqinvari* and the Terek; I also must begin my letter from this, yes, I must, but how? What in the world has been left unsaid?" (Vazha Pshavela 1961 [1892], 127) So too, Bavreli, writing about a completely different part of Georgia, with completely different rivers, still feels the need to locate himself and the rivers of this new landscape of Ottoman Georgia with respect to the "already spoken about" Terek River, as we will see in the next section.

Map 2: Rivers and cities mentioned in the text.

Chavchavadze's travels are along the Terek River which flows from Georgia into Russia (top center), while Bavreli's travels are in the areas between the Chorokhi and Mtkvari rivers in the southwest area of the map.

"In the Land Described by Rustaveli": Realism in a Land of the Fantastic
While the self-assured young writer-aristocrat Ilia Chavchavadze found in the Dariel Gorge a literary terrain "already written about," densely populated with the voices of other writers, for his *Letters of a Traveler*, the socially marginal writer S. Bavreli is a self-conscious, lonely literary traveler, finding in Ottoman Georgia a silent, deserted literary land-scape "not yet written about." In order to populate this lonely literary landscape with voices, in his early literary adventure "A Journey by Boat on the Choroxi" (published in Chavchavadze's own literary journal *Iveria* in 1878), Bavreli echoes Chavchavadze by using an animated, expressive landscape to create intertexts with literary forebears:

> Some sort of mournful expression lay on nature and

brings sorrow to men, here amid high bullet-coloured cliffs the Choroxi, blue like lapis lazuli, leaps quickly and makes a noise like some sort of strange complaint—it is in a hurry to go far away and you would think it is saying 'farewell!' to the cliffs. The fortress and the cliffs echo this noise. I became lost in thought and a daydream took me so that I thought myself in the land described by Rustaveli. But nevertheless the strange voice of the Choroxi drew me. I wanted to understand what it was saying to me, but I could understand nothing, it had become so foreign/strange [gaucxoebula], that its language too now is no longer understandable to us.[5]

Bavreli sees in the strange, almost fabulous landscape, of the Choroxi River the "land described by Rustaveli." Citing Shota Rustaveli's twelfth-century poem, the *Vepxistqaosani* (The Knight in the Panther's Skin), a poem that takes place in fantastic lands of the Orient but which was believed to be a covert representation of Georgia itself, allows Bavreli to capture the uncanny sense of familiarity crossed with strangeness of the Ottoman Georgian landscape. But as a literary device, to invoke Rustaveli, the apical ancestor of all Georgian writers and the prototypical object of *kritika,* was to locate a writer's work within an august lineage. If the genius Rustaveli was a "mirror of his people," as all writers sought to be, for Bavreli, he was also something of a fun house mirror in which the familiar was made strange.

The other literary reference here is of course Chavchavadze's own *Letters of a Traveler*. Like the semifabulous landscape of Ottoman Georgia, the babble of the Choroxi River is the voice of a Georgia that has become strange, unintelligible, but it also reminds us of the theriomorphic roar of the Terek in *Letters of a Traveler.* Just as Chavchavadze, in his struggles to understand the complaint of the Terek, eventually turns the theriomorphic roar of the Terek River into an intelligible human voice, finally incarnated in the Terek-drinker Lelt Ghunia, so Bavreli sees the Choroxi, a river which speaks in a strange, garbled voice and appears to be saying farewell to its familiar cliffs and hurrying far away like the people of Ottoman Georgia itself.

The "strange voice" of the Choroxi allows Bavreli not only a point of departure for writing, but also, to define his role as writer as a kind of service. Figuring his role as a writer as a translator, a mediator, he wonders how he can translate the estranged and strange voice of the Ottoman Georgia (figured by the Choroxi), if he cannot even understand the strange voice of the Mtkvari River (a river which flows through Georgia, which Bavreli uses here as elsewhere as a figure for Georgia and its people) (map 2). He compares his mediating role in concrete terms as a translator translating between a child who has forgotten Georgian during a long stay in Russia and his mother:

> In this case, I and the Choroxi were in the same situation, as a youth returning from Russia to his mother after a long absence. I, your slave and servant, am a witness of this incident. One beautiful day, which are common in Kartli, I was rolling towards Imereti on the railroad. On the train I met a youth, who having returned from Russia was going home; I gathered that he was happy to be going home. Without blushing he told me, "I have forgotten Georgian, I don't know how I can talk to my mother!" He asked me for help in this difficult situation. I helped him. The mother, broken-hearted from happiness threw her arms around the neck of her child and the child too around his mother, but the problem was that could not tell each other their feelings. Then I took it upon myself to play the mother's part, sometimes the part of the child. . . . But even so I couldn't understand anything the Choroxi was saying, but what would I understand from the Choroxi, when I can't even understand anything the Mtkvari has to say? . . .[6]

For a writer as obsessed with the act of writing as Bavreli, even something as prosaic as the technology of writing is worthy of comment. As a writer, desirous of describing this fantastic scenery of the Choroxi gorge, Bavreli segregates himself from the other passengers and the picturesque scene he is to describe, seating himself in the corner of the boat beside the Ottoman navigator and takes out his new fangled "chemical" pen.

> I took paper out of my travel *chakmaji* and a newly-

invented chemical pen. I had to describe the Choroxi. As I was getting ready and writing about the Choroxi, my Ottoman marveled.

—You are writing in Georgian [*gurji-ja*], uncle? Our Mullahs, even our lords cannot write with metal and water, how in the world can you write! . . .[7]

Bavreli laboriously attempts to explain the technology that produces this wondrous method of writing without quills and ink, but "with metal and water," using Ottoman vocabulary. From the technological wonder of the European pen used to write Georgian, they move to the exoticism of a book written in Georgian using Tatar letters:

—This is a pen made in such a way, that there is *boia* (*c'amali* [medicine; dye]) inside, which makes writing with water possible, I explained to him. Where are you from, brother?

—I am from Maradidi. Our *kovi* (*sopeli* [village]) is down below. My *bap'oa* [sc. grandfather, West Georgian *babua*] also knew *gurjija* [Georgian] *iazi* (*ts'era* [writing]). *Rahmatlogi* (*cxonebuli* [The departed one, sc. the grandfather]) wrote well.

—You don't know? You didn't learn?

—Yes, sir, I know *musulmanja* [Moslem writing], not *gurjija* [Georgian writing]. We have *katabi* [book(s)] of such a kind, that in them *Gurjija* [Georgian] words are written with Tatar letters.[8]

Technical aspects of writing, from European writing implements to Oriental alphabets, both become objects of wonder when they are used to write Georgian. Bavreli's European chemical pen, which writes Georgian "with metal and water," is paired with the Ottoman's *katab*, in which Georgian is written with Tatar letters. This familiarity (Georgian language) crossed with a kind of exotic difference ("Muslim" or "Tatar" writing) produces a kind of uncanny effect that parallels the strangeness of the Choroxi River, a quondam Georgian river which babbles in an unfamiliar tongue, the "fabulous speed" of travel on which (G. Qazbegi 1995, 114), parallels the railroad in Imereti.[9]

But this is not the only way that Ottoman writing is strange. Bavreli, more or less without comment, establishes that his own version of Lelt Ghunia, Osmana, the riverboat sailor of his narration of travel on the Choroxi, is a typically superstitious Georgian peasant. For Bavreli, writing is a secular act; he positions himself within a universe of writing that at all points belongs to materialism and realism, but for an Ottoman peasant, writing itself belongs to a semisacred sphere, its uses belonging to the order of superstition:

> Superstition is widespread here [sc. in the Choroxi river valley]; they believe with conviction in the existence of chinkas and devils in dark and abandoned places. For protection against these [creatures] the Mollahs give them spells—talismans, I have seen inside in the spell there is a small piece of paper, on which are written some words from the Quran. They save this paper in a rag folded into a triangle and they sew it onto the back [sc. of their clothing].[10]

Writers like Bavreli might use writing to banish creatures of superstition with scientific realism, but the local peasants use writing to banish them with phrases copied from the Quran. The apotropaic devices they use represent an unfamiliar use of writing grounded in an unfamiliar religion, an alterity like that of the Ottoman words that sprinkle the speech of the peasant. However, the creatures that populate their superstitious imagination are familiar Georgian spirits, chinkas [*ch'ink'a*], which are commonplace in West Georgia (even though Bavreli pretends ignorance of them).

Spying the ruins of a small tower and a wall on the riverbank as they glide along, Bavreli asks about them. He discovers that once there was a bridge there, but that there was a fort there too, and the peasant adds a touch of mystery to these ruins by noting, "Within there are many chinkas":

—What is a chinka?
—A chinka is a devil.
—Then how do you know that there are chinkas there?
—I know, sir, once a certain *iolchi* (*mgzavri* [traveler])

was coming to his own *kovi* [village]. It was night. *Magier*
(*turme* [apparently]) there chinkas met up with him,
ast'prula! They apparently brought him into that fortress
and they apparently made him dance and were telling
him,

This is how they *at'ik't'ik'eben* [lit. make babble]
A traveler as late as you

Apparently, they were having a wedding and they were
making a *quimass* (*xavits's* [porridge]), they had in the
house a great big empty *qazana*. All of them were stick-
ing their fingers in it and crying out: "Let no one say,
that here be his *Baraka!* . . . The *qazana iavash-iavash*
(*nela* [slowly]) is filled and they are to throw the traveler himself in too, but had he not called upon Allah,
he would have been boiled right then and there, *hama
allaxi,* when they heard it apparently, the chinkas *bitun*
(*sul* [all]) fled."[11]

Bavreli is simply eliciting what amounts to Georgian folklore, just as
on the plane of form, the unfamiliar terms of the Ottomanized dialect
are transcribed and glossed, so too on the plane of genre, this is a typical folktale illustrative of peasant superstitions about chinkas, fantastic
creatures who inhabit ruins and torment travelers. Just as the Georgian
dialect contains some obvious Tatar words, so Islam enters as a kind
of source of apotropaic folk magic, either using writing or invoking the
name of Allah. The form and content of the tale are Georgian, not a matter of religious alterity but secular identity of folklore and fairy tales,
the chinka is Georgian, Allah is not.

The peasant, who defines a chinka in quasi-religious terms as a species of devil [*eshmak'i*] might disagree, but in intelligentsia discourse, the
preternatural world of folk spirits represents a secular folk discourse of
"superstition" belonging neither to the supernatural or religion proper
(Orthodox Christianity nor Islam) nor to the natural world defined by
secular intelligentsia writers like Bavreli (on superstition as an object
of secular discourse see Asad [2003, 35]). Initially diagnosed as part of
a set of "harmful customs" to be banished by either religious or secu-

lar enlighteners, by Bavreli's period these "superstitions" were already being recuperated as a secular component of a shared folklore, a part of the national patrimony (shared, after all, by Christian and Muslim Georgians). Thus, these marginal spirits take on a central role in defining the intelligentsia practice of writing in relation to folk "customs": The spirits of such a discourse, defining a secular zone epistemically opposed both to natural (scientific) and supernatural (religious) domains, represent both the superstitious lack of enlightenment of the peasant to be banished by the intelligentsia, but also a set of national folkloric traditions to be transcribed by them.[12] Though they do not exist either in supernature or nature, they nevertheless take on a lively existence in the secular sphere of folk or national culture (customs and beliefs).

Bavreli's conversation with the Ottoman boatman about chinkas sits on a watershed between these different approaches to describing peasant "customs" and "superstitions." In the more materialistic and naturalistic realism of the 1860s–1870s, peasant stories about such spirits are diagnostic of a painful absence of scientific enlightenment and part and parcel with the "harmful and impoverishing customs" which everywhere strangle the "life" of the peasantry. By the 1880s, in the wake of the turn to a self-consciously "ethnographic" reading of realism centering on the mountainous regions of Georgia, the preternatural world of chinkas and kajis has become as topical a theme for Georgian writers as writing about the natural world of the peasants who believe in them, belonging to the secular and national culture of the peasantry. Thus, the mere existence of Bavreli's factual report of a conversation with his Ottoman boatman about chinkas is as much an example of "writing about writing" as their discussion of technologies of writing itself, for simply to report a factual narration about fantastic creatures like chinkas presupposes a specific kind of answer to the question, "What should I write?" and the related questions "What is realism?" and "What is real (life)?" to which I turn next.

Writing and Life: Realism

Writers like Bavreli accorded a certain urgency to their task, for writing (and writers) responded to the urgency of "life." To write was to write about "life," and to write about life was to write about "the people" (who typically could neither read nor write themselves), and eventually to write "for the people" (as part of a growing campaign to spread literacy beginning at that time). Early correspondents of *Droeba* like Mose (Ingilo) Janashvili saw themselves as living on the precipice between two epochs, an "old life" and a "new life." To build a new life, the writer must be critical with respect to the old life, and literature must assume a practical, utilitarian role with respect to the new one, writing and "theories" must be grounded not in "air" but in "life" (*cxovreba*): "my desire is that literature must obey life. Every word must be adapted to life; our life and present questions must be researched."[13] "Life" is a key word defining the field of intelligentsia activity of all kinds.

What is meant by "life"? The words used in Georgian, typically *cxovreba*, *qopa*, or *qopa-cxovreba*, have some of the same specific nuances of the Russian word *byt* in the same period:

> Loosely translated, *byt* encompassed all of the following English terms: 'daily life', 'domesticity', 'lifestyle' or 'way of life'. Prior to the Revolution the term *byt* had largely ethnographic implications, and was used to describe differences in daily life represented by traditional ethnographic subjects such as Siberian aboriginal groups, as well as traditional European peasant societies. With the Revolution and the problem of constructing a new socialist society the word *byt* assumed increasing political significance.... (Buchli 1999, 23)

But activism directed at changing "life" does not begin with the Russian Revolution; it is an abiding and defining concern for intelligentsia in Georgia from the period of Emancipation at least. For writers like Ingilo writing in the Emancipation period which coincided with the beginning of *Droeba*, "life" was the present period that was fettered by the harmful "customs" from the past. By the socialist period, however, "life" had become identified instead with the past in the present. Life, then, was the dead weight of the past which stood opposed to future revolution, the future. As Boym notes, by the late nineteenth century, "life" had come to mean that which was resistant to revolutionary change by the avant-garde, under the influence of symbolists and early revolutionaries in the late nineteenth century who saw *byt* as "the reign of stagnation and routine, of daily transience without transcendence . . ." (Boym

1994, 30). In an influential series of formulations, Trotsky essentially identified *byt* as a mixture of the present "given conditions" and the past "customs," but is heavily slanted toward the past.

> Daily life [*byt*], i.e. conditions and customs, are, more than economics, 'evolved behind men's backs,' in the words of Marx. Conscious creativeness in the domain of custom and habit occupies but a negligible place in the history of man. Custom is accumulated from the elemental experience of men; it is transformed in the same elemental way under the pressure of technical progress or the occasional stimulus of revolutionary struggle. But in the main, it reflects more of the past of human society than of its present. (Trotsky 1973, 29)

For Ingilo, too, writing in the 1860s, life is a category defined in terms of the times (*droeba*): Life is cleft in twain by an epochal divide between the "old, extinguished life" and the "new life." In one sense, life might include the past life and customs (the old life), but in another, life (including what Trotsky would call "given conditions") is identified with the present and directly opposed to customs, the past life. The opposite of life and the present is custom and the past, the duty of writers is to describe life with a view to changing life, in particular by identifying and eliminating bad customs among the people:

> The duty of the writers is that they don't put cotton in their ears and close their eyes to everything that is happening in life, good or bad, then they must put their hand to the task and pronounce it in literature, and in this way cut off the roots of the bad customs of the people . . .[14]

For Ingilo, customs are the remnants of the old life that must be destroyed to build the new one. For another writer (Chkotua), customs were similar to Tylorean "survivals"; they are the "result" (*shedegi*) or "trace" (*kvali*) of the past conditions of life that are retained in the present life, but no longer make sense in terms of the conditions of present life:

> There is many such a custom [*chveuleba*] that has re-
> mained in the life [*cxovreba*] of the people, whose original
> idea and significance we no longer understand, which we
> consider to be almost laughable or ridiculous. . . . Really,
> what is 'custom'? Custom is the result of the life [*cxovrebis
> shedegi*] of a people or a private individual, it is the trace
> [*k'vali*], in which is imprinted the past conditions of life.[15]

However, the collection of such customs could be regarded as having
a certain utility. Another author (Antimozi) describing customs among
the Mingrelians notes, "It has been said many times, that there are
among us such customs, which clearly portray for us the effect of the
people of old, who lived among us at different times, on our own people
[*xalxi*]. For this reason we consider it to be very useful to collect the
customs, superstitions, and fables [*zghap'rebi*] of our people: these bring
great utility for the writer of the history of our people."[16]

For writers as different as these, life is a category of the present
tense; customs are products, effects, or traces of a past life. The utility
of customs is always weighed in terms of the present life: customs are
"harmful" if they have negative consequences for contemporary life of
the people; they are "useful" if, for example, they help us understand the
past life of the people. This has a particular effect on the descriptions of
customs of the people, of course, for they are described often because
they have crucial moral and material effects. Life was the ultimate
ground of reality, and the duty of a realist author was to study life; the
duty of a critical realist author was to help remove the old life and bad
customs and find a new life.

"Harmful" and "Useful" Customs

The relation of writing to life was therefore materialistic in its ontology, realistic in its epistemology, and utilitarian in its teleology. This
definition of writing in relation to "life" explains the specific epistemic
and aesthetic mode that characterized "writing about life": a scientific
realism which differs little from that in Russia in the same period, as
summed up by Frierson:

> The characteristic approach [to the description of the

life of the peasants] was a commitment to what they understood to be scientific principles: rationalism, empiricism, and objective realism. Their sideward glance was
directed at romanticism an as inadequate attitude that
failed to penetrate 'reality' and thus did not offer useful
guidance on the pressing concerns of transforming Russia . . . The structure of their accounts of village life . . .
bespoke their effort to appear scientific. Each typically
opened with a description of the physical setting of the
report or sketch, thus establishing the major features of
the geographic, climatic, and economic environment.
They were striving for what was essentially a positivistic
account of peasant society. (Frierson 1993, 27–8)

A typical Georgian example of such correspondence is an early letter to
Droeba about the West Georgian region of Racha in 1868 by U. Uximerioneli. He begins by ruminating on the status of Racha as a kind of *terra
incognita* for what he calls "Georgians, that is, readers of *Droeba*," since,
like many of the early correspondences to *Droeba* in the 1860s, Racha is
located in West Georgia, and is thus relatively mysterious and unfamiliar to the largely East Georgian urban readers of *Droeba*. Thereafter, this
correspondence is structured much like an eighteenth-century natural
history, making a steady descriptive progression from the material and
natural to the moral and human orders, from natural history to civic
history. The first letter moves from the geographical location of Racha
in the mountains, the geography of Racha itself, its isolation resulting
from mountainous location, resulting frequent landslides and resulting
poor condition of roads, climate, quality of local mineral water and soils,
cereal and wine production, the need for the population to search for
work elsewhere half the year because of the shortage of land, the reputa-
tion of Rachan craftsmen in the plains of Georgia, and the general de-
mography of Rachan villages.[17] With the second letter, we have moved
to the human order, civic history, with a description of both the physical
and moral character of the Rachans, compared to other Georgians, including desirable properties like industriousness, balanced, however, by
a lengthy discussion of their proclivity to superstition (to be discussed
below), a description of religious festivals, the ethnic makeup of Racha,
and the establishment of village courts of justice. Here, the letter trails

off, unable to finish this discussion, for fear of boring the reader with what is already a long discussion.[18]

In fact, this early correspondence was singled out for praise by the writer signing himself T. Akaki Tsereteli (T stands for Tavadi "lord"; Tsereteli is a noble), for illustrating a happy exception to the rule in *Droeba*'s correspondence to that point, which was, in Akaki Tsereteli's opinion, confined to long lists of tedious facts about the material situation of the region. First, Tsereteli praises *Droeba* for being the first newspaper to contain local correspondence at all, but complains at the same breath that the correspondents themselves do not pay attention to the right kinds of details about their regions: "its correspondents do not pay attention to real and necessary matters and write such stories for us, that if we didn't know them we wouldn't be missing anything, and knowing them gains us nothing! . . ."[19] What then, counts as useless knowledge for Tsereteli?

> Well, my good man, why do we need to know whether a lot of wine was produced in Imereti this year or not? . . . In Imereti if a lot of wine is produced, they drink a lot, if not, they gulp down water. . . . Such correspondences, that is, those that talk pointlessly, it is best that they not be printed in a quality newspaper![20]

The editors, of course, took major exception to Akaki Tsereteli's light-minded dismissal of "material conditions", for example, of the importance of the wine harvest in Imereti:

> It is strange, how the author of the article does not understand this clear truth, that a good wine harvest has a big influence on the public commonwealth, especially among us [Georgians]. It is true, that there are those, who if they have a lot, they 'gulp down' a lot; but the author should have taken into account that majority, who sell extra pitchers [of wine] and exchange them for a couple of pairs of sandals a year.[21]

One can see in the difference between the lord Tsereteli and the editors of *Droeba* here a pervasive divide on what constituted items worthy of narration, Tsereteli preferring less talk about the material conditions of life and more talk about the customs, the editors of *Droeba* arguing for the importance of material conditions of life for the people. Implied here is also an emergent divide between what the local correspondent wanted to write about their locality, and what the elites in the city (whether the editors or readers like Tsereteli) wanted to know about the life of the peasants.

The question of what was important to write about was directly related to the question about what to do about it. Here, the local correspondents and the editors of *Droeba* frequently disagreed. One correspondent from Racha, one of many who wrote against the inordinate expenses of funerals, took the materialist and economic view (so disliked by Tsereteli) to an extreme, providing an exact (and extremely detailed) accounting of the crippling expenses that funerals represent for peasants, eventually arriving at the princely sum of 208 rubles and 80 kopeks.[22] This correspondent not only criticizes these customs for being harmful, impoverishing, and pointless, but also because they are, in his opinion, not Orthodox, but survivals from "our ancestors, who apparently at one time were followers of another religion" that have remained unchanged until today. The goal of this local correspondent in tabulating such a complete list of charges (down to the last kopek), like so many others, is to enlist the aid of external agencies in eliminating these harmful and impoverishing customs, in this case advocating the government use force to eliminate them (since the people are opposed to abandoning the customs of their ancestors). He asks, "What opposition could there be for local government to make the people abandon such customs by force; this will please both the people themselves and the people of other estates too. They know, don't they, that this custom is harmful and impoverishing for them?!" Here the editors, in a footnote, take a major exception to the elimination of customs by force, advocating instead that village teachers and priests should attempt to enlighten the peasants.

This letter is a relatively early example of what constitutes an utterly banal form of "local" correspondence, demonstrating how materially and economically crippling such "savage customs" (*mxecuri chveuleba*) are (with a particular criticism of the depredations of the priests) for nobles and peasants alike. As an editor to *Droeba* would despair in the following years, letters about "harmful and impoverishing customs" such as this form a huge and popular genre among reform-minded local correspondents. In fact, they form the bulk of "local correspondence":

> When we look over correspondences printed in lo-
> cal newspapers, we will read 365 times a year at least,
> if not more, about useless expenses, which the people
> pay in burying the dead, on New Year's celebrations, on
> weddings, or other kinds of gatherings. In the opinion
> of correspondents, these gatherings form the primary
> cause of the poverty of our people and if priests by
> preaching and teachers by teaching can help wipe out
> these harmful customs, then the welfare of the people
> will be greatly promoted.[23]

If Tsereteli and the editors of *Droeba* disagreed on the relative importance of describing the moral versus material aspects of custom, the correspondence from the village seemed unanimous in seeing such customs as being materially impoverishing and morally harmful. The customs in question were primarily those related to funerals, including both the crippling material expenses but also the dubious moral practices such as ritual wailing, customs especially characteristic of West Georgia (Imereti, including Racha, Mingrelia, Svaneti), which was becoming clearly identified as a veritable hotbed of backwardness.[24] The litany of local correspondence was in favor of eradicating this or that harmful and impoverishing custom. In response, the editors of *Droeba* often used their editorial page to point out that "custom" was not always "harmful and impoverishing."

Facts versus Fables: Ghost Stories As Superstition

In his criticism of the correspondence to *Droeba*, Akaki Tsereteli singles out the Rachan correspondent Uximerioneli above as an example of what a newspaper like *Droeba* should write about, specifically singling out his description of "the customs of the people." The customs that interest, or rather distress, Uximerioneli are, indeed, not materially impoverishing ones that distress other correspondents, but primarily moral ones: superstitions. According to Uximerioneli, the primary moral problem of the Rachans is that they are a very superstitious people. As a scientifically minded person, he is distressed by their superstitious tendencies to attribute preternatural agencies to natural phenomena. Before even illustrating this superstitious tendency, Uximerioneli apologizes to his scientifically and serious-minded readership that he is about to relay the sort of story that the peasant regards as a factual "narration" (*naambobi*) about the forest inhabitants, but the reader will surely recognize as a "fable" or "fairy tale" (*zghap'ari*), something which, if they have heard such a story before, they can pass over unread:

> Among the Rachans superstition is very widespread. Apparently different phenomena of nature have frightened the people (*xalxi*) and it has created ideas about the existence of some sort of evil men of the forest, which they call kajis, chinkas and women with tails [i.e. witches]. I want to relate here one story [*naambobi*, a narration] about these inhabitants of the forest, and I ask the reader, if he has ever heard fables [*zghap'rebi*] like this one, that he omit this section and not trouble himself with reading it.[25]

However much Tsereteli apparently enjoyed his account, Uximerioneli (like most correspondents of his time) is a reluctant, even apologetic, narrator of ghost stories and fairy tales (*zghap'rebi*). With his reluctance and apologetics for even so much as a retelling of this dubious material, the author establishes a crucial distance between a scientific epistemic stance shared by the author and the reader, and that of the superstitious peasants, who present fables (*zghap'rebi*) as narrations of fact (*naambobi*).

Like any good ghost story, the story begins with a frame narrative of travelers arriving at a local inn (*dukan*) on a dark and stormy night. Because of the lack of beds and the noise coming from a stream nearby, they spend a sleepless night in the inn. At dawn, the owner of their horses, who had been delayed and came after them, finally appears at the door, and from him we get our first ghost story:

> He knocked, we opened the doors for him, we looked at him: this man is very pale in color, and he is holding a big rifle in his hands. As soon as he came in, he called out: 'In

my entire life I have never experienced such difficulties as these, what devil made a fool of me, that I spent the night in such a cursed place. The whole road, I swear, I didn't take a breath, the whole time I was looking this way and that and I had the rifle at the ready in my hands; and God protected me, if he hadn't then, as you also well know, these forests and cliffs are completely full of devils and tempters.'

'There,' he continued, 'where there is a lovely meadow, there I encountered a lovely woman. I called out to her: "Who are you, tell me, a devil [*kaji*] or a man [*k'aci*]?" She mumbled something incomprehensible and didn't reply to me and went along with me for about 40 strides and then, when I looked she was no longer accompanying me, I crossed myself and called out "Fie on the Devil, Fie on the Tempter!" I made sure the tempter had vanished, so too did your enemy vanish!'[26]

Such is the first Rachan ghost story, told with conviction of truth and faithfully transcribed. Our main narrator now breaks frame to insert a parenthetical comment: "this 'tempter,' in our opinion, was a young Mingrelian shepherd, whom we ourselves had met along the road and who did not understand Georgian." Mingrelian boys who do not speak Georgian, in the dark, might well be mistaken for feminine demons by a frightened and superstitious peasant. But this naturalizing diagnosis of superstitious mistaken identity remains as yet unspoken in the *dukan*, but is only shared as an aside with the other "Georgians, that is, readers of *Droeba*." Speaking out loud, another traveler instead identifies this tempter as a dangerous form of witch who might have struck him mute or made him lame.

But as it happens, this was not the only frightening forest creature our traveler encountered that night; he continues, "At this accursed place at the same time, a kaji came twice with a roar and a scream like wildfire down from the cliffs and made a crashing noise flow through the trees in the forest. At that moment I aimed my rifle, fired it, and the kaji fell over into the water with one voice and one scream." This second story causes those present to cross themselves, and some of them have their hair standing on end and elicits a general diagnosis in the *dukan*:

that Racha, of all places in Georgia, is *particularly* densely populated by witches and kajis:

> 'No, there are kajis and witches in our land,' the same one began, 'so many as are found nowhere else. There where there are caves in the cliff, from there a kaji threw a rock at me and nearly broke my head open; as I passed by again a little later and under the clear, star-studded sky a devil threw water and snow at me from the cliff, may God curse his mentioner.'

> 'Really, I swear,' added another traveler, 'The kajis know how to do marvels; if it is good weather, they throw snow at you and if it is bad weather they pelt you with dry earth and rocks.'[27]

Here the narrator can no longer restrain himself, and breaks into their conversation in the *dukan* to retell their stories to them in terms of what really happened in scientific terms of nature and not superstitious fable: the kaji who came down from the cliff with a roar and a scream through the woods was an avalanche, and "as far as the throwing of rocks is concerned, rocks fall from cliffs really often and we also have been hit in the back, but we very much doubt, that kajis and witches threw them! . . ."

It is as if he had not spoken at all. His attempts to naturalize the preternatural world instead elicit more of what he calls *zghap'rebi* (fairy tales) and *arak'ebi* (fables) that take us deeper into the peasant cosmology of preternatural beings, moving from allegedly factual narrations of kajis in Racha to similar narrations of chinkas in neighboring Imereti. Significantly, when repeating the man's factual narration in indirect discourse, the writer replaces the particle *rom* ("that"), which introduces a noncommittal evidential value, with *vitom* (which we have already seen is used for narrating one's own dreams and narrations presented as factual by others (*naambobi*) which the reteller judges to be dubious or false like *zghap'rebi*):

> 'A kaji is a kaji, isn't it? I am not one who has seen one,' begun an Imeretian traveler, who, like an attorney,

sometimes pointed his finger at us, sometimes pointed it upwards and waved it this way and that, 'but a man among us had a chinka, and this I know for a fact.' He told his tale [*zghap'ari*], which we have heard many times in Imereti: allegedly [*vitomc*] a man had caught a chinka in the forest and he clipped its nails, and he made it help him as a servant at home. On one Sunday, when the owner of the house had gone to pray, this chinka tricked his son into telling him where the clipped nails of the chinka were hidden. The chinka took out his nails and he pasted them back on his own hands and feet and supposedly this made his strength come back and he stole off. The youth, on the other hand, was supposedly thrown into boiling water by the chinka. 'So I heard, I wasn't there to witness it myself.' Our traveler finished his narration [*naambobi*]. Earlier he had been trying to convince us that supposedly he had seen a chinka himself. In general they are all like this, they tell such fables [*arak'ebi*] and whoever you ask, no one can tell you that they themselves have actually seen witches and kajis. Such fairy tales [*zghap'rebi*] and superstition are very wide-spread in all of Racha and Imereti, too.[28]

Uximerioneli is seemingly embarrassed at even retelling these fairy tales, and it is noteworthy that this narration is virtually unique in the period; I have found no other transcriptions of fairy tales until the ethnographic boom of the 1880s. So why does he retell ghost stories and fables at all? On the one hand, this retelling establishes the epistemic solidarity of the readers of *Droeba* (who recognize these stories as fairy tales, even if they enjoy them) as opposed to the superstitious folk (who cannot recognize the retelling of their own fairy tales in the naturalistic terms of science). Two orders of narrators are created in correspondence (correspondents and peasants), and two orders of narrative (written and oral, factual narration and fairy tale), each belonging to two absolutely opposed epistemes (science and superstition; naturalist and animist); each populated by its own typical narrative agencies (avalanches and kajis, respectively); recreating the opposition between "society" ("Georgians, that is, readers of *Droeba*," those who write correspondence and do not believe in kajis) and "the people" (those who they write correspondence about, who tell stories about kajis). At the same time, by narrating his own failed attempts to explain the stories in naturalist terms, in terms of Mingrelian shepherds, avalanches and not kajis, first as an aside to readers of *Droeba*, second, to the peasants themselves enlighten them, a foray of the discourse of *Droeba* into the West Georgian village *dukan*, he shows that there can be no dialogue and no reciprocity of perspectives between these two spheres of circulation. The naturalistic discourse of the correspondent to *Droeba* is passed over in silence by the peasants in the West Georgian *dukan*, just as Uximeri-oneli suggests his retelling of their fairy tales can be passed over unread by the reader of *Droeba*.

Fables As Cultural Facts: Ghostly Ethnographies

Just two years after our Rachan correspondent made embarrassed excuses for retelling the *zghap'rebi* and *arak'ebi* of the peasants in the Dukan, Umikashvili's call for the collection of folklore in villages in 1871 called upon collectors to include those, along with a wide range of other "folk" genres (*saxalxo*) which are also "national" (*saero*) genres, "what the peasant men of the village sings and says." These included (1) poems (*leksebi*), either sung during work or play; (2) fairy tales (*zghap'rebi*), stories (*ambebi*) of heroes, fables (*arak'ebi*); (3) proverbs (*andazebi*); (4) poems (*shairebi*); (5) blessings for sickness (*shelocva ram avadmqopebisa*); (5) prayer either from the period of idolatry (*k'erp'oba*) or Christianity, but the latter only if the people have remade in a specific way (*tavise-burat gadauk'etebia*); and (7) riddles (*gamocanebi*). One notes in passing that intelligentsia writing about the secular sphere of folk customs is extremely carefully segregated from the sphere of "religion" (a category that includes Christianity and Islam, but not, for example, paganism or idolatry). Thus, while all customs left over from the time of idolatry be-long to the "folk," Christian prayers are "folk" only when they have been remade in a non-Orthodox "pagan" fashion; Orthodoxy itself is not part of the sphere of the "folk," nor is it (unlike idolatry!) within the purview of secular "custom" or "superstition," that is, a secular topic that the secular intelligentsia can write about. Accordingly, by the late 1870s, the situation had changed enough that Bavreli felt that precisely such stories about chinkas from his boatman were interesting and worth recording, dutifully transcribed with appropriate attention to their form, just as Umikashvili in 1871 suggested in his call for folklore by correspondence.

This particular *secular* sphere of "customs and superstitions" is a privileged sphere for intelligentsia writing about the folk. Importantly, such beliefs did not belong to the sphere of religion but did belong to the sphere of national culture (after all, chinkas are found both among Orthodox and Muslim Georgian peasants). Just as their role as enlighteners required them to teach the peasants the benefits of scientific naturalism, their role as cultural workers required them to document the mistaken superstitious beliefs of the peasantry, which nevertheless were an important aspect of national culture. Even in the nineteenth century, then, intelligentsia found in folklore and folk superstition a domain in which they could both define themselves in opposition to the unenlightened folk (who sought supernatural explanation where natural explanation was required) and also unify themselves to those same folk with a secular narrative sustained by an emergent concept of a "national culture," in which folklore and mythology would play an important role.

In the earlier period of realism of the 1860s (typified by Uximerioneli's correspondence) which privileged discussion of "life" over "customs," stories about kajis and chinkas are reported with apologies and reluctance, primarily to show that the people are superstitious and unaware of natural causation, embedded in a larger naturalistic narrative that attended to, for example, the material plight of the people of Racha (lack of land that causes them to engage in guest work elsewhere). By the 1880s, there is something of a sea change in favor of ethnographic realism, and the pages of *Droeba*, and later, Iveria, are full of ethnographic, folkloric, and other accounts of the "moral" life of the people. In 1888, a description of folk beliefs in West Georgia about kajis, for example, could be taken up instead as an unapologetic study of folk beliefs, without any concomitant description of their material conditions of "life." The basic epistemic divide between enlightened society and the people is not challenged by this relativistic description of custom and belief, rather, it could be argued that it is even firmer. In the spirit of "liberal" models of dialogue discussed above, Uximerioneli at least attempted to persuade the peasants he wrote about that there were other forms of explanation; he not only wrote about their superstition, he talked to them and argued with them. On the pages of Iveria, firmly within the universe of "conservative dialogues" with the peasants, the peasants are much more hermetically sealed in their epistemic universe, but the writers are much more willing to show the inner logic of that universe: now, ideas about kajis are interesting in themselves, not merely as a sign of the superstitiousness of the people.

With folkloric and ethnographic reportage characteristic of the 1880s, superstition is transformed as a negative property of the "material order" (ignorance of real material causes) into a positive property of the "moral order" (folklore), revelatory of Georgianness. At the same time that the fantastic kaji is redeemed as a form of folklore, it nevertheless remains constitutive of the epistemic horizons of *folk* discourse, the written about, and not educated society/intelligentsia discourse (their writers), ultimately to be overcome. The fantastic and the folk are mutually constituting: realism can report the fantastic, but not participate.

With this redirection of realism, we can see the transformation of mistaken, fantastic, folk beliefs into historical facts about the folk, as Figal (1999, 134, see also Foster 2009, chapter 4) notes in a parallel case with the codevelopment of the folkloric and the fantastic in Japan, "[A]lthough the content of tales and legends were not historical facts . . . , the very telling of and belief in such stories among people were historical facts that could and should be dealt with in a cultural history . . ." That is, the discourse of the folk and the discourse of the fantastic could be mutually constituting (under the secularizing rubric of "custom, belief" of the folk other) *and* opposed (under the rubric of folk superstition, backwardness, or a strictly materialist discussion or a strictly realist one).

Thus, a description of folk beliefs about kajis in Imereti in Iveria in the 1880s will be a very different thing from what we have seen from *Droeba* in the 1860s. From the very start, we are brought into the universe of discourse of the *zghap'ari* (fairy tale), taken on its own epistemic terms as *naambobi* (factual narration). First, we are given a description of the Imeretian kaji:

> A kaji, in the viewpoint of the folk, is similar to a man and with a big enormous body, ugly to look at and it expresses horror itself at its own appearance, it has a body covered In hair, and, of course, does not wear clothing;

on its chest it has spines, which, when it becomes angry, it releases.[29]

The kaji is distinguished from the humans it otherwise resembles by physical monstrosity and nudity, but it is distinguished from other devilish creatures, such as the chinka, partially by time and place of operations: the chinka is defined primarily in temporal terms, the kaji primarily in spatial terms:

> The kaji does not have a time of coming and going, like for example, the chinka, and it is always here. The kaji is very distinct from the chinka. The chinka is more like a domestic/interior [shinauri] creature and does harm to domestic animals, objects and furniture, the kaji, however, is wild/exterior [gareuli], it does not come near the house and does not harm anything domestic [shinauri]; it harms the man himself, if a kaji runs into a man on the road, it begins to wrestle with him, if it defeats him, it doesn't kill him, but it really 'daaquebs' (daamt'revs ['thrashes']) him.[30]

In this clear, almost structuralist analysis, the chinka and the kaji are almost perfect opposites, each haunting half the key cultural division between the household/domestic/tame/inside (shinauri) and the wild/exterior spaces (gareuli): the kaji haunts the latter and avoids the haunts of the chinka. The appearance of the chinka in domestic spaces is according to time of day, while the kaji is restricted by time but more particularly a creature located in spatial terms and subdivided according to more specific details of its hauntings:

> The folk do not really know where the chinka lives, but the kaji, in the opinion of the folk, lives in big cliffs, caves and desolate places, in creeks and in water. According to the place of habitation, the kaji is of two types: one is of water [a dweller in water], the second, of dry land [a dweller on dry land]. Since by its own activity the kaji resembles a man a great deal, for this reason the folk have called the kaji by the different names 'water man'

and 'forest man'. Kajis of the two breeds walk about on the earth from twilight to the cock's crow; afterwards they hide themselves in their own places. At night they wander about here and there and avoid humans. If a kaji of the dry land runs into a man, then he begins to fight with him and there are many examples of this among the people; the water kaji does not fight much with men and I couldn't find a single example among the people of a water kaji fighting with a man.[31]

Kajis obey specific rules; for example, when one sees a kaji, one should greet it in the normal Georgian fashion *"gamarjoba!"* ("Victory!") before the kaji has a chance to do so. If one does so, and if the kaji forgets itself and gives the normal reply greeting *"gagimarjos!"* ("Victory to you!"), then, as the greeting itself implies, you will win the following fight. They are also afraid of the sound of bells and particularly the sound of iron objects. The author gives several illustrative stories of fights with kajis as reported by the people. If one wins such a fight, then it is possible, as with a chinka, to take the creature home, but this is pointless, for unlike a chinka, the kaji, a wild spirit, cannot be domesticated:

Even though a kaji can be caught, still it cannot domesticated, that is, it cannot be kept it at home by cutting its hair and toenails, as for example with a chinka. The folk do not remember such an example of anyone managing to domesticate a kaji. Whoever catches a kaji, it is said, that kajis will never again come near anyone of their surname.[32]

Other than tricking them with greetings or beating them in a fight, kajis are, like other Georgians, fond of wine, but kajis cannot hold their wine, unlike humans:

Aside from chance encounters, some kajis actually chase after humans. In such circumstances, if it has caught up with you, you must pour wine for the kaji, and, because it likes wine a lot and wine has a greater effect on it, it will not refuse and it will soon become drunk. The moment it gets drunk it falls asleep.

Then a man can easily save himself.[33]

While the chinka is a domestic creature that can be domesticated and turned into a servant by physically removing some of its "wilder" physical features (cutting its nails and/or hair), the kaji cannot be so domesticated. However, as with an interaction with a stranger, who represents a potential enemy or a potential guest, the kaji's malevolence can be domesticated by either physical prowess (as an enemy) or by sociable means, by greetings, and by traditional Georgian forms of hospitality (offering them wine). The chinka is the fantastic image of serfdom, of domestic servants, animals, or children turned into wild malevolent beings, who can in turn be enslaved; the kaji is the fantastic image of the stranger, a perfect stranger from whom nothing can be gained and with whom no permanent relationship other than avoidance can be formed.

Even though, in many ways, kajis are the opposites of normal humans (kajis are often marked by doing things backward and speaking backward in other folkloric accounts), there are uncanny similarities between kajis and normal people, as this writer notes. In fact, kajis do not represent the opposite of society (they do not lack a social order), but an antisociety; they themselves have a society in the desolate wastes (ruins, caves, forests) which at all points mimics that of humans. In one story, for example, the hero kills two kajis who are brothers, and later witnesses their funeral, which involves the same kinds of ritual wailing characteristic of Imeretian peasants. That is, the society of "men of the forest" is still very much a society. It is antisociety, but not an absence of society. The author concludes,

> From this example, by the way, it also appears that the kaji by his actions and manner of living very much resembles a man. The kaji is tall in body, portly and has small arms, [but] like a man he has as customs: lamenting the dead. So consider the following, that kajis even have a political order and life, too. They have the very same sort of elders as in the society of men; they have one main elder, whom all kajis pay respect to . . .[34]

The kajis have not only become the object of folkloric study but of ethnographic study as well, they live in communities just as mysterious to, and yet uncannily similar to, those of the (Western) Georgian peasant, as the (Western) Georgian peasant is mysterious to the (Eastern Georgian) intelligentsia.

The Fantastic As Metaphor for the Real: Peasants As Kajis

"This 'tempter', in our opinion, was that young Mingrelian shepherd, which we ourselves had met along the road and who did not understand Georgian."[35]

One could, in fact, study the folkways of the kajis much as one would study the folkways of the peasants who tell stories about kajis. For kajis have customs, political orders, and social life very much like those that the ethnographers at this time are scouring Georgia to document among the peasants. In fact, the custom this author uses to illustrate the parallelism between the customs of kajis and the customs of humans is precisely the custom most often treated as epitomizing the backwardness of West Georgian peasants relative to East Georgian ones: lamenting the dead (t'irili), a harmful moral practice embedded in a series of equally "harmful and impoverishing" material expenditures. Thus, kajis in fact seem to resemble the (West Georgian) peasants who tell stories about them, they are the more uncultured, more natural, and wilder equivalent of those peasants. In the same way that West Georgian peasants tell stories about kajis, writers in Droeba tell stories about West Georgian peasants (who are telling stories about kajis).

The most famous piece of Georgian writing in which kajis figure is Rustaveli's Vepxistqaosani, the twelfth-century poem in which kajis serve as the villains. Like their nineteenth-century versions, kajis are imagined in the Vepxistqaosani not as fantastic (superhuman or subhuman) others, but humans on the same order as the heroes. This Rustavelian figure of the kaji as a nonsupernatural other crops up, once again, in the appropriation of Ottoman Georgians into Georgia. Amid the many attempts to map the fictive space of Rustaveli's poem onto the map of Georgia, it involved an identification of parts of the Ottoman Georgian city of Batumi with the fantastic fortress of the kajis in Rustaveli's twelfth-century poem. Naturally, such identification of spaces from the privileged national narrative with recently reconquered territory of Georgia leads to a powerful way of synthesizing these spaces with the national narrative. But of course, such syntheses have other consequences, including the jarring connection for many Georgians of the period of a human form of alterity with a supernatural/superstitious form of alterity.

This invocation of Rustaveli is the device used in one travel account that appeared alongside that of Bavreli in the pages of *Droeba* of 1879, by A. N__dze. This account chronicles a sea voyage from Poti in Mingrelia south to Batumi, in which the writer realizes two dreams of his, to see the sea and to see "our newly united Georgia as well."[36] He gives a leisurely description of Poti, which he terminates, because "the Georgian readers of *Droeba* will not need to be introduced to Poti, for all will know about it."[37] Finally they depart, having a rough sea voyage to Batumi. Finally, the sea calms and at the same time Batumi comes into view. Quoting from Rustaveli's medieval poem, the *Vepxistqaosani*, the writer and an acquaintance of his identify Batumi with the semifabulous city *Kajetis Cixe* (The fortress of the land of kajis), wherein dwell the semifabulous creatures, the kajis, with whom the heroes of the poem must do battle to save the beautiful princess. If this is the land of *Kajeti*, the writer's friend reasons, then the inhabitants must therefore be kajis themselves:

> My interlocutor pointed out some emaciated, pallid young boys and told me:
> —Look, those are the inhabitants of the Fortress of Kajeti, whom Rustaveli in his undying poem calls Kajis!
> I couldn't make out the devilish (*kajuri*) in them at all: the appearance of the face, disposition of the body would really make you think of village dwellers of the Axalcixe district; their language however was almost Mingrelian. When I announced my doubt about this, he brought out a copy of the 'vephis tqaosani,' from which he read aloud to me the following:
> Their name is called Kaji, because they are banded together,
> Men skilled in sorcery, exceeding cunning in the art,
> Harmers of all men, themselves unable to be harmed by any;

They that go out to join battle with them come back blinded and shamed.

[Wardrop translation, stanza 1225]

—Who knows that exactly about these people it was said? I asked.

—First wait, from below let me read to you:

For this reason all those that dwell roundabout call them Kajis,

Though they, too, are fleshly men like us.

[Wardrop translation 1226][38]

In folklore, the kaji is a social being, living in a "society of nature" that at each step is parallel to the society of humans. Here, on the authority of Rustaveli, the kaji moves a further step from preternatural alterity to social alterity; the kaji is now a Mingrelian boy (as we saw before, in naturalistic debunking explanations of the kaji in a meadow in Racha, who, the author thought, was probably just a Mingrelian shepherd boy who did not know Georgian): "They are fleshly men like us." Fleshly like us, yes, but perhaps not quite exactly like us.

In contemporary Georgia, too, the figure of the kaji continues to serve as a figure of the ignorant rural folk (or especially, ex-rural urban folk) in relation to the educated intelligentsia (Manning 2009c). The primary contemporary meaning of kaji, outside of fairy-tale books in Georgia, is precisely in the meaning of "peasant, villager, lumpkin," with a particular sense something like a villager who is out of place who is in the city and wants to become a city dweller.

However, while it may seem there is no connection between the "fantastic" use of the term for a supernatural entity and the "slang" use for a natural one, beyond a simple metaphoric extension, we can see that the ways in which the fantastic was constitutive of the folk, that believing in kajis defined the universe of discourse of the folk in epistemic terms as being a discourse of the fantastic, as opposed to the real, could collapse into a more direct linguistic identification of the folk with the objects of their erstwhile belief. The elision of the folk into the fantastic allows the intelligentsia discourse of realism to remain in place, even as it moves from talking about the materially real, the natural, to valorizing mistaken folk beliefs as being nevertheless facts to be analyzed. But at the same time, it creates an unbridgeable epistemic divide between the writer and the written about (the folk and folk beliefs), almost as unbridgeable as the divide between the folk speaker and the fantastic objects spoken about. The folk come to be a bit more like kajis than chinkas; in that, like kajis and unlike chinkas, they can never really be domesticated.

VIII: FELLOW TRAVELERS:
LOCALISM, OCCIDENTALISM, AND ORIENTALISM

> For nearly the whole route I did not depart from the
> devoted Mtkvari, you would think that the Mtkvari was
> also one of our fellow travelers![1]

In his earliest travels in 1878, Bavreli finds himself two fellow travelers:
a Russian chinovnik and the "devoted" Mtkvari River, which flows along
their route. As fellow travelers, the Russian chinovnik (bureaucrat) and
the Georgian river each stand as figures for imagined horizons against
which Bavreli constitutes himself as a "traveler." Against these horizons
the landscape they traverse comes to have very different, mutually unintelligible meanings. Like most of the Georgian travelers of his time,
Bavreli is an ambivalent traveler, never traveling very far from "home."
Accordingly, Bavreli defines his own travel as being local by providing
himself with two kinds of fellow travelers: human and nonhuman. On
the one hand, the extremely circumscribed space-time of his own travels are defined in opposition to the space-times that define the rather
more cosmopolitan journeys of his human (Russian, Georgian, Armenian) fellow travelers, variously defined in terms of imperial service,
military campaigns, or long-distance trade. On the other hand, Bavreli
personifies the landscape of the locality itself, particularly the rivers,
the Mtkvari and the Choroxi, which, after all, like him, travel, but always
with respect to a concrete and determinate landscape. By emphasizing
his difference from these cosmopolitan human fellow travelers and
his kinship with his local nonhuman fellow travelers, Bavreli valorizes
a specific form of travel, a travel that is circumscribed by locality and
nature. This chapter seeks to locate this self-consciously *Georgian* form
of travel and traveler in relation to other "European" forms of travel
and fellow travelers against which Georgian travelers self-consciously
defined themselves, as well as the different space-times in which Georgians traveled: localist travel within Georgia, archaeological travels into
the Georgian past, Occidentalist travels into the European future, and
finally, Bavreli's own Orientalist travels in Ottoman Georgia.

We return to Bavreli's early travels by the banks of the Mtkvari. Even as Bavreli and the Russian chinovnik travel together through the same concrete landscape, they experience these places as being part of very different journeys. For his fellow traveler, this place, by the banks of the Mtkvari in Georgia, is simply one of many more or less equivalent places he might have been appointed, equivalent because they are far from the imperial metropole: "my fellow traveler had recently finished school and they had appointed him for service 'somewhere' [sadghac] and he was on his way to this 'somewhere' . . ." The Russian traveler experiences "here" as a vague and indefinite "somewhere"; somewhere in an empire of more or less equivalent somewheres, somewhere where someone like him, whose travels form a career defined by his service to empire and the boundaries of that empire, has been sent to serve. The chinovnik is one of those Andersonian absolutist functionaries, whose travels, indeed whose life, is a career path that is defined at the intersection by algebraic variables of rank (chini) and place, producing senses of abstract equivalence between fellow travelers based on this very same algebra of rank and place:

> Sent out to a township A at rank V, he may return to the capital at rank W; proceed to province B at rank X; continue to vice-royalty C at rank Y; and end his pilgrimage in the capital at rank Z. . . . The last thing the functionary wants is to return home for he *has* no home with any intrinsic value. And this: on his upward-spiralling road he encounters as eager fellow pilgrims his functionary colleagues, from places and families he has scarcely heard of and surely hopes never to have to see. But in experiencing them as travelling-companions, a consciousness of connectedness ('Why are we . . . here . . . together') emerges (Anderson 1991, 55–6)

But no such consciousness of connectedness is obtained between this chinovnik and Bavreli, who is not such a fellow variable within the abstract algebra of empire. In fact, it is precisely because of their differences that they value each other as fellow travelers. Bavreli admits to the reader that he is happy that his fellow traveler is *chiniani* ("having rank," that is, an official) since this will simplify his own travels considerably; the fact of the matter is that Bavreli lacks the funds necessary for travel. For his part, the chinovnik admits that he values Bavreli's company precisely because he is a "local" (*akauri*, one from "here"), who can explain aspects of the locality to him.[2] For Bavreli, what the chinovnik experiences as a somewhat vague and indifferent "somewhere" is strongly centered as a familiar "here," near his home and his travels, for the most part, are in and around his home region. In fact, in these very "travel notes," Bavreli is "traveling" (if we can call it that) *home*,[3] to the very village, Bavra, near Axalcixe, near the border with Ottoman Georgia, from which he takes his nom de plume, to his home, "in the house of a poor peasant."[4]

On his journey on the Ottoman Georgian river Choroxi, too, Bavreli casts a sideward glance at the very different itineraries that separate him from his human fellow travelers—including a Georgian nobleman, an Armenian merchant, and a pair of Russian officers—even as he shares the same boat along the same river with them. In a manner that recalls Chavchavadze's alignment of himself with Lelt Ghunia, Bavreli aligns himself with the Ottoman boatman, who agrees to take him on the journey for a lesser rate of four rubles, because, as he says in his heavily Ottomanized Georgian, dutifully transcribed, as always, by Bavreli:

'*bahli* (*diax* [Yes]) I will take you. *Hama* (*magram* [but]) *gurji* (*kartveli* [Georgian]) *ki* (*rom* [if]) you were not, I would not have taken you at that *bahat* (*pasat* [price])]'[5]

Despite the great difference between their dialects, the boatman's sense of a kind of kinship with a Gurji like Bavreli reflected concretely in the lower price of passage, in contrast with one of the other travelers, an Armenian merchant, who, as it turns out, must end up paying a higher-than-normal price.[6] The Georgian nobleman and the Armenian merchant turn out to be old acquaintances, and Bavreli reports their overheard conversation at length.[7] From characteristic details of dress, movement, down to the macaronic Russian-and-Armenian-inflected speech of the merchant, it becomes clear that these two are almost comic stereotypical representatives of their species, their presence pointing to very different itineraries, very different worlds of motivation that divide them even as they share the same boat. The Georgian nobleman, who served at the front at Kars, deep inside Ottoman Georgia, is returning home to Poti via Batumi. The Armenian merchant is going to Istanbul via Batumi. The Armenian merchant, who plays the role of comic sidekick to the Georgian nobleman, complains that his noble friend's journeys expanding the boundaries of empire are defined by a motivation of *chini* ("rank"), a motivation he does not understand, for his own extra-imperial travels are defined by money, he frankly admits: "*t'o* [Armenian-derived familiar address term] All you talk about is ranks (*chini*), tell me, did you make any money?"[8] Yet for all their differences, these two yet represent, like Bavreli, a kind of "local," in contrast to the other two travelers, Russian officers, one of whom is a dissolute drunk, with red eyes from loss of sleep from playing cards and drinking, a picture of absolute indifference to the journey which arbitrarily brings him to yet another arbitrary "somewhere" in the Russian Empire, and hence spends much of the journey playing cards with the other officer and the merchant.[9] Each of these fellow travelers is an emissary from a different space-time, grounded in the horizons of different imaginaries and motivations, against which Bavreli can define himself as a "local" traveler.

Fellow travelers are defined not only by comparability of their conception of how the same or similar objective itinerary maps onto the wider phenomenological and motivational horizons of their travels ("space-time"), but also by the comparability of their subjective aestheticized reactions to the landscape with those of other travelers. Along a well-traveled itinerary, such as the Dariel pass which everyone must cross who wishes to go from Russia to Georgia, one is never alone; there is no dearth of literary fellow travelers for a writer like Chavchavadze to keep him company. But Bavreli has no literary fellow travelers with whom to share his aesthetic appreciation of the sublime, the picturesque, and the beautiful in the landscape, he only has his Russian chinovnik, and there is nothing comparable in the thoughts of these two. Enraptured by the natural landscape along the banks of the Mtkvari River, Bavreli imagines another traveler, who is also a painter, who, however rushed he might be, still he would tarry involuntarily to paint the landscape on paper:

> —imagine an isle, which divides the Mtkvari in two, a bridge crosses one branch of the Mtkvari from the bank to the isle, between whose abutments the Mtkvari runs seething with foam; a little further there is an old fort on a high cliff, to the right a village spreads out, a pretty

forest and gardens, wild plum trees blooming with new flowers like white cotton and many similar decorations of nature. But oh! I, unfortunate one, where can I, with my weak pen, describe the beauty of my motherland![10]

But his reverie is interrupted by his actual fellow traveler, the chinovnik, who raises his voice to scatter his "sweet thoughts," which turn on speculations about the quantity and type of game animals that can be found in the local forests.

The two travelers share the same road, even the same cart, but their minds are in different worlds. In contrast to the Russian chinovnik, Bavreli's private thoughts and nature seem in harmony, a harmony which is figured by the Mtkvari River, who had been until just now merely a salient feature of the natural landscape along the route, but now becomes an anthropomorphized, yet inarticulate fellow traveler, a familiar old acquaintance from his youth, whose mood here, however, has changed; here the river is unfamiliar, troubled, and angry:

> What my fellow traveler was thinking, where his thoughts were running to, I do not know even now; mine however were flying very far and to such a place, for which I would sacrifice my whole youth for this moment; if only this thought and dream were to come true, I would have considered myself the most blessed of beings. . . . The cooing of the Mtkvari led us from temporary sleep. Oh how it made me happy, when I saw my old acquaintance and friend, the Mtkvari! It made me happy, but what to do, because this no longer was that Mtkvari, which I had seen in my boyhood—It now longer seemed to have that purity, that freshness, that peacefulness. The agitated Mtkvari was running along so angrily and so wrathfully grumbled, that my heart almost broke. That is the matter and misfortune, that I couldn't understand and do not know, what was the reason for its trouble. . . . I asked its beautiful banks 'why, why is it so angry?'—There was no one to answer.[11]

The Mtkvari moves from being a stable aesthetic figure connecting the natural beauty of the landscape along the journey, to an anthropomorphic figure, a moody and inarticulate fellow traveler. The Mtkvari is also a literary intertextual figure, allowing Bavreli to compare his travels *here* beside the Mtkvari to literary travelers like Chavchavadze elsewhere beside the Terek. Like the Terek for Chavchavadze, the anthropomorphic Mtkvari as fellow traveler stands for Bavreli's own organic connection as local and *intelligent* to the landscape and by extension, its people (in contrast to the official, who represents a competing field of imperial elites for the local intelligentsia). This is the same Mtkvari which Bavreli elsewhere (above) contrasts to the Choroxi, a semifabulous river which has become unfamiliar, and speaks in a strange, foreign accented voice, a figure for Ottoman Georgia, a river which is pictured as saying farewell to the familiar cliffs of its headwaters as it heads away into Ottoman Georgia, much as the population of Ottoman Georgia are leaving their homes en masse fleeing the Russian conquest. In explicit comparison and contrast to Chavchavadze's anthropomorphic, sublime Terek, Bavreli refashions the Mtkvari into a patriotic Georgian, who refuses to go abroad, who refuses, in effect, to *travel* at all:

> However angry the Mtkvari may be, still I love it. While the Terek brings many into rapture with its noise and terrible rush, with its richly adorned banks and it awakened many feelings in people, but no, I don't love that; I came to hate the Terek without seeing it, for the Terek is not devoted to the fatherland, as is the Mtkvari. The Terek runs off from the fatherland into foreign countries and beautifies the lands of others, and not our own . . . I love the Mtkvari because it is self-sacrificing and devoted to the fatherland.[12]

If the Terek is two-faced and treacherous (again recalling Chavchavadze's characterization), seeking to go to foreign lands, the Mtkvari is devoted and patriotic, a river that flows through and for Georgia alone. Just as Chavchavadze used the figure of the Terek River to make geopoetic arguments and invoke oppositions of imaginative geography, such as that between Europe and Asia, Georgia and the Caucasus, so Bavreli extends this language of rivers both to intertextually link his own travels here to those of a more famous aristocratic writer elsewhere and to extend this imaginative geography in space into Ottoman Georgia, producing a threefold opposition between the Mtkvari (the familiar European Georgia), the Choroxi (the alienated Ottoman Georgia), and the Terek (the Caucasus, or perhaps the cosmopolitan imperial space of a chinovnik in Russian service like the man seated next to him, including many Georgian chinovniks and even Russian-educated Georgians [the original meaning of tergdaleuli] like Chavchavadze himself besides) (see map 2 for the locations of these three rivers).

But the comparison has an unintended reading, too: the Mtkvari could be taken as a figure for "travel" in the Georgian sense, at least the Terek, and the Choroxi too, is a traveler in the normal sense, it seeks out foreign lands, but the Mtkvari never goes anywhere at all. The Mtkvari as "fellow traveler" is a figure for the predicament of the Georgian traveler, who travels but does not ever leave Georgia, a river whose circulation is like the circulation of Georgian travel writers, circulating within the imagined unity of Georgia. Bavreli and the Mtkvari are fellow travelers through much of their travels, though neither could be said to "travel" since they are never very far from home.

Traveling Home: The Localist Georgian Traveler

Like the Mtkvari River itself, Georgian travel writers seem to be loath to actually leave Georgia. No better illustration of this tendency can be found than the inaugural call for submissions for the popular journal *Mogzauri* ("Traveler") which reads in part:

> The editors of *Mogzauri* asks lovers of Georgian history-archeology, and geography—ethnography, to send to the editors articles of general interest about the history, archeology, geography and ethnography of Georgia.[13]

As one contemporary commentator noted, to illustrate his point that "the contemporary Georgian does not like to travel, he doesn't like looking around as does a European": "We could not get used to traveling. Just consider we even founded the journal *Mogzauri*, but not even it could make us love traveling."[14] Georgians are defined in opposition to Europeans as the local to the cosmopolitan, those who stay at home versus those who travel.

Georgian travel seems to be a contradiction in terms. The feuilleton-ist Sano tried his hand at writing a letter of his travel from Tbilisi to Baku. He begins by discussing his title:

> Feuilleton
>
> ---
>
> Notes of a Georgian Traveler
> (From Tbilisi to Baku)
>
> I made up this title on purpose for today's letter. Were I to have written only 'Notes of a Traveler', the readers would think that some real traveler had really aimed at some scientific or social idea and intended such a journey to investigate it, as European travelers are wont to do for us.[15]

Sano is not a real traveler, a European traveler, but a Georgian one, just as this is not a real travel letter but a feuilleton. As a feuilleton version of a traveler letter then, meandering digression is the order of the day, every ancillary topic is covered, everything pertaining to the journey except the journey itself. We do not hear so much about the landscape as about its absence: everything the writer might have wanted to see cannot be seen; the journey for some reason is always at night, so one can see little or nothing from the windows; the railway itself is so devised as to wind a tortuous path through remote and deserted places, avoiding each potentially interesting human settlement by a number of miles, so that even important cities like Ganja (unless you actually go out of your way to see it on purpose) only appear in the distance from the railway station "only as about ten dim candles and lamps and nothing more."[16] The price of the ticket, too, almost double what it should be, is blamed on the no doubt sublime, but invisible, mountainous landscape which the route is at pains to avoid: "It is the fault of Mount Kazbek and Elbrus, that you pay 12 roubles to Baku instead of six, you arrive from Tbilisi into Baku, in such a way that you can't see even one mountain ridge."[17]

But as the title warns, this journey which is not a journey is made by a travel writer who is not a travel writer (but a feuilletonist) and, indeed, not a real European traveler, but a Georgian traveler. And here is the greatest oxymoron, as the reader, surely, will already know, the main thing about contemporary Georgian travelers is that there is no such thing:

> So as to not raise a false hope in the reader, I just now added in, that the traveler is a Georgian man, and you will be aware, won't you, how our urbane fellow-countryman travels. I should have said in the title, that this Georgian traveler was "of our times", so that it would be even clearer, with whom the reader is dealing, but the title came out too ugly and long and for this reason in the manuscript itself I am informing you of this quality of the traveler.[18]

The Georgian traveler is neither the familiar figure of the serious, scientific European traveler nor the Georgian traveler of old, when apparently, long ago, Georgians used to be of a more curious and cosmopolitan nature, believing themselves to be part of humanity in general and therefore loving knowledge, and accordingly, Georgians used to travel to far-off places in the East: "In this old times, as I was saying, we see the Georgian man not only in Persia, but Afghanistan, India, China, and elsewhere. He goes there to pray or to make war or to trade, he remains one, three, ten years. He sees many new things, new relationships, different wonders of nature and then, armed with new knowledge and experience, returns to his homeland, and imparts his mental treasury to friends and strangers."[19] Travel for the contemporary Georgian traveler is nothing quite so bold, and its aims are much more modest. "Travel" and "traveler" are used, Sano says, when someone puts on a coat and hat and sets out on the road, "from let's say, a small village to a large village or a city. The distance traveled will be from 30 to 60 versts [kilometers, more or less]."[20]

The distance traveled by the contemporary Georgian "traveler" are modest, and so are his goals. Much of the time this travel is forced upon the unwilling traveler, who must travel to the office of some police superintendent in a larger village or city by some specific date on some bureaucratic or police matter, lest they have to make a much longer trip to Siberia. If the reasons for such travel are not understandable to the traveler, at least there is a reason the reader will understand. But what of voluntary travel? What is its point?

But for the most part Georgian travel means meandering from one place to the next, pointlessly, for no reason. The only reason for travel is for Georgian man to show his in-laws his abilities, for example . . . to annihilate their wine. It could be that he has in-laws or friends who live at a distance, but the Georgian man nevertheless will dare to travel, so he can ascertain in detail, what quality of wine they have. This is typically the main goal, that a Georgian man leaves off his own supra and goes to the supra of others to devour everything. . . . Our fellow countryman returns from far travels and all his reminiscences are where he drank how many *stakans* [glasses] and *q'anc'i* [drinking horns] on Monday, who did he compete with in drinking wine on Tuesday . . .[21]

The Georgian man does not travel to learn, to find out new things, to learn the good and bad aspects of himself or others; his desire for new knowledge "is apparently buried in some deep gorge somewhere." As a result, it is no wonder "why we do not have any descriptions of not only of other countries, but of our own homeland," and all the while foreigners from God knows where "practically kill themselves to see our lovely country . . . at the same time our Georgian man, however, often only knows his own village and those places which can be seen from this village and which his eye can reach."[22] Thus, to the Georgian, slumbering in his own backyard, all the "wondrous victories of human ingenuity" in this age of mechanical wonders, like the use of steam-powered transport for travel on dry land and sea, have no "spiritual importance" for the Georgian man, "neither the steam train, nor the steam ship nor the telegraph have brought hardly any utility into our spiritual life." The Georgian man makes no use of the inventions of the nineteenth century that annihilate space and time (Schivelbusch 1977, 33), because, frankly, he doesn't want to go anywhere and is not interested in understanding or seeing anything, not only in other countries, but practically in his own country either.

How do we reconcile this model of travel with what we tend to view as being the *essence* of travel? European travel writing is a genre generated at the margins of self and other, familiar and foreign. Therefore travel writing requires traversing an imaginative geography and recapitulating the oppositions that inform such an imaginative geography, along the way finding them manifested "on the ground" in representative figures that tend to confirm the basic otherness of the territory traversed in relation to one's home. In general:

> Travelers, then, impose on the foreign a demand that it should in some way proclaim itself as different from the familiar. At the same time, they define their own task as one of grasping that difference. Travel writings regularly note the disadvantages of those travelers who, for whatever reason, are unresponsive to alterity. (Chard 1999, 3)

Georgian travel writings like that of Sano, at least, are willing to do that last bit, for travel is mostly an opportunity to lambaste oneself, or other Georgians and Russians, for their unresponsiveness to alterity. Thus, it is not as though Georgians were somehow unaware of this definition of what it meant to travel, or had some competing definition. As Georgian writers like Sano and Proneli make abundantly clear, Georgians know perfectly well what it is, it is just that they don't want to do it. The project of Georgian travelers, by and large, does not involve interest in exploring the foreign, the unfamiliar, or the different. The Georgian traveler, too, because of the unstable position of Georgia between enlightened Europe and exotic Asia, shows little desire to explore the indeterminate position of Georgia within this space, the exoticism of Asia has no allure for him (and in any case any Tbilisian could find "Asia" in the bazaars of his hometown, as our feuilletonist reminds us in the preceding chapter), and Europe remains more of a geographical expression of modernity as such than a concrete destination. These places largely stand for categories or positions in a space of progressive teleology, ways of classifying or criticizing the locality, of finding fault with "useless" intelligentsia in the locality; they are not places to actually visit. In a way, too, the local peregrinations of Georgian travel letters are just an extension of the existing genre of correspondence. Just as correspondence allows stationary readers *of Droeba* located in this or that corner of Georgia to become writers *to Droeba*, so travelers are simply correspondents who are now themselves in motion, like the newspapers they read and the letters of correspondence they send back.

Both are equally circumscribed by locality.

Even in places like Ottoman Georgia, the Georgian traveler often seeks the *familiar* in the strange landscape. Here and there, Georgian travelers find the familiar preserved in the form of Christian ruins, customs, superstitions, even alleged practices of "secret Christianity" practiced among the ruins of old Christian churches. Alongside ethnographic notes on the Georgianness of the inhabitants, the most extensive descriptions are devoted to the ruins of old churches, usually attributed to the illustrious empire of Queen Tamar. But in general, Ottoman Georgia fascinates not because of its Oriental alterity, as it would European traveler, or even the picturesque assemblage of the ancient Georgian ruins and the exotic Ottoman present, but because of the ruins of Georgianness, both moral and material, that preserve a sense of familiarity in the landscape. Here, in the erstwhile center of Georgia's past glory, ruins of Georgia's past are common, perhaps more common than in Georgia itself: "in the district of Ardahan, wherever a person goes, they encounter old remains at every step: ruined churches and castles."[23] Accordingly, the traveler to Ottoman Georgia travels in time, not in space, and the most typical kind of correspondence is ultimately the genre of "archaeological travel."

Georgian travelers define themselves not so much as travelers in space, as in time. This emerges most clearly if we compare the two most distant places that Georgians traveled to in the 1870s: Ottoman Georgia and Europe. Georgians who traveled to Ottoman Georgia were above all archaeological travelers, travelers seeking an image of a lost Georgian *empire* under Queen Tamar: their landmarks are the ruins of Georgian churches, which, more than anything else, attract attention and give license for their travels and were textualized as a kind of monumental palimpsest. At the same time, it might be said that travel to Europe was travel to the future; there, in Europe, one went to witness the destination of a progressive civilizational teleology, to see world exhibitions and find models for progressive reform of Georgia, and most of all, to read newspapers.

Traveling to the Past: The Archaeological Traveler
Bavreli, taking his leave after dinner with some local Tatar inhabitants in Ardahan, extracts from the locals a strange promise:

> We took our leave. My last request was that, whatever old relics [*nashti*] there were: fortresses, churches and halls, that they not destroy them. They gave me their promise. I left.

He then lectures the reader on the moral significance of these material ruins:

> It will not be unseemly, for those who have possession of [these ruins] to pay attention and issue commands to others, that these remains [*nashtebi*] which have remained from the old life, that they will not ruin and destroy them even more. Maybe our future [generations] won't be as cold-hearted as we are; maybe these ruins, witnesses of our past life, will have influence on them and they will become sign posts showing them the way for another life. . . .[24]

Bavreli's peculiar request needs to be understood within a broader episteme arising in the 1870s, a period in which the "archaeological journey" becomes a special subgenre within the broader genre of travel letters, a subgenre especially associated with Ottoman Georgia. By the 1870s, Georgian Romantics had made ancient churches into secular objects that were already becoming hybrids of the Romantic discourse of *ruins* (eliciting a subjective lyric response) and a newer archaeological discourse that treats churches as historical national *monuments* (eliciting a historical, memorial response) (see Manning 2008). As monuments, these old Georgian churches stood in opposition to the new Russian ones as icons of differences in monumental time, in which the temporality of Georgian orthodoxy and Georgian empire encompasses that of Russian Orthodoxy and Russian Empire by an order of aeons. Vaxtang Orbeliani's (1812–1890) poem, "Two Buildings," from the same period (1881) contrasts a contemporary (Russian) freshly painted building to an old Georgian one from the period of Tamar, which is encrusted with weeds. The first building has weak walls which are easily destroyed, and even its ruins will quickly disappear into the earth: "it has no past, nor will it have a future." The second one, including a "holy church," while abandoned and overgrown with weeds, has no fear of the flow of time, "it stands heroically, built by the hands of heroes," and "if someday its walls are destroyed, its remnants (*shtenni*) will remain forever," "because a great past has a great future." If the Russian "imperial sublime" (Ram and Shatirishvili 2004) emphasizes the spatial vastness of empire, projected both on vertical and horizontal spatial axes, by which the Russian Empire both encompasses and surveys from a great height colonies like Georgia, the Georgian imperial sublime instead is projected onto the canvas of time, encompassing the Russian Empire on a temporal order of aeons.

In late Romantic poems, we already see signs that old churches are moving from the aesthetic order of ruins to the epistemic order of monuments, from the subjective lyricism of Romantic poetry to the dispassionate disciplinary empiricism of Georgian archaeology, from the period of "romanticism" to the period of "realism" (Lotman 1984, 142). Romantic ruins are mysterious, illegible, hieroglyphic; archaeological positivism would replace this mystery with historical knowledge as surely as it would remove the moss from the facade to read the inscriptions beneath (Edwards 1999, 16). The new archaeological understanding assimilated old churches to the category of monuments (*dzegli*), which included verbal texts (including both written monuments like Rustaveli's poem *Vepxistqaosani* as well as oral texts passed from mouth to mouth) as well as other secular buildings like fortresses, all of which were felt to be traces (*k'vali*), remnants (*nashti*), signs (*nishani*) of a once great Georgian civilization, to be monuments and witnesses of the culture of a Georgian nation.[25] Each kind of monument (architectural, textual, customary, oral) would become the object of a corresponding emergent academic discipline (archaeology, philology, ethnography, and folklore), both within imperial academies as well at the amateur level in the Georgian popular press. Each emerging discipline (archaeology, ethnography, folklore, philology) constituted itself with respect to a specific sort of empirical object but were understood to be homologous in methodology and aim (compare van der Veer 2001, chapter 5). The work of archaeology in piecing together the scattered ruins of the nation (associated with rulers like Tamar, to whom in the popular tradition in Russian and Ottoman Georgia these monuments were usually ascribed) were likened to the philological work of reconstructing from various existing manuscripts a singular, authoritative Ur-text of the national epic poem (associated with a contemporary of Queen Tamar, the poet Shota Rustaveli). All these new disciplines were also united in having a single transcendent object; they were all disciplines of "the nation," each revealed a specific kind of national specificity. Accordingly, each disciplinary object, each "monument," could be assigned, once and for all, on the basis of original authorship, to exactly one such transcendent historical national unity.

These changes in the epistemic order occurred around the same time as the Russian conquest of territories of Ottoman Georgia in 1877–8. These territories had formed the center of Tamar's empire in the twelfth century, but had been under Ottoman rule for over two centuries. As we have seen, Ottoman Georgia had become the site of a major current of irredentist fantasy of the cultural and political reunification of these "long separated brothers," Ottoman and Russian Georgia. In the period leading up to the war, and in the immediate aftermath, Russian imperial spies and archaeologists (all of them Georgians) and Georgian newspaper correspondents, respectively, scoured the countryside of Ottoman Georgia, finding little that was Georgian there other than ruins of churches. Even if the people often no longer resembled Georgians in language and especially religion, the ruined churches that dotted the landscape were signs that the land itself, if not the people, belonged to Georgians.

With the "archaeologization" of churches, the interpretive custody of old churches passed by slow degrees from Orthodoxy to the nation, from religious sites of worship of God to secular monuments of the nation. Georgian travelers in Ottoman Georgia like Qazbegi and Bavreli continually drew attention to the nature and quality of ruins, particularly of churches, always searching for telltale inscriptions that would permit identifying them as "Georgian," but rarely tarrying as their forebears might have done to emit a lyric groan or melancholy sigh. Since local Georgians were usually Muslims (hence Bavreli calls them "Tatars" above), these churches had ceased to be Georgian religious objects and were now freely appropriable as secular objects belonging to the Georgian nation. Georgian travelers like Bavreli worried that the local Muslim population would destroy these ruins to use the old stones for building purposes and requested that they not do so. But as the Ottoman Georgian Tatars fled these conquered lands, Georgian writers worried that the emptied-out landscape was filling up with Armenians, and they were even more scandalized that some such churches were being appropriated by the local Christian populace as Armenian apostolic churches, often accusing the local Armenian population of intentionally hiding or defacing Georgian inscriptions (e.g., Bakradze 1987 [1878], 41).[26] Accordingly, every church was scoured for signs of Georgian inscriptions that would establish once and for all that a given church was part of the Georgian, and not Armenian, religious, and therefore national, patrimony.

In this discourse, the appropriation of ruins of churches was strongly *textualized*, ruins were seldom *illustrated* as parts of sublime landscapes but were more often *transcribed* as textual objects. Bakradze's *Archaeological Journey to Guria and Ajaria* (published in Russian in 1878, describing a journey to Ottoman Georgia that took place in 1873), shows a strongly textualizing approach to monuments. The only illustrations of churches in his book are a paltry few drawn by Giorgi Qazbegi (1839–1921) during an earlier espionage mission in Ottoman lands (published in 1875), while his own illustrations, numbering over a hundred, are all transcriptions or illustrations of inscriptions found on these churches. This "textualizing" shift is registered even in late Romantic poetry from the period. Vaxtang Orbeliani's poem "There Is a Place" (*Aris Adgili . . .* ; Orbeliani 1879) about Gelati Monastery, the burial place of Tamar, begins with a description that otherwise shows all the typical affect-laden qualities of the Romantic ruin, the sublime and deserted surrounding landscape, the moonlight, and especially "the moss of a thousand years" that decorates it. However, the ruin is first of all a monumental *text*: "Its walls . . . are a notebook" (*amis k'edeli . . . aris rveuli*), that tell the tales of thousands of years, of its glorious builders, specifically, of Tamar.

Just as the architectural landscape is read as monumental text, textual monuments are read into the landscape. Travelers to Ottoman Georgia make the strange Ottoman Georgian landscape familiar by seeing in it illustrations of passages from the epic poem by Rustaveli. As we saw above, one traveler thinks to see in the Ottoman Georgian city of Batumi a fabled city from Rustaveli's poem;[27] while Bavreli, daydreaming on a boat floating down the Choroxi River in Ottoman Georgia, thinks himself to be "in the land described by Rustaveli."[28] The two kinds of monuments, ruins, and texts move from metaphoric to metonymic parallelism: Ottoman Georgian churches are themselves searched for signs of texts, inscriptions, and old books in Georgian. At the same time, parts of the Ottoman Georgian landscape are searched for scenic spots that Rustaveli had in mind when writing his epic poem. The ruins authored by Queen Tamar and the epic poem authored by Rustaveli become two series of monuments, architectural and literary, that, taken in tandem, allow the imagining of Georgia, an ancient Georgia whose center was Ottoman Georgia.

To further reinforce this metonymic alignment of the archaeological and philological orders of monuments, the first deluxe illustrated print edition of Rustaveli's epic poem (1888) made this connection explicit by having the decorative borders and capitals of this textual monument be drawn from the decorative reliefs found in old churches. As the introduction to the edition itself notes, "Almost every monastery and fortress,—Mcxeta, Uplis-cixe, Betania, Kutaisi, Gelati, Sapara, Kabeni, Axtali, Pitareti, Samtavisi, Ateni—has its part [c'ili], has imprinted its mark [k'vali], in this book" (Kartvelishvili 1888, 325). On this simple, decorative level, this text stands as a kind of print microcosm of the national macrocosm. Here the monumental text contains within it parts (c'ili) and marks or traces (k'vali) of the order of architectural monuments which mark the historical territory of Georgia, thus linking together the order of circulatory textual monuments (the first print edition of the poem) with the immovable order of archeological monuments as an *intertextual* series.

The assimilation of churches to the quasi-textual order of the "monument" was also a decisive move to transform them into objects of a secular intelligentsia discourse. On the eve of conquest, the intelligentsia project for Ottoman Georgia was an explicitly secular one, which emphasized only putative commonalities (a common culture and language) between Russian Georgians and Ottoman Georgians, ignoring or downplaying the religious divide between them as Christians and Muslims. This approach was in explicit opposition to state-sponsored programs of proselytism as represented by the Society for the Restoration of Orthodoxy (see above).[29] The assimilation of churches to the authorship of the monarch Tamar alongside the secular epic poem by her contemporary Rustaveli represented, in effect, a claim by the secular Georgian intelligentsia for authority over these monuments and their interpretation. As time goes on, such intelligentsia discourses about churches as monuments of culture become ever more explicitly critical of the Russian Orthodox Church.

Lastly, the fact that these old churches were ruined temples in distant lands deserted by Georgians made visits to them into pilgrimages as well as expeditions. Starting with the travelers of the 1870s, "archaeological excursions" and "archaeological descriptions" have become a distinct genre within the broader category of travel letters, and by the 1890s, churches had become exemplary subjects for the nascent social practice of amateur photography. While "archaeological excursions" have a solid non-Romantic epistemic alibi, the fact that the ruins surveyed were always *Georgian* ones showed that the aesthetic discourse of the Georgian imperial sublime was always a factor. One Georgian travel writer and amateur photographer (Alxanishvili, whom we met above), summarizing his own motives for traveling to Ottoman Georgia, pointed to precisely this sense of the sublime one could only feel there, in Ottoman Georgia, the erstwhile center of a large Georgian empire:

> The reason for our travel was to inspect and photograph, along with inscriptions, old remains [*nashtebi*], signs [*nishnebi*] of a strong and lively life of Georgia that once existed here. Lo, he who wishes to feel the strength of the Georgians in the past must travel to these places.[30]

What a Georgian *intelligent* might experience in these places of secular pilgrimage is a kind of Georgian "imperial sublime," a melancholy sublime mingled with the picturesque, in which one surveys the strength and life of a quondam Georgian empire fallen into ruin and decay. In Artvin, Bavreli has met up with some young Georgians who have bought wine and they go into the ruins of Artvin's ruined fortress, which stands on the cliffs overlooking the Choroxi, to drink it. Here they find the ruins of a complex technology of wine storage (a series of interlinked wine jars [*kvevri*]), which attests that "once Georgians lived here." Appropriately, here they spread their tablecloth [*supra*] and drink their wine. One of his "chirruping" companions offered the following toast in the register of this "imperial sublime":

> Brothers, let us drink to the memory of those brave heroes, of our ancestors, who once apparently lived here and battled for the freedom of their families before violent and barbaric enemies! May God will that their

good feeling be passed on to us! May God will it! Cheers, Cheers!

He offers that the "chirrup" of his companions will not be pleasant for every ear, "but fortunately, no one was listening other than the sheer cliffs, and only they joined in our song."[31] Toasting the ancestors among the ruins, with only sheer cliffs to listen and answer, produces the sublime and melancholy sense of loneliness and loss of past glories that characterizes the Georgian "imperial sublime." (I owe the idea of a specifically Georgian "imperial sublime" to Zaza Shatirishvili.)

Perhaps the most striking difference between travel letters about Ottoman Georgia in the 1870s and the explosion of ethnographic writings about the mountains of Georgia in the 1880s is the way that the material aspects of the landscape, in particular ruins, dominate over the moral characteristics of the contemporary inhabitants in the former, and not the latter. It might be added that the material ruin stood as a handy figure for the moral condition of Georgianness among the Ottoman Georgians, whose Georgianness was much like a ruined building, able to be deciphered in shards and fragments of language and custom and perhaps even practices of "secret Christianity," but nowhere found in its original, integral form. One commentator from Ottoman Georgia in 1882, complaining about the general disinterest of Georgians in "their brothers" and distorted picture presented in the press about the moral condition of the people, treating them just as if they were like any other tribe of Georgians, advised that, in reality, only in their external appearance and among the monuments of language, specifically oral texts, could the Georgianness of the people be clearly descried, "—all the rest, which constitutes the specific characteristics of Georgians and by which they are differentiated from other neighboring peoples has been smashed to smithereens . . ."[32] But if the order of material ruins stood as a metaphor for the moral ruins of Georgianness of the Georgians living on these ruins, there was also, as Bavreli suggests above, an indexical, metonymic effect: perhaps these material ruins, associated in the popular memory with the figure of Queen Tamar, could act as a form of the Georgian "imperial sublime," act to instill memory of Georgianness, of a lost Georgian empire associated with the name of Queen Tamar, among the people. Alongside this secular "imperial sublime," in which Georgians experience their past glories by pilgrimage to the ruins of Ottoman Georgia, Georgian intellectuals imputed other ennobling moral effects of material ruins on the Ottomans themselves.

Alongside the way that these ruins served as a secular reminder for the Ottomans of their Georgianness, their prior belonging in a large Georgian empire, there was also frequently imputed to the Ottoman Georgians practices (based, it appears, on local Muslim folklore or rumor) of "secret Christianity" revolving around these abandoned ruins in the woods.[33] For the most part, the local accounts place these practices in the past, part of a narrative of conversion, while the Georgian accounts move them into the present tense. For example, Bavreli quotes one Georgian Muslim interlocutor as reporting of his own people that they *used* to practice secret Christianity:

> We used to be Georgians [*Kartvelebi*, presumably in the sense of 'Christians'], I learned this from my grandmother. That dearly-departed one knew Georgian, and read and wrote it like water. God, who seeks out his *qulebs* (*monebs* ['servants']), undoubtedly looking down upon them from above, our grandparents saw, that Islam was the true faith and accepted it, but among them many Georgians [*Kartvelebi*] remained, and secretly retained their old faith.—They say that by night they would go into the woods and there they would pray in the church. They say that the remains [*nashti*] of that church are even now in the woods. Our people learned this and caught them all at once.[34]

In a sense, imputing to Georgian Muslims practices of "secret Christianity" points to a similar "return of the repressed" in their own secular interpretation of monuments: by these means the Georgian intelligentsia can construct the population and the ruins simultaneously as belonging overtly to a secular Georgian order (nationality without religion), and simultaneously give both the monuments and the people a covert religious (Christian) dimension which again links religion to nationality.

The moral effects of Christian monuments on other set of Muslim Georgians (the Ingilos, living in contemporary Azerbaijan) is also the theme of a set of fictional travel notes written by Droeba correspondent Mose 'Ingilo' Janashvili. These fictional travel notes present themselves

as a survey of the Georgian ruins of this erstwhile part of Georgia
(Saingilo) by a group of fictional Georgian travelers (fictional because,
as Janashvili points out, other than himself, no other Georgian has ever
traveled there). Like many real Georgian travelers in Ottoman Georgia on which he is modeled, one of these travelers narrates the sort of
"imperial sublime" that the ruins would provoke in any Georgian (if,
presumably, any Georgians ever decided to actually go there):[35]

> 'Lo, those remains [*nashti*],' [one of the travelers said]
> said, pointing to the ancient ruins of a temple, 'surely
> can awaken in the heart of a Georgian man warm love
> towards the glorious ancestors and at the same time
> venom towards their many enemies . . .' 'Here,' he con-
> tinued, 'at one time was a great city, named Qumi. We
> are convinced of this not only by the traditions passed
> done word of mouth by the tongues of the people, but
> also by our [historical chronicle] "The Life of Kartli" . . . In
> the laps of these lovely mountains apparently once life
> bloomed.'[36]

While the primary purpose of this set of travel letters is to describe
the ruins of this sublime landscape from the imaginary perspective of a
group of Georgian travelers, Ingilo *also* has his narrator comment on the
parallel moral effects of these same material ruins on the "Lekified" (Lek
is the general east Georgian ethnonym for a wide range of Daghestanian
Muslim mountain groups) people of the village of Belokani:

> One thing makes us happy, this traveler went on, that
> all these Lekified people have a great love towards our
> ancestors. This love has apparently remained in them
> with the help of all these manifold beautiful remnants
> [*nashtebi*], which here before our eyes smile at us now. All
> the local villages and forests are full of such remnants.
> For example, Belokanians have before their eyes diverse
> churches, the traces [*k'vali*] of the ruined dwellings of
> Georgians and so on. You cannot imagine with what
> delight and love they recall our queen Tamar, a woman
> whose like never yet been born nor will be.[37]

The abandoned churches in the woods, the churches, along with other material signs of Georgianness like fruit trees and grapevines gone wild,[38] serve not only as historical evidence of the Georgianness of the people for the archaeological traveler, but also, more importantly, a reminder for the people themselves.

Travels to Europe: The Occidentalist Georgian Traveler

Unlike a Russian traveler, who, though uncertain of their Europeanness among Europeans, still can confidently project themselves as a European traveler in Asia, Georgians cannot safely assume a European point of departure as the "familiar" to contrast with the obvious "foreignness" of the East. As Sano implied, European travelers are "real travelers," and Georgians are not travelers nor, it seems, Europeans. An Orientalist Georgian traveler like G. Qazbegi is certain of the validity of a basic cosmological divide between Europe and Asia and can assign everything exhaustively a place within this imaginative geography, except himself. Indeed, throughout his description of Ottoman Georgia, the implied interlocutor is a European science which knows nothing about and has never seen these lands (and *still* has not, since Qazbegi does not identify himself as a European) (e.g., Qazbegi 1995[1875], 29, 70, 100, 134).[39] Perhaps this insecurity of position within the master dichotomy that organizes most nineteenth-century imaginative geographies (Orientalism) leads Georgian travel writers and travelers to beg the question, or even avoid the question, of where they stand in it. Georgian travel writing of this period (before the Russian revolution), when it travels abroad (which is rarely), does not head *east* or *south* (since for the Russian empire, Asia is as much south as it is east). It heads *north* (to the imperial metropole) and *west* (to Paris), and then rarely.

European travelers, safe in their knowledge of self, can afford to revel in the alterity of the Oriental other. Travel in the Orient defines the European as European, but the historical mission of the Georgian intelligentsia is predicated on a nonidentity between Georgians and Europeans. After all, the defining mission of the Georgian intelligentsia was to mediate between Georgia and Europe, to bring Georgia *into* Europe:

Among us the mission of the Georgian intelligentsia

after the end of serfdom was—the development of the diverse national life into European forms.[40]

The intelligentsia mission is an almost platonic demiurgic one of transformation, to mediate between the unchanging (because perfected) forms of European life and the obdurate and diverse materials of Georgian national life. This is still the master narrative of the Georgian intelligentsia, as it has been, virtually without a break, for over a century. Because the historical role of the intelligentsia is to _bring_ Georgia _into_ Europe, the first step of this "intelligentsia mission" is to _go to_ Europe.

The problem is, of course, that Georgians really don't like to travel, even to Europe. This is something which Sergi Mesxi (editor of _Droeba_) finds even in his own character: at the beginning of his journey to Europe, remonstrating in part with himself, Mesxi chides all would be intelligentsia reformers who wish to make pronouncements on progressive and enlightening reforms in their own society, who have not seen with their own eyes the model upon which all such reforms must be based, Europe, but rather make their unpersuasive pronouncements based on "knowing two cities in Russia and Tbilisi and Kutaisi," and from their apartment in Sololaki [a neighborhood in Tbilisi] "preach to Georgians that they should stop sleeping, put their hands to new tasks and a new life and adopt the life of Europe, that life, which you yourself have not seen and not gotten to know?"

For Mesxi, the very alterity of Europe (opposed now to Russia and Georgia both) recommends itself as a source of _models_ for liberal reform. Unlike traveling in Asia, journeying to Europe one experiences an alterity which is also universality, a set of models to be adopted by all. The life of Europe is the best representative of life in general, and the life of France is the best representative of life in Europe:

> I wanted to see that Europe, whose life, that a man might really assess it, composes the life of the whole world. And that France, which, for its part, is the best representative of the life of Europe. I wanted a little, even in passing, to become acquainted with and catch sight of the life of those peoples, whom many envy, whose various arrangements and rules others imitate. Where would I see

all these things if not in Western Europe, and in its best corner, France![41]

European forms of life stand to Georgian customs as the future to the past, whereas the role of the intelligentsia is to describe and critically assess Georgian customs, relicts of past life, as to whether they are "harmful and impoverishing" (and therefore to be eliminated) or not, the intelligentsia role with respect to Europe is to understand these European forms with a view to their eventual adoption in Georgia.

If Paris will be the prototypical incarnation of the pinnacle of Europeanness, "the best representative of Europe," his first stop along the journey is the World Exhibition in Vienna, where he will find his own progressive Eurocentric cosmology incarnated in a microcosmic display, from which the whole imaginative geography in which Mesxi is traveling concretely is quasi-ritually displayed to be taken in, if not at a glance, at least in the course of a couple of days. Such a "world picture" represented a condensed, almost fairy-tale microcosm version of the imaginary journey that Mesxi was undertaking:

> Universal expositions represented this 'single expanded world' in a microcosm, celebrating the products of industry and technological progress and displaying the entire human experience. Other cultures were brought piecemeal to European and American cities and exhibited as artifacts in pavilions that were themselves summaries of cultures . . . World's fairs were idealized platforms where cultures could be encapsulated visually—through artifacts and arts. . . . (Celik 1992, 1)

Mesxi is very familiar with the conventions and expectations of such a spectacle, he is almost a connoisseur. (He has virtually memorized the arrangement of the earlier French (therefore better) exhibition, for example, from a newspaper account). Accordingly, Mesxi is disappointed with the Vienna world exhibition:

> Every exhibition must be organized so that the viewing and recognition of the displayed objects is possible and made easy not only for knowledgeable persons and

experts, but for everyone. Everyone should be able to see easily, which art has risen to a higher level in which country and which people are more practiced in which art. This is the first and foremost condition of every exhibition and if this cannot be fulfilled, such an exhibition, you must know, cannot bring any benefit to human arts.[42]

Mesxi, a confirmed Francophile, compares it unfavorably with the French exhibition of 1867 (which, again, Mesxi himself did not actually *see*). Unlike the Vienna exhibition, in which the different peoples of the earth had separate exhibitions laid out iconically in terms of their relative disposition on the globe, in the French exhibition, the circular building was laid out into galleries with two intersecting principles of organization, one that gathered together all the arts of a single people, the other which was by individual sphere of art or science, and the individual peoples were laid out as a progressive narrative within that sphere, allowing comparison of the relative achievements of different peoples in the same branch of arts. Compared with the ideal exhibition found in Paris, the Vienna Exhibition is a disaster: this European representation lacks Europeanness (it is disorderly and chaotic, very unlike the straight and clean streets that he remarks upon everywhere as being impressive characteristics of European cities), and therefore, it also fails as a representation of the world, because you can't find anything specific anywhere, and as a representation of progress, it fails, because the incoherent representation fails to represent the ordering of the whole:

> The Vienna Exhibition, however, is arranged almost completely unsystematically, incoherently: The Exhibition occupies a very large space, but in this space often similar things that belong together are displayed in completely different houses. One part of the machines, or industrial objects is in one building, the other part is somewhere else entirely; some of the crafts of one people are displayed in one place, some somewhere else entirely. So a man's brain becomes confused, the catalog cannot help you at all, you go around all day, look around and

you can't arrange anything into or see any kind of order.[43]

Mesxi is not only interested in seeing a general map of human progress, he wants to know where Georgia and the Caucasus are located on
that map. But because the map is so confusingly laid out, it takes him
two days of searching before he finds it, and upon finding it, he is dis-
mayed, mostly because it is nothing new. It turns out to be the very
same exhibit that was displayed at the Moscow Polytechnic the year before, and he has nothing to add to what the *Droeba* correspondent said
about that exhibit a year before (what that was, he does not say), adding
that he will say only two words about the exhibit, and will say that later!
He leaves Vienna disappointed.

In letter 7, Mesxi finally lays eyes on the city of his dreams, Paris.
From the outset, Paris itself presents itself as a "fairy-tale" spectacle
like a world exhibition, a sublime vision with its corresponding subjective states of astonishment and pensiveness, except here it is a sublime
spectacle of infinitude, a city that cannot be taken in by the eye, streets
that are infinite, houses that are like towers.

> The first time a man lays eyes on Paris, the first time he
> step on its ground, has a stupefying and pensive effect
> on the mind of a man. His eye sees a city too vast for
> the eye to encompass, like the city of a fairy-tale, the
> endless straight streets, the six and seven storey houses
> raised like towers and rising above these houses the even
> higher churches, towers and monuments. . . . You feel
> that every foot of this city's earth is watered with blood
> shed for the freedom of France. You feel that you are on
> that ground, in that city, which is at one and the same
> time the head and heart of all France, where political and
> social life pulses. . . .[44]

Meshki's stupefaction at encountering his own Occidentalist fanta-
sized fairy-tale city, the sacred center of Europe, is such that he can only
compare his own Westernizer's fantasy come true with its corresponding antipode within this Orientalist imaginary, a Muslim (whom he
characterizes as "worshippers of Mohammed") who first completes the
hajj to their holy city. While presenting his journey as an Occidental-

ist inversion of an Oriental's hajj to Mecca, Mesxi does not become a Westerner, but insists on his nonidentity, presenting himself as "A man from the East":

> I do not know, what would happen to and with what feelings the worshippers of Mohammed enter their holy city – Kaba [sic]; but I think, that their feelings must be very similar to the feelings of a man who has first arrived from the East in Paris![45]

Paris is a fairy tale come to life, but Mesxi wants to correct the existing Georgian fairy tale about Paris, that it is a city whose "contemporary" life is typified by its public, social life ("theatres, a myriad ballets, evenings, concerts..."), in much the same way that he argues elsewhere, Georgian pseudo-intellectuals reduce European progress and enlightenment to a matter of Parisian hats and dresses. He summarizes as follows:

> We all, who are raised on our own kind of books, have created an obstinate idea, about "contemporary" Paris and its life. There [mand, i.e., where his readers are, Georgia] from every side we hear "Paris is such a city, such a crazed life exists there, so many entertaining, diverting, and attractive things are found there, that not only is study impossible there, but a restful life and generally thoughtful work too."[46]

"This is a mistaken and false idea from beginning to end," Mesxi tells us; there are plenty of things to do in Paris, like any city, he adds, but also here as elsewhere there are many serious people who want to work or study, especially since all forms of entertainment turn out to be quite expensive, while living the life of the mind in Paris turns out to be very cheap. But for Mesxi, the life of Paris that attracts him is not the social life of popular entertainments, for he is an intelligent; for him the only life is the political life, the Paris he wants is the revolutionary Paris. For Mesxi, the editor of *Droeba*, the political life of a country to be assessed by looking at its newspapers, and here Mesxi is certain that "Paris" (and not Germany) is the answer to the question, "Which has the first place in the description of the political life of the people?"[47]

Leaving Paris behind, a city which is, even now, the motherland of freedom and the newspaper for Mesxi, he is saddened, comparing himself to a bride oppressed by her mother-in-law, who has had a brief respite of relative freedom as a guest, and now has been recalled back into servitude. He recalls that he began his journey with the consolation that in travel, at least, he can leave behind all those "persons, affairs, and interests which always fill my heart, which always remind me of my shortcomings and 'our' difficult circumstances." In short, in particular, it becomes clear that the main benefit of leaving Tbilisi is to escape *other* Tbilisians, "at least I will rest and I will no longer see various people and events such as have a deadening effect on me," he thinks.[48]

But alas, other Tbilisians can travel too, and he dedicates his eighth and final letter (like Chavchavadze's travel letters, Mesxi's journey is divided into eight stages) to discussing the problem of going to Europe and finding other Tbilisians there. In Poti, as he is taking his seat on the boat that will take him across the Black Sea to Europe, he runs into an acquaintance from Tbilisi (whom he will later call Polkovnik), who, after exchanging greetings, takes a seat next to him and begins to ask Mesxi about his itinerary. The deadening prospect of having a boorish fellow countryman as his constant companion raises its ugly head:

> —Where are you headed?
> —To Vienna.
> —To the exhibition?
> —To the exhibition.
> —Very good, I am going there too. From there do you intend to go somewhere?
> —To Paris.
> —Even better: I'm also going to Paris. Then we are fellow travelers. It's very nice to have a fellow traveler on the road![49]

Mesxi realizes he is in for a long voyage as his new travel companion "twitters away a whole hour with incessant chatter," so he takes out a book and slowly begins leafing through it, and somehow signals with a glance to his chattersome travel companion that he is no longer paying attention to his chatter and wishes to be left alone. His companion somehow gets the message, stands up, and seats himself with some other acquaintances, and other than brief greetings, they remain separate for the remainder of the voyage. In Odessa, Mesxi sneaks off the boat, hoping never to run into this friend again. The plan is a success, he makes it alone to Vienna, and thence to Paris. In Paris, however, his luck runs out: one evening while he is out walking and window-shopping with a French student along the Boulevard des Italiens, he hears a familiar voice greet him in Russian. There is no help for it, he must obey his fate; he exchanges cards with his traveling companion from Poti, Polkovnik, and they meet up once or twice for meals.

This Polkovnik appears to be a dreadful boor. In restaurants, he takes it amiss whenever the *garcon* serves anyone else seated in the restaurant, "some simple merchant or who knows, even a clerk!" ahead of him, stewing in anger through the meal, "only from time to time looking over at the *garcon* wrathfully, as if to he wished to instill fear and trembling in his heart with his blazing glare."[50] After an imagined slight having to do with the dessert tray, Polkovnik rages, "What can a man do? Here is their *égalité*! Wherever you step, everyone has written on their face *liberté, égalite, fraternité*! Here is their liberty, unity [sic] and brotherhood, that they don't know how to pay respects to their betters and they lack manners!"[51]

In short, Polkovnik understands very well how service in a French restaurant enacts in everyday life the revolutionary principles of *liberté, égalité, fraternité*, it's just that he is allergic to these things. He requires a more aristocratic standard of service. After reporting another horror story of *égalité* at another restaurant, where the two servers have the temerity, after they are done serving the guests, to sit themselves down at their side *the very same host's table* and begin eating, Polkovnik describes his attempts to instruct them in manners by yelling "Garcon!" every time they sit down, but his attempts to instruct French waiters in the fundamentally aristocratic etymology of *service* are in vain, and he decides he must leave this intolerable country.[52] And true to his word, he does leave Paris, spending three days in London, upon returning counsels Mesxi to return home to our "blessed land." Thus, after spending three days in Vienna, a week in Paris, and three days in London, "now, when he returns home, without a doubt, he will say 'I traveled Europe. The people of France are in decline, Germany is 10 times more advanced in every respect, England is a wealthy country,' etc. etc."[53]

Ardanuji by Moonlight: The Orientalist Georgian Traveler
If intelligentsia like Mesxi travel to Europe to see the future Western world they dream for Georgia, to travel to Ottoman Georgia is, in terms of imaginative geography, to travel in the opposite direction, or rather two opposed directions: to the exotic East (despite the fact that they are literally moving to the southwest); but also, as we have seen above, into the Georgian past. The land of Ottoman Georgia has once been, and is now again, Georgian, and yet, like the babble of the Choroxi, it and its people have become strange, Oriental, and even the familiar Mtkvari changes its tone in Ottoman lands: "If no one were to tell you that this is the Mktkvari, you wouldn't know you were looking at the Mtkvari. That noisiness, that haughtiness, that strength, here changes into peacefulness." Accordingly, Bavreli's descriptions seem torn between localism, his desire to see a familiar fragment of Georgia in the contemporary land and its people, and not merely content himself with the Georgian ruins that dot the land, and a desire to give himself over to the exoticizing Orientalism of a European traveler. Sometimes, in the wooden houses and green fields of an Ottoman village, he thinks to see a fragment of Imereti: "the villages around here, their buildings and the nature, too, is almost Imereti.[54] At other times, he poetically adorns the features of nature with Asiatic dress: "the darkness of night hid the local area under its curtain, as a chador unfairly hides a beautiful Tatar woman."[55] "The sun crossed over towards the mountains. In the light of the sun's rays the blue peaks of the mountains were painted pleasingly with a chador of snow."[56]

In this strange yet familiar landscape, Bavreli frequently divides the landscape into elements of two discrete temporal series, the Georgian past, figured usually as a ruined church, and the Ottoman present, which is figured variously in the landscape, the contemporary buildings, or the people. This produces a picturesque contrast, in which Christian ruins and Oriental gardens are equally important scenic elements which compose a picturesque assemblage:

> From afar Grtvani appears as a beautiful city, decorated with gardens. Olive groves further beautify the city. . .
> . It was in the evening at the time of prayer. A Tatar in a white *chalma* had gone up onto a great cliff and was

offering a prayer to Allah . . . The houses of the village [of Lomasheni] are almost entirely hidden from view by the olive gardens. It has a pretty location. One side looks out over the Choroxi river, on the other side are high cliffs. Above Lomasheni (one verst away) there stands an old church.[57]

The two are ordered as a temporal opposition within the picturesque whole, as the order of ruins belongs to the melancholy lost world of Christian Georgia, while the gardens and olive groves, the praying Muslim to the Ottoman present.

At the same time, Bavreli is at times a strictly picturesque traveler, seeking after spots whose contrasts are important not because they illustrate the contrasts of an Orientalist imaginative geography but only because they give rise to picturesque aesthetics. The neighborhood of Artvin seems to abound in such picturesque spots:

Up to this point you have seen the Choroxi from afar, here, now we come close. Hither and there are little islands, narrow places, where red sand, collosal boulders appear. At one point the Choroxi has so narrowed the road by the cliff, that if a traveler doesn't dismount, he cannot pass. . . . Another picturesque [*samxatvro*] spot is the end of Artvin's bridge—on one side high mountains, olive gardens below, on the other side an old fortress on sheer cliffs. In the narrows between two cliffs sits a place like a little hamlet, with pretty shops. Above a rainbow-shaped bridge over the Choroxi. The Choroxi by the bridge is slow and deep. Below the bridge stand a thousand different kinds of *qaighi* (*navebi* ['boats']) and some of the Ajarians are hauling cattle in the boats quickly, some are unloading cattle from the boats.[58]

Elsewhere, albeit rarely, Bavreli moves decisively from the flattened affect and deadened nature of realism to a more Romantic Orientalist description that invests the landscape with expressive and fantastic elements. If in his descriptions of Lomasheni and Artvin Bavreli gives reign to his feeling for the Orientalist picturesque, at Ardanuji he gives full flight to his fancy, making the city into a locus of the Orientalist *fantastic*:

> We came into Ardanuji. The remains of an old church on
> a high cliff, an equally old wall of mortared stone, which
> surrounds this small city, encircled by high harsh cliffs
> and bald mountains, gives Ardanuji a sort of fantastic
> appearance.[59]

Finally, we meet up with Bavreli in the town where we first found him, dreaming up the news in the town of Ardanuji, a town which in a slightly earlier letter represented for him an empty desolate exile, almost an afterlife, from the circulatory universe of Tbilisi. Before, Ardanuji was situated in an Orient whose primary features distinguishing it from European Tbilisi was the absolute stasis and absence of circulation and life. Now Ardanuji instead comes to represent an positively valued *fantastic* land in which Bavreli can freely invest the landscape and people with all those expressive elements that he would not be able to if he were in Imereti in "European" Georgia, whose life and problems require a more prosaic realism. Ardanuji is, after all, part of a strange dreamlike land from the fantastic medieval stories of Rustaveli.[60] It is in a "New Land (Seen in Dreams and Awake)" (the title, after all, of his long *feuilleton* taking place in Ardanuji); a land caught between empiricism and imagination, waking life and dreams. It is in *the Orient*.

"This little city," Ardanuji, standing a day and a half west of Ardahan, "used to be ours, and even now it has become ours once again. If it is ours, we should know what kind of city it is. Here I will describe it for you."[61] His description dwells lovingly on the pretty streets, the wood and stone houses so close together that "you would think they are all descended from one mother and thus they have a great love for one another," and then moves on to the ruins, the cliffs, the surrounding nature.[62] Having set off this "pretty little city" in description, after a brief prologue in which he extols the beauty of autumnal moonlit nights in Georgia, he invites the reader to imagine the equal or greater beauty of such a night in Ardanuji, he moves from simple description to rapture:

> Who has not seen somewhere in Georgia beautiful
> moonlit Autumnal nights and has not been given over

then to daydreams? . . . Ardanuji has one of the most beautiful of these beautiful nights. Jupiter has not given to me a place in his Parnassus, I am not gifted by the heavens above with a fountain of rhythms pleasing to the ear, that I might have sung with verse my love for nights around here, which leads a slave of a weak nature like me into amazement.[63]

Bavreli ends his description of the landscape of Ardanuji with a portrait of the city by moonlight, as the city has moved from culture to nature, the noisy din of humanity changed to a still image of a landscape without the bustle of humanity.

Behold it has become dark. Twilight has spread its shadowy sheet. All of the inhabitants of this small city have sought out their own homes. Silence! That noisiness, that great bustle, the rumble of carriages, the ringing laughter in the circle of women – conversation, the seductive whispers of delicate educated women – is not present here! Here nature reigns!

I am sitting, like a bird who has fallen into a foreign land and from an open window I delight in the beauty of nature. Behold the full moon has risen too and dresses nature with a light like that of its brother. Then you will think that the stars too have begun to flicker and whisper. . . .[64]

From his window perch, he takes in his surroundings with rapt wonderment. His description takes in the way the moon lights up the snowy peaks of far mountains of Iasamani to the east, the high and steep cliffs of mount Kuardeba to the right, to the west the peaks of Varishxeti. He moves from mountains to nearby places, to fires appearing like earth-born stars in a little village nearby, "wrapped in fresh air," the high cliffs of Qomrali, which looks out directly across to another cliff: "They look at each other with some sort of secret sorrow." Finally, his gaze returns to the city itself by moonlight, and he finishes this rapturous description so:

Lo, the city itself. The river's reproachful muttering can be heard. From time to time the barking of dogs destroys the silence, to the right appear the ruins of an old tower; hither white houses, from whose windows can be seen laughing Tatar women; secluded by day, by night they enjoy fearless freedom.

Lo, a mullah has gone up onto the minaret and gives the call to prayer. Oh, what a pleasing voice it is! Every rise and fall of his voice, stanzas strung together like pearls strikes a man's heart strings and makes him tremble. In that voice is expressed national sentiment [*nacionaluri grdznoba*]. Only Orientals can feel it. This will not please the good taste of a European. . . .[65]

In this final description, Bavreli gives full reign to a firmly sentimental, Orientalist description of Ardanuji. Here there is no attempt to use ruins as a key to decode the past; ruins are ruins, by moonlight, alongside the minaret, both are equally picturesque. Bavreli, always an ambivalent interlocutor, very unlike the later travelers, in his rapture moves into awe and wonder, typically European aesthetic responses to the Orient. But at the same time, in a move that is extremely rare for Georgians, he elides his own lyric subject position subtly into that of the Oriental: his enjoyment of the voice of the mullah's call to prayer, in which is portrayed "national sentiment" [*nacionaluri grdznoba*], moves him. Since it expresses "national sentiment" and therefore can only move Orientals, it will not appeal to European canons of taste, therefore, Bavreli, perched on his window in a moonlit night in Ardanuji, suggests perhaps that he himself has become, or always was, an Oriental. In some sense, this is always a position available to Georgians, who ambivalently position themselves with respect to Ottomans as Europeans and yet simultaneously oppose themselves to "real" European travelers (compare G. Qazbegi, Sano, above). But even if Georgians, then as now, treat Europe as a "shifter" in which they are now included, now excluded (on Europe as a "shifter" see Gal 1991), nevertheless, Georgians of that time, as well as now, are not similarly willing to accept the converse, that they themselves may be in some sense, in some contexts, Orientals.

This is what makes this Orientalizing moment so peculiar. His apperception of space as a Georgian, a shifting position as a traveler, himself an Oriental, traveling in the Orient, moves briefly from ambivalence to full identification with the Orient. And Ardanuji, a town that a moment earlier his correspondence is defined a desolate no-man's-land beyond the pale of Occidentalist circulatory civilization, is now transformed into an aestheticized Orientalist fantasy. Bavreli is similarly ambivalent, now seeing in Ardanuji a lifeless desolate place of exile from the European world of circulation, now seeing in it a place in whose autumnal moonlit nights he can lose himself momentarily in the "national sentiments" inscrutable to Europeans and pleasing only to the Oriental soul. We might ask the question, then: Who was Bavreli, a man who we know to be from a town on the borderlands of European and Ottoman Georgia?

CONCLUSION: A STRANGER FROM A STRANGE LAND

Bavreli is truly a "hero of our times." Only at this time and place could this nobody become somebody within the world of the Georgian press. I have argued that we don't *need* to know who he is, in a sense, because unlike, for example (Prince) Akaki Tsereteli or (Prince) Ilia Chavchavadze, nothing he says is dependent for its interpretation on knowing anything about him. Understanding the conditions of possibility of his speaking to the Georgian press does not depend on knowing who he is: his name, his rank, his background. I have chosen Bavreli as the hero of this book for several reasons, but one of them due simply to the way that he is uniquely a product of the possibilities of his times. Histories of Georgian print culture and political culture of this period are often histories of great men (and often written from the socialist period onward as if they emanate from those who have been canonized as great geniuses, thinkers, and social activists like (Saint) Ilia Chavchavadze), and yet, I am arguing, the essence of Georgian print and political culture in this period is the agency it afforded to *nobodies*: the nineteenth-century Georgian press was truly a revolutionary liberal press allowing more or less egalitarian access to forums for public debate, open to aristocrats like Chavchavadze and nobodies like Bavreli alike.[1] Bavreli is both a nobody in the sense that he comes from humble origin, a nobody whose voice could never have been heard in "society" in the aristocratic sense, but also, because he was the kind of "nobody" created by the device of pseudonymity/anonymity itself: it is worth remembering that the very first literary pseudonym, chosen by Odysseus to fool the enraged Cyclops, was *outis* ("nobody"), a name he later foregoes because his pride will not allow him to not announce his true name and thus not take credit for his heroic deed. Unlike aristocratic "society," in which one's print persona is essentially an extension into the world of print of one's embodied aristocratic status, "society" in the intelligentsia sense was precisely founded on affording a distinction between embodied status and print persona. Bavreli, a nobody, a stranger, was perfectly at home in a print culture consisting of anonymous "strangers" and pseudonymous "nobodies." My evidence for this claim is S. Bavreli himself. However, someone might suspect that this was one of those pseudonymous nobodies behind which was hiding someone famous: I can only prove my point in the end by discovering who Bavreli was, if only to show that he was a nobody. This book was not written to be a detective story, but it seems appropriate to end it as one. Let us follow the clues.

For the compilers of encyclopedic "decoders" of the cryptonymic universe of pseudonyms of the nineteenth-century press, Bavreli remains an enigma. Grishashvili's (1987) pseudonym lexicon has no entry for him at all: here he is a complete nobody. G. B-dze's unpublished manuscript *kartuli pseudonimebi* (Georgian pseudonyms) has an entry for him which gives some of the places and times he published, but the identity of the writer himself is a question mark:

> *Bavreli, S. "Iveria" 1879; "Jvari Vazisa" 1906*   ?

Apparently, whoever he was, he was not well-known in Tbilisi society, aristocratic, or intelligentsia, or his name would surely have been known to these assiduous intelligentsia name collectors. He was clearly an authentic outsider. We are thrown back on his pseudonym, which tells us this much: that he was from Bavra, a town in the Axalkalaki region on the boundaries of Ottoman Georgia. Knowing this, we are not surprised that he appears to be fluent in Tatar as well as Georgian and Armenian. Georgian scholars I know, on this basis, surmised that he might be a *prangi*, a Georgian Catholic who are common in this region. But that was the extent of what I knew when I wrote the bulk of this book.

As I was completing the manuscript in 2009, however, making use of the Georgian Parliamentary Library's new database to search for dictionaries, I discovered the library itself had a new pseudonym database. Seaching for S. Bavreli there, I discovered we did indeed know his name (Solomon Aslanishvili/Aslanov), and that, moreover, there was an archival *fond* for him, and that the previous year (2008), a book of his collected writings had come out.

Some basic biographical details, then, are known: Solomon Aslanishvili was born in 1851 in the village of Bavra in the Axalkalaki district on the border of Ottoman Georgia, into a Georgian Catholic (*prangi*) family. He received formal schooling rather late, at the age of fifteen, in a local Catholic parish school. Among his teachers there was the well-known Georgian publicist Ivane Gvaradze (known for writing under the pocud oɪɪyɪɪɪ *Vlnme Mesxı* ["some Mesxian"]). Later, he himself became a teacher at the same school, where he was known to be a liberal and suspected of having Georgian nationalist tendencies (Metreveli 2008, 17–19). His period in Ottoman Georgia we already know from his writings, beginning with a large number of writings in 1878–1880, but a trickle of publications thereafter continuing to give towns in Ottoman Georgia, especially Ardanuji, in his dateline into the 1890s. What he was doing there, and why he stayed so long, let these remain a mystery for a moment. We know he married and settled there, but we do not know the name of his wife. We know his eldest daughter Tamar was born in Kutaisi in West Georgia in 1888, while two other daughters Elene (Lenichk'a) and Maragarit'a and a son, Shalva (born in 1896), were born in Ardanuji (Metreveli 2008, 21). He apparently remained there until the twentieth century, when a conflict broke out between him and the local district boss (a certain Shubinskoi), who defined Bavreli as an enemy of the state. This conflict that grew so vicious that Shubinskoi apparently tried to have Bavreli killed using a hired assassin! Somehow Bavreli survived, but his persecution at the hand of the local authorities continued and he ended up being reassigned to a well-known hardship post (Julfa in Azerbaijan), from which he eventually returned with the help of friends, ending up first in Kutaisi and finally ending up in Tbilisi, where he died in 1924 (Metreveli 2008, 21–23).

Making a visit to the National Manuscript Center, I finally had before me the sum of what we know about S. Bavreli the person, the man behind the public persona (*Fond* 150). I had hoped there would be a wealth of unprinted manuscripts, perhaps rough drafts that could show me the difference between what Bavreli had intended and the censored work. But there were none, and with a few exceptions, there are almost no unpublished works. However, in the clippings, notebooks, and assorted scraps of paper, we see the lively world of the consumption, if not production, of Georgian print culture writ large, and also signs of its material poverty. One folder (150/7) contains his calling card on which is written his name in Russian (Aslanov) and Georgian (Aslanishvili), another folder (150/9) contains clippings of photolithographs of historical monuments and printed poems by well-known aristocratic poets like Raphiel Eristavi and Akaki Tsereteli. Alongside scrapbooks of clippings from the press are books of handwritten transcriptions of stories (150/17), poems (150/18), popular songs (150/19) by various authors, handwritten grammar notebooks for Russian (150/20) French (150/24), as well as notebooks with word lists, French-Russian (Georgian) (150/22), and Tatar—Georgian

(150/21), as well as one which has a short story written on one side, and a French-Georgian word list on the other (150/10), which point once again to the range of his linguistic interests.

Some more detailed glances at items from the collection with biographical asides:

No. 2 A sheet of paper

On one side, dated 1898, Ardanuji, is a collection of his son Shaliko's baby words with their translations. On the other side, an elegiac poem written on the occasion of Ilia Chavchavadze's murder (in 1907). Clearly, as we will see again, paper was at a premium: events from public life and his private life a decade apart appear on opposite sides of the same sheet of paper. Like many linguists I have known, Bavreli's linguistic interest in transcription of alterity of speech applies even to his personal life, touchingly, to the baby speech of his own son:

> *pa — upala — ghmerti* ("god")
> *ghodolo — mghdeli* ("priest")
> *ma — p'uri* ("bread")
> *naa — ts'q'ali* ("water")
> *k'o — q'veli* ("cheese")
> . . .

No. 4 A manuscript of a textbook for teaching Georgian to Ottoman Georgians (*Sakitxavi Tsigni Gamahmadianebuli Kartvelebisatvis* ["A Lesson Book for Muslimized Georgians"])

It seems natural to move from his transcription of his son's own halting attempts to learn Georgian to his desire to spread this language among the Ottoman Georgians. Again and again we have seen that Bavreli was a linguist, but here we see Bavreli attempting, on his own, to do that which he complained that Georgian intelligentsia were unwilling to do—engage in practical pedagogical work to reclaim the lost Georgianness of Ottoman Georgia. Bavreli clearly saw himself as an enlightener; after all, we know he worked as a teacher in a Catholic parish school until 1876. During his time in Ardanuji, he established a private school to teach Georgian to Muslim Georgians (and Bavreli's writings are filled with criticisms of the condition of schools in both Russian and Ottoman Georgia, it is a topic he took great interest in) (Metreveli 2008, 20). This book apparently represents only a fraction of the pedagogical materials he created to bridge this divide: he completed a "Georgian-Ottoman Dictionary for Muslim Georgians" which he sent to the Society for the Propagation of Literacy in Tbilisi, which was not published, and subsequently the manuscript was lost (Metreveli 2008, 26).

The material form of the textbook draws our attention: we recall that Bavreli sitting on the boat on the Choroxi wondered at the idea of writing Georgian with Ottoman script, and here he has reversed the association. In figure 6 (page 11 of the textbook) the top of the page presents the Georgian alphabet (top) alongside the Ottoman (Arabic) alphabet (bottom), showing equivalences, and at the bottom of the same page "Ottoman" (top) and Georgian (bottom) words for numbers are both written in the Georgian alphabet, which is enhanced with some diacritics to provide for the specificities of Ottoman, like accents:

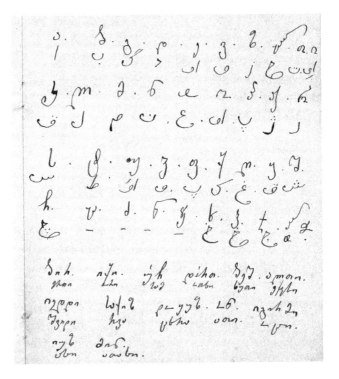

Figure 6
Page from a manuscript of a textbook for teaching Georgian to Ottoman Georgians (Sakitx-avi Tsigni Gamahmadianebuli Kartvelebisatvis ["A Lesson Book for Muslimized Georgians"])

[Ottoman]	zich.	iki.	úch	dórt.	besh.	alti.
[Georgian]	erti	ori	sami	otxi	xuti	ekvsi
	one	two	three	four	five	six

No. 8 A formal request by Solomon Aslanishvili to restore his old surname Leonidze

The Aslanishvili family were part of a large group of Georgian Catholics (*prangi*) who had been resettled in Bavra in Russian Georgia from the village of Veli in the Ardahan district Ottoman Georgia in the wake of the 1828–29 Russo-Ottoman War (Metreveli 2008, 17). So much we know from his later writings (1906, Aslanishvili-Bavreli 2008, 186–199) in the Georgian Catholic journal, *Jvari Vazisa*. In the confusion, the family's documents were lost, and with it their surname, and the Russian officials simply gave the family a patronymic *Aslanov* (Georgian *Aslanishvili*) based on the name of the head of the household *Aslani*. Aslanishvili is no more Bavreli's real family name than Bavreli is; indeed, it was precisely upon moving to Bavra that they became Aslanishvilis.

Bavreli's familiarity with, and partial identification with, Ottoman Georgia, comes from his biographical, and not historical, identification with the region. For other Georgians, the residents of Ottoman Georgia are distant imagined ancestors (historical memory), but for Bavreli, drinking a toast to the ancestors among the ruins of Artvin may well have been drinking for very recent known ancestors (biographical memory). Bavreli's travels in Ottoman Georgia are not only to a place he himself will call home for the next two decades, but they are also to his ancestral home. A Catholic exile from Ottoman Georgia with an "Ellis Island" surname, he is even more a man from the margins than we originally suspected: he is a stranger from a strange land.

No. 9 A Scrapbook

A seemingly unremarkable item in the collection is a scrapbook of clippings including both photolithographs of landscapes, printed poems by Georgian authors, and black-and-white drawings. From the perspective of Western twentieth-century print culture, such a scrapbook is absolutely unremarkable, making it difficult to imagine both the novelty of the genre of scrapbook in the period, the sea changes it indexes with respect to the organic composition of print culture in terms of images relative to printed words, and the aspirations it indexes for a richer, more image-intensive material culture of print in an impoverished and marginal print culture like Georgia. As Beverly Gordon points out, the genre of scrapbook is a novel genre of the Victorian era, a period of "scrapbook mania" which indexed both an astonishingly exuberant proliferation of both industrial commodities as a whole and especially a proliferation of printed images (Gordon 2006, 39). This explosion of printed images resulted from new process techniques: photolithograph, chromolithograph, halftone, etc. (Beegan 2008), many of which were used for the first time in Georgian print culture to produce the luxury 1888 illustrated edition of Rustaveli's *Vepxistqaosani*, a fact that the editor of this edition was careful to point out (Kartvelishvili 1888, 325). In Georgia in this period, illustrations defined a sphere of rarity and luxury within print culture exemplified by luxury editions like this, editions well out of the price range of any but the highest aristocracy. Compared to the exuberance of scrapbooks in Victorian print culture on the popular level, however, Russian and Georgian print culture offered only paltry affordances for this form of consumption. Mostly what we sense when we look at Bavreli's collection is the material poverty and consequent enforced logocentrism of Georgian print culture of the late nineteenth century, which consisted almost entirely of printed *words* and almost no *images* of any kind until the twentieth century (the twentieth-century journal *Mogzauri* ["Traveler" 1901–4] for example, was one of the first to include extensive use of half-tone photographs of Georgian places and especially ruins, while the newspaper *Cnobis Purceli* ["Information Pages" 1896–1906] introduced a pictorial supplement beginning in the same period [1901–1906]).

While Bavreli's existence as a writer is certainly a product of a somewhat ascetic print revolution consisting solely of words, the paltry gleanings of his scrapbook express an aspirational quality pointing to a desire for a materially richer print revolution: not just bread but also roses, not just words but also images. This aspiration is one he expressed directly in one of his unpublished writings about the significance of old ruins (150/15, published for the first time in Aslanishvili-Bavreli [2008, 202–206]), for a Georgian print culture that would be materially rich (with [colored] illustrations as well as text). This text primarily dwells on plans of a young acquaintance of his to photograph the ruins of Ottoman Georgia and publish them in a Russian journal (a very common motivation for travel described above under the rubric of "archaeological travel"), for which he asked Bavreli to serve as a local guide. This event gave Bavreli an occasion to see and describe in words an old ruined church at Opiza, which forms the bulk of the manuscript.

But it is the frame of the text that is most interesting. Bavreli's frame narrative is a conversation with a Georgian friend, who, having heard that an *illustrated* Georgian journal (*Teatri* "Theater" 1885–1890) was coming out, reports a dream in which he opens the door to the postman who is carrying a huge bag full of Georgian newspapers, among them *Teatri*, whose title appears in gold letters. He dreams himself impatiently opening his copy of *Teatri* to find on the first page of one a portrait of (historical figure) Gorgaslani, on the third page of the third issue a portrait of Queen Tamar, on the fifth page of the fifth issue a portrait of Shota Rustaveli reading his *Vepxistqaosani* aloud to Queen Tamar, these illustration along with many other pictures from Georgian everyday life, all done by Georgian artists!

Such is the dream of Georgian print culture in the period, but the actuality represented by *Teatri* is disappointing; in the whole of 1886, only two pictures appeared (Aslanishvili-Bavreli 2008 [ND], 203). The dream for such a materially rich aesthetically saturated "fairyland" print culture (Gordon 2006) elicited by the announcement of an illustrated Georgian journal is dashed to pieces by the poverty of the actuality of Georgian print culture, a frustrated dream that is indirectly indexed in Bavreli's scrapbook itself.

No.11 An undated "Album of poems"

The album contains a loving transcription of the two poems between Grigol Orbeliani and Ilia Chavchavadze that epitomizes the debate between the "fathers" and the "sons" in the 1870s: Chavchavadze's satirical poem *Gamocanebi* ("Riddles") that provoked the debate (transcribed on pages 4–8 of the album), followed by Orbeliani's response, *Pasuxi (Shvilta)* ("Answer [to the Sons]") (pages 9–11), followed by Chavchavadze's *Pasuxis Pasuxi* ("Answer to the Answer," pages 11–15). Certainly for Bavreli, as for others of his generation, this debate (discussed above) was formational to their identity as a generation. We could deduce this much from his writings. Flipping to page 15, we see the title of another poem written out, followed by a blank page. The unwritten poem's title is *Pasuxis Pasuxis Pasuxi* ("An Answer to the Answer to the Answer").

What did Bavreli intend to write for his own generation in answer to Chavchavadze? We will never know, except that he thought that this debate was not yet finished, and that a person like himself might have something more to say. There is room on the page, in the album, to write a lengthy response. Perhaps the most important thing is not what he would have said, but simply that he imagined that the debate was not closed; it was open to yet another response and open to even someone like him to give that response. The idea that every reader was in turn a potential writer and not a passive "audience," I have argued, is foundational to intelligentsia publicness and correspondence. In essence, the answer he might have given in poetry we can deduce at least partly from his correspondence, supplying this answer has been the topic of this book.

Figure 7

Page from an undated booklet consisting of a handwritten French grammar written in Georgian on one side (recto), a Georgian-Russian grammar on the other side (verso), written on official post office forms

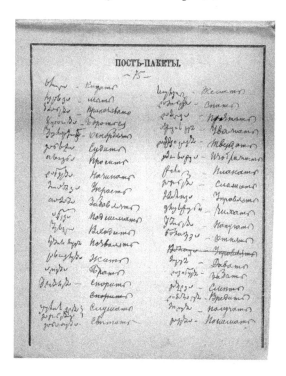

Figure 7 (cont.)

No.16. An undated booklet consisting of a handwritten French grammar written in Georgian on one side (recto), a Georgian-Russian grammar on the other side (verso)

At first glance, from the handwritten text, there is nothing here that we did not already know, that Bavreli had a strong interest in languages and was a linguistic polyglot. Again, it is not the text but the materiality of the text that draws our attention. We sense that paper was at a premium, for this book, like many of his other writings, is on recycled paper. In fact, the whole book is written in the empty spaces between printed words on official forms, specifically official post office forms (figure 7).

At last, we know what Bavreli was doing all this time, the occasion for his travels to Ottoman Georgia. He was not a paid professional correspondent, since such a thing simply did not exist in the nineteenth-century press, he was a post-and-telegraph employee (Metreveli 2008, 19–23). He was stealing paper from work, then, for his own writings. We do not know what his precise rank and job was, but we can make some guesses. Since he left his previous job as a teacher to work in this branch of state service around 1876, immediately before the war, we can surmise he was a telegraph operator. Partly this is because the two networks were not amalgamated into a single post-and-telegraph system until years later in reforms begun in 1884. Partly this is because this particular form of state service was made available to persons without rank, such as Bavreli, by reforms of 1874 which turned the telegraph into a civilian organization (Prigara 1991[1941], 30).

Partly this is because his linguistic skills, evidenced by this very archive item (a Georgian-French grammar on the recto side (left side in figure 7), and a Georgian-Russian grammar on the verso side (right side in figure 7)), included those that were job requirements for a telegraph operator, including knowledge of the languages (French and Russian) that are commonly found on this channel (telegraph) (for a fascinating discussion of the alignment of linguistic codes [English, French, Turkish] to alphabets [e.g., Roman, Turkish] to telegraphic codes [Wheatstone, Morse, Continental] through transcription and retranscription, see Bier 2008, 180–184). Bavreli's figuration of himself as linguist, translator, and mediator are not merely poses, but very literally requirements of his job. After all, like the earlier competing Ottoman telegraph, the Russian telegraph line was at least partially dedicated to transmitting messages between Britain and India, thus the need for telegraph operators on both lines to know European languages like French or English (Bektas 2000, 685–8). As Bektas notes, the Ottoman telegraph encouraged "general literacy and the study of foreign languages. Most of the telegraph staff, both local and foreign, were required to speak French. The Ottoman telegraph department for this reason recruited its staff predominantly from the Translation Bureau" (Bektas 2000, 688). Interestingly, Bektas (2000, 688) notes that Ottoman telegraph operators were often drawn from Ottoman minorities, such as Armenians, who could find room for advancement in this new technology and practical application for their existing multilingual repertoires in a situation that often required considerable translation abilities. Bavreli himself, a Georgian minority from a marginal multilingual region, provides a close analogy to this tendency (and certainly represents himself as first and foremost a translator, real and metaphoric). In essence, telegraph operators on either side of the Ottoman-Russian frontier, as translators coming from marginal ethnic groups, are remediations of the Ottoman *dragoman* (Bektas 2000, 675, cf. Georgian *tarjimani* "interpreter, dragoman"; on Ottoman Dragomans more generally, see Rothman 2009).

If Bavreli is a post-and- telegraph operator, it is appropriate for him to write grammars of these languages, knowledge of which is a job requirement, on appropriated postal forms. But one cannot resist the metaphors this coincidence affords: Bavreli is writing in the empty spaces on stolen official forms, just as he is writing local correspondence in the spaces between telegraph stations and times between long-distance official telegraph messages.

We might never have guessed this from his writings alone. Throughout his writings, there are only a few places where he mentions telegraphs and telegrams at all, compared to the amount of attention he lavishes on Ossetian postal riders and their stations, roads, and bridges. These are the infrastructural channels that *interest* him, because they are the channels by which he sends and receives correspondence to and from *Droeba*. By contrast, the telegraph doesn't seem to interest him, it appears, because the messages it carries have nothing to do with him or the locality; for the most part, he is a merely a relay for messages that originate in distant places and are usually intended for equally distant places. The telegraph was indeed annihilating, or if you prefer, compressing, space and time, for someone somewhere, but not for anyone in the locality (see Bier 2008, 175–177 on the asymmetric distribution of space-time compression afforded by the telegraph in modernity). Like the chinovnik he briefly travels with, these messages are from "somewhere" and they are going "somewhere," merely passing through "here." Just as some of his own writings are written in the empty spaces on official postal forms, so the very idea of locality grows in the gaps between these distant somewheres, in the distance one must still traverse on bad roads on horse or foot between distant telegraph stations.

In fact, one assumes the novelty of the technological sublime of the telegraph would wear off quite quickly for a telegraph operator. So we imagine Bavreli, bored out of his skull, sitting at a telegraph/postal desk in Ardanuji. We imagine that this job, a new technology from a point of view of the "technological sublime," which gives career opportunities to a whole class of cosmopolitan "new men" like Bavreli who have the linguistic and technical skills to use the technology, primarily affords him a good deal of time, and free paper, to compose local correspondence to *Droeba*. Certainly Involvement with the telegraph shows Bavreli to be part of a new layer of the emergent intelligentsia, a technical intelligentsia, who yet remain part of the traditional intelligentsia of writers. But in the process of entering the autonomous public of print culture as an *intelligent*, he erased his technical identity as telegraphist along with his name. So far from killing off local correspondence, and along with it the very idea of locality, these new technologies like the telegraph that are said to "annihilate" or "compress" space and time, only do this for some people who live somewhere else: the idea of locality, local correspondence, grows and proliferates in the gaps between telegraph stations. The cosmopolitan space-time of the telegraph does not annihilate the local space-time of correspondence, it produces it as a residuum. In the case of Bavreli, the telegraph, moving forward into Ottoman Georgia simultaneously along with the postal network, affords him an opportunity, a time, and a space to write and a locality to write about. In a sense, his technical identity as a telegraph operator, a career path that only became possible after reforms of 1874 allowed an unranked person such as himself to enter this service, afforded him indirectly with the ability to enact his literary identity as an *intelligent*, to be a writer, a local correspondent. However, in his technical identity as a telegraphist, Bavreli is merely a human part of the infrastructure, the channel or medium, of other people's messages, alongside the nonhuman infrastructure of wires and stations. Like the locality itself, he is simply part of the "in between" space between distant somewhere: the space-time that is annihilated or compressed for those someones somewhere else. His role there is in principle no different from that of Ossetian post riders in the postal network on which his own correspondence to *Droeba* depends. By contrast, as a writer/correspondent, a role he plays parasitic on his professional role as telegraphist, he is the sender and receiver of messages, and in his correspondence, the locality itself now becomes something more than a space to be traversed on the way to somewhere else.

ENDNOTES

INTRODUCTION
1. Accessed March 16, 2011, http://www.georgia.travel/.
2. Georgians in the contemporary period make a distinction between "traditional intelligentsia" and "modern intellectuals".
3. St. Chreladze, "Chveni Mtis Xalxi: Sabibliograpio Cerili" (Our Mountain People: A Bibliographic Letter). *Iveria* (1892): 1, 1.
4. See Ram 2007, Manning 2009c, Manning and Shatirishvili 2011.
5. I am indebted to Shunsuke Nozawa for directing my attention to the way that being a "nobody" is itself a crucial way to engage in print culture both as writer and as one written about. One might, indeed, look at the process of becoming a famous "somebody" in print culture often requires a prior period of "self-emptying," of becoming a "nobody" (See Buurma 2007, Nozawa 2011, 2012). For Nozawa (2012), the stance of being a "nobody" in Japanese virtual media subcultures and encoded in the pseudonym (or even a complete absence of pseudonym or other individuating sign (e.g. tripcodes in IRC chat), see also Knuttila (2011), Coleman (2012)) "most saliently articulates the subcultural modality of being-in-society: nobodyness. Not simply the anonymous, but the *insignificant* and the *unspectacular*." Not merely a category of anonymity ("nobody-in-particular") characteristic of participation in publics, Nozawa productively links this stance to in a particular way of being ordinary, unspectacular, and insignificant, even unworthy of being noticed and talked-about: "The ordinary refers to nobodies, not nobody-in-particular but real, particular nobodies: the hitherto forgotten and unimportant, those *otherwise* 'unnoticed' non-memorable and non-notable for some stretches of time" (Nozawa 2011: 5). This connection between nobodyness in the sense of anonymity and nonbodyness in the sense of insignificance discussed by Nozawa resonates strongly with the world of 1860s Russian and Georgian print culture, in which a new class of anonymous "nobodies" (like Bavreli) began to notice and write about the previously insignificant "real particular nobodies" that surrounded them (the peasantry). As we will see, Bavreli was a "nobody" in both these senses.

CHAPTER ONE
1. Notes on transcription. In the interests of legibility, I use a simplified transcription system for both Russian and Georgian that omits similar-looking diacritics from both (the soft sign from Russian and the glottalization from Georgian); these marks are meaningful only to Georgianists who will know where to supply them (I supply them only in italicized Georgian words that

are not proper names of persons, places or things [titles of works], and not transcriptions of Russian words to avoid confusion)). Contemporary Georgian does not use distinctive capitalization, but since Georgian in the *Droeba* period made use of it, I will follow the *Droeba* convention and use capitalization where appropriate following the international conventions. In the interest of avoiding as many digraphs as possible, I will transcribe Georgian using *x* for voiceless velar fricative [x] instead of *kh*, *c* for voiceless alvealor affricate [ts]. Where there is a widely accepted transcription, for example for proper names (Bakhtin, Tsereteli), I will use that instead.

2. Ghunia is the proper name. Lelt (lit. "of the reeds") functions much as a surname.

3. The fortunes of this "Caucasocentric" geopoetics in the political and cultural projects of early twentieth-century Georgian elites, and in particular the maverick Georgian linguist Nikolaj Marr, are explored in detail in Cherchi and Manning 2002.

4. Here Nikolaj Marr's observations of the transformation of the disappointed "social movement" in Georgia (associated in particular with the hopes inspired by the successes of the revolution in Guria in West Georgia) into a more nationalist one between the two revolutions of 1905 and 1917 are apropos (for a discussion, see Cherchi and Manning 2002 and more generally Suny 1988). For the Guria revolution more generally and its antecedents, see Stephen Jones 2005.

5. Chavchavadze's attempt at realism, moreover, was partially grounded in actual empirical description, exhibiting a different level of intertextuality, some of the terms are glossed in philological footnotes, as well as some whole phrases derived from a mountaineer named Ivane Gulashvili (according to Chavchavadze's notebook of 1871) (Itonishvili 1963: 70).

6. Russian colonialism, like the responses of the colonized, varied widely across the empire at different times and places, making difficult simple comparisons even with the empire, let alone with colonial situations elsewhere. For perspectives on Russian colonialism, see, for example, the papers in Brower and Lazzerini 1997, Khalid 2000, Jones 2005. For Russian colonialism in Georgia and the North Caucasus, see Jersild 1997, 1999, 2002; Jersild and Melkadze 2002). For the exceptionally privileged position of Georgian gentry, see Suny (1979). For Russian colonial representations of Georgia and the Caucasus, see Layton (1992, 1994, 1997) and Ram and Shatirishvili (2004). Whereas Russian intelligentsia trace their genealogy to an emergent group of de-classe intellectuals (*raznochintsy*), Georgian intelligentsia arose out of a much more solidly urban gentry milieu, and to this day, many postsocialist Georgian intelligentsia see their heritage as being essentially aristocratic (but see Jones 2005, chapters 1–2).

7. The turn to "folk language" in this text could not be for purposes of intelligibility and popular accessibility, but rather for its exemplary formal otherness. The extreme and self-conscious difficulty of Ghunia's speech makes it an in-

adequate vehicle for popular dissemination; rather, the dialectisms of Ghunia strongly resemble in difficulty the classical language against which Chavchavadze inveighed elsewhere.

8. Chavchavadze reproduces a notable calumny against Georgian masculinity ("the timid Georgians ran," from Lermontov's famous *Demon* (1983 [1842]: line 242), a Romantic poem also set in the Dariel gorge), mitigating its force by placing the quotation in the mouth of a drunken Russian officer.

9. An anonymous reviewer suggests that Layton's thesis concerning the feminization of Georgia in Russian literature is simplistic, offering that it could be viewed instead as an emasculation (and physical elimination) of Georgian males from Russian literature about Georgia as a heightened attention to the feminine.

10. For Pushkin also (1997 [1829]: 76), the peaceful shepherd characterizes the Aragvi in Georgia versus the dangerous robber mountaineer tribesman characterizing the Terek gorge in the Caucasus. The sudden transition and absolute contrast between the gloomy mountain vales of the Caucasus (and the Terek) to the pleasant pastures of Georgia (and the Aragvi) is a familiar *topos* of the journey, noted by Griboyedov (1917 [1859/1818]: passage 6), Pushkin (1998 [1835]: 144) and Lermontov (1983 [1829–1842]: section III–IV), among others.

11. In contrast to Chavchavadze's contemporary poem *Achrdili* "Phantom" (1977 [1859–1872]: 133–151), also set in the Dariel gorge, it features both the Terek (as the Caucasus) and the Aragvi River, and the latter is explicitly identified with Georgia ("Our Aragvi," ibid: IV–V).

12. An anonymous reviewer notes that certainly many other Russian Romantics show equal interest in the natural and cultural features of the landscape and populate the landscape with figures and voices of the inhabitants. However, they are nowhere near as loquacious as Chavchavadze's interlocutor, who becomes a central human interpreter of the meaning of the nonhuman landscape.

13. The distortion of dialect itself works by systematic principles. Wherever a form of Moxevian, or some other nearby dialect, *in some distribution* is distinct from a standard form, this form is generalized to all distributions, in accentuation, phonology, and morphology of nouns and verbs alike. The result is systematic and intentional difficulty of dialect achieved by a hypertrophy of dialectisms that mark each and every word as being distinctively "dialect" in form, maximally distinct from the standard dialect. An example chosen at random will give some idea; each major constituent bears at least one (almost all words bear a distinctive dialectal accent marker) and sometimes two or more distinctive features of "dialect" phonology or morphology. The whole text is like this:

Ghunia: *rái arn mt'eróba, tu éri érobs? caríal mshvidába mic'áchic gveqópis*
Standard: *ra aris mt'roba, tu eri erobs? carieli mshvidoba mic'ashic gveqopa.*
Gloss: 'What are enemies, if a people is free? We'll have enough empty peace in the ground.'

14. Chavchavadze's choice of terms for native institutions may be tendentious, since he uses the term *eri* (people, folk, nation), redolent with nationalist connotations, where the corresponding Moxevian term would have had *temi* (village community). According to the Moxevian writer A. Qazbegi, the correct term for what Chavchavadze calls the *eroba* is *temi* (village community) or *temoba*. The Moxevian *eroba* is not an institution or a collectivity but a place, Qazbegi defining it as a village square (Aleksandre Qazbegi [A. Mochxubaridze], "Moxeveebi da imati Cxovreba" (The Moxevians and Their Life). *Droeba* (1880) 167, 2). What Chavchavadze refers to as the "people's council" (*erta sabch'o*) is called by Qazbegi more prosaically the "gathering of the *temi*" (*temis qriloba*) (Qazbegi, "Moxeveebi," 164, 2), though he also makes reference to a "judgment place" (*sabch'eo*), a building outside the church where the community gathered for certain other matters (Qazbegi, "Moxeveebi," 164, 2).

15. Chavchavadze believed that ethnographic studies of "folk customs which pertain to economic and juridical life," institutions like the Moxevian *sabch'o* and *eroba,* to be more pressing than purely folkloric collections of poetry popular at the time and which this text also pioneers (Chavchavadze 1887: 191).

16. Qazbegi's own description of the "meeting of the community" (*temis qriloba*) held at the monastery of the Trinity is virtually identical to Ghunia's description of the "people's council" (*erta sabch'o*): "Here was held the village gathering. Here they decided their own affairs, here they tried the cases of plaintiffs, and no Moxevian would dare to appear to be in opposition to against the will of the people decided here. Now, it is true, this monastery has lost its old significance" (Qazbegi, "Moxeveebi," 164, 2).

17. Chavchavadze's mistaking Lelt Ghunia for an Ossetian would not have been an isolated incident. The Moxevian writer Aleksandre Qazbegi complained that: "The greater part of reading society thinks that 'Xevi' is Ossetia and its inhabitants Ossetians . . . [However, Moxevians] are pure Georgians and know no other language than Georgian" (Qazbegi, "Moxeveebi," 156, 1).

18. In what is clearly one more dig at the assimilationist strategies of the older generation of Georgian gentry, such as Grigol Orbeliani and Aleksandre Chavchavadze, both of whom were in Russian service.

19. The rhetorical "de-Europeanization" of Russia in this work stands in interesting counterpoint to the appropriation of Russian voices as positive representatives of European modernity *against* the backwardness of local society among "native" intelligentsia elsewhere in the empire, particularly the Islamic cultural reform movement of Jadidism (on which, see Khalid 1997, 1998; see also the relevant papers in Brower and Lazzerini 1997; Jersild 1999). In part, this is a function of Chavchavadze's generally quite ambivalent posture toward modernity in general (which was noted by contemporaries (Suny [1988] 130–1).

20. The term "ethnographic letter" comes relatively late (the mid-1880s) as part of the title differentiating self-consciously "ethnographic" materials from the mass of other correspondence from rural Georgia, though the term is used

quite early in correspondence (c. 1868 in *Droeba*). To give some idea of the rate of expansion of the genre, the paper *Droeba* (1866–1885) had around nine ethnographic contributions before 1871 (less than two per year); from 1871–1880, there were thirty-five such contributions (3.5 per year); and from 1881–5, twenty-two more (4.4 per year). In *Iveria* (the institutional successor to *Droeba* as a daily newspaper from 1886–1906), during the period when Chavchavadze was editor (1886–1991), there were 117 such contributions (nineteen per year)! Virtually, none of these ethnographic letters had Ottoman Georgia as their topic.

CHAPTER TWO

1. An anonymous reviewer queries the exact historical transition between Romanticism and realism in Georgia. Naturally, these well-known stereotyped generational periodizations admit of many exceptions (both Pushkin and Lermontov have notable texts which show realist tendencies), but in the main, as Urbneli's text shows, the Georgian writers of the 1880s had already reached a point where they could confidently contrast their humanistic, realist aesthetics to the largely Romantic aesthetics of nature that characterize the aristocratic writers of the 1840s generation like Aleksandre Chavchavadze or Grigol Orbeliani. Chavchavadze, writing in the 1870s, shows tendencies which point in both directions.

2. It should be noted that Georgian railways did not connect Russia with Georgia directly until the twentieth century, and no railroad ever ran through this passage. The railways of this period allowed access to Russia primarily indirectly through the Black Sea port of Poti. In a period in which railways were annihilating space and time elsewhere producing a kind of aesthetic of 'technological sublime,' traffic between Russia and Georgia through the Dariel primarily proceeded through the rather more technologically picturesque means of the Russian post cart, from post station to post station on roads constantly being threatened by erosion from the bare hills above and the roaring rushing Terek alongside.

3. Qazbegi, "Moxeveebi," 156.1.

4. Qazbegi, "Moxeveebi," 2.

5. Certainly, as an anonymous review comments, earlier Romantic writers like Pushkin did concern themselves with the infrastructure of the crossing, often by contrasting the Russian road with the vagaries of the torrential Terek which continuously destroyed the road. Griboyedov's notes continuously draw attention to the horrible state of the road. The point I am making is more a matter of the primarily aesthetic focus of writers in the Romantic period (who, Urbneli alleges, are *only* interested in the nature of the crossing) and those of the self-consciously "realist" period like Urbneli (who are primarily interested in the human dimensions of the crossing, figured by the Russian road). The same reviewer correctly also cautions that it is not possible to read the objec-

tive state of the roads from the texts without considering the aesthetic and polemic intent of the author. However, that said, it is clear from numerous accounts that the roads in the period of Griboyedov's or even Pushkin's crossing were virtually nonexistent (making the use of wheeled transport difficult to impossible) and the dangers to traveler still very real, concerns that have largely been banished by Chavchavadze's period where regular roads and post stations have been set up.

6. Qazbegi, "Moxeveebi," 2–3.

7. N. Xizanashvili (N. Urbneli), "Mgzavris Shenishvnebidgan" (From the *Notes of a Traveler*). *Droeba* 1883, 129, 2 .

8. Xizanashvili, "Mgzavris," 2.

9. Xizanashvili, "Mgzavris," 3.

10. Xizanashvili, "Mgzavris," 3.

11. Because the body of this state consists largely of military and postal bureaucrats, we might call this a "bureaucratic sublime" (a term used by John [1995: 11] in reference to the North American postal network).

12. An anonymous review objects that the Russian imperial project in the Caucasus should not be viewed as a form of colonialism, but a political or cultural project of modernization or Europeanization, albeit sometimes violently imposed. This is also a familiar critique from Russian intellectuals of the applicability of the term colonialism, Orientalism, or even imperialism to the Russian context (for a lively recent debate between Russian and Western scholars on this issue, see Grachev and Rykin 2007, Morrison 2007). For a debate about the applicability of Orientalism, see Khalid 2000, Knight 2000 and Todovora 2000; for authors that assume, as I do, its general applicability *mutatis mutandis* to the Caucasus, see Layton (1986, 1992, 1994, 1997), Jersild (1999, 2002). Naturally, colonialism (like Orientalism and imperialism) is a term that, like essentially every other term of comparative analysis, eludes easy and unchanging definitions except by ostension, but consider how much more elusive than these is the invariant core of term "modernity," a term which is nearly always defined either extremely abstractly or by simple ostensive definition (a long list of things that seem to go together). Therefore, replacing colonialism with modernization doesn't get us anywhere; we jump from one morass of comparisons and definitions to another, particularly since colonialism is almost always defined as a developmental project located within a generally liberal narrative of progress, is it strange that the child (modernization) resembles the parent (colonialism)? My feeling, with Morrison 2007, is that the attempt to make a distinction here is based more on a desire to euphemize and so not offend contemporaries than any real attempt to understand the past. If French colonialism can be compared to British colonialism, differing as they do along so many dimensions (arguably as many or more than the Russian case differs from the British case), then there is no question that the Russian situation can be productively compared with either of these: certainly all these at one point or another phrased themselves as

civilizing, or what is basically the same thing, modernizing projects, and all of them imposed this civilization, or what is the same thing renamed, modernity, by force.

13. X. M. "Sami Kvira Imeretshi (Mgzavris Dakvirveba)." (Three Weeks in Imereti [Research of a Traveler]. *Droeba* [1872] 18, 2).

14. X. M. "Sami Kvira," 2.

15. I am obviously oversimplifying the complex ways that the categories of the sublime, the beautiful and the picturesque are opposed in debates from the period (see Hipple 1957 for a classic survey). One key difference between the categories is that the sublime is first and foremost an aesthetic category which arrives on the scene with a fully specified aesthetic theory, while the picturesque is a largely extensional collection of picturesque objects and qualities in search of a unifying theory. The picturesque is defined by its extremely common collocation with the word "assemblage": a picturesque assemblage typically denotes an assemblage of diverse and contrasting elements including both humans and nonhumans. So for example, a picturesque landscape, like a pastoral landscape and unlike a sublime landscape, is always one that contains both human and nonhuman elements, and the most stereotypical picturesque object is a ruin, an object which is not only a characteristic feature of a picturesque landscape, but in itself is a picturesque assemblage of human and nonhuman, culture and nature, artificial and organic (on ruins as typically picturesque elements see Andrews 1989: 41–50, Yablon 2009: 43–49). When I speak of "picturesque technologies," then I am talking about those that are dilapidated, antiquated, and falling apart (thus exposing themselves *as* assemblages) as opposed to "sublime technologies" which are new and still able to incite awe (and largely function as "black boxes" whose internal workings are a mystery). I note in passing, because I don't know where else to put it, that the view of technology coming out of Actor-Network Theory (the work of Bruno Latour and John Law, for example), with its emphasis on heterogeneous assemblages of human and nonhuman actors, seems to be an analytic view of technologies as "picturesque assemblages" rather than sublime "blackboxes" more typical of older technology studies.

16. I am using "subaltern" not in the sense of "utterly abject" but in its original sense of denoting a kind of noncommissioned officer, a state of being subordinate to someone else but also superordinate to someone else (something like "second-in-command").

17. This, incidentally, shows that the concern of an anonymous review that "realism" is strictly speaking a literary phenomenon and only secondarily applicable to "extraliterary" activities like ethnography is not shared by Georgians of the period. Given the tendency of realism to privilege de-aestheticized "life" (the subordination of art to life or reality) over aesthetic "beauty" (the pervasive aestheticization of life) said to be characteristic of "romanticism" (Paperno 1988: 8), one might argue that factual descriptions of life, including genres like ethnography, are in fact the primary genres of "realism," and

literary forms strictly secondary and parasitic. We find that virtually all the "mountain writers" of the 1880s (Aleksandre Qazbegi, Vazha Pshavela, Urbneli) turned their hand to first to ethnography, often before they turned their hand to literature.

18. St. Chreladze, "Chveni Mtis Xalxi: Sabibliograpio Cerili" (Our Mountain People: A Bibliographic Letter). *Iveria* (1892) 1, 1.

CHAPTER THREE

1. Uximerioneli, "Korrespondencia Rachidam Daba Oni" (Correspondence from Racha, Oni District). *Droeba* (1868) 23, 1.
2. Before the *Droeba* period (1866–1885), Georgian language newspapers in the Caucasus were spotty in their coverage, and most of the significant newspapers were official Russian ones like *Kavkaz*. Before *Droeba*, the motley assemblage includes *Berdzneba da Ucqeba* (1763–1787), *Sakartvelos Gazeti* (1819–1821), *Tpilisis Ucqebani* (1828–1832), *Kavkasiis Mxareta Ucqebani* (1845, a short-lived Georgian addition to a Russian language newspaper *Zakavkazskii Vestnik*, 1836–1864), *Ciskari* (1852-1-1853; 1857–1875), *Gutnis Deda* (1862–1876), *Sakartvelos Moambe* (1863), *Sakartvelos Sasuliero Maxarobeli* (1864). Until the late 1850s, there is no continuous coverage for any of these, and none of them had *Droeba*'s universal scope of coverage. *Droeba* remained the central newspaper until the 1880s, virtually all competitors until that time having more specific aims (literary, village, etc.).
3. There were many other correspondents, of course, but for readers of *Droeba*, correspondence from Ottoman Georgia was largely synonymous with "Bavreli" in this period. No other author wrote quite so much or quite so well as Bavreli.
4. S. Bavreli. "Axali Kveqnis Ambavi (Sizmarshi da Cxadshi Nanaxi)" (The Story of a New World [Seen in Dreams and Awake]). *Droeba* (1879) 2, 1.
5. Bavreli, "Axali Kveqnis," 1.
6. Bavreli, "Axali Kveqnis," 1.
7. Bavreli, "Axali Kveqnis," 2.
8. Bavreli, "Axali Kveqnis," 2.
9. D. Mikeladze, "Peltoni: Surati Osmalo Sakartvelos Cxovrebidgan" (*Feuilleton*: A Picture from the Life of Ottoman Georgia). *Droeba* (1873) 2, 1–3.
10. Mikeladze, "Peltoni," 1.
11. Mikeladze, "Peltoni," 2.

CHAPTER FOUR

1. A reviewer points out that different forms of the supra are shared across social classes in Georgia and indeed are felt to index a national attribute of hospitality. My point is that while the supra is not the exclusive attribute of the aristocracy, there is no question that they are the group who exhibit hospitality and commensal feasting (the supra) in the most exemplary manner, indeed,

this is, in part, how they found their "representative publicness" (compare Valeri 2001 more generally).

2. My specific treatment of ritual forms of commensality like the supra as being in essence infrastructures is inspired by Mars and Altman (1991); my more general treatment of hospitality as being in effect an infrastructure for other forms of circulation is inspired by Munn (1986: 55–6); my discussion of infrastructures of sociability is more generally indebted to Elyachar 2010.

3. This spurning of Persian forms in Orbeliani's lyric was only characteristic of his public poetry; his private "bohemian" poetry instead typically used precisely these Persian lyric forms like the *muxambazi* (Manning 2004, Ram 2007, Manning and Shatirishvili 2011). It is arguable that Chavchavadze missed the political charge of adopting lyric forms for Romantics of this period, which allowed them to express a "lyric subjectivity" coeval with Russians and other Europeans (Ram and Shatirishvili 2004, Manning 2008).

4. S. Bavreli, "Patara Shenishvnebi Artaanzed" (Some Small Notes on Ardahan). *Droeba* (1878) 212, 2.

5. This interest in roads is not unique to Qazbegi, however, the theme of the condition of roads and roadlessness represents a major theme of Georgian print culture in this period and up to the present day:

> [In the nineteenth century] [r]oads [in Georgia] remained unpaved and impassable for much of the winter. There were almost no maps, and most people were too scared or too poor to travel. In the 1840s, Viceroy Vorontsov complained that the roads between east and west Georgia were so bad that it took months to transfer goods from the Black Sea port of Redut-Qale to Tiflis. Things were not much better in 1902, when a report on Kutaisi *guberniia* (province) declared that 'during spring, autumn and winter [the roads] become impassable.' There were a few highways, but they were 'worn out and torn up, overrun with potholes and often without bridges.' (Jones 2005: 12)

Whereas we seldom notice the quality of a really good road, and like the rest of the infrastructure of our culture of circulation, we notice roads only when they are absent or are bad, the joy Qazbegi experiences at seeing a truly *good* European road is something that we can scarcely identify with.

6. S. Bavreli, "Mgzavris Shenishvnebi (Axalkalakidam Artahanamdis)" (Notes of a Traveler [From Axalkalaki to Ardahan]). *Iveria* (1878) 26, 9–11.

7. S. Bavreli, "Artaanidam Artvinamdin (Mgzavris Shenishvnebi)." (From Ardahan to Artvin [Notes of a Traveler]). *Droeba* (1879) 28, 2; "Xi-Xi-Xa-Xa" (Hee Hee Ha Ha). *Droeba* (1879) 78, 1–2.

8. S. Bavreli, "Mahmadiant Sakartvelodam (From the Georgia of the Mohammedans)." *Droeba* (1880) 172, 1–3.

9. Bavreli, "Mahmadiant," 1–3.
10. S. M. (Sergi Mesxi), "Sadili Axlad-Shemoertebul Kartvelebisatvis" (A Dinner for the Newly Reunited Georgians). *Droeba* (1878) 239, 1.
11. S. Mesxi, "Dghiuri" (Diary). *Droeba* (1878) 232, 1.
12. Mesxi, "Dghiuri," 1.
13. Mesxi, "Dghiuri," 1.
14. S. Mesxi, "Osmalos Sakartvelo" (Ottoman Georgia). *Droeba* (1875) 76, 1.
15. S. M., "Sadili," 1.
16. S. M., "Sadili," 1.
17. S. M., "Sadili," 2.
18. S. M., "Sadili," 2.
19. Gardmoxvecili, "Xma Mahmadian Sakartvelodam (Cerili Redaktortan)." (A Voice from Mohammedan Georgia [A Letter to the Editor]), *Droeba* (1882) 70, 1–2.
20. Il. Alxanishvili, "Javaxeti. " *Iveria* (1893) 231, 3.
21. It is clear, for example, that *pace* Habermas (1991: 12), the middle orders of British nineteenth-century society were very much concerned with a kind of embodied claim to publicness ("respectability"), which, while differing from aristocratic modes in the specific claims it made, was not only crucial for organizing differential access and belonging to public spaces (Kaviraj 1997, Otter 2002), including the very coffeehouses of which Habermas is so fond, but also, as an embodied attribute, was a precondition for the lower orders participating in disembodied debates of the public sphere (Manning 2004b).
22. S. M. [Sergi Mesxi], "Axlad-shedzenili Sakartvelo: Cerili Meore da Ukanaskne-li" (Newly Regained Georgia: Second and Final Letter). *Droeba* (1878) 52, 1.
23. Mesxi, "Axlad-Shedzenili," 1.
24. Alxanishvili, "Javaxeti," 3.
25. The figures are from Wikipedia with the usual caveats. http://en.wikipedia.org/wiki/Circassian_Genocide#Genocide_Question.
26. A. N__dze, "Peltoni: Mgzavris Shenishvnebi Gamahmadianebuls Sakart-veloshi" (*Feuilleton:* Notes of a Traveler in Ottoman Georgia). *Droeba* [1879] 150, 2. The same author has similar conversations elsewhere (N__dze, "Pel-toni," *Droeba* [1879] 166, 2).
27. Mesxi, Sergi. 1880. "Mahmadianta Gakristianeba" (The Christianiza-tion of Mohammedans). *Droeba*, 219: 1.
28. The theme of "secret Christianity" (usually gendered as a specifically female practice) is a continuous theme about Ottoman Georgians found in virtually all accounts (and again, there is never any indication of how, if it was in fact a secret, its presence was known), along with, for example, shared customs and language and the idea of a shared historical memory not only of having once been Christians, but also having once been subjects of the Georgian empire and of Queen Tamar. In *Iveria* of 1877, before the war was over and before any correspondents could reach the area, a long historical and ethnographic description of the various regions of Ottoman Georgia was serialized (*Iveria*

1877), there are references to "secret Christianity" attested in virtually every such region ([Editorial], "Osmalos Sakartvelo" [Ottoman Georgia], *Iveria*, 1877, 8, 11; 18, 10; 20, 8–9; 21, 8–9). During a brief return of interest to the region in the 1890s, a serialized semifolkloric account of the "Tatarization" (*Gatatreba*) of these same regions makes continuous and repeated reference to the same themes of "secret Christianity" (Z. Ch., "Zeda Acharis Gatatreba" [The Tatarization of Upper Ajaria]. *Iveria* [1895] 155, 3; 156.2; "Sxaltis Xeobis Gatatreba" [The Tatarization of the Sxalta Valley]. *Iveria* [1895] 172, 3; "Acharis Gatatreba" [The Tatarization of Ajaria]. *Iveria* [1895] 176, 3; "Betlemis Midam-oebis Gatatreba" [The Tatarization of the Betlemi area] *Iveria* [1985] 177, 2–3; "Kaxabris, Ach'aris, Shua-Xevis da Xulos Gatatreba" [The Tatarization of Kaxabari, Ajaria, Shua-Xevi and Xulo]. *Iveria* [1895] 182, 2). Secret Christianity represents, in effect, a sort of "return of the repressed," what Georgian intelligentsia discourse suppressed to produce a secular basis of "nationality" returns in the form of "secret Christianity" imputed to the Muslim other, in much the same way that the failure of the secularization project is blamed on the "fanaticism" of the Muslim other.

29. This was quite general, alongside the discourse of lukewarm public Islam and secret Christianity of the Ottoman Georgians, Mose (Ingilo) Janashvili claimed that since the Muslim Georgian Ingilos had been converted to Islam by force, they had never really left Christianity behind, and so they remained "Christians at heart [*gulit*], superficially [*pirat*] Mohammedans." Mose (Ingilo) Janashvili, "Ingiloebis Chivili imaze, rom isini Ingiloebshi Kalebs Satxovnelat ver Shouloben" (The complaint of the Ingilos that they cannot find wives among the Ingilos). *Droeba* (1866) 42, 2.

30. S. Bavreli, "Artaanidam Artvinamdin (Mgzavris Shenishvnebi)." (From Ardahan to Artvin [Notes of a Traveler]). *Droeba* (1879) 25, 3.

31. S. Bavreli, "Axali Kveqnis Ambebi" (Stories of a New Land). *Droeba* (1879) 17, 2).

32. S. Bavreli, "Mgzavris Shenishvnebi" (Notes of a Traveler). *Iveria* (1878) 24, 16. It should be noted that the term *Kartveli* does not have anything like a stable referent in this period in any case. In addition to meaning something like "Christian Georgian" (opposed to Tatari), the term *kartveli* can be used by writers of Bavreli's period to indicate East Georgians of the Gubernate of Tbilisi as opposed to *Imereli* "Imeretian," often used to denote West Georgians of the Gubernate of Kutaisi (Cherchi and Manning 2002: 40).

33. Guriateli, "Batomis Mazris Kartvelebis Azrebi" (The Thoughts of the Georgians of the Batumi District). *Droeba* (1880) 131, 2.

34. Erti Mgzavrtagani (One of the Travelers), "Cerili Acharidam" (Letter from Ajaria). *Droeba* (1880) 215, 3.

35. Editorial (Sergi Mesxi). "Sakartvelo: Axalcixis Kartvelebi" (Georgia: The Georgians of Axalcixe), *Droeba* (1876) 20, 1.

36. (Editorial), "Sakartvelo," 1.

37. S. Bavreli, "Haerostatit Tantali Mahmadian Sakartveloshi" (A Journey by

Aerostat in Muslim Georgia), *Droeba* (1879) 208, 3.
38. S. Bavreli, "Haerostatit Tantali (Mahmadiant Sakartvelodam)" (A Journey by Aerostat [from Ottoman Georgia]), *Iveria* (1891) 75, 2.
39. While after the initial contact period there is virtually no ethnographic interest in any aspect of Ottoman Georgia, one correspondent (Gardmoxvecili, "Xma," 2–3) makes a strong argument that among the material and moral "ruins" of Ottoman Georgia textual monuments of folk creativity should have a privileged role in disclosing lost Georgianness similar to the archaeological study of material monuments, but unlike ethnography: "These very people's mental products themselves will best answer these questions for the reader, that is, their poems, proverbs, stories, and other sayings. All such as these, in my opinion, are windows, in which the people creating them are portrayed clearly and lucidly their qualities and defects in their entirety. In ethnographic and other accounts, it is not possible that there will not be errors, for an external observer collects and writes down accounts in which he expresses his own ideas and discussions, in which he explains and elucidates every aspect and every kind of phenomenon of the life of the people in his own peculiar way."

CHAPTER FIVE
1. Erti Kulasheli Valdebuli Glexi, "Micvalebulis Dasaplavebis Cesi Imeretshi" (The Rules for Burying the Dead in Imereti). *Droeba* (1872) 16, 3.
2. Erti, "Micvalebulis," 3.
3. (Anonymous). "Upals Germaniidam Cignis Momcers" (To the Lord Writing a Letter from Germany). *Droeba* (1869) 11, 3–4.
4. Imeda Kistauri. *Droeba* (1978) 249, 1.
5. Erti, "Micvalebulis," 3.
6. Erti, "Micvalebulis," 3.
7. The first footnote is an ethnographic one, glossing a description of the population of the village of Kulashi which says that there are ninety-six noble families, and simply states that all the nobles have the same surname (Mikeladze). The second is more of a linguistic order, glossing the use of the word *mozare* in the text, describing the role of singers in funeral ritual, states that "a *mozare* is a singer of a different funeral voice [*gansxvavebulis saglovo xmis*]." Lastly, the third footnote glosses the term *archivi*, where *archivi* (a dialect word for "portion") is glossed more specifically in terms of what portions of the animal in each case count as a portion in this case for the officiating priest, including certain cuts of each type of animal along with wine, bread, and *ghomi* (essentially the same thing as grits).
8. I use the term "transcription" with caution, for clearly, the writers in question were more often than not writing *as if* they could transcribe the speech of the peasantry, though we know from, for example, Umikashvili's notes, they often recomposed it as best they could, or in the case of Lelt Ghunia, the entire voice

of the peasant is assuredly as much a fabrication as the quasi-dialect itself. I thank Miyako Inoue for this point.

9. A swazzle is an example of one of the many mechanical devices inserted into the mouth used by puppeteers to produce an alterity between their own natural voice and the voice of specific puppet characters. The swazzle, for example, produces the voice of Punch (http://en.wikipedia.org/wiki/Swazzle).

10. Boyer argues that the invocation of "the censor" acts as a "figure whose ideational crudity and penury reciprocally defines the identity of productive, creative intellectuals" and allows one to "situationally, however fleetingly, locate and distance oneself from the social, institutional and professional contexts of intellectual practice that mediate one's own epistemic labors" (Boyer 2003: 539).

11. Petre Umikashvili, "Saxalxo Simgherebisa da Zghaprebis Shekreba" (The Collection of Folk Songs and Stories), *Droeba* (1871) 22, 1.

12. Petre Umikashvili, "Xalxshi Rogor Unda Movpinot Kartuli Cignebi?" (How Are We to Circulate Georgian Books among the People?), *Droeba* (1872) 24, 1.

13. Umikashvili, "Saxalxo," 2.

14. Umikashvili, "Saxalxo," 2.

15. Umikashvili, "Saxalxo," 2.

16. Umikashvili, "Saxalxo," 2.

17. Umikashvili, "Saxalxo," 2.

18. Although, interestingly, the very people, the Xevsurs, whose poetry is memorialized in this volume (Shanidze 1931), had a completely different view, recognizing individual authorship, indeed, often writing their names or pseudonyms directly into their poems, and spoke of "writing" these poems, as well.

19. Umikashvili, "Saxalxo," 2.

20. Umikashvili, "Saxalxo," 2.

21. Umikashvili, "Saxalxo," 2.

CHAPTER SIX

1. Ucnauridze, "Acharuli Peltoni" (An Ajarian *Feuilleton*), *Droeba* (1880) 246, 1.

2. Something like this specific version of the Ottoman word is a stock Russian (*muxajirstvo*) and Georgian (*muxajiroba*) expression for Muslim emigrations or deportations from the Russian empire.

3. The specific alterity of the peasant in both the referential content of what he is saying and the specific forms used is insistently constructed as being specifically a Muslim one: *allax kebimdar* (*ghmertia moc'qale* ["God is merciful"]), *mesebisaa* (*sarcmunoebisaa* ["It is of religion"]), *muxajirat* (*gadasaxlebas* ["To emigrate"]), *izini* (*neba* ["will" sc. of Allah]), *emri* (brdzaneba ["command"]).

4. Ucnauridze. "Acharuli," 2.

5. Ucnauridze. "Acharuli," 2.

6. For example, Krazana, "Peltoni: Cerilebi Acharidam "(Letters from Ajaria),

Droeba (1880) 114, 1–2; Guriateli, "Batomis Mazris Kartvelebis Azrebi" (The Thoughts of Georgians of the Batumi District), *Droeba* (1880) 131, 1–2; Erti Mgzavrtagani, "Cerili Acharidam" (A Letter from Ajaria), *Droeba* (1880) 215, 1–3.

7. Ucnauridze. "Acharuli," 3.
8. Anonymous (Giorgi Tsereteli), "Mgzavris Cignebi" (Travel Letters), *Droeba* (1867) 12, 3.
9. "Mgzavris Cignebi," 12, 4.
10. "Mgzavris Cignebi," 12, 4.
11. "Mgzavris Cignebi," 36, 4.
12. "Mgzavris Cignebi," 37, 4.
13. "Mgzavris Cignebi," 39, 3.
14. "Mgzavris Cignebi," 12, 3.
15. "Mgzavris Cignebi," 39, 3.
16. "Mgzavris Cignebi," 39, 3.
17. Certainly Tsereteli gives short shrift to the theory Chavchavadze puts in the mouth of Lelt Ghunia and which was enshrined in noble dogma (Suny 1988) and later national dogma even today, that, in essence, serfdom had been an essentially benign relationship of mutual respect and rewards rather than an oppressive form of pillage dressed up as hospitality.
18. Akaki Tsereteli makes explicit comparisons of Georgian *t'irili* (ritual wailing) with Homeric Greek practices in several places: Akaki, "Motkmit Tirili" (Crying with Keening), *Droeba* (1875) 85, 1; Akaki. "Mcire Ram" (Something Minor), *Iveria* (1901) 161, 1.
19. A. N__dze, "Peltoni: Mgzavris Shenishvnebi Gamahmadianebuls Sakart-veloshi" *(Feuilleton: Notes of a Traveler in Ottoman Georgia)*, *Droeba* (1879) 150, 1.
20. S. Bavreli, "Navit Mogzauroba Choroxze" (A Trip by Boat on the Choroxi), *Iveria* (1878) 2, 71.
21. I thank Miyako Inoue for this formulation.
22. Sano, "Kartuli Mcerloba Chveni Mter-moqvareni" (Georgian Literature: Our Friends and Enemies),, *Iveria* (1889) 55, 1–3.
23. Sano, "Kartuli," 2.
24. Anchisxatisebneli *"Peltoni: Salxinod"* (Feuilleton: For Entertainment), *Iveria* (1888) 172, 3.
25. A feuilleton describing the small city of Ozurgeti, for example, finds that it "can be distinguished from the rest of the cities of Georgia only by location and, possibly, size." Like all such small cities, there are four *dukans* (taverns) for every inhabitant, and of course, a local intelligentsia, whose discussions, interests, and prejudices are much the same as those of the intelligentsia in the rest of the Georgian cities from which Ozurgeti can barely be distinguished (Sano, "Peltoni: Kartvelta Shoris" [Feuilleton: Between Georgians], *Iveria* [1888] 49, 2).
26. Al. Xoncli, "Sakvirao Peltoni" [Weekly Feuilleton"], *Droeba* (1882) 217, 1.

27. Xoneli, "Sakvirao," 1.
28. Xoneli, "Sakvirao," 1.

CHAPTER SEVEN
1. S. Bavreli, "Artaanidam" (From Ardahan), *Droeba* (1878) 143, 1.
2. Bavreli, "Artaanidam," 1.
3. Bavreli, "Artaanidam," 2.
4. Sano, "Peletoni: Kartvelta Shoris: Chveni Inteligencia" (Feuilleton: Among Georgians: Our Intelligentsia). *Iveria* (1889) 237, 1.
5. S. Bavreli, "Navit Mogzauroba Choroxze" (A Trip by Boat on the Choroxi), *Iveria* (1878) 2, 62.
6. Bavreli, "Navit," 63.
7. Bavreli, "Navit," 68–9.
8. Bavreli, "Navit," 68–9.
9. We should remember that for Georgians, their peculiar and unique alphabet is just as important a linguistic expression of Georgianness as the Georgian language itself, certainly, as we will see, it plays an important role in deciphering the historical meaning of ruins (which "speak Georgian," even if the people do not). Within the Russian Empire, the Georgian alphabet was an acceptable display of national difference within imperial cosmopolitanism, and certainly not suppressed any more than the Georgian language was; for example, the imperial spy Qazbegi notes that they carved their names in the trees at one camping spot in both Russian and Georgian letters. For conservative writers like Chavchavadze's *Iveria*, whose discourse, as we have seen, is a selective reading of existing travel accounts to produce a sense of maximal identity (up to and including religion), the fact that Laz speakers are highly literate in their language, but write with *Arabic* characters, is unfortunate, making their literacy strange, illegible, to "us": "In Chaneti [Laz territories] literacy is very widespread, but unfortunately for us instead of Georgian characters they use Arabic ones" ("Osmanlos Sakartvelo" [Ottoman Georgia], *Iveria* [1877] 23, 7). According to Giorgi Qazbegi, very few know how to write in Georgian in Ajaria (Qazbegi, 1995: 61).
10. Bavreli, "Navit," 75–6.
11. Bavreli, "Navit," 77.
12. The idea that these beliefs would later form a coherent set of beliefs or fragments of a "mythology" or an erstwhile local folk religion (usually called here as elsewhere "animism" [see Pelkmans 2006: 130] that could be assimilated to the category of a "world religion" comes later [compare Stewart 1991]; for a parallel Orthodox example on the creation of "world religions," see for example Asad 2003, Masuzawa 2001, 2003). The status of local forms of "paganism" or "animism" in Georgia is disputed throughout the entire modern period, in some cases, such as among the Xevsurs, It is treated either as a lapsed form of Christianity or an autonomous folk religion. Nor did everyone agree that these

animist systems constitute a sphere of "religion." Soviet authors in particular treated "animistic" folk systems that do not feature a dualistic separation of supernature and nature as not being "religions" by definition (animism is the next best thing to scientific atheism!) For contemporary Georgians, they as often as not form part of a secular national patrimony (in books titled *Georgian mythology*) (see Manning 2006). It is interesting, however, that while the Xevsur folklore with its grand mythological narratives of heroes and demons has been elevated to a national mythology, the rather more prosaic creatures of the plains, the chinka and especially the kaji, is deemed fit only for children's books and seem neglected within this discourse.

13. Ingilo (Mose Janashvili), "Kiziqelebi Ingiloebshi" (Kiziqis among the Ingilo). *Droeba* (1868) 17, 4.

14. Ingilo, "Kiziqelebi," 4.

15. D. Chkotua, "Ori Chveuleba Apxazetshi" (Two Customs in Abxazia). *Droeba* (1872) 30, 1.

16. Antimozi, "Droebis Korespondencia" (Droeba Correspondence). *Droeba* (1875) 54, 2.

17. Uximerioneli, "Korrespondencia Rachidam Daba Oni" (Correspondence from Racha, Oni District), *Droeba* (1868) 23, 1–2.

18. Uximerioneli, "Korrespondencia," 23, 1–2.

19. T. Ak. Tsereteli (Tavadi Akaki Tsereteli), Up. Redaktoro! (Lord Editor!) *Droeba* (1869) 41, 1.

20. Tsereteli, "Up. Redaktoro!", 1.

21. Editorial footnote to Tsereteli, "Up. Redaktoro!", 1.

22. M. A. Sh., "Micvalebulis Tirili da Amis Xarji Rachashi" (The Mourning of the Dead and Its Costs in Racha). *Droeba* (1870) 5, 3.

23. Editorial, "Erti 'Mavne da Gamagharibebeli' Chveuleba" (One "Harmful and Impoverishing" Custom). *Droeba* (1886) 41, 1.

24. Ritual wailing (*tirili*) typical of West Georgia and some plains in the highlands was, after the material expenses of weddings, a constant theme of correspondence, description, and commentary. Rather than attempt to summarize this correspondence, I will note that Akaki Tsereteli in his early writings (1875) writes somewhat critically of the practice, particularly the insincerity of the practice of *motkmit tirili* with hired professional keeners (Akaki, "Motkmit Tirili" [Crying with Keening]. *Droeba* [1875] 85, 1), while in 1901 he is already writing in defense of the custom against condemnations by religious authorities, indeed comparing this form of folk circulation to the publication of an obituary in a newspaper (Akaki, "Mcire Ram" [Something Minor]. *Iveria* [1901] 161, 1–3).

25. Uximerioneli, "Korrespondencia," 24, 1.

26. Uximerioneli, "Korrespondencia," 24, 1.

27. Uximerioneli, "Korrespondencia," 24, 1.

28. Uximerioneli, "Korrespondencia," 24, 2.

29. Korncli, "Peletoni: Kaji Xalxis Shexedulebit Imeretshi" (*Feuilleton*: The *Kaji* in

the View of the Folk in Imereti). *Iveria* (1888) 177, 1.
30. Korneli, "Kaji," 1.
31. Korneli, "Kaji," 1.
32. Korneli, "Kaji," 1.
33. Korneli, "Kaji," 1.
34. Korneli, "Kaji," 2.
35. Korneli, "Kaji," 2.
36. A. N__dze. "Peltoni: Mgzavris Shenishvnebi Gamahmadianebuls Sakart-veloshi" (*Feuilleton:* Notes of a Traveler in Ottoman Georgia). *Droeba* (1879) 149, 1.
37. A. N__dze. "Peltoni," 2.
38. A. N__dze. "Peltoni," 1.

CHAPTER EIGHT
1. S. Bavreli. "Mgzavris Shenishvnebi" (Notes of a Traveler). *Iveria* (1878) 24, 12.
2. Bavreli, "Mgzavris," 24, 10.
3. Bavreli, "Mgzavris," 24, 9–10.
4. Bavreli, "Mgzavris," 25.11.
5. Bavreli, "Navit," 64.
6. Bavreli, "Navit," 66.
7. Bavreli, "Navit," 64–66.
8. Bavreli, "Navit," 65.
9. Bavreli, "Navit," 68.
10. Bavreli, "Mgzavris," 11.
11. Bavreli, "Mgzavris," 11
12. Bavreli, "Mgzavris," 11
13. (Editorial). *Mogzauri* (1901) January 1, 1.
14. A. Proneli, "Naxuli da Gagonili VII : Vardzia" (Seen and Heard VII: Vardzia). *Iveria* (1904) 134, 2.
15. Sano, "Peletoni: Shenishvnebi Kartveli Mgzavrisa (Tpilisidam Bakomde)" (*Feuilleton:* Notes of a Georgian Traveler [From Tbilisi to Baku]). *Iveria* (1888) 234, 1.
16. Sano, "Kartveli Mgavrisa," 3.
17. Sano, "Kartveli Mgavrisa," 3
18. Sano, "Kartveli Mgavrisa," 1.
19. Sano, "Kartveli Mgavrisa," 1.
20. Sano, "Kartveli Mgavrisa," 1.
21. Sano, "Kartveli Mgavrisa," 1–2.
22. Sano, "Kartveli Mgavrisa," 2.
23. S. Bavreli, "Patara Shenishvnebi Artaanzed" (Some Little Notes on Ardahan). *Droeba* (1878) 211, 1.
24. Bavreli, "Patara," 212, 2.
25. E. G M. Zemokartleli, "Chveni Dzveli Cxovrebis Dzeglebi" (The Monu-

ments of Our Old Life). *Droeba* (1875) 93, 1–2.

26. Il. Alanishvili, "Javaxeti." *Iveria* 1893 227, 2.
27. A. N__dze. "Peltoni," 3.
28. Bavreli, "Navit," 62.
29. For example, the editor of *Droeba*, Sergi Mesxi, issued editorials against such church-sponsored conversion activities among the Ottoman Georgians, noting that the Ottoman Georgians were already fleeing Russian rule for fear of such forcible conversions, and that, in any case, religion was a matter of "conscience," and that economic, administrative, and cultural work were preferable to religious conversion in these regions. (Sergi Mesxi, "Mahmadianta Gakristianeba" [The Christianization of Mohammedans]. *Droeba* [1880] 219, 1).
30. Il. Alxanishvili, "Javaxeti." *Iveria* (1893) 227, 2.
31. S. Bavreli, "Axali Kveqnis Ambebi" (The Stories of a New Land). *Droeba* (1879) 18, 3. Literally "gave us our bass line," the reference is to polyphonic choral singing, but also am intertextual reference to Orbeliani's poem *Saghamo Gamosalmebisa* "Night of Farewell" (1959 [1841]: 58–9), set in the Dariel passing, also quoted by Chavchavadze in his *Letters of a Traveler*, where the cliffs answer the roaring of the Terek with their echoing base line.

sheghamda . . . marto vzi chmunvit;	Twilight . . . Alone I sit in grief;
chemi chivili vis esmis?	Who hears my complaint?
daqruvda are . . . mxoloda	The spot became silent . . . only
kma ismis zogjer gushagis.	A sentry's voice sometimes is heard.
mxolod hschans, mtani mdumared	All that appears are mountains silently
aqudebulan catamdis,	Resting on the sky,
da qazibegsa saamod	And above *Qazibegi* pleasantly
zeda varskvlavi dahnatis!	A star shines down!
cqalni mtit dakanebulni,	Waters rolling down from the mountains,
upskrulsa ikargebian,	Are lost in the abyss,
tergi hrbis, tergi ghrialebs,	Terek rushes, Terek thunders
kldeni bans eubnebian!	The rocks give back its bass!

32. Gardmoxvecili, "Xma Mahmadian Sakartvelodam (Cerili Redaktortan)." (A Voice from Mohammedan Georgia [A Letter to the Editor]). *Droeba* (1882) 70, 1–2.
33. Z. Ch., "Zeda Ach'aris Gatatreba" (The Tatarization of Upper Ajaria). *Iveria* (1895) 155, 3; 156.2; "Sxaltis Xeobis Gatatreba" (The Tatarization of the Sxalta Valley). *Iveria* (1895) 172, 3; "Ach'aris Gatatreba" (The Tatarization of Ajaria). *Iveria* (1895) 176, 3; "Betlemis Midamoebis Gatatreba" (The Tatarization of the Betlemi Area). *Iveria* (1985) 177, 2–3; "K'axabris, Ach'aris, Shua-Xevis da Xulos Gatatreba" (The Tatarization of Kaxabari, Ajaria, Shua-Xevi and Xulo). *Iveria* (1895) 182, 2.

34. S. Bavreli, "Artaanidam Artvinamdin" (From Ardahan to Artvin). *Droeba* (1979) 27, 1.

35. This entire serialized Feuilleton which is an imaginary journey through the ruins of Saingilo, a Muslim Georgian province very far from Ottoman Georgia, is a reaction to the newfound interest in the Georgian press in the Muslim Georgians of Ottoman Georgia. His frustration with the indifference of the Georgian public to these Muslim Georgians, and their obsession with the new ones, is expressed directly: "From then [1865, when he began writing to Droeba about the Ingilo] it has now been thirteen years and not even one Georgian has set foot in the direction of Saingilo, everyone is rushing off to Ottoman [Georgia]. Lord D. Bakradze has published his noteworthy work on Ajaria—what would result if he set his feet in the direction of Saingilo as well and looked around here too." Ingilo (Mose Janashvili), "Mogzauroba Saingiloshi" [A Journey in Saingilo]. *Droeba* (1878) 237, 2.

36. Ingilo, "Mogzauroba," 234.1.

37. Ingilo, "Mogzauroba," 235.1.

38. Ingilo, "Mogzauroba," 234.1–2.

39. E.g. "which for the time being no European has yet seen" (Qazbegi 1995 [1875]: 100).

40. Archil Jorjadze, "Ra aris Inteligentsia?" (What Is the Intelligentsia?). *Cnobis Purceli* (1901) 1438, 2.

41. S. Mesxi. "Peltoni: Kartveli Evropashi (Xami Mgzavris Shenishvnebi da Pikrebi)." (*Feuilleton:* A Georgian in Europe [Notes and Thoughts of an Inexperienced Traveler]). *Droeba* (1874) 405, 1.

42. Mesxi. "Kartveli Evropashi," 405, 3.

43. Mesxi. "Kartveli Evropashi," 405, 3.

44. Mesxi. "Kartveli Evropashi," 407, 1.

45. Mesxi. "Kartveli Evropashi," 407, 1.

46. Mesxi. "Kartveli Evropashi," 407, 1.

47. Mesxi. "Kartveli Evropashi," 407, 1.

48. Mesxi. "Kartveli Evropashi," 407, 2.

49. Mesxi. "Kartveli Evropashi," 407, 2.

50. Mesxi. "Kartveli Evropashi," 407, 3.

51. Mesxi. "Kartveli Evropashi," 407, 3.

52. Mesxi. "Kartveli Evropashi," 407, 3.

53. Mesxi. "Kartveli Evropashi," 407, 3.

54. S. Bavreli. "Artaanidam Artvinamdin" (From Ardahan to Artvin). *Droeba* (1879) 27, 1–2.

55. Bavreli, "Artaanidam," 26, 1.

56. Bavreli, "Artaanidam," 29, 1.

57. Bavreli, "Artaanidam," 29, 3.

58. Bavreli, "Artaanidam," 29, 3.

59. Bavreli, "Artaanidam," 27, 2.

60. Bavreli, "Navit," 62.

61. S. Bavreli. "Axali Kveqnis Ambebi (Sizmarshi da Cxadshi Nanaxi)" (The Stories of a New Land [Seen in Dreams and Awake]). *Droeba* (1879) 4, 1.
62. Bavreli, "Axali Kveqnis," 4, 1–2.
63. Bavreli, "Axali Kveqnis," 4, 3.
64. Bavreli, "Axali Kveqnis," 4, 3.
65. Bavreli, "Axali Kveqnis," 4, 3.

CONCLUSION
1. My remarks here are inspired by the work of Shunsuke Nozawa.

REFERENCES

Anderson, Benedict. 1991. *Imagined Communities*. London: Verso.

Anderson, Benedict. 1998. "Nationalism, Identity, and the World-in-Motion: on the Logics of Seriality." *Cosmpolitics: Thinking and feeling Beyond the Nation.*Edited by Pheng Cheah and Bruce Robbins. 117-133. Minneapolis: University of Minnesota Press.

Andrews, Malcolm. 1989. *The Search for the Picturesque*. Stanford: Stanford University Press.

Aslanishvili-Bavreli, Solomon. 2008. *Ts'erilebi "Osmanlos Sakartveloze."* Tbilisi: Art'anuji Press.

Asad, Talal. 1973. "Two European Images of Non-European Rule." *Anthropology and the Colonial Encounter*. Edited by Talal Asad. 103–118. New York: Ithaca Press.

Asad, Talal. 2003. *Formations of the Secular: Christianity, Islam, Modernity*. Stanford: Stanford University Press.

Bagby, Lewis. 2002. Lermontov's *A Hero of Our Time: A Critical Companion*. Evanston: Northwestern University Press.

Bakhtin, Mikhael. 1986. *Speech Genres and Other Late Essays*. Austin: University of Texas Press.

Bakradze, Dimitri. 1987. *Arkeologiuri Mogzauroba Guriasa da Ach'arashi*. Georgian translation of Bakradze (1878). Batumi: Sabch'ota Ach'ara.

Barth, Fredrik. 1969. *Ethnic Groups and Boundaries*. Boston: Little, Brown and Company.

Bauman, Richard. 2004. *A World of Others' Words: Cross-Cultural Perspectives on Intertextuality*. Boston: Blackwell.

Bazilevich, K. V. 1999 (1927). *The Russian Posts in the XIX Century*. Translated by David Skipton. N.p.: Rossica.

Beegan, Gerry. 2008. *The Mass Image: A Social History of Photomechanical Reproduction in Victorian London*. New York: Palgrave McMillan.

Bektas, Yakup. 2000. "The Sultan's Messenger: Cultural Constructions of Ottoman Telegraphy, 1847–1880." *Technology and Culture* 41: 669–696.

Bektas, Yakup. 2001. "Displaying the American Genius: The Electromagnetic Telegraph in the Wider World." *British Journal for the History of Science* 34.2: 199–232.

Bier, Jess. 2008. "How Niqula Nasrallah Became John Jacob Astor: Syrian Emigrants aboard the *Titanic* and the Materiality of Language." *Journal of Linguistic Anthropology* 18.2: 171–191.

Boellstorff, Tom. 2008. *Coming of Age in Second Life: An Anthropologist Explores the Virtually Human*. Princeton: Princeton University Press.

Boyer, Dominic. 2003. "Censorship As a Vocation: The Institutions, Practices, and Cultural Logic of Media Control in the German Democratic Republic." *Comparative Studies in Society and History* 45: 511–545.

Boym, Svetlana. 1994. *Common Places: Mythologies of Everyday Life in Russia*. Cambridge, MA: Harvard University Press.

Brower, Daniel and Edward Lazzerini, eds. 1997. *Russia's Orient: Imperial Borderlands and Peoples, 1700–1917*. Bloomington: Indiana University Press.

Brooks, Jeffrey. 1978. *When Russia Learned to Read: Literacy and Popular Literature, 1861–1917*. Princeton: Princeton University Press.

Buchli, Victor. 1999. *An Archaeology of Socialism*. Oxford: Berg.

Burbank, Jane. 1996. "Were the Russian *Intelligenty* Organic Intellectuals?" *Intellectuals and Public Life*. Edited by Leon Fink et al., 97–120. Ithaca: Cornell University Press.

Buurma, Rachel. 2007. "Anonymity, Corporate Authority, and the Archive: The Production of Authorship in Late Victorian England." *Victorian Studies* 50.1, 15–42.

Carey, James. 1989. *Communication As Culture*. Revised Edition. Routledge.

Çelik, Zeynep. 1992. *Displaying the Orient: Architecture of Islam at Nineteenth-Century World's Fairs*. Berkeley: University of California Press.

Chakrabarty, Dipesh. 2000. *Provincializing Europe: Postcolonial Thought and Historical Difference*. Princeton: Princeton University Press.

Charachidzé, Georges. 1968. *Le système religieux de la Géorgie païenne: analyse structural d'une civilisation*. Paris: Maspero.

Chard, Chloe. 1999. *Pleasure and Guilt on the Grand Tour*. Manchester: Manchester University Press.

Chavchavadze, Ilia. 1977 (1859–1872). "Achrdili" (Phantom). *Ilia Chavchavadze I*, 133–151. Tbilisi: Sabchota Sakartvelo.

Chavchavadze, Ilia. 1977 (1861–1871). "Mgzavris Cerilebi" (Letters of a Traveler). *Ilia Chavchavadze I*, 253–274. Tbilisi: Sabchota Sakartvelo.

Chavchavadze, Ilia. 1977 (1871). "Gamocanebi" (Riddles). *Ilia Chavchavadze I*, 88–91. Tbilisi: Sabchota Sakartvelo.

Chavchavadze, Ilia. 1977 (1872). "Pasuxis Pasuxi" (Answer to the Answer). *Ilia Chavchavadze I*, 97–101. Tbilisi: Sabchota Sakartvelo.

Chavchavadze, Ilia. 1977 (1887). "Xalxis Chveulebata Shescavlis Shesaxeb" (On the Study of Folk Customs). *Ilia Chavchavadze II*, 357–359. Tbilisi: Sabchota Sakartvelo.

Chavchavadze, Ilia. 1977 (1887). "Ra Mizezia, Rom Kritika ara Gvakvs" (What Is the Reason that We Do not Have Criticism?). *Ilia Chavchavadze II*, 131–135. Tbilisi: Sabchota Sakartvelo.

Chavchavadze, Ilia. 1977 (1892). "Cerilebi Kartul Literaturaze" (Letters about Georgian Literature). *Ilia Chavchavadze II*, 164–196. Tbilisi: Sabchota Sakartvelo.

Cherchi, Marcello, and Paul Manning. 2002. *Disciplines and Nations: Niko Marr vs. His Georgian Students on Tbilisi State University and the 'Japhetidology'/ 'Caucasology' Schism*. The Carl Beck Papers: The Center for Russian and East European Studies, University of Pittsburgh.

Cody, Francis. 2009. "Daily Wires and Daily Blossoms: Cultivating Regimes of Circulation in Tamil India's Newspaper Revolution." *Journal of Linguistic Anthropology* 19(2), 286–309.

Cody, Francis. 2011a. "Echoes of the Teashop in a Tamil Newspaper." *Language & Communication* 31: 243-254.

Cody, Francis. 2011b. "Publics and Politics." *Annual Review of Anthropology* 40:37-52.

Coleman, Gabriella. 2012. "Our Weirdness is Free: The Logic of Anonymous—Online Army, Agent of Chaos, and Seeker of Justice" http://canopycanopycanopy.com/15/our_weirdness_is_free

Confino, Michael. 1972. "On Intellectuals and Intellectual Traditions in Eighteenth- and Nineteenth-Century Russia." *Daedalus* 101(2): 117–150.

Coombe, Rosemary. 1996. "Embodied Trademarks: Mimesis and Alterity on American Commercial Frontiers." *Cultural Anthropology*, 11.2: 202–224.

Dianina, Katia. 2003a. "The Feuilleton: An Everyday Guide to Public Culture in the Age of the Great Reforms." *Slavic and East European Journal*, 47.2: 186–208.

Dianina, Katia. 2003b. "Passage to Europe: Dostoevskii in the St. Petersburg Arcade." *Slavic Review*, 62. 2: 237-57.

Donath, Judith. 1998. "Identity and Deception in the Virtual Community." Electronic document, accessed March 21, 2011, http://smg.media.

mit.edu/papers/Donath/IdentityDeception/IdentityDeception.pdf.

Edwards, Catharine. 1999. "Introduction: Shadows and Fragments." *Roman Presences: Receptions of Rome in European Culture, 1789–1945.* Edited by C. Edwards. 1–18. Cambridge: Cambridge University Press.

Eisenstein, Elizabeth. 1983. *The Printing Revolution in Early Modern Europe.* Cambridge: Cambridge University Press.

Ellis, Markman. 2008. "An Introduction to the Coffee-House: A Discursive Model." *Language & Communication,* 28.2: 156–164.

Elyachar, Julia. 2010. "Phatic Labor, Infrastructure, and the Question of Empowerment in Cairo." *American Ethnologist,* 37.3: 452–464.

Fabian, Johannes. 1983. *Time and the Other: How Anthropology Makes Its Object.* New York: Columbia University Press.

Figal, Gerald. 1999. *Civilization and Monsters: Spirits of Modernity in Meiji, Japan.* Durham: Duke University Press.

Foster, Michael Dylan. 2009. *Pandemonium and Parade: Japanese Monsters and the Culture of Yokai.* Berkeley: University of California Press.

Freshfield, Douglas. 1869. *Travels in the Caucasus and Bashan.* London: Longmans, Green and Co.

Freshfield, Douglas. 1896. *The Exploration of the Caucasus.* Two volumes. London: Edward Arnold.

Frierson, Cathy. 1993. *Peasant Icons: Representations of Rural People in Late Nineteenth-Century Russia.* Oxford and New York: Oxford University Press.

Gal, Susan. 1991. "Bartok's Funeral: Representations of Europe in Hungarian Political Rhetoric." *American Ethnologist,* 18.3: 440–458.

Gal, Susan, and Kathryn Woolard. 2001. "Constructing Languages and Publics: Authority and Representation." *Languages and Publics: The Making of Authority.* Edited by Susan Gal and Katherine Woolard. 1–12. Manchester: St. Jerome.

Gleason, Abbott. 1991. "The Terms of Russian Social History." *Between Tsar and People: Educated Society and the Quest for Public Identity in Late Imperial Russia.* Edited by Edith Clowes et al. 15–27. Princeton: Princeton University Press.

Goffman, Erving. 1974. *Frame Analysis: An Essay on the Organization of Experience.* Cambridge, Mass.: Harvard University Press.

Gordon, Beverly. 2006. *The Saturated World: Aesthetic Meaning, Intimate Objects, Women's Lives, 1890–1940.* Knoxville: University of Tennessee Press.

Grachev, Ifor and Pavel Ryzkin. 2007. "A European's View of Asiatic History." *Anthropological Forum* 4. 402–415. Electronic document, accessed November 11, 2011, http://anthropologie.kunstkamera.ru/en/index/8_3/.

Graham, Steven. 1911. *A Vagabond in the Caucasus.* London: John Lane.

Grant, Bruce. 2009. *Captive to the Gift: Cultural Histories of Sovereignty in Russia and the Caucasus.* Ithaca: Cornell University Press.

Greenleaf, Monika. 1991. "Pushkin's 'Journey to Arzrum': the Poet at the Border." *Slavic Review,* 50.4: 940–953.

Greenleaf, Monika. 1994. *Pushkin and Romantic Fashion: Fragment. Elegy, Orient, Irony.* Stanford: Stanford University Press.

Griboyedov, A. C. 1917 (1859/1818). "Ot Mozdoka do Tiflisa (Oktyabr 1818)" (From Mozdok to Tiflis [October 1818]). *Polnoe Sobranie Sochinenii A. C. Griboedova.* volume 3, 30–34. Petrograd: Nauka.

Grishashvili, Ioseb. 1963 (1926–7). *Dzveli Tbilisis Lit'erat'uruli Bohema* (The Literary Bohemia of Old Tbilisi). Grishashvili, Ioseb, *Txzulebata Krebuli Xut Tomad,* 3, 125–305. Tbilisi: Sabch'ota Mts'erali.

Grishashvili, Ioseb. 1969. "Psevdonimebisa da Kriptogramebisa Amoxsnisatvis" (Decoding Pseudonyms and Cryptograms). *Mnatobi 5.* Reprinted in Grishashvili *Psevdonimebis Leksik'oni,* 7–14. Tbilisi: Mecniereba.

Grishashvili, Ioseb. 1987. *Psevdonimebis Leksikoni.* Tbilisi: Mecniereba.

Habermas, Jurgen. 1991. *The Structural Transformation of the Public Sphere: An Inquiry into a Category of Bourgeois Society.* Cambridge, MA: MIT Press.

Halliday, M. A. K. 1976. "Anti-Languages." *American Anthropologist.* 78.3: 570584.

Hastings, Adi and Paul Manning. 2004. "Introduction: Acts of Alterity." *Language and Communication,* 24.4: 291–311.

Herzfeld, Michael. 1987. *Anthropology through the Looking Glass: Critical Ethnography in the Margins of Europe.* Cambridge: Cambridge University Press. 1987.

Herzfeld, Michael 1997. *Cultural Intimacy: Social Poetics in the Nation-State.* New York: Routledge.

Hipple, Walter. 1957. *The Beautiful, the Sublime and the Picturesque in Eighteenth-Century British Aesthetic Theory.* Carbondale: The Southern Illinois University Press.

Holst-Warhaft, Gail. 1992. *Dangerous Voices: Women's Laments and Greek*

Literature. London: Routledge.

Hubbard, Thomas. 1998. *The Pipes of Pan: Intertextuality and Literary Filiation in the Pastoral Tradition from Theocritus to Milton.* Ann Arbor: University of Michigan.

Huurdeman, Anton. 2003. *The Worldwide History of Telecommunications.* Hoboken, NJ: Wiley and Sons.

Inoue. Miyako. 2006. *Vicarious Language: Gender and Linguistic Anthropology in Japan.* Berkeley: University of California Press.

Itonishivili, V. 1963. *Ilia Chavchavdze da Sakartvelos Etnograpia.* Tbilisi: Sak SSR Mecnierebata Gamomcemloba.

Jenkins, Henry. 2006. *Convergence Culture: Where Old and New Media Collide.* New York: New York University Press.

Jenny, Laurent. 1976. "La stratégie de la forme." *Poétique,* 27: 257–281.

Jersild, Austin. 1997. "From Savagery to Citizenship: Caucasian Mountaineers and Muslims in the Russian Empire." *Russia's Orient: Imperial Borderlands and Peoples 1700–1917.* Edited by Daniel Brower and Edward Lazzerini. 101–114. Bloomington: Indiana University Press.

Jersild, Austin. 1999. "Rethinking Russia from Zardob: Hasan Melikov Zardabi and the 'Native' Intelligentsia." *Nationalities Papers,* 27.3: 503–517.

Jersild, Austin. 2002. *Orientalism and Empire: North Caucasus Mountain Peoples and the Georgian Frontier.* Montreal-Kingston: McGill-Queen's University Press.

Jersild, Austin and Neli Melkadze. 2002. "The Dilemmas of Enlightenment in the Eastern Borderlands: The Theater and Library in Tbilisi." *Kritika,* 3.1: 27–49.

John, Richard. 1995. *Spreading the News: The American Postal System from Franklin to Morse.* Cambridge, MA: Harvard University Press.

Jones, Stephen. 2005. *Socialism in Georgian Colors: The European Road to Social Democracy 1883–1917.* Cambridge, MA: Harvard University Press.

Karbelashvili, Andre. 1991. "Europe-India Telegraph 'Bridge' via the Caucasus." *Indian Journal of History of Science,* 26.3: 277–281. (http://www.new.dli.ernet.in/rawdataupload/upload/insa/INSA_1/20005ac0_277.pdf)

Kartvelishvili, G. D. 1888. "Gamomtsemelisagan" (From the Publisher). *Vepkhist'q'aosani Rustavelisa.* Stamba I. Martirosiancai: Tbilisi.

Kaviraj, Sudipta. 1997. "Filth and the Public Sphere: Concepts and Practices about Space in Calcutta." *Public Culture,* 10.1: 83–113.

Keane, Webb. 2003. "Semiotics and the Social Analysis of Material Things." *Language and Communication,* 23.3–4: 409–425.

Kelty, Christopher. 2005. "Geeks, Social Imaginaries, and Recursive Publics." *Cultural Anthropology,* 20.2: 185–214.

Khalid, Adeeb. 1997. "Representations of Russia in Central Asian Jadid Discourse." *Russia's Orient: Imperial Borderlands and Peoples 1700–1917.* Edited by Daniel Brower and Edward Lazzerini, 188–202. Bloomington: Indiana University Press.

Khalid, Adeeb. 1998. *The Politics of Muslim Cultural Reform: Jadidism in Central Asia.* Berkeley: University of California Press.

Khalid, Adeeb. 2000. "Russian History and the Debate over Orientalism." *Kritika,* 1.4: 691–700.

Knight, Nathaniel. 2000. "On Russian Orientalism: A Response to Adeeb Khalid." *Kritika,* 1.4: 701–715.

Knuttila, Lee. 2011. "User Unknown: 4chan, Anonymity and Contingency." *First Monday* 16.10. http://firstmonday.org/htbin/cgiwrap/bin/ojs/index.php/fm/issue/view/350

Kockelman, Paul. 2007. "From Status to Contract Revisited: Value, Temporality, Circulation, and Subjectivity." *Anthropological Theory,* 7.2: 151–176.

Komaromi, Ann. 2004. "The Material Existence of Soviet Samizdat." *Slavic Review,* 63.3: 597–618.

Kopytoff, Igor. 1986. "The Cultural Biography of Things: Commoditization As Process." *The Social Life of Things.* Edited by Arjun Appadurai. 64–94. Cambridge: Cambridge University Press.

Kotthof, Helga. 1995. "The Social Semiotics of Georgian Toast Performances—Oral Genre As Cultural Activity." *Journal of Pragmatics,* 24: 353–380.

Larkin, Brian. 2008. *Signal and Noise.* Durham: Duke University Press.

Latour, Bruno. 1992. "Where Are the Missing Masses? The Sociology of a Few Mundane Artifacts." *Shaping Technology/Building Society: Studies in Sociotechnical Change.* Edited by Wiebe E. Bijker and John Law. 225–258. Cambridge, MA: MIT Press.

Latour, Bruno. 2005. *Reassembling the Social: An Introduction to Actor-Network-Theory.* Oxford: Oxford University Press.

Laurier, Eric and Chris Philo. 2007. "'A Parcel of Muddling Muckworms': Revisiting Habermas and the English Coffee-Houses." *Social & Cul-*

tural Geography, 8.2: 259–281.

Law, John. 1987. "Technology and Heterogeneous Engineering: The Case of Portuguese Expansion." *The Social Construction of Technological Systems: New Directions in the Sociology and History of Technology.* Edited by W. E. Bijker, T. P. Hughes, and T. J. Pinch, 113–134. Cambridge, MA: MIT Press.

Layton, Susan. 1986. "The Creation of an Imaginative Caucasian Geography." *Slavic Review*, 45: 470–8.

Layton, Susan. 1992. "Eros and Empire in Russian Literature about Georgia." *Slavic Review*, 51.2, 195–213.

Layton, Susan. 1994. *Russian Literature and Empire: The Conquest of the Caucasus from Pushkin to Tolstoy.* Cambridge and New York: Cambridge University Press.

Layton, Susan. 1997. "Nineteenth-Century Russian Mythologies of Caucasian Savagery." *Russia's Orient: Imperial Borderlands and Peoples 1700–1917.* Edited by Daniel Brower and Edward Lazzerini. 80–99. Bloomington: Indiana University Press.

Lee, Benjamin. 2001. "Circulating the People." *Languages and Publics: The Making of Authority.* Edited by Susan Gal and Katherine Woolard. 164–181. Manchester: St. Jerome.

Lee, Benjamin and Edward Li Puma. 2002. "Cultures of Circulation: The Imaginations of Modernity." *Public Culture*, 14.1: 191–213.

Le Galcher-Baron, Valérie. 1993. "L'invention de la Montagne en Géorgie: Le 'Realisme Romantique' d'Alexandre Q'azbegi." *Revue des Études Géorgiennes et Caucasiennes*, 8–9: 151–174.

Lermontov. 1983 (1840) *A Hero of Our Time.* Translated by Irwin Paul Foote. London: Penguin.

Lermontov, Mikhael. 1983. (1829–1842) "The Demon: an Oriental Tale." *Mikhael Lermontov: Major Poetical Works.* Edited and translated by Anatoly Liberman. 355–415. Minneapolis: University of Minnesota.

Levi-Strauss, C. 1963. *Totemism.* Translated by Rodney Needham. Boston: Beacon Press.

Loraux, Nicole. 2006. *The Invention of Athens: The Funeral Oration in the Classical City.* New York: Zone Books.

Loraux, Nicole. 1998. *Mothers in Mourning.* Ithaca: Cornell University Press.

Lortkipandize, Ioseb. 1987. Introduction to Grishashvili. 3–6.

Lotman, Juri. 1984. The Theater and Theatricality As Components of

Early Nineteenth-Century Culture. *The Semiotics of Russian Culture*, 141–156. Ann Arbor, Michigan: University of Michigan.

Maine, Henry Sumner. 2002. (1861) *Ancient Law*. New Brunswick, NJ: Transaction.

Manning, Paul. 2004. "Describing Dialect and Defining Civilization in an Early Georgian Nationalist Manifesto: Ilia Ch'avch'avadze's *Letters of a Traveler. Russian Review*, 63.1: 26–47.

Manning, Paul. 2004b. "The Streets of Bethesda: the Slate Quarrier and the Welsh Language in the Welsh Liberal Imagination." *Language and Society*, 33.4: 469–500.

Manning, Paul. 2006. "Idolaters without Images and Images of Idolatry: Orthodox and Intelligentsia Discourses about the Georgian 'Pagan' Mountain Peoples." Paper presented at the American Anthropological Association, San Jose, November 2006. Electronic document, accessed March 15, 2010. http://dangerserviceagency.org/workingpapers.html.

Manning, Paul. 2007. "Love Khevsur Style: The Romance of the Mountains and Mountaineer Romance in Georgian Ethnography." *Caucasus Paradigms: Anthropologies, Histories, and the Making of a World Area*. Edited by Bruce Grant and Lale Yalçın-Heckmann, 23–46. Berlin: LIT Verlag.

Manning, Paul. 2007b. "Rose-Colored Glasses? Color Revolutions and Cartoon Chaos in Postsocialist Georgia." *Cultural Anthropology* 22.2: 171–213.

Manning, Paul. 2008. "Materiality and Cosmology: Old Georgian Churches as Sacred, Sublime, and Secular Objects." *Ethnos* 73.3: 327–360.

Manning, Paul. 2009. "Just like England: On the Liberal Institutions of the Circassians." *Comparative Studies in Society and History*, 51.3: 590–618.

Manning, Paul, 2009b. "Can the Avatar Speak?" (Review essay) *Journal of Linguistic Anthropology*, 19.2: 310–325.

Manning, Paul. 2009c. "The City of Balconies: Elite Politics and the Changing Semiotics of the Postsocialist Cityscape." *City Culture and City Planning in Tbilisi. Where Europe and Asia Meet*. Edited by K. Van Assche, J. Salukvadze, N. Shavishvili, 71–102. Lewiston, New York: Mellen Press.

Manning, Paul and Zaza Shatirishvili. 2011. "The Exoticism and Eroticism of the City: The 'Kinto' and His City." *Urban Spaces after Socialism: Ethnographies of Public Places in Eurasian Cities*. Edited by T. Darieva,

W. Kaschuba, and M. Krebs. 261-281. Frankfurt: Campus Verlag.

Mars, Gerald and Yochanan Altman. 1991. "Alternative Mechanisms of Distribution in a Soviet Economy." *Constructive Drinking.* Edited by Mary Douglas. 270–279. Cambridge: Cambridge University Press.

Marx, Leo. 1964. *The Machine in the Garden: Technology and the Pastoral Ideal in America.* London: Oxford University Press.

Masuzawa, Tomoko. 2000. Troubles with Materiality: The Ghost of Fetishism in the Nineteenth Century. *Comparative Studies in Society and History* 42(2): 242–267.

Masuzawa, Tomoko. 2005. *The Invention of World Religions: Or, How European Universalism Was Preserved in the Language of Pluralism.* Chicago: University of Chicago Press.

Meneley, Anne. 1996. *Tournaments of Value: Sociability and Hierarchy in a Yemeni Town.* Toronto: University of Toronto Press.

Metreveli, Rion. 2008. "Solomon Aslanishvili-Bavreli." *Cerilebi "Osmanlos Sakartveloze."* Aslanishvili-Bavreli, Solomon, 17–33. Tbilisi: Artanuji Press.

Mikadze, Givi. 1984. *Psevodnimebis Leksikoni* (A Lexicon of Pseudonyms). Tbilisi.

Mikadze, Givi. 1998. *Kartul Psevdonimta Samqaroshi* (In the Universe of Georgian Pseudonyms). Tbilisi.

Montag, Warren. 2000. "The Pressure of the Street: Habermas's Fear of the Masses." *Masses, Classes and the Public Sphere.* Edited by Mike Hull and Warren Montag, 143–4. London: Verso.

Moore, Robert. 2006. "Disappearing, Inc.: Glimpsing the Sublime in the Politics of Access to Endangered Languages. *Language & Communication.* volume 26.3–4: 296–315.

Morrison, Alexander. 2007. "What Is 'Colonisation'? An Alternative View of *Taming the Wild Field.*" *Anthropological Forum* 4, 402–415. Electronic document, accessed November 11, 2011. http://anthropologie.kunstkamera.ru/en/index/8_3/.

Morson, Gary Saul. 1981. *The Boundaries of Genre: Dostoevsky's Diary of a Writer and the Traditions of Literary Utopia.* Evanston: Northwestern University Press.

Mostashari, Firouzeh. 2001. "Colonial Dilemmas: Russian Policies in the Muslim Caucasus. *Of Religion and Empire: Missions, Conversion and Tolerance in Tsarist Russia.* Edited by Robert Geraci and Michael Khodarkovsky. 229–249. Ithaca: Cornell University Press.

Munn, Nancy. 1986. *The Fame of Gawa: A Symbolic Study of Value Transformations in a Massim (Papua, New Guinea) Society.* Durham: Duke University Press.

Nozawa, Shunsuke. 2011. *The Advent of Readers: The Project(ion) of Memory and the Semiotics of Everyday Life in Japanese Personal Historiography.* Dissertation, Department of Anthropology, University of Chicago.

Nozawa, Shunsuke. 2012. "The Gross Face and Virtual Fame: Semiotic Mediation in Japanese Virtual Communication." *First Monday* 17(3)http://firstmonday.org/htbin/cgiwrap/bin/ojs/index.php/fm/article/view/3535/3168

Nye, David. 1996. *American Technological Sublime.* Cambridge, Mass.: MIT Press.

Orbeliani, Grigol. 1959. (1874) "Pasuxi Shvilta" (Answer to the Sons). *Txzulebata Sruli K'rebuli*, 67–72. Tbilisi: Sachota Mcerali.

Orbeliani, Grigol. 1959. (1827–1870) "Sadghegrdzelo" (A Toast). *Txzulebata Sruli K'rebuli*, 87–106. Tbilisi: Sabchota Mcerali.

Orbeliani, Grigol. 1959 (1841). "Saghamo Gamosalmebisa" (Night of Farewell). *Txzulebata Sruli K'rebuli*, 58–59. Tbilisi: Sabchota Mcerali.

Orbeliani, Vakhtang. 1879. "Aris Adgili. . . ." Electronic document, accessed September 7, 2007. www.nplg.gov.ge/gsdl/ cgi-bin/library.exe.

Orbeliani, Vakhtang. 1881. "Ori Shenoba." Electronic document, accessed September 7, 2007. www.nplg.gov.ge/gsdl/cgi-bin/library.exe.

Orjonikidze, Iza, ed. 1997. *Evropa tu Asia?* (Europe or Asia?). Tbilisi: Literaturis Matiane.

Otter, Chris. 2002. "Making Liberalism Durable: Vision and Civility in the Late Victorian City." *Social History* 27.1: 1–15.

Paperno, Irina. 1988. *Chernyshevsky and the Age of Realism: A Study in the Semiotics of Behavior.* Stanford, Calif.: Stanford University Press.

Pelkmans, Mathijs. 2006. *Defending the Border: Identity, Religion and Modernity in the Republic of Georgia.* Ithaca: Cornell University Press.

Prigara, S. V. 1981 (1941). *The Russian Post in the Empire, Turkey, China, and the Post in the Kingdom of Poland.* Translated by David Skipton. N.p.: Rossica.

Pshavela, Vazha. 1961 (1892). "Rame-rume mtisa" (Something or Other about the Mountains). *Vazha Pshavela, T'oml 5*, 127–136. Tbilisi: Sabch'ota Sakartvelo.

Pushkin, A. 1997 (1822). "Prisoner of the Caucasus." *Alexander Pushkin*. Translated by A. D. P. Briggs, 58–74. London: J. M. Dent.

Pushkin, A. 1997 (1829). "The Caucasus. *Alexander Pushkin*. Translated by A. D. P. Briggs, 76–77. London: J. M. Dent.

Pushkin, A. 1998 (1835). "A Journey to Arzrum." Translated by Ronald Wilks. *Tales of Belkin and Other Prose Writings*, 131–195. London: Penguin.

Qazbegi, Giorgi. 1995 (1875). *Sami Tve Turketis Sakartveloshi*. Georgian translation of original Russian version of 1875. Batumi: Achara.

Quirk, John and James Carey. 1989. "The Mythos of the Electronic Revolution." *Communication As Culture*. Revised Edition, 87–108. London: Routledge.

Ram, Harsha. 1998. "Russian Poetry and the Imperial Sublime." *Russian Subjects: Empire, Nation and the Culture of the Golden Age*. Edited by Monika Greenleaf and Stephen Moeller-Sally, 21–49. Evanston, Ill.: Northwestern University Press.

Ram, Harsha. 1999. *Prisoners of the Caucasus: Literary Myths and Media Representations of the Chechen Conflict*. Electronic document, accessed March 15, 2011. http://iseees.berkeley.edu/sites/default/files/u4/bps_/publications_/1999_01-ram.pdf.

Ram, Harsha. 2003. *The Imperial Sublime: A Russian Poetics of Empire*. Madison, Wis.: University of Wisconsin Press.

Ram, Harsha. 2007. "The Sonnet and the Mukhambazi: Genre Wars on the Edges of the Russian Empire." *PMLA* 122. 5, 1548–1570.

Ram, Harsha and Zaza Shatirishvili. 2004. "Romantic Topography and the Dilemma of Empire: The Caucasus in the Dialogue of Georgian and Russian Poetry." *Russian Review* 63.1: 1–25.

Remer, Gary. 2000. "Two Models of Deliberation: Oratory and Conversation in Ratifying the Constitution." *The Journal of Political Philosophy* 8: 68–90.

Remer, Gary 2008. "Genres of Political Speech: Oratory and Conversation, Today and in Antiquity." *Language & Communication* 28: 182–96.

Robbins, Bruce. 2007. "The Smell of Infrastructure: Notes toward an Archive." *Boundary* 2 34(1): 25–33.

Rothman, E. Natalie. 2009. "Interpreting Dragomans: Boundaries and Crossings in the Early Modern Mediterranean." *Comparative Studies in Society and History* 51(4): 771–800.

Said, Edward. 1978. *Orientalism*. New York: Vintage.

Saqvarelidze, Rusudan. 1956. *Kartuli Teatris Istoriidan* (From the History of Georgian Theater). Tbilisi. Xelovneba.

Schivelbusch, Wolfgang. 1977. *The Railway Journey*. Berkeley: University of California Press.

Seremetakis, C. Nadia. 1991. *The Last Word: Women, Death and Divination in Inner Mani*. Chicago: University of Chicago Press.

Shanidze, Akaki. 1931. "Tsinasitqvaoba" (Foreword). *Kartuli Khalkhuri Poezia: Khevsuruli*. Edited by Akaki Shanidze, 04–031. Tbilisi: S. M. U. S.

Spitulnik, Deborah. 2000. "Media." *Journal of Linguistic Anthropology* 9 (1-2): 148-151.

Star, Susan. 1999. "The Ethnography of Infrastructure." *American Behavioral Scientist* 43: 377–391.

Stewart, Charles. 1991. *Demons and the Devil*. Princeton: Princeton University Press.

Suny, Ronald. 1979. "Russian Rule and Caucasian Society in the First Half of the Nineteenth Century: The Georgian Nobility and the Armenian Bourgeoisie." *Nationalities Papers* 7: 53–78.

Suny, Ronald. 1988. *The Making of the Georgian Nation*. Bloomington: Indiana University Press.

Taylor, Charles. 1975. *Hegel*. Cambridge: Cambridge University Press.

Taylor, Charles. 1995. "Liberal Politics and the Public Sphere." *Philosophical Arguments*. Charles Taylor, 257–287. Cambridge, MA: Harvard University Press.

Taylor, Charles. 1989. *Sources of the Self: The Making of the Modern Identity*. Cambridge, MA: Harvard University Press.

Taylor, Charles. 2002. "Modern Social Imaginaries." *Public Culture* 14.1: 91–124.

Taylor, Charles. 2004. *Modern Social Imaginaries*. Duke: Durham University Press.

Todd, William Mills. 1986. *Fiction and Society in the Age of Pushkin: Ideology, Institutions, and Narrative*. Cambridge, MA: Harvard University Press.

Todorova, Mariia Nikolaeva. 2000. "Does Russian Orientalism Have a Russian Soul? A Contribution to the Debate between Nathaniel Knight and Adeeb Khalid." *Kritika* 1.4: 717-727.

Trotsky, Leon. 1973. *Problems of Everyday Life*. New York. Pathfinder

van de Veer, Peter. 2001. *Imperial Encounters: Religion and Modernity in*

India and Britain. Princeton: Princeton University Press.

Valeri, Valerio. 2001. "Feasting and Festivity." *Fragments from Forests and Libraries*. Valerio Valeri, 1–14. Durham: Carolina Academic Press.

Voloshinov, Valentin. 1986. *Marxism and the Philosophy of Language*. Translated by Ladislav Matejka and I. R. Titunik. Cambridge, MA: Harvard University Press.

Wardrop, Oliver. 1888. *The Kingdom of Georgia: Notes of Travel in a Land of Women, Wine and Song*. London: Sampson Low, Marston, Searle and Rivington.

Warner, Michael. 1990. *Letters of the Republic: Publication and the Public Sphere in Eighteenth-Century America*. Cambridge, MA: Harvard University Press.

Warner, Michael. 2002. "Publics and Counterpublics. *Public Culture* 14.1: 49–90.

Wedeen, Lisa. 2008. *Peripheral Visions: Politics, Power, and Performance in Yemen*. Chicago: University of Chicago Press.

Xarazi, Mamia. 1995. "Giorgi Qazbegi." *Sami Tve Turketis Sakartveloshi,* 7–12. Batumi: "Achara."

Xizanashvili, N. 1940. *Etnograpiuli Nacerebi*. Tbilisi: SakSSr Mecnierebata.

Yablon, Nick. 2009. *Untimely Ruins: An Archaeology of American Urban Modernity, 1819–1919*. Chicago: University of Chicago Press.

dialogue
conservative 91, 148, 193,
202, 203, 243, 313n9;
liberal, 91, 185, 193,
201-203, 242; dialogue in
the feuilleton, dialogue of
the feuilleton 26, 91, 167,
187, 188, 190, 191, 195,
210; quoted, quoting 187
Dolidze, Andro 172
Donath, Judith 165
dreams 97-101, 239, 248, 276,
282, 283, 293, 306n4
Droeba ("Times") 11, 15-19,
22, 24, 78, 81, 82, 84-89,
91, 96-99, 101, 104-106,
109-111, 113, 116, 117,
123, 129, 131-135, 141,
143, 152, 156-158, 162,
163, 166, 172, 176, 182,
184, 188, 189, 191, 193,
207-209, 212, 214, 230,
233-236, 238, 240-243,
246, 248, 261, 270, 272,
276, 277, 297, 298,
300n1, 302n14, 303n20,
306n2n3, 316n29,
317n35

Emancipation (of serfs) 19, 24,
33, 34, 78, 155, 161, 170,
175, 176, 193, 196, 197,
199, 200, 207, 230
embodiment 94, 95, 125; disembodied 11, 27, 93, 94, 11,
112, 113, 124, 125, 142,
159, 164, 168, 181, 185,
308n21

Emin-Afendi 150
enlightenment 29, 34, 35, 47,
48, 53-57, 122, 196, 216,
217, 229, 277
Eristavi, Raphiel 288
Ermolov (Yermolov), A. P. 62, 63
ethnography 59, 66, 187, 257,
264, 305n17, 306n17,
310n39
ethos 164, 165, 168, 201-203
Europe
as narrative 10, 12-15; as
model 11, 13, 38, 73, 75,
114, 124, 273
Evangulov, Bughdan 174
exotic 93
expressive, expressivism 26, 30,
41, 42, 48, 58, 114, 131,
198, 223, 281, 282

Fabian, Johannes 93
fantastic, 100, 185, 187, 219-
220, 225, 228, 229, 243,
246, 247-250; airship,
108; land, 223; the Ori-
ent, 224, 281-282
Feuilleton
as space in newspaper
85, 163, 184, 189, 191;
as genre 67, 81, 82, 105,
107, 172, 188, 209,
210, 213, 214, 218,
221, 222, 258, 282,
306n9, 308n26, 311n1,
312n19n24n25n26,
313n4, 314n29,
315n36n15, 317n35;
as boundary work 188,

Ximshiashvili, Sherif 119
Ximshiashvilis, the dynasty 118,
        119

Zakavkazskii Vestnik 306n2
Zhukovskii, Vasilii 43
Zubalov (Zubalashvili), A. 135,
        136, 137

CPSIA information can be obtained
at www.ICGtesting.com
Printed in the USA
BVHW03s0840130618
518949BV00006B/110/P

9 781618 118318